FINEST HOUR

Tim Clayton & Phil Craig

Hodder & Stoughton

Typeset by Palimpsest Book Production Limited,
Polmont, Stirlingshire
Printed and bound in Great Britain by
Clays Ltd, St Ives plc

Hodder and Stoughton
A division of Hodder Headline
338 Euston Road
London NW1 3BH

Friday 10

There was terrific
excitement this morning
at about 4am. when
all the guns in the
neighbourhood got going.
"A" flight got 5 germans
before breakfast. Dickey
hel of my flight got
into combat and got hit
by several shots, one
a graze in his leg. Angus
landed in Belgium OK.
One of "A" flight got a badly
cut eye when a bullet smashed
his cockpit cover. The
days total bag was 16
I did not fly at all
as I am too inexperienced
but am I browned off.

FINEST HOUR

To Avice and Peter Clayton, Christine and Mike Craig:
our parents.

Contents

Illustrations

Illustrations

Endpapers
Pages from Denis Wissler's 1940 pocket diary (*Edith Kup*)

Section 1
Paul Richey (*Diana Richey*)
Denis Wissler (*Edith Kup*)
Page Huidekoper in a London street (*Page Wilson*)
Marian Holmes at Chequers (*Marian Walker Spicer*)
Armourers with a Hurricane of No. 85 Squadron at Seclin airfield near Lille, 10 May 1940 (*Imperial War Museum*)
Iain Nethercott's two-pounder pom-pom on HMS *Keith* (*Iain Nethercott*)
Ernie Leggett in drummer's uniform, Gibraltar 1938 (*Ernie Leggett*)
Peter Vaux representing the 4th Royal Tank Regiment in a motorbike trial in 1939 (*Peter Vaux*)
Corporal Bob Burroughs (*Peter Vaux*)
Mark VI light tanks on exercise in France, early 1940 (*Imperial War Museum*)
Martin McLane and the note to his wife (*Martin McLane*)

Section 2
David Low, 'All Behind You, Winston', *Evening Standard* 14 May 1940 (*Centre for the Study of Cartoons and Caricature, University of Kent, Canterbury*)
Bob Doe of No. 234 Squadron with Spitfire 'D for Doe' and ground crew (*Alfred Price*)
Spitfires climbing beneath a German reconnaissance plane (*Alfred Price*)
Pilots of No. 501 Squadron at Hawkinge (*Alfred Price*)
Pilots of No. 85 Squadron 'B' Flight (*Edith Kup*)
HMT *Lancastria* sinking, photographed from HMS *Highlander* (*HMT* Lancastria *Association*)
Survivor from the *Lancastria* aboard HMS *Highlander* (*HMT* Lancastria *Association*)

Maps

Prologue

This book began in the kitchen of Sam and Rose's house near the Thames estuary, listening to him talk about war at sea and her about East London in the Blitz.

Sam Patience is the only living survivor of the *Jervis Bay*, a lightly armed merchant vessel that, in November 1940, steamed towards a German battleship to try to save its convoy. Heroism, self-sacrifice: the story had it all and it was why we had come to meet him. But for Sam, 1940 contained much more. He shipped British gold to Canada, he watched the Royal Navy cripple the French fleet at Oran, he was torpedoed by a French submarine.

In the months that followed we heard other stories. Some of the people we met had talked about their experiences before, but many had not. The war, and particularly 1940, evoked powerful feelings: usually of pride, but sometimes other emotions intruded. For most, nothing since had been so vivid or so intense.

The people whose stories make up this book were at school or at work in 1938 when Prime Minister Neville Chamberlain returned from Munich with the promise of 'Peace in our time'. There was a feeling of great relief because no one wanted a repeat of the Great War, the 'war to end all wars'.

Some thought that a stand should have been made at that moment and were ashamed at the betrayal of Czechoslovakia. Others said that Britain was not prepared for war after years of low spending on armaments. In particular, there were nothing like enough modern warplanes. Weapons production immediately accelerated.

In September 1939, Hitler invaded Poland. France and Britain declared war. Chamberlain's radio broadcast announcing the fact was immediately followed by an air-raid warning. Terror bombing and gas were the great fears. The Soviet Union, in alliance with Germany, seized part of Poland and invaded Finland.

A British Expeditionary Force and some squadrons of the Royal Air Force were sent to France. The French put their faith in the Maginot Line, an immensely strong system of underground fortifications running from France's border with Switzerland to the border with Belgium. Along the Belgian frontier the British troops trained, dug trenches and built pill-boxes.

For the Royal Navy there was no phoney war. After ferrying the BEF to France, it blockaded Germany and established a convoy system for merchant shipping. In April Germany invaded Norway, bypassing the Navy's attempts to intercept their fleet at sea. British and French troops were landed but made little headway. The Navy did well in several fierce actions but it was felt that the whole campaign had been bungled from the start.

Meanwhile, on the French border, nothing of note had happened for months.

In northern France, May 1940

Ken Lee: Age 23, Pilot Officer, No. 501 Squadron, flying Hurricanes, based in Britain, transferred to a base near Reims on 10 May.

Ernie Leggett: Age 20, Private, 2nd Battalion, Royal Norfolk Regiment, stationed in Orchies near the Franco-Belgian border.

Martin McLane: Age 28, Platoon Sergeant-Major, 2nd Battalion, Durham Light Infantry, stationed in Nomain near the Franco-Belgian border.

Iain Nethercott: Age 19, Able Seaman, serving in the destroyer HMS *Keith*, a flotilla leader, Dover Patrol.

Paul Richey: Age 23, Flying Officer, No. 1 Squadron, flying Hurricanes, based near Reims in eastern France.

Peter Vaux: Age 23, Second Lieutenant, 4th Battalion, Royal Tank Regiment, stationed in a training camp near Paris.

Denis Wissler: Age 19, Pilot Officer, No. 85 Squadron (later No. 17 Squadron), flying Hurricanes, based near Lille.

Map 1   British Expeditionary Force (BEF) Area of Operations, May 1940

Entries from the diary of Denis Wissler,
May 1940

Saturday 4th
'. . . I joined 85 squadron . . . The mob seem damn nice. I am in 'B'
Flight, blue section. There are few sanitary arrangements and no system
of having a bath, so everyone goes into Lille about once a week and has
one at a Hotel. I am sleeping in a room with seven other officers and all
of us on our camp kits between blankets . . .'

Sunday 5th
'I did my first patrol today, it was in answer to an alarm, but nothing
was seen and we returned after about 30 mins . . . This is a very quiet
sector and only about three enemy planes have ever been seen the whole
war, but we all hope that it will warm up soon.'

Monday 6th
'. . . The Duke of Gloucester visited the aerodrome and had tea in the
Mess. I played pontoon and Monopoly, losing 70 odd francs on the latter
and winning 30 on the former. Sunbathed most of morning . . .'

Tuesday 7th
'Did no flying today at all, but I had to remain at 30 mins readiness all day. It was a beautiful day and I got as sunburned as I have ever been before . . . I went into Lille and got a little pissed.'

Wednesday 8th
' . . . showed . . . a concert party over a 'Hurricane' and around our dispersal point. Then went to their show which also had the R.A.F. Central band, the whole was damn good. I was Orderly officer and in the evening I had to investigate a couple of shots, but nothing was seen or heard so I let it go.'

Thursday 9th
'I went on patrol again today and went up to 25,000 ft for quite a while. I really thought that our section had found something as we were being directed by the Controller who was getting very excited. However nothing was seen and we returned home. Nothing else happened during the day apart from some patrols, and directly after dinner I went to bed.'

Chapter 1

10–14 May

The pilots awoke to the urgent battering of anti-aircraft fire. Richard 'Dickey' Lee, Benjy Angus and 'Paddy' Hemingway tumbled out into the dawn. Denis Wissler followed them to the door of their sleeping quarters. 'Look, up there!' High above the control tower there were orange flashes in the sky over Lille. Somewhere a phone was ringing. Moments later Lee was sprinting across the dewy grass of Seclin airfield to his Hurricane: VY R. VY for 85 Squadron, R for Richard. Angus and Hemingway followed. 'B' Flight took off, first Lee then the others. Further away a section of three planes from 'A' Flight was already racing along the strip.

All through Friday, 10 May, they flew patrols in sections of three. Armourers, in shirtsleeves in the baking heat, hauled out case after case of machinegun belts. Dusty fuel bowsers trundled across the airfield, ready for the next time the planes came back. Refuelled and rearmed, the fighters roared up again into the haze. All day the sun beat down and the score mounted. 'A' Flight claimed five before breakfast. The ground crew cheered and slapped the pilots' backs. Some photographers were there, snapping away for the government. They photographed the armourers at work, they photographed the pilots as they landed, and they photographed 'A' Flight as a group, minus one pilot who was now in hospital with a cut eye after a bullet smashed his cockpit cover.

Denis Wissler had been with the squadron for a week. He did not even know the name of the man in hospital. His own flight, 'B' Flight, had done well too. 'Dickey' Lee came back with several holes in his aircraft and a graze to his leg, but by the end of the day he had been awarded two kills. Benjy Angus, the Canadian, had baled out over Belgium. He phoned through later to say that he was OK. No one had been killed or even seriously injured, and the total claim for the day was sixteen. Bombers everywhere, with little in the way of fighter protection.

Wissler hadn't flown. Squadron Leader Oliver had told him gently that he was too inexperienced for combat. He'd spent the day scanning the skies enviously from outside the officers' mess.

Someone was hammering on the door of the billet. Private Ernie Leggett pulled the curtain from the window and looked outside. In the grey first light, Company Sergeant-Major Gristock was barking instructions. As his head cleared, Leggett searched frantically for his wristwatch and stumbled out on to the Rue de la Gare, where the men stationed in Orchies were already mustering. There was a thunder of guns from the direction of Lille and a red glow in the sky over the airbases less than ten miles away. Sergeant Gristock ordered the company out on parade. One hundred and twenty men of the 2nd Battalion, Royal Norfolk Regiment stood to attention as he shouted: 'Get your kit together, we're moving out now.'

They were no more than a mile from Orchies, about halfway to the forest of Marchiennes, when German bombers flew over fast and low and plumes of smoke rose from their billets around the station. The men climbed out of the ditches by the road, dusted themselves down, looked back for a few moments and hurried on towards the safety of the trees.

Rabbits bolted at the sound of marching boots. The oak trees reminded Leggett of home. He was a country boy, raised in a scattered hamlet called Clippesby a couple of miles from Filby Broad. He used to walk two miles to school in one direction and a mile to church in the other. His father was a farm labourer; his brother had been crippled in an accident and could no longer work. At eleven Leggett passed the exam that entitled him to go to Yarmouth grammar school, but his parents could not afford the uniform.

Farm work was hard to find and so Leggett, aged sixteen, joined the Army. As well as learning infantry drill, the boy soldiers were trained as bandsmen. Leggett loved his leopardskin and drum. Each week he saved some of his ten shillings' pay to send to his mother. Army life suited him; he was tall and strong and he liked to look smart. He had shot rabbits with his brother from earliest boyhood and now he won marksman's badges for both rifle and 'Bren' light machinegun. The Bren fired five hundred rounds per minute and could slice through the trunk of a tree. But shooting at anything other than targets had seemed a distant prospect during three happy years in Gibraltar. Then war had come. 'We were the boys who met the enemy eye to eye and we would have to do the fighting. It suddenly sunk into our brains, not only me but other people as well – "what the hell have we done?"'

All day the soldiers shuffled about, talking in hushed voices, brewing tea and waiting for their marching orders. Sunlight flickered through the shielding canopy of trees. Leggett felt his stomach turning over with anxiety. He was determined to do his best. The only thing that unnerved him was the thought of close combat. 'I just couldn't bear anything to do with bayonets – using one or, even worse, being stabbed by one. We'd been taught all about it – how to push it in, twist it and rip it out – and just the idea of it made me feel cold inside.'

They would move under cover of darkness. As the light faded, Captain Barclay, Sergeant-Major Gristock and some of the other sergeants came out carrying hurricane lamps. Barclay said, 'Right-ho, lads, gather round, I've got something to tell you.' 'A' Company knelt round their captain in the gloom. It was his last words that they remembered: 'Now more than ever your training will stand you in

9

good stead. Keep your heads down and your spirits high, and from now on when you aim your rifle to shoot, you shoot to kill.'

Impressed with these ominous instructions, the company formed up and marched away into the darkness. They crossed the Belgian frontier by back lanes and then met their transport. During the night they travelled unscathed but the roads were crowded and they were still in their lorries at dawn. German reconnaissance found them. 'We heard the planes coming and we were given the order "everybody out" and we tumbled out of the back into the ditches and when we got back there was one man on the floor. A single bullet through the head had killed him. That was the first dead man I had ever seen in my life and of course it upset all of us.'

Sergeant-Major Gristock told his men to pull themselves together. But he looked up at the skies anxiously. Why was it that German aircraft could attack British infantry with such impunity? Where was the RAF?

The RAF was busy shooting down German planes all over northern and eastern France. But there were nothing like enough of them to cope with the hundreds of air attacks. The first light of day on 10 May had brought bombs screaming down on airfields and barracks all over France, Belgium and Holland. Within hours half of the Belgian Air Force and nearly all the Dutch was destroyed on the ground. German paratroops and glider forces were landing behind the front line. Waalhaven airport near Rotterdam was seized. Six RAF Blenheim fighter-bombers of 600 Squadron were sent there to destroy any aircraft on the ground. Only one returned home.

The British Royal Air Force in France was under French command. Orders were slow to arrive and hesitant when they came. 'At all costs avoid bombing built-up areas' was one injunction. Plans were quickly made to attack the advancing German units. But sending Britain's lumbering and lightly armed bombers against enemy forces protected by mobile anti-aircraft guns and fighter cover was to invite disaster. Later that day four waves of eight Fairey Battle light bombers attempted to disrupt a German column advancing through Luxembourg. Thirteen were destroyed and all the surviving planes were damaged. It was hard to know where the main effort should go when every unit was calling for fighters and bombers simultaneously. And it proved almost impossible to guide fighters and bombers to the same place at the same time.

The RAF's remaining bombing force was practically eliminated in a series of attacks on the German armoured divisions advancing through the Ardennes. On 11 May eight Fairey Battles attempted to bomb near Sedan. Seven were shot down. The RAF followed up with Blenheims. Five out of six were shot down. More Blenheims had been lost to German bombing in the morning. Of 114 Squadron's eighteen, neatly lined up on their airfield near Reims, six were destroyed and the rest made unserviceable.

Paul Richey was a pilot with No. 1 Squadron based near Reims. He had been in the Champagne country since the previous September, spoke fluent French and had made many friends in the villages around the British airfields. On Friday, 10 May he got up at 3 a.m. At 5 a.m. his flight patrolled over Metz and shot down a single Dornier bomber. At midday they tried to rendezvous with Fairey Battles over Luxembourg but, though they waited, the bombers did not appear. Later in the day the squadron was moved to a new base at Berry-au-Bac. They arrived to discover there was, as yet, no telephone link and no tankers to refuel their Hurricanes.

The tired pilots dozed in the oppressive heat. Then they saw twenty German planes approaching – Heinkel bombers. One peeled off and flew lazily towards them. 'Then we heard it – first a whisper, then a faint whistle that rose to an unearthly shriek that filled and split the heavens as if all the devils in hell had been let loose.' Richey threw himself underneath a lorry as a stick of bombs overshot into a neighbouring field where French villagers were ploughing. The shock of the explosions made the lorry bounce up and down on its wheels.

> We found them among the craters. The old man lay face-down, his body twisted grotesquely, one leg shattered and a savage gash across the back of his neck oozing steadily into the earth. His son lay close by in a state I will not describe. Against the hedge I found what must have been the remains of the third boy – recognisable only by a few tattered rags, a smashed boot and some splinters of bone.

Richey and his fellow pilots got some rifles and shot the stricken horses. 'I imagined the German bomb-aimer, heading for his base at 18,000 feet, entering in his log: "Military Objective bombed, Berry-au-Bac, British airfield".'

Next morning No. 1 Squadron got their fuel and their revenge. They ran into a formation of thirty Dorniers escorted by fifteen of the feared Messerschmitt 110 fighters, christened 'Destroyers' by the Luftwaffe. The six Hurricanes caught the Messerschmitts by surprise and saw several go down in flames. Richey claimed two kills but then found himself alone with three enemy planes and was himself shot down. As he drifted to earth at the end of his parachute he was surprised at how natural and peaceful everything became. He spent the night in the French village where he landed, and it was not until he returned to Berry on 12 May that the experience began to unsettle him: 'At this stage I began to feel peculiar. I had a hell of a headache and was jumpy and snappy. . . . I dared not speak for fear of bursting into tears.' An old lady in whose house he was billeted took him aside and said passionately, '*Vous êtes destiné à vivre*,' but Richey was not convinced and that night found his sleep disturbed by thoughts of death:

> Scarcely had I dropped off when I was in my Hurricane rushing head-on at a 110. Just as we were about to collide I woke with a jerk that nearly threw me out of bed. I was in a cold sweat, my heart banging wildly about . . . I shall never forget how I clung to the bed-rail in a dead funk.

'Get your men ready, we will be moving into Belgium.' Martin McLane's mortar platoon hauled their boxes of ammunition and their heavy mortars into a lorry. Just as they were about to go, an officer ordered McLane to take temporary charge of a frontier control point at Mouchin. His men and his mortars went forward without him and McLane spent the rest of 10 May directing traffic.

McLane was born in Bycker, Newcastle. He was the son of a shipyard worker, brought up in a part of the world where the men who worked the steel imagined themselves wrought from the same substance. He should have been building ships, but in the early 1930s there were not many ships to build. Unemployment drove him into the Army, where tough, resourceful lads were welcomed. Like Ernie Leggett, he found that he enjoyed the life. He was small and stocky with the build of a front-row forward, soon to be his position in the battalion rugby team. When the opposition made a mistake it would be McLane who was first to the muddy ball, winning possession for his team, as the other forwards drove over in support. The Army soon spotted his potential and promoted him first to corporal, then to sergeant, then to platoon sergeant-major. He could look after himself, could McLane, and the men respected him for it. They were a hard lot, his Durham lads, shipyard men like himself, and miners too. But they didn't dare take their sergeant on.

He had drilled them into a solid unit and he was sure that they would do the job when the time came. The 2nd Battalion Durham Light Infantry was one of those front-line units that got the best equipment the Army had, the half-track Bren gun-carriers and the motorised mortar platoons. McLane was interested in new equipment and he had made the mortar platoon his own. His two three-inch mortars gave local artillery support to the whole battalion. It was quite a responsibility, and that was why he was wondering what he was doing standing around directing traffic. What was more, the Germans couldn't have chosen a worse day to start. One of his mortars had a worn-out tripod. He had applied for a replacement from stores and they had sent him something else by mistake. It was certain that only one of his mortars would work. He needed time to find a good site and bring up ammunition and night-sights and yet here he was manning a checkpoint.

He thought of his wife Annie and their new baby. He had seen his little girl only once. He took the worn photograph of them both out of his pocket, as another column of lorries rumbled by. They weren't lorries from his own division any more, he could tell because their own 2 Division lorries were marked with crossed keys painted white on the bumper. He seemed to have been left there and forgotten. He got on his motorcycle and rode north in search of his men.

As a child Ernie Leggett had sat in his family's pew at St Peter's, Clippesby, gazing at the large stained-glass window over the altar. The crossed keys of St Peter fascinated him. Silver over gold, they seemed to shine when the sun hit them from the east. When he'd arrived in France his battalion had been put into 2 Division. All around him, on shoulder flashes and painted on to half-tracks and lorries, were the same crossed keys. Leggett had thought it was a good omen.

He had been travelling now for twenty-four hours, with several stops to shelter from strafing German planes. The Norfolks had tried firing their rifles and Bren guns back up at them, and once they were sure that they had hit something, but they had still seen no sign of a French or British fighter. Then, as they left their lorries near Wavre, they encountered a new kind of terror. 'We heard these Stuka dive-bombers and they had sirens on their wheels and as they came down they made this terrific hellish noise, screaming. Also the bombs which they let loose had sirens in their tails and it was the most hellish terrific noise you could ever encounter. And I threw myself down on the bank spread-eagled and I shook just like a jelly. We all did, we couldn't help it.'

The British government was in crisis even before it was hit by news of the German offensive. On 7 May, during a passionate debate about the previous month's fighting in Norway, Conservative Prime Minister Neville Chamberlain had sat, head bowed, whilst former supporters called upon him to resign and the Labour opposition chanted 'Go, Go, Go!' At first he tried to fight it out, attempting to build a cross-party coalition. But the Labour Party refused to serve under the man they blamed for years of appeasing Hitler and for eight months of insipid wartime leadership.

Chamberlain had two obvious successors: Foreign Secretary Lord Halifax and Lord of the Admiralty Winston Churchill. Both were from wealthy landed families, but there the similarity ended. Halifax was urbane, well read and icily logical. He had served as Viceroy of India, the most prestigious administrative post the British Empire had to offer, and carried with him a sense of earnestness and piety that led to the nickname of 'Lord Holy Fox'.

Winston Churchill had accumulated many nicknames but the word 'holy' hadn't featured in any of them. Sometimes a reformer, sometimes a reactionary, he'd been in and out of office since 1906. In Parliament he was widely seen as a maverick. But Churchill had consistently warned about Hitler and called for British rearmament. And he spoke well on the radio.

Halifax, the consummate 'insider', was the choice of London's political and social élite. A great friend of the royal family, he had been granted the rare privilege of a key to the Buckingham Palace gardens so that his daily walk to work might take him through the grounds. But Halifax sat in the House of Lords and felt this would make it difficult for him to control the more disorderly House of Commons. When Chamberlain offered him his chance, he demurred.

Churchill seized the opportunity. Supported by the leaders of the Labour Party, he accepted Chamberlain's suggestion that he form a coalition government. Halifax and Chamberlain were both offered seats in a new five-man War Cabinet along with Labour leader Clement Attlee and his deputy Arthur Greenwood. The news broke on the morning of 10 May.

To fight a difficult and protracted war, Britain needed leadership and a common purpose. But the 1930s had been a decade of division, depression and drift. Capital and labour, rich and poor, employed and unemployed – the scars ran very deep. Poverty, poor health and decrepit housing scarred the old industrial cities. Churchill, a former Home Secretary, had once been denounced by the Left as a strike-breaker. Now he went out of his way to bring the representatives of this other Britain into his war effort. He appointed the former trade union boss Ernest Bevin as his Minister for Labour.

Churchill faced a huge challenge. Hitler's previous enemies had been overwhelmed as much by psychological pressure as military force. Men will only face Stukas and bayonets for so long when they feel it is in a lost cause. From the moment he took office, Churchill placed morale at the heart of his policy-making. His primary aim, whatever his own private anxieties, and there were many, was to spread confidence – within his Cabinet, through the machinery of government, then outward into the nation. But it wouldn't be easy. On the first evening of his administration, Churchill's personal detective wished him luck. 'I hope that it is not too late,' the new Prime Minister replied. 'I am very much afraid that it is.'

There were military policemen at every junction as Martin McLane rode his motorcycle through the forest of Soignes, looking for his battalion of Durham Light Infantry. He waved to a final Redcap, who directed him up a minor road. Soon after, McLane arrived at La Tombe, an isolated hamlet on a hillside above the little River Dyle. Here, south-east of Brussels, on what military planners had called the Dyle Line, the British Army was moving into defensive positions prepared for them by the Belgians. There they would hold the Germans. But it was immediately clear that the Belgian defences did not amount to much and McLane found that his mortar platoon had been ordered to dig trenches. Furious, he demanded that they should go forward to site the mortars – or, rather, mortar. No new tripod had been delivered while he had been away.

One man carried the base, another the barrel. The rest carried six bombs each plus their kit. Each bomb weighed ten pounds and there were three to a case. With this load they struggled down a winding path through thick beech woods to the front line. As he trudged through the trees, McLane was still cursing the new company commander under his breath. The captain was a schoolteacher, a Territorial recently shipped in to take charge of Headquarters Company. This company had all the best kit – the Bren-carriers, the signallers and the mortars – and this new captain had no idea how to use it. He didn't seem interested in what a mortar could do given proper communications and transport. They should have promoted one of the regular lieutenants, who would have known what to do.

As they reached the river there was a sudden change in scenery. They were in the park of a country house. McLane quickly assessed the terrain. Ahead of him a straight track led over an ornamental bridge to a village on the other side of the river. Immediately to the left a wooded spur of the hill commanded the riverside. Farther left and away to the right were open water meadows. Behind him on a grassy hill stood a beautiful country house. It looked like the ideal vantage point. The carrier platoon, which had been scouting, returned. They had seen the Germans coming only about a mile away. The engineers had been waiting for them to come back over the bridge and were now preparing to blow it up.

McLane walked up the path towards the house. It was lined with ornamental railings. The whole place was absolutely beautiful. He thought about days out and picnics with Annie. He'd got a letter from her a few days before. It was the last one he would receive for some time now that they were going into action. A few months back he'd had to warn her that the officers read all the letters to check on morale. She'd said that thinking of some of the things she had written and then the officers reading it all had made her blush. She wrote very loving letters, did Annie.

Before he reached the top of the path a bullet whistled past. McLane could hear it as clear as day. Snipers! You could see right across the valley from up here. He pulled out his binoculars. There were German motorcyclists on the road across the river. This would be a great spot to put the mortar but absolutely obvious to the enemy. It would be a magnet for their mortars and artillery. He crawled away a bit until he was no longer silhouetted and then walked on to the house, went round to the side door that faced away from the Germans, and knocked. A small man with a goatee beard, not much taller than McLane, opened the door. McLane could hear that inside the family was having dinner. 'You want to vamoose tout de suite, Allemands coming.' The Belgian said nothing, but hurried off. McLane was not sure that he had been understood, but feeling that he had done the decent thing, he went back down the hill, taking care to keep out of view until he got back to his men.

He decided to site the mortar behind some sheds in a clump of trees just off the straight track. It was not the ideal position but he could see the main road on the far side of the river from there. Scores of refugees, their belongings piled on carts, were trudging by. The bridge, he noted, was too close to where 'D' Company had dug in to land mortars on it, but at a pinch he could hit the meadows beyond to the left, and he had a clear view to the right. He told the men to dig in. As he turned to report to Headquarters he saw a car racing down the drive away from the château. It turned right through some trees and disappeared. 'See,' he told his corporal, 'told you I could speak French.'

As McLane's platoon dug in behind the River Dyle, they saw waves of German bombers passing overhead and flying on towards Brussels.

85 Squadron still wouldn't let Denis Wissler fly and so he was writing up his diary. He became aware of a distant drone. It must be the Hurricanes returning again. Then he realised the note was wrong. Bombers! He sprinted for his life. Two bombs landed thirty feet from him, demolishing the sleeping quarters. In the rubble they found a body. A cook was pulled out alive, whimpering with pain. Another bomb hit the adjutant's car. His driver had been blown to pieces. In the evening Wissler wrote: 'I came nearest to death today than I have ever been . . . I was in the Ante-Room and my God did I run . . . There was a raid into Germany, which our chaps convoyed, and Dickey Lee has so far not returned. We are going to sleep by the aeroplanes in a Nissen hut tonight.'

Dickey Lee had doubled his score to four on 11 May before disappearing somewhere deep in Belgium, now a long way behind enemy lines. He was the squadron's hero. Tall and handsome, he looked every inch the dashing young air ace. Lee was twenty-three and had graduated from the RAF College at Cranwell in 1937. He had been in France since the beginning of the war. He knew his Hurricane inside out and had even flown stunts in a George Formby film. Wissler, by contrast, had joined up on 10 July 1939, the eve of his nineteenth birthday, and he knew he looked his age. He had completed his basic flying training in April and was only in France because he had drawn the short straw when one of eight trainee pilots was required to go. He had little more than two hundred hours experience of flying and only a handful of these had been in a Hurricane.

Mounting casualties brought him his chance, and on Sunday, 12 May Wissler finally represented 'B' Flight in more than just late-night bar games. Straight away, he found that flying patrols wasn't easy. On the first one he got lost. He landed at an airfield that turned out to be a French base, got directions, flew home and did another sortie. They didn't find any enemy but the tension and excitement quickly unsettled him. On the evening of 12 May, from new quarters in Lesquin, he scrawled, 'I now have had 6 hours sleep in 48 hours and haven't washed for over 36 hours. My God am I tired? And I am up again at 3 am tomorrow.'

Monday morning brought good news. Dickey Lee turned up. He had crashed, been captured, escaped from a hayloft, borrowed some clothes from a peasant, and picked his way through enemy lines. Typical. Wissler flew two more patrols that day. On the second his flight was bounced by Messerschmitt 109s, the fastest and most deadly German fighter plane. The squadron leader was shot down but baled out. Fleeing for the clouds, Wissler found himself alone and disoriented. He landed at an airfield that turned out to be Cambrai and a French engineer told him that his plane was gushing oil. While English ground crew were summoned to find the fault, Wissler ate in the 'very pukka' French mess, acutely conscious of his own dishevelled state, and then finally got a good night's sleep.

Taking off without being bombed, handling tight manoeuvres without stalling, finding his way back to the airfield and landing the plane among shell craters demanded all the skill he could yet command. Pilots like Dickey Lee or Paul Richey had three years of flying behind them, and six months to learn the geography of northern France. Wissler had to try to master all these things in four days while, simultaneously, the Luftwaffe was doing its best to kill him. No wonder he was tired.

Within days of coming to power, Churchill was juggling military resources, attempting to boost war production and dealing with a panic-stricken ally. Across London there were many who thought he was singularly ill equipped for the job. Churchill's enemies called him unstable, impetuous and absolutely the wrong man to trust with weighty matters of state in a moment of unsurpassed crisis. Some of those who had served under him in the First World War remembered the disastrous landings he'd masterminded at Gallipoli.

They predicted more of the same. Such fears were amplified when Churchill announced that he would combine the role of Prime Minister with running the Ministry of Defence. He also proclaimed that he would lead a special defence committee made up of himself and the Chiefs of Staff, putting him in day-to-day, hour-to-hour command of Britain's armed forces. Clearly this was not going to be Parliament's war, or even the Cabinet's war – it was going to be Churchill's war.

At first he spent very little time in Downing Street, preferring to remain at the Admiralty whilst the Chamberlains packed their bags. Waiting for him inside Number 10 was a nervous twenty-year-old secretary called Marian Holmes. Holmes had been with Chamberlain for three years. He had been a gracious, considerate employer who stopped work at 6 p.m. and retired after a simple dinner to his private rooms to read. She was dreading her first encounter with her new boss: 'The staff at Number Ten had grave misgivings about this man. They'd heard rumours about how he was impossible to please, difficult to work for, that he was a man used to giving orders but unaware of the practicalities of carrying them out.'

Lord Halifax had turned down his chance to form a government. Nevertheless, some of his followers were free with their scorn about the man who had taken control of the nation. 'Rab' Butler was Halifax's deputy at the Foreign Office. In the presence of John 'Jock' Colville, Chamberlain's assistant private secretary, Butler called Churchill 'a half-breed American whose main support was that of inefficient but talkative people of similar type'. Butler despaired that 'the good clean tradition of English politics . . . had been sold to the greatest adventurer of modern political history'. Colville, who was about to start working for the new Prime Minister, wrote in his diary that 'Everybody here is in despair at the prospect . . . [Churchill] may be able to speed up our creaking military and industrial machinery, but it is a terrible risk, it involves the danger of rash and spectacular exploits . . .'

Churchill's critics were sceptical about his lifestyle and way of working. The new Prime Minister liked to be at the centre of a fluid group of advisers, ministers and generals who would together embark on late night brainstorming sessions sustained by huge dinners, cigars and champagne. 'The Crazy Gang', one senior official called them. Inspired by the atmosphere (or, some said, by the alcohol), Churchill's mind would race, enthusiastically leaping from topic to topic, and a plethora of memos, directives and letters would result. Halifax, Butler and many others distrusted Churchill's fondness for boisterous dining partners like Canadian newspaper proprietor Max Aitken, Lord Beaverbrook, or the MP and financier Brendan Bracken.

But to his admirers Churchill represented hope, inspiration and a pure galvanising energy. Here, at last, was a natural leader, someone who would revitalise the nation and trample on the toes of the slow, shabby and pusillanimous Britain of recent years. Violet Bonham-Carter, whose father, Herbert Asquith, had led the nation into the First World War, wrote to Churchill during his first week in office: 'My wish is realised and I can face all that is to come with faith and confidence. I know, as you do, that the wind has been sown and that we must all reap the whirlwind. But you will ride it, instead of being driven before it. Thank heaven that you are there and at the helm of our destiny.' And whatever his detractors might say about over-confidence, Churchill more than anyone knew the size of the task before him. He had spent years cataloguing British military weakness. Now he would have to make the best he could of the paltry resources available.

Three days after taking office, he addressed the House of Commons for the first time as Prime Minister. In the first of hundreds of bravura performances, he announced in a grave and trembling voice that: 'I have nothing to offer but blood, toil, tears and sweat. We have before us an ordeal of the most grievous kind. We have before us many, many long months of struggle and of suffering.'

Chapter 2

14–20 May

The British Army's three-inch mortar could be devastatingly effective. Each shell burst scattered fragments of red-hot metal across a radius of fifty feet in open ground. If the shell landed on a hard surface the effect was even more deadly, with shards of stone added to the shrapnel. The mortar was versatile; it could lay down smoke to cover an attack or a retreat. It was just about portable too, but needed lorry support for ammunition and spares.

Martin McLane had dug and camouflaged an observation trench with a clear line of sight along the path that led to the bridge over the River Dyle and the German positions beyond. From here he could shout instructions to his crew, twenty yards away hidden behind some farm buildings. McLane then went back to his battalion headquarters to get the night-aiming equipment, megaphone, lamps and more ammunition, only to find that his support trucks, which he had left carefully hidden in a wood, had been sent back to the brigade support base fifteen miles to the rear. After an argument with the company sergeant-major, he applied for more ammunition and left. It did not arrive until next morning. It took twenty-four of his men to carry the 144 rounds three-quarters of a mile to the mortar post.

Around noon on Tuesday, 14 May the Germans made their first

attack. McLane ranged his mortar on the houses over the river, switching direction every so often to cover 'C' Company on his right. It was just like the drill: take off the safety cap, drop the shell down the barrel and cover your ears. Bang! Shells lobbed towards the enemy. One every five or six seconds. McLane shouted out orders: 'Range 240, elevate fifteen degrees, fire!'

Across the river he could see German soldiers blown high into the air. He felt a professional satisfaction in a job well done. The forward companies had only taken light casualties and, as the Germans retreated, the whole 2nd Battalion, Durham Light Infantry enjoyed the sensation of a first battle won.

At dawn on 15 May the Durhams realised that German sappers had got underneath the demolished bridge over the Dyle during the night. It was at most fifty yards in front of their positions – far too close for McLane to fire on it without risk to his own side. It was a straight bridge with a straight track leading up to it. The approach was very exposed, but a young platoon leader, Second Lieutenant Annand, did not hesitate:

> He ran with his grenades, dodging here and here, dodging and dodging and scooting down, moving around, and he got to the edge of this bridge and he just unloaded his grenades. And he caused devastation in that area. Now I don't know who was in there, but you could hear them yelling. You don't think that a soldier dies peacefully, they yell and scream when they're hit and wounded, have no doubt of that, they scream for their mothers a lot of them. But you could hear the screams coming from the place, with the men badly hit.

During the day the Germans got under the bridge again and Lieutenant Annand cleared it once more, earning the first Army Victoria Cross of the campaign. To McLane's right the Germans stormed a pill-box but 'C' Company took it back. The battle for the River Dyle was getting fiercer, but the Durhams were standing firm and Martin McLane was proud of his men.

Paul Richey was getting angry: 'We had started out open-mindedly making full allowance for alleged German atrocities', but on 14 May a crowd of French refugees trudged past the pilots' mess at Pontavert. They spoke of being bombed and machine gunned:

> This child's father had been killed by a strafing Hun; that young woman's small daughter had had her brains blown out by a bomb-splinter and so on. It was heart breaking to see these pathetic people, hungry, tired, with fear in their eye, fleeing before the relentless invader ... There was a stony silence in the mess when we told our story. Then a disillusioned Johnny almost reluctantly said, 'They are shits – after all.' From this moment our concept of a chivalrous foe was dead. We suddenly saw the war in a grimmer, uglier and no doubt truer light – and we realised we were not just fighting Germans, but Nazis.

Richey's flight of five or six planes was regularly attacking large groups of German bombers, with Messerschmitt 109s high above waiting to swoop. On Wednesday, 15 May, after just such an unequal fight, Richey was shot down for the second time in three days. Having hitched a lift back to Reims, he met some pilots from No. 73 Squadron and heard about some encouraging signs of respect from the Luftwaffe. His friend 'Cobber' Kain claimed to have come across a lone German bomber whose entire crew baled out at the sight of the Hurricane before a single shot was fired.

Later, after the eighth bombing raid on their airfield at Berry-au-Bac, the No.1 Squadron pilots were relaxing in the garden of the mess. They cheered as they watched an aircraft shot down in a distant fight. Then they realised it was a Hurricane: 'We watched, hypnotised, as the spinning aircraft crawled slowly down the cloud mountain, flicking round and around like a dead leaf floating from a tall tree. We tensed as we waited for the white blob of a parachute to appear . . . But nothing happened . . . and as it dropped and dropped to the base of the cloud, so did our hopes fall; until finally it disappeared in the evening shadow, leaving only its signature – a crooked trail of smoke down the sky – to mark its last flight.'

A kind of bloodlust took over Richey:

> . . . we hadn't wanted this bloody awful war that the Huns seemed to think so glorious. We had been forced to fight. And now that we are fighting, we thought, we'll teach you rotten Huns how to fight. We'll shoot your pissy little fighters out of the sky, we'll rip your dirty great bombers to shreds, we'll make you wish to Christ you'd never heard of the aeroplane!

Somewhere in the huge oak forest that covered the hills south of Brussels and north of the River Dyle, Second Lieutenant Peter Vaux was waiting for some orders. He was the reconnaissance officer with the 4th Battalion, Royal Tank Regiment, so he had been sent to the forest in advance of the tanks to work out the best places to put them when they arrived.

The previous four days had been exhausting. On 10 May he had been at Pacy-sur-Eure, south-west of Paris. He had been woken at six by the technical adjutant with the news that 'The Germans have gone into Belgium and you're off to Brussels at once'. Within two hours his eight-hundredweight truck had rumbled over the cobbles, heading north. Towards evening they crossed the Somme at Amiens. The roads were crowded. Columns of lorries were crawling north and cars with mattresses on the roof were trying to get south. The occupants looked very scared. Looking out at distant flashes of gunfire and hearing the rumbling, echoing sound of bombs, Vaux thought of his father, a mining engineer who had come back from Malaya to fight in 1914. He too would have heard the sound of shells as he approached the front. He probably marched up the same road.

Peter Vaux was twenty-three. Born in 1916, he had been

conceived on leave. His father had been a tunneller, laying mines under German trenches. He must have been very brave.

Vaux had grown up in Devon. At eighteen he had gone to Sandhurst Military College. In 1938 they had been taken on a battlefield tour through Flanders. The place names were already familiar, and they had trained in this area too. They drove through Doullens and swung on to the Arras road. Vaux knew his roads; a reconnaissance officer should. He had got the lorry safely to Brussels and they had picked up the map reference for where the tanks were to be placed.

But since the tanks had arrived from their train two days previously they had heard nothing from Headquarters. He wondered if his father had felt as he did now. 'It wasn't fear, or not quite, it was a kind of anticipation and excitement and a sense of going into the unknown. We felt we were a good army, we'd been well trained, and we wanted to get at the enemy.'

The tank crews sat tight in the wood, unable to see anything and with no news of what might be happening elsewhere. Distant rumbles of gunfire raised the level of anxiety:

> It was all really rather alarming. This great forest was a creepy sort of place at the best of times. There was an aeroplane which crashed in the middle of the forest and hit someone's ammunition dump so there was the most almighty explosion. Then a man arrived in our midst from nowhere and said he was the last survivor of some artillery regiment. And we didn't really know where these Germans were that were supposed to have decimated this man's regiment. He said they were at the other end of our wood. But, of course, at that stage we didn't realise that when someone said they were the last survivor of something it often meant they had been the first to run away.

Communication was a problem throughout the British Army in France. The Germans had mobile radio sets and could call down instant artillery and air support. Each British battalion also had a radio, but the enemy could intercept radio transmissions and so their use was forbidden prior to actual combat. Expecting a static, defensive war, the Allies had laid some fixed land-lines, but these quickly proved vulnerable to bombing or sabotage. Very soon communication at almost every level relied on dispatch riders and runners.

As he was in charge of the battalion's only three-inch mortar, Martin McLane should have been kept informed of developments in the battle, but no runner came from Headquarters. Then, as he was away seeking information, a ferocious German attack overran 'C' Company's forward positions, outflanking the mortar. McLane's men fell back with what they could carry, leaving the mortar's baseplate embedded in the ground. But they still had the base of the second mortar, so McLane hurriedly reassembled his weapon and shelled the fields by the river where the Germans had broken through. Unknown to McLane, a counter-attack had already been launched.

He saw the men in khaki too late. Suddenly there were shells exploding amongst them – his shells, the ones he had dragged up from the lorry. Sick with horror and shame, McLane pulled out his revolver. He meant to shoot himself but his men were too quick. 'One of them just hit my hand. "Not worth it," he said.' The men shouted at their sergeant. They told him that they needed him.

On the evening of 15 May orders finally came through to both McLane and Peter Vaux, still waiting with his tanks in the forest. To their astonishment both were ordered to retreat to the south-west. Vaux was told to meet tank transporters at the railway station in Halle. But it had been bombed flat. With no prospect of a train, the tanks and their support vehicles set out down the road towards Lille. There was no transport available for Martin McLane's men either, so they hauled their mortar on to a cart and attached it to an old horse they found in a barn. Slowly they wound down the valley, away from their first battlefield and towards Brussels.

General Lord Gort, commander of the British Expeditionary Force, had just been told that the main German armoured force had broken through to the south. The attack on the River Dyle had been a feint, designed to draw the British Army north into a trap. To keep the line straight, Gort's French superior had ordered a redeployment to the River Lasne. The BEF's long retreat had begun.

David Low's cartoon in the *Evening Standard* was called 'All Behind you Winston'. It had Chamberlain, Halifax and the rest of the Cabinet all grimly rolling up their sleeves and marching determinedly behind their new leader at the head of a vast mass of the British people. Certainly, some were behind Churchill. Labour's Ernie Bevin threw himself into the new administration, bullying union leaders and forcing through agreements to curb strikes and suspend long-cherished working practices.

And Churchill, despite his sixty-five years, seemed to have the power to energise a moribund bureaucracy. Marian Holmes was startled by the energy of her new employer. With Chamberlain it had been slow, slow, slow. Churchill's way of doing business was totally different:

> he was to be seen striding down the garden path with his chin jutting out and a sense of resolve, and a contagious air of confidence. And very soon the whole attitude to him changed to one of absolute admiration and it's difficult to describe adequately the change – it was as if a superhuman current of electricity had gone through Number Ten Downing Street.

But were they really all behind him? Churchill's first few appearances in the House of Commons were received with grudging and half-hearted acclaim from the Conservative benches. And Whitehall was full of politicians and civil servants who looked on aghast as Churchill brought his loud, pushy friends into Number 10 and offered them jobs in his government. Private secretary 'Jock' Colville had yet to make up his mind about his new master: 'I spent the day in a bright blue new suit from the Fifty-Shilling Tailors, cheap and sensational looking, which I felt was appropriate to the new government.'

Shock at the speed of the German advance was keenly felt in Washington. A war like that of 1914 had been expected, and the French were thought to have a fine army. There would be time for America to decide what to do. But suddenly there was nothing but news of collapse and retreat and something close to panic gripped the State Department.

Throughout May, Secretary of State Cordell Hull received cables from various embassies reporting wild speculation about German intentions and secret weapons. One from Havana, an important intelligence centre, mentioned transcontinental supersubmarines, huge new bombers, 'air torpedoes' and other horrors lifted, it seemed, from the pages of H.G. Wells. Germany appeared sinister and brilliant and quite unstoppable.

In Washington's emerging nightmare, Italy would soon run the Mediterranean, Hitler would control Europe and the old British and French Empires while Japan would dominate the Pacific and China. And all this would happen before America had begun to shake itself from decades of weakness and isolation.

As the news from France worsened and the cable traffic into Washington grew ever more fevered, all that stood between America and a world dominated by her enemies was the ambiguous figure of Winston Churchill. Aware that Churchill was the most belligerent member of Chamberlain's Cabinet, President Franklin D. Roosevelt had been secretly corresponding with him since the beginning of the war. Roosevelt had spoken of his desire to help Britain to the limits of his power. But his power was severely limited. Congress was wary of any foreign policy commitments and highly suspicious of the European powers, who had already dragged America into one terrible foreign war and then refused to honour their war debts.

A presidential election was due in November. Would there be votes in a large increase in military support for Britain? It seemed unlikely. And many in Washington wondered if Britain, and the man who now led her, was even worth supporting. Perhaps America, ill prepared for war herself, should look first to her own defence rather than waste resources on a lost cause.

Contrasting attitudes towards Churchill would dominate America's reaction to the crisis. Roosevelt had sent diplomatic troubleshooter Sumner Welles on a mission to London just before the Germans attacked on 10 May. Welles's first impression of Churchill was widely discussed in Washington. The great man had greeted the American party at the private flat in the Admiralty smoking a huge cigar and 'drinking a whiskey and soda', having 'consumed a good many whiskeys'. According to Welles's account, Churchill first offered the sternly teetotal American ambassador, Joseph Kennedy, a glass, and then went on to deliver a 'cascade of oratory, brilliant and always effective, interlarded with considerable wit', declaring that 'we will win the war and that is the only hope of civilisation'.

The Cabinet discussed the situation in Europe. According to Secretary of the Interior Harold Ickes, talk soon turned to the character of the new British Prime Minister:

> the President said that he supposed that Churchill was the best man that England had even if he was drunk half of his time. Apparently Churchill is very unreliable when under the influence of drink . . . At any rate I am glad that Chamberlain is out. I had no hope in my own heart so long as this inept man was at the head of the British government. To his small clique in the British Empire under his leadership has been due the terrible situation in which the world finds itself today.

If Washington was initially unsure about Churchill, it had even less confidence in some of his ministers. A sense that the British government was divided percolated back to America. In March Rab Butler, Lord Halifax's deputy at the Foreign Office, had walked in St James's Park with James Moffat, another of Washington's top diplomats. Moffat recalled that Butler seemed very keen on peace, was understanding towards the Nazis and had then told him that there were forces more constructive than Churchill in Britain. What was the State Department supposed to make of that?

Such uncertainty affected Roosevelt's reaction to Churchill's immediate appeals for aid. Five days after becoming Prime Minister, Churchill cabled the President asking for the immediate loan of fifty mothballed old destroyers and for other military assistance. He warned starkly that 'the voice and force of the United States may count for nothing if they are withheld too long. You may have a completely subjugated Nazified Europe established with astonishing swiftness.'

Thus was established the main political dynamic of 1940: Churchill pleading for help and warning Roosevelt that America's front line lay in Europe, Roosevelt agonising about Britain's prospects and the kind of help that could be given without forfeiting public opinion and the support of Congress.

The news from France suddenly worsened. Churchill learned that the Germans had crossed the Meuse at Sedan. At first the French generals were unruffled. Late during the night of 14 May, the capitulation of Holland was announced on the radio. Churchill had known this was coming. The Dutch Queen, Wilhelmina, had just been evacuated on a British destroyer. Then soon after 7 a.m. in the morning of 15 May Churchill received an alarming phone call from Paul Reynaud, the French Prime Minister, who was very excited. He announced that tanks were pouring through at Sedan and that 'the road to Paris was open'. Churchill was reassuring, but Reynaud remained insistent that 'the battle was lost'.

Churchill rang up General Georges, commanding the French forces in the field, who seemed quite relaxed and told him that the gap had been plugged. At 3 p.m. on 16 May Churchill flew to Paris to find out for himself what was going on. The mood of the French generals had changed. Using a map, they now quite calmly revealed a dangerous dent in the front that stretched almost to Reims. Churchill's request to be shown the position of the strategic reserve was met with a shrug of the shoulders. There was none. Out of a window Churchill could see bureaucrats burning official papers in a courtyard. Somebody clearly did not expect to be in Paris for very much longer.

Churchill returned to London and the first of many depressing messages from Roosevelt. He could not ask Congress for permission to hand over any destroyers at the moment. It was politically impossible.

Aware of the need to keep up morale in Whitehall and beyond, Churchill knew the value of even a token gesture from America. He mentioned his expectation of American aid at every opportunity. But what he said was based more on wishful thinking than any real evidence of support from Washington.

Once the bad news broke, it got rapidly worse. On 17 May newspaper headlines announced that Brussels had fallen and that German tanks had broken through the Maginot Line. The supposedly impregnable Maginot Line, a series of mechanised forts and tunnels upon which France had pinned her faith, stretched from Switzerland to the Ardennes. But northward from there, along the border with Belgium, the 'Line' was only pill-boxes and barbed wire put in place over the previous winter. It was through these improvised defences that the Panzers had smashed.

The news shocked the world. In Ottawa the Canadian Prime Minister, William Mackenzie King, wrote in his diary that day: 'Situation very serious . . . They have not anything like the supply of planes or engines for planes that they should have – quite inadequate . . . the Blitzkrieg might lead to destruction of Britain and France within the next few weeks.'

The 2nd Battalion, the Royal Norfolk Regiment, was screening the withdrawal to the river Lasne. During 16 May Ernie Leggett's company remained dug in under shellfire. That night they skirted the old battlefield of Waterloo as they withdrew to the Brussels-Charleroi canal. They marched seventeen miles because their transport had got lost in the forest. The night march and the accumulated tension of the last few days brought them close to collapse: 'People say that you can't march while you're asleep – well I can tell you here and now you can march while you're asleep because I've done it – and all my company did it! The only time you wake up is when you bump into the man ahead of you or the man behind you bumps into you. Marching along asleep in the darkness.'

When they reached their new positions at eight in the morning they had hardly had breakfast when the order came to fall back further, this time to the River Dendre. Shattered as they already were, they marched all though the day along roads now crammed with civilian refugees:

> Villages and towns had just been brought to the ground. And there was water and smoke, and fires in the streets. And I can still remember that terrible smell of death after a bombing or shelling had occurred. And people were in these houses, they hadn't been taken out and there was still that horrible stench which we had to go through. As we went past some woods all the trees had been uprooted, the tops had been shelled away, and it was just like walking through a hell.

Leggett scavenged for food, taking raw swedes from the fields: 'In their cellars they used to cure meat and we were able to help ourselves to an extent to that. The only water we had to drink was water out of the ditches which we were able to boil.'

In order to get past the slow-moving civilians, the soldiers took to the fields. And so, when German aircraft attacked, it was mostly the refugees they hit:

> We saw horses and carts and people and everything blown sky high. Most bodies were mutilated, blown to pieces. We could shoot the animals – we saw a horse which had its guts open

and we shot it – but the people, we couldn't stop and help them. We couldn't give them first aid. We saw them go up in the air and just pieces flying everywhere. We were all right. We were in the fields. We then realised what the enemy was – what mentality they had. They had no need. All they did was just murder. We realised that some of the propaganda we'd heard previously was coming true to life.

They reached their latest river defence line in the evening and dug shallow trenches. But they were told to retreat again, this time to Tournai. The transport was reported lost so they stumbled off on foot.

Martin McLane's Durhams were also retreating and also, now, on foot. The wheel had come off their improvised horse-drawn mortar transport. At first they tried to carry the weapon. Then they disabled and buried it.

They settled into a rhythm: five miles, a short rest, perhaps a cup of sweet tea, then another ten, trudging along roads that were choked with refugees, eyes open for bombers:

I was just shattered for the want of sleep. Men would just keep marching in a line when the rest turned the corner. They were in a kind of trance. The poor pathetic people that were walking along the roads, you had to see them to believe them. Old horses and carts, farm carts, big ones, little ones, all loaded up with their family possessions. All the people looking frightened and desperate, walking along the roads, not knowing what was happening, not knowing what to do. They had dog carts laden up with stuff, they had bicycles laden up with stuff, the men were carrying big loads on their backs, the children were plodding along the side of the road. Old people they were collapsing exhausted and people were trying to recover them. You could see them huddle about the person and they'd eventually lift her or him onto a cart, and they'd move off on the road.

On 15 May Denis Wissler's luck almost ran out as 'B' Flight scrambled in another last-minute attempt to intercept German bombers: 'I crashed taking off in a Hurricane, overturned, the cabin cowling collapsed, and I was pinned underneath. The crew were very prompt getting me out but they had to dig in order to release the escape panel. All I had time to do was to duck my head, and even so we can't understand how I did not break my neck or back. The machine is a complete write-off.' The field had been very uneven. When the plane turned over the cockpit had ended up over a hole in the ground. But for this piece of luck Wissler would have broken his neck. Instead, for three days he was nursing a sore back and in too much pain to fly. So he was able to enjoy 85 Squadron's new quarters in a château that had once belonged to the famous Duke of Marlborough.

There he saw his first burns case. He had met the man as they had travelled up on the train together to Lille to join the squadron. He had chattered endlessly. The previous day he had baled out with his plane on fire, his face completely scorched and blackened. He wouldn't be talking again for some months.

From the château garden Wissler watched three Hurricanes take off to attack a hundred passing bombers and saw the Canadian Benjy Angus become the squadron's first pilot to be killed. Before the day was out another pilot was dead and one missing. They buried Angus in the local cemetery at Frétin.

Since he could not fly, Denis took over as 'Ops B', helping to control the pilots from the ground. He got to know more about what was going on: 'There is a dreadful flap on at the moment,' he wrote in his diary for Friday, 17 May, 'the Germans are pushing on all fronts. We have all instructions ready for an immediate leave, and for the disposal of stores.' The senior pilots had been fighting constantly and were now red-eyed with tiredness. Sergeant Allard, who had ten kills to his credit, had fallen asleep at the wheel over German territory and had been woken only by shouts over the RT. When he landed and failed to get out of the plane they thought at first that he was dead. He was asleep again, so deeply asleep that at first no one could wake him. Dickey Lee and Paddy Hemingway were in a similar state and they were all sent home for a rest. On 18 May Derek Allen was killed, shot down for the third time, and Noel Lepine was missing. Two other senior pilots had been involved in a car crash. One was dead and the other in hospital. A newly arrived Canadian flight lieutenant was commanding what was left of the squadron.

Sunday, 19 May was Wissler's first day back flying: 'We left Seclin aerodrome in a great flap, and moved about 40 miles to Merville. I flew in a lot of patrols, one an offensive. I, or at least we, were fired on by A/A fire. The aerodrome was bombed after a low flying attack by Me 109s. Once again I was about 20 yards from the bombs, sitting in my aircraft trying to start the engine.'

Paul Richey had now shot down three enemy aircraft but was beginning to wonder how long he could reasonably expect to remain alive. He spent an evening getting drunk with a French air-gunner in a bar near Amiens. 'At midnight I dragged myself to my feet and shook hands with the Frenchman. We wished each other the luck we knew we needed. He was killed the next day.'

At night Richey fretted sleeplessly. 'I lectured myself severely and called myself a yellow dog. In reply I confessed that I was afraid. All right I said, get it under control. I was often afraid before a job, and although none of us admitted it, I knew we all felt the same.' But once in the cockpit, training and concentration drove the fear away:

> From then on there was no time to think of anything but finding the enemy, searching every cubic inch of air, and seeing him before he saw me. When I did see him, all the tension and concentration in my body focused in a wild leap of my heart, a flicking-over in the pit of my stomach. It always made me swallow hard a couple of times. After that it was a simple matter: sights switched on, range and wing-span indicators checked, gun button on fire . . . then into action,

37

body taut against the straps, teeth clenched, thumb on the gun button, narrowed eyes intent on getting that Hun in the sights and holding him there. I felt my pounding heart turn into a block of ice. Not in fear. My brain became coldly-clear, and in an instant I was transformed into a cool, calculating killer.

You'd think an aerial combat was a hot-blooded, thrilling affair. It isn't. I've never felt a fighter in a fight – except, perhaps, in the moment of victory, when I experienced a savage, primitive exaltation. It's not very pleasant.

Sunday, 19 May was Paul Richey's last day of flying. He was sick of retreating and felt that with reinforcements the RAF could have driven the Luftwaffe out of France. As it was he found himself outnumbered yet again as the remnant of his squadron swooped down to attack a formation of Heinkel bombers. 'I was wondering why he showed no sign of being hit, because I knew I was hitting him. He had nearly caught his formation up when grey smoke streamed from both his engines, then from his wing-roots and fuselage, and in a second he was completely enveloped. I felt that savage thrill again and said: "And that's for luck, you sod" as I fired a final burst into the burning mass.'

Suddenly, in his moment of victory, Richey heard a loud explosion and felt blood gushing down the side of his chest. He had been hit in the shoulder and couldn't move his right arm. Shocked, half paralysed and with his Hurricane stuck in a dive, Richey struggled with his controls and with himself. 'I could hear myself grunting and straining to move. Then suddenly I heard myself scream. Muffled but clearly audible, I heard myself say it, then shout it, then scream it: "God! God! I'm going to be killed! God!"'

Regaining control and flying one-handed, Richey managed to land in a field. Smoke rose from the floor of his cockpit. He released the canopy and staggered out. French villagers handed him to an ambulance unit that had run out of morphine. Hours of pain followed until he finally reached a field hospital.

As I was carried out of the bright sunlight into the cool

darkness inside, a vision with blonde hair in the uniform of the American Ambulance Corps pressed my hand, in which I still clutched my blood-stained flying helmet, and said, 'It's going to be alright'. I thought she had the sweetest voice I had ever heard and was more beautiful than anyone I had ever seen. My eyes filled with sudden tears, and all I could manage in return was a twisted smile of gratitude as I thought fervently 'God Bless America'.

The following morning Denis Wissler's squadron prepared to leave France. The pilots were shattered, they could no longer get supplies through, and the Germans were about to overrun their new airfield. All but twenty of the ground crew and a handful of pilots were sent by van towards Boulogne. Wissler was off duty when the squadron launched its six remaining Hurricanes in a final mission during which three more pilots were killed. One of the dead was the new Canadian CO, who had led the squadron for a single day. The surviving pilots of 85 Squadron flew home to Northolt with three Hurricanes and a transport plane. The squadron claimed ninety confirmed victims, but in killed, wounded and missing they had lost seventeen pilots in ten days. Wissler scribbled in his diary: 'I came home last night. Bath, bed, booze.'

On 19 May Churchill made his first broadcast speech, carried live to radio stations all around the world. Had they heard him, 85 Squadron's survivors might have smiled sadly when he spoke about the great successes of the RAF, but like millions of other listeners, they would still have thrilled to the absolute defiance in his voice. It was a fighting speech, crackling with hatred of Hitler and 'the foulest and most soul-destroying tyranny that has ever darkened and stained the pages of history'.

'Jock' Colville, Churchill's assistant private secretary, had not looked forward to serving his eccentric new master. But he was now revising his opinions. 'It is refreshing to work with somebody who refuses to be depressed even by the most formidable danger that has ever threatened this country,' he wrote that evening in his diary. 'Whatever Winston's shortcomings, he seems to be the man for the occasion. His spirit is indomitable and even if France and England should be lost, I feel he would carry on the crusade himself with a band of privateers.'

After four days on the road, Ernie Leggett's battalion had most of a night and a day's rest behind the Belgian town of Tournai. Then around dusk on 20 May it was ordered into the line again along the River Escaut where a major attack was expected soon. Leggett's section took up position under sniper fire, darting from building to building. They found themselves in a cement factory right on the towpath. It was a towering building that had been recently bombed and there were holes in the roof and walls. From the corner of a balcony at the front, Leggett could dimly make out woods on the opposite bank. The Germans must be over there. They set up the Bren gun, dragging up tables and boxes for cover. They made sure they had plenty of ammunition ready, and set sentries. Then they cleared some space in the debris on the floor, wrapped themselves in blankets and tried to get a few hours' fitful sleep.

The first tank brigade had been moving south-west as fast as the refugees and the bombers would allow. Each day Peter Vaux was ordered to take his troop of four Mark VI light tanks east to look for the Germans. They went into areas that were strangely deserted:

> Just the odd person who looked out of the window as we went by. Otherwise doors open and flapping. Trams stationary and empty; cars, which I suppose had run out of petrol, which were empty too. Dogs, running about; cows in the fields which clearly hadn't been milked. That certainly was a creepy experience. Travelling through this empty countryside. Because of course you didn't know really

whether it was empty. Were the Germans over the next hill, round the next corner? And there was no one to ask.

On the fourth day Vaux finally came across a lone French anti-tank crew. The sergeant in command said he was waiting for the Germans, who were not far behind them. Vaux took his troop forward carefully and, crossing a ridge, suddenly saw an armoured column ahead. Spraying the leading motorcyclists with machinegun fire, he withdrew. Vaux radioed a report and retired. As he passed he told the French sergeant: 'They're about two miles and coming. Are you sure you won't move?' The answer impressed Vaux deeply. 'No, no, no. I will stay and I will see these people off.' The Frenchman had retreated as far as he was going to go.

Peter Vaux found his regiment at the village of Petit Vimy, a few hundred yards from the huge, melancholic memorial to the Canadian dead of the Great War. He got his tanks refuelled and his men fed and then reported to his commanding officer. Lieutenant-Colonel Fitzmaurice informed him gently that his news about the German motorised column was out of date. He had already been told that the Germans had broken through near by and had been ordered to counter-attack near Arras. 'Is it the real thing, Colonel?' 'Yes, Peter, it's the real thing this time.'

Affectionately known to all his men as Fitz, the colonel had fought near by in the First World War. After studying maps and planning the morning's attack, the time came to sleep. Fitzmaurice insisted that Vaux took the only bed. 'You'd better get some sleep. You've had four heavy days. I need you tomorrow.' The colonel overruled the young man's protests and bedded down on the floor.

While Peter Vaux slept in his colonel's bed, Ernie Leggett was curled up thirty miles away next to his Bren gun by a window of the cement factory. Both men, the Sandhurst officer and the Norfolk farm labourer's son, knew that they would face their first battle in the morning.

Chapter 3

20–22 May

P resident Roosevelt did not know what to make of America's man in London. Ambassador Joseph Kennedy was not a career diplomat: he had been by turns a banker, a player of the stock market, a producer of movies and an importer and distributor of hard liquor. Starting out in the tough world of Boston politics, he had made a lot of money and won a lot of influence during the boom-bust interwar years. He had donated generously to Democratic Party campaign funds, twice helping put Roosevelt in the White House. But he was also one of the President's potential rivals, and both men knew it. And they differed most in their attitude to the war in Europe.

Kennedy had been in London since 1938. Journalists, British and American, could not get enough of him and his large, glamorous family. In print and in private, Kennedy made no secret of his support for appeasement. He grew close to leading members of the right-wing 'Cliveden Set', led by Lady Nancy Astor, a strong believer in good relations with Nazi Germany. It was at Astor's London home that Kennedy first met Charles Lindbergh, the famous aviator and champion of American iso-lationism. Lindbergh, himself an admirer of Hitler and the new German military, became a friend and confidant. Kennedy, like

Lindbergh and his Cliveden friends, thought that the war was a huge mistake.

Twenty-year-old New Yorker Page Huidekoper was Kennedy's secretary: 'Lindbergh wrote a big report about the German airforce and its potential and it was very, very pessimistic about what would happen and that confirmed Joe Kennedy's feelings.'

Impressed by Lindbergh, and by his own pre-war visits to Germany, Kennedy felt it was his duty to warn Washington that backing Britain meant backing the losing side. Immediately after the war had started he advised Roosevelt that 'England passed her peak as a world power some years ago and has been steadily on the decline. Regardless of the outcome, war will only hasten the process.' Britain was the past, Germany the future. America would have to learn to live with Hitler. If Germany won the war quickly many expected Kennedy to run for President later in the year, on the basis that he was the best man to deal with the new master of Europe.

A file of overheard Kennedy remarks, labelled 'Kennediana', was carefully assembled by the British Foreign Office and samples were leaked to the press and visiting American politicians. British diplomats went out of their way to describe Kennedy as a 'defeatist' in the hope of lessening his influence in the White House. In April 1940 Roosevelt had sent diplomat Sumner Welles to London to get a second opinion about the situation in Britain. But now, with the American ambassador in Paris sending back equally bleak cables, Kennedy's predictions seemed about to come true.

American fears about Britain's chances were magnified by a German propaganda coup. CBS's Berlin correspondent, William Shirer, was allowed to go to the front. His dramatic radio reports reached a huge audience. On 20 May he caught up with the forward Panzer columns and advanced with them. He was amazed by the ease of their progress: 'It is a gigantic impersonal war machine, run as coolly and efficiently, say, as our automobile industry in Detroit.'

On the way back Shirer was shown some English prisoners and

was surprised by their poor physique compared with the Germans he had been with earlier. 'The English youngsters, I knew, had fought as bravely as men can. But bravery is not all; it is not enough in this machine-age war.' Shirer's daily reports, broadcast and rebroadcast across the world, caused consternation in London. In America some of Shirer's listeners asked whether there was any point sending aid to a country about to be overrun by the invincible Nazi war machine.

Page Huidekoper did not think like that. She was impressed with the British friends she had made in the two years since she moved to London, many of whom were now serving in the military. She was particularly fond of the family she had lodged with over the past eighteen months. It was Hurricane pilot Paul Richey's family. Paul's father George was a much-decorated lieutenant-colonel who had fought in five wars for his king and country. In photographs he sits ramrod straight, the epitome of the old values of duty, Empire and sacrifice.

Colonel Richey's two sons, Paul and Michael, did not share all their father's opinions. Page Huidekoper had joined the Richey brothers and their large circle of friends in many passionate arguments about the rights and wrong of war and patriotism, ideology and appeasement. Like many of their generation, the Richeys did not want to see a rerun of the Great War, nor did they automatically feel their father's devotion to the British Empire. But both agreed that Hitler must be confronted. Paul's chosen route was the RAF. Michael, who held strong pacifist beliefs, had decided to serve on board a naval minesweeper – thus allowing him, he hoped, to take part in the war without having to kill.

The lance-corporal shook Ernie Leggett roughly by the shoulders. It was 5 a.m., Tuesday, 21 May. A section of the 2nd Royal Norfolks was huddled up in blankets against the walls of the first floor of the cement factory. Dust was floating in the rays of early morning sunshine that shone through the gaping holes in the walls. From behind a barricade of tables and desks the corporal was keeping a close watch on the woods across the river. Leggett joined him and peered over the balcony. He had a good view, to the left and right as well as forward.

Captain Barclay had found some clever concealed positions for 'A' Company, even if they were thinly spread. Leggett's platoon was in the centre, holding the factory and its outbuildings. Company headquarters was over to the right in and around some ruined nineteenth-century cement ovens. The rough towpath stretched away to either side. Leggett's building was one of the most modern of the industrial sites that littered the untidy riverside. Some had evidently fallen into decay even before the recent shelling. There were great rugged structures a century or two old, looking like ruined abbeys or castles. Railways linked the working factories to the main line. Cranes stood ready for absent canal barges. There were clusters of houses with little networks of garden walls. Every so often Leggett could pick out a hint of khaki – or the glint of a rifle trained on the woods opposite.

For a moment it was quiet in the morning sunshine. The birds seemed to have stopped singing. Leggett could hear the wind in the long grass. His father would be going out to the fields now. Cutting the marsh hay, this time of year, Leggett thought, and looking up at the same hazy sky, probably thinking of his son, the boy soldier gone to war.

Sudden movement caught his attention. There were German officers on the opposite bank, calmly discussing their task and giving orders. Within seconds bridging parties were dragging boats out of the woods and down towards the water. The moment at last. Leggett raised his rifle but the corporal quietly stopped him. 'Wait. Barclay told us to wait for his signal.'

They were very cool, these men in grey. Surely they knew that the opposite bank was occupied by British troops. But they seemed to think they could just strut around in the open. Captain

Barclay's hunting horn rang out and concentrated British rifle fire hit the Germans. Some scattered, some dropped to the ground. Leggett picked his target carefully. A German soldier was crawling towards the canal a little to the right. Leggett saw him get up to run and squeezed the trigger. The German dropped and didn't move. Leggett gazed to make sure that the first man he had shot was really dead. A hand patted the marksman's badge on his arm, the corporal's hand. 'There's more than one out there. Take this for a while.' Leggett found himself fitting the stock of the section Bren gun into his shoulder. He was panting for breath.

Suddenly, to his left, Private May grunted, almost in surprise. Then he slumped to the ground. In Gibraltar they had shared a music stand and now he was dead. Leggett looked at the blood trickling from the ugly hole in his temple. *'Our Father, which art in heaven, hallowed be Thy name . . .'* Leggett could hear himself whispering the prayer, half under his breath. Machineguns and mortars opened up from the woods across the river. Half-track vehicles tore through the undergrowth as the Germans surged forward. *'. . . Thy kingdom come, Thy will be done . . .'* They were everywhere. Firing before he even realised, Leggett swung the juddering Bren down and across and tried to control and aim the weapon with pressure from his right shoulder. He was shouting his survival prayer now, clear and unembarrassed. Other men were shouting too, all kinds of nonsense.

The Bren was spitting spent shell cases all over the room as Leggett held the trigger down for a few seconds, released it, then held it down again. German soldiers fell before him. Some seemed to fly backward into the tree line as the force of his bullets took them. He aimed left and scattered a group trying to drag an assault boat to the bank. Those that did not drop dived for the tree trunks. But there wasn't much cover. As Private Bartrum slammed in magazine after magazine, Leggett poured fire across the river and into men now cowering behind an abandoned half-track. Soon he saw signs of panic. They were pulling back, well back into the wood. And they were leaving a lot of dead and injured behind.

Leggett's hands were shaking as he laid the Bren gun down on the now bloodstained cement floor. Once again he could hear the birds and the wind in the grass.

Leggett put his fleeting feelings of guilt to one side. He had won, he and his comrades had won. They could hold this position for ever. They all agreed on that. It felt good, it felt like being a soldier. From the first floor of the cement factory came a muffled cheer.

Churchill was working harder than at any other time in his life. Marian Holmes was amazed at her new boss's capacity for detail and the powers of concentration he could muster at all hours of the day and night. Work would begin in bed, would continue in a bathrobe, would proceed through breakfast and lunch, pause for an afternoon nap and then continue through regular black-tie dinners and run on late into the night. Secretaries would wilt, chauffeurs would drive through red lights to make up lost time. Every day the Prime Minister worked his way through a mountain of official papers, then sent out a blizzard of requests for more information, for clarifications, for someone to be brought to him urgently. Special labels were printed up bearing the slogan 'Action This Day'.

Sometimes Churchill was so absorbed that he didn't notice people leaving or entering a room or even that they were talking to him. When Holmes was first properly introduced he completely ignored her presence:

> Then, without any warning, he started to dictate. He was unaware of everything around him except this crucial matter he was dealing with. So I quickly seated myself at a desk with a silent typewriter – it was always kept at the ready – and I typed away at this directive. It was not easy to hear Churchill because often he'd abandon his dentures, he had a slight speech impediment and he might be smoking a cigar. So I typed away and he said, 'Give me', and I just took the directive over to him

48

and went to the door. And there was this explosion behind me. 'Where are you going? I've hardly started!' And then he looked up and I was transfixed: his whole fantastic, cherubic face changed to this marvellous smile and he said, 'Oh, I am so sorry, what was your name?' I said, 'Miss Holmes.' 'Oh sit down.' And he continued to look at me over his glasses: 'You must never be frightened of me when I snap. I'm not thinking of you, I'm thinking of the work.'

Tuesday, 21 May was a typical morning, a blur of meetings and memos, cabinets and committees. As Ernie Leggett and his comrades held the Germans on the banks of the River Escaut, Churchill wrote once again in an attempt to encourage the French Prime Minister, Paul Reynaud. 'I feel more confident than I did at the beginning of the battle; but all the armies must fight at the same time, and I hope the British will have a chance soon.' Churchill was preoccupied with the business of spreading confidence. Some called it hoping for the best, but he was also planning for the worst. Turning from his message to Reynaud, he chaired a Chiefs of Staff meeting at 10 a.m. The first item was the Prime Minister's request for a study of likely German invasion techniques.

One junior member of Churchill's government was making his own arrangements. Harold Nicolson wrote to his wife, Vita Sackville-West, at their home in Kent:

> I don't know whether the government have prepared any scheme for evacuation, but you should think it out and try to prepare something. You will have to get the Buick in a fit state to start with a full petrol-tank. You should put inside it some food for 24 hours, and pack in the back your jewels and my diaries.

Peter Vaux had woken up at Petit Vimy that same morning knowing he was going to take part in the first British counter-attack of the campaign. His commander, Colonel Fitzmaurice, who had spent the night on the floor beside him, had been ordered to attack the German armoured divisions that were assaulting Arras and to cut the Arras–Cambrai road. Vaux quickly dressed and swallowed a cup of strong coffee. In the orchard opposite, crews were loading ammunition and fuel into the tanks. Beyond them loomed the imposing bulk of the Vimy Ridge, site of so much bloody fighting in the Great War.

Thinking that the Luftwaffe might expect him to take the main road, Colonel Fitzmaurice sent Vaux off to find a place where the British tanks could ascend Vimy Ridge across open country. Vaux took a motorbike. The climb up to the ridge was very steep and on both sides of the crest he encountered the trenches and shell-holes preserved as a monument to the fighting during his father's war. At the top was the Canadian war memorial. It was a sobering sight, and it was impossible terrain for armoured vehicles. They would have to start out on the road and then cut right. He motored back down the hill. As he got off his bike outside the colonel's house, fitters and mechanics were making final checks and adjustments to the tanks.

The Mark I infantry tank was the mainstay of Vaux's 4th Battalion, Royal Tank Regiment. It was not a great advance in anything but shape on the tanks of the First World War. Affectionately christened the 'Matilda', it was armed only with a machinegun, held a crew of two and could reach a sedate eight miles per hour. It was adequate for infantry support but not much use if it met anything with a proper cannon. But the Matildas did have one great quality: their defensive armour was very thick. By 21 May, after their punishing, four-day journey along the cobbled roads from Brussels, the 4th Battalion had thirty-five Matildas left fit for battle.

To give them some punch against enemy armour, their sister battalion, the 7th, who were to form the right wing of the attack, had loaned them six of the more powerful Mark II tanks. These boasted a two-pounder gun as well as a machinegun and carried a crew of four. The armoured force was completed by Peter Vaux's four Mark VI light tanks with a crew of three, two machineguns, a maximum speed of 35 mph and practically no armour at all. The colonel had decided that he and the adjutant, Captain Cracroft, would each take one of the light tanks. Peter Vaux was feeling 'sort of tense and knotted inside'. He was no longer commanding a troop: he had a bigger responsibility. He had to map-read for the battalion. He focused on the map until he knew every junction off by heart. One mistake and he could lose the battle all on his own.

About midday the column skirted a vast French military cemetery. Most of the tank commanders made a point of looking the other way. Occasionally, away to the right, Vaux caught glimpses of the 7th Battalion's tanks, but there was no sign of the infantry that were supposed to be at their rear. He munched a sandwich. Near Dainville, the right hand troop engaged some German tanks and drove them off. Then, to Vaux's relief, they reached the start line, the Arras–Doullens railway. He had got them there without a hitch.

The line had fanned out to a frontage of three-quarters of a mile, and the leading tanks waited for stragglers to catch up. For the first time since they had been tuned in under the trees near Brussels, the tanks switched on their radios. Nearly all had been jolted away from the correct frequency as they rattled over the Belgian cobbles. Apart from Vaux's light tanks, which had been using their radios while scouting, only a handful could now communicate. But it was too late to do anything about it.

As they prepared to attack, shells began exploding near by. The level-crossing gates were down and a bell was ringing as if a train was about to pass. For a moment the tanks paused like dutiful motorists:

> And it took an old soldier, one of the squadron commanders, to drive straight through those gates and send them flying in all directions. And that stopped the bell ringing and then everybody went through and over and round the gates and up a small slope the other side through some scrub and we reached the top going as fast as poor little Matildas could go. And there suddenly at the top in front of us was a whole stream of German lorries and trucks and half-tracks, and motorcyclists. No tanks. And they were as astounded as we were.

The British tanks immediately opened fire and German vehicles burst into flames before them. 'There was a German motorcyclist just in front of me and he was kicking away at this bike to make it start and it wouldn't start and there he was with a vein standing out on his forehead and my gunner was laughing so much he couldn't aim the gun and shoot him.' German soldiers frantically unhitched anti-tank guns and brought them to bear on the Matildas. But their shells could not penetrate the thick British armour. Some of them ran away. One leapt on top of Peter Vaux's tank, but someone shot him off.

As they burst through the German column, Vaux was most struck by the incredible noise. In the absence of decent radio communication his role changed from map-reader to messenger. 'I was kept very busy by the Colonel dashing about the battlefield finding the three squadron commanders, giving them certain instructions to move a bit more up to the left or the right or close in or whatever. And they would tell me what their situation was and I'd come back and tell the Colonel.' This was hardly machine-age war, but the British still kept pressing forward. They had already torn a great hole into the side of a major German column and sent many of the enemy fleeing in panic. And thus far they had hardly taken any casualties themselves. Then a particularly large German tank came into view and Colonel Fitzmaurice sent Vaux to find an equally large French Somua tank they had passed earlier and summon it forward to help.

Having started 21 May telling the French Prime Minister that he was confident, Churchill found his mood changing as the day wore on. The problem of getting any coherent news from France caused his morale to sag. Jock Colville wrote in his diary, 'I have not seen Winston so depressed, and while I stood by him, trying to get M. Reynaud on the telephone, he said: "In all the history of war, I have never seen such mismanagement."'

Then followed a psychological rhythm that was to become very familiar to Churchill's staff. A few moments of silent brooding, perhaps a walk around the office or out into the garden. Then a surge of renewed energy, a memo or two, a barked order for more information or to have someone put through to him on the telephone. That afternoon Churchill decided that he had to go to France again. They needed him there.

By the mid-afternoon of 21 May the Germans on the River Escaut knew where their opponents were. On the first-floor balcony of the derelict cement factory, Ernie Leggett peered over the barricade of desks and tables while the other two members of his Bren gun crew filled magazines with bullets and piled up cases of ammunition. There was little to be seen among the trees. Near by, shells were falling again. They screamed and banged a lot but they weren't that accurate. Dust from the dry towpath mingled with the paler dust of cement that rose in clouds around the factory buildings. It was the mortars which were doing the damage. They had worked out where the English fire was coming from and they were picking out the positions one by one. Leggett would hear a dull pumping sound from somewhere in the wood and the next moment there would be an explosion. The explosions would creep closer as the Germans corrected their aim with the help of spotters up in the trees. They had already landed one shell at the far end of his floor and two of the lads had been killed. Another had been carried downstairs screaming. Leggett had tried not to listen.

It was hot now. The Norfolks had already repelled two big attacks. But the corporal was dead, picked off by a sniper when he'd raised his head while replacing the overheating barrel of the Bren gun. As they dragged his body to the other side of the room, Leggett had prayed again under his breath.

Carefully Leggett peered out from the balcony to the right. There was machinegun fire coming from the wrong direction.

'Then, about 120 yards away I saw a body. I didn't know who it was, a body crawling with his rifle in front, towards the river, over open ground.' An English soldier was stalking the machinegun nest that the Germans had set up on 'A' Company's right flank. The machinegunners hadn't seen the Englishman. Every few seconds he edged closer and closer towards the German gun, inches above the ground, supported on his elbows. Then Leggett saw a second machinegun setting up close by on the German side. The Englishman couldn't see this. Leggett watched fascinated as the soldier crawled closer, inch by inch. Then, suddenly, he stood up, lobbed a grenade and shot the machinegunners as they scattered. Such bravery. At that instant the other German machinegun opened up and he toppled. Leggett felt a cheer die in his throat. It looked as if someone had sawn his nameless hero in half. And then bullets hit the desk in front of Leggett. He ducked and trained his rifle through a crack. He did not know it until later but he had just seen his company sergeant-major, George Gristock, win the Victoria Cross. He died later of his wounds.

From the hills that overlooked Tournai and the valley of the River Escaut, Martin McLane surveyed Ernie Leggett's battlefield. He and his platoon of Durham Light Infantrymen had spent the previous afternoon searching for food. It had been a harrowing experience: 'All around there were herds of beautiful cows that had been killed. Those that were alive were crying for the want of somebody to milk them, because their udders were completely full.' Still, by raiding houses and taking vegetables from fields, they had managed to put together the first decent meal they had had in a week.

They knew the Germans were going to attack when they started to shell nearby houses. The Durhams watched buildings disappearing in clouds of dust. It was the tall buildings, McLane

Paul Richey

Denis Wissler

Above right Page Huidekoper
in a London street

Above far right Marian Holmes
working at Chequers

Right Armourers with a
Hurricane of 85 Squadron at
Seclin airfield near Lille,
10 May 1940

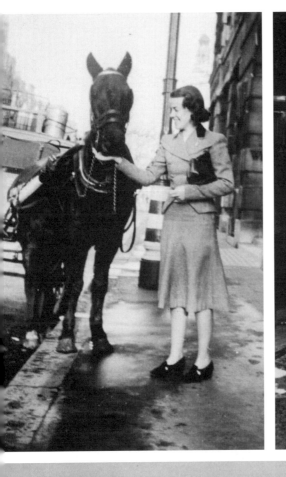

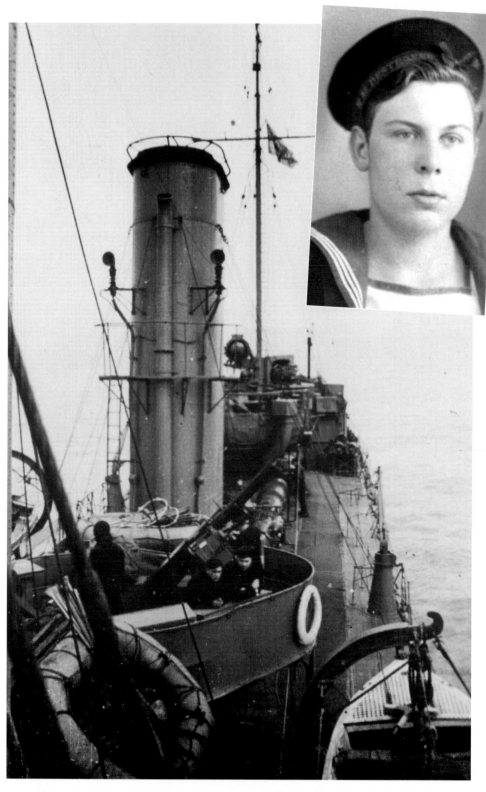

Iain Nethercott's two-pounder pom-pom on HMS *Keith*. Nethercott is the sailor on the far right, under the gun barrel, and inset above

Ernie Leggett in drummer's uniform, Gibraltar 1938

Peter Vaux representing the Royal Tank Regiment
in a motorbike trial in 1939

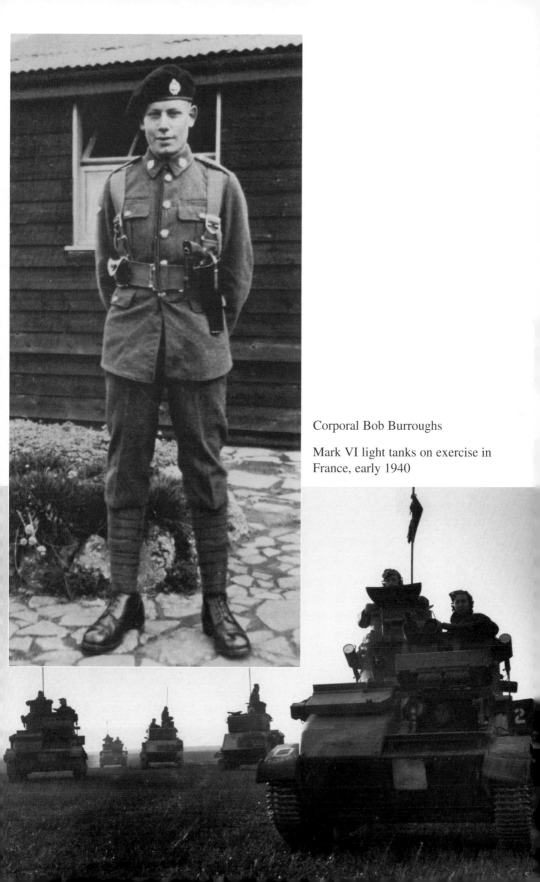

Corporal Bob Burroughs

Mark VI light tanks on exercise in France, early 1940

Martin McLane. The photograph, taken in 1932 when he was twenty,
is the one he left with his daughter so that she would recognise him on his return.
The note to his wife was written on this luggage label while on a train
immediately after his return from Dunkirk

noted, which were going down. They were picking on the places that the Royal Artillery observers would be using to spot targets for the British guns. Then they heard the bridge over the river at Tournai being blown up with a massive explosive charge. Debris flew high into the air. It was clear that things were set for a fight. But they were so exhausted that they slept soundly through every explosion that troubled the rest of the night.

They were woken early and prepared to go forward to fight. But Lieutenant Gregson stood the company down again. They were in reserve this time. Many of McLane's men were soon asleep again. They needed the rest and he was not going to disturb them. Better that they should be fresh when they were needed. If they were called down now it could be bayonets. That's what the reserve battalion was for. To counter-attack any breakthrough at the charge.

Now he could see and hear the shelling of the buildings on the front line. He could see mortar fire going into the factories along the canal. If only he still had his own mortar. He wanted another opportunity, a chance to use it better.

What a moment for the tank to break a track! Peter Vaux felt that he had to get back to the colonel. He hadn't brought the French tank. Just as he was speaking to its commander, shells had fallen near by and the Somua had driven off. Shells were still falling. He hadn't been able to find the Frenchman again so he called the colonel up on the radio but there wasn't an answer. So he looked for him. 'I moved about that battlefield quite a lot and the whole atmosphere had changed in that last half-hour. There was a lot more smoke, a lot more firing and there were bigger guns that were firing and somehow it was a rather awesome feeling. It was rather like when there's a tremendous thunderstorm overhead and you're waiting for the lightning.' Now the track had broken and they had just spent ten minutes mending it. There was firing coming from behind in the village of Achicourt, which shouldn't be happening because the tanks had already driven the Germans out of there. Eventually the track was repaired and they drove on.

Things were very confusing. At a crossroads, Vaux saw a lorry with a big 'G' on it and in sudden realisation shouted, 'G for German, shoot,' and the lorry exploded. Later Vaux realised that 'G' was not the first letter of the German word for German, but he was glad he had made the mistake. His gunner swung the turret round to fire at the German driver, who ran off.

> He was zigzagging down the street with tracer bullets flying on each side of him. And he disappeared into a garden. And we hadn't hit him so we stopped firing. And unbelievably a woman came out of one of those houses and emptied a bucket into a dustbin and went in again. She must have watched the whole thing from her kitchen window and waited her turn to come out and empty her bucket into the dustbin.

Vaux continued driving towards the east. Not far away he saw a British tank burst into flames. The commander jumped out and was machinegunned the moment he hit the ground. Vaux increased speed. When he reached the cover of a sunken road he got out of the tank and peered over the top of the bank: 'I could see that there was a lot of shooting in front so the rest of the tanks must have been there.' He soon reached the Cambrai road astride the crest of the ridge, and there in front were the tanks he had been looking for on the downward slope. Vaux called up the colonel again but got no response so he tried the adjutant, Captain Cracroft. This time he was successful. Cracroft told him to come and join him. Vaux said, 'Where are you?' and Cracroft replied, 'I'm right in the front at the bottom of the valley in front of all the tanks. Come down here.'

Vaux obeyed and turned down into a hayfield. The tall grass exuded a heady perfume as he flattened it in the heat of the afternoon. Through the haze Vaux could see about twenty tanks from his battalion. It was only as he reached them that he began to feel uneasy. There was something odd about them:

They weren't moving. None of them were moving. You would have thought some of them would have been moving. And then when I looked more closely I saw that some of the turrets were crooked on the tank, they'd been hit and driven to one side. And then I saw that the chap in the turret was lying dead, hanging, with his head hanging down on the top, same with the driver. There were one or two like that. There were others where two men were lying beside the tank. Some of the tanks were smoking slightly. And it dawned on me that all these tanks were dead, the whole lot. They all had names. Devil, Dauntless, Dragon . . . And I knew who was in which tank and there they were lying dead and I felt absolutely shattered. These were my friends, people I'd been in the regiment with for two years ever since I arrived there as a nipper as it were. And there they were.

Among them was the colonel's tank with the front smashed in.

Vaux found the adjutant with another tank trying to break the trails of some German anti-tank guns while shooting up their crews, who were trying to find shelter in a potato field. It was almost farcical. They couldn't break the guns and they couldn't get the elevation of the machineguns low enough to shoot the men, though Cracroft picked off one with his pistol. Suddenly shells began to fall around them and Cracroft said, 'Come on, it's time for us to go; and we'll pick up any of those chaps we can as we go.' The three vehicles turned around and motored back up and out of the valley of shattered British tanks. At the colonel's tank they paused while the adjutant ran across, but he returned shaking his head. And now, with his back to the enemy, the full weight of defeat bore down on Vaux. The regiment had been destroyed and his friends were dead. And they had to leave them, dead, in the fading after-noon sunshine and the sweet-smelling hay. 'It seemed wrong to be leaving the bodies lying there in and on the smouldering tanks.'

And as if he were sharing the same thought, the adjutant stopped and turned his turret round to give the woods at the top of the hill a last defiant burst of machinegun fire. The other tanks joined in and to Vaux's amazement German soldiers fell out of the branches, spotters for the artillery that had shattered his regiment. For the first time, Vaux enjoyed killing. 'You bastards, it serves you right,' he said.

They had a contingency rendezvous at the crossroads at Achicourt. Eventually the three tanks, by now carrying a number of survivors from the hayfield, were joined by about nine others. The supporting infantry were also in the village, enduring a prolonged Stuka attack. The light was failing. As it grew darker, Very lights kept shooting up to the right and left. The Germans were moving round their flanks. The tank crews were just considering pulling out when they all heard the sound of approaching tanks. The adjutant walked over to wave them in and then ran back as he realised they were German. Both sides opened fire but they were too close to hit each other. The Germans withdrew and the British made a speedy decision to do the same. Achicourt was in total confusion. The two armies kept bumping into each other in the dark and no one knew what was around the next corner. The tanks got separated from each other crossing a curving bridge clogged with infantry, vehicles and even some stray German motorcyclists.

Vaux's gunner had swapped places with a major whom Vaux had picked up in the hayfield. He was called Major Fernie and, as he was now the senior officer present, he, Peter Vaux and Vaux's driver were the last to leave the village. As they drove off, the major was trying to raise Headquarters on the radio, but he was having difficulty mastering the unfamiliar controls of the light tank. Vaux, meanwhile, was now the gunner so he went down to check the ammunition. There was none left; they had shot off all thirty-two belts. Whilst he was down below and the major was struggling with the radio, the driver, Corporal Burroughs, was in command. When they got to the main Arras–Doullens road, instead of turning left and then right as the other tanks had done, Burroughs turned left and kept going. When Vaux came back up they were alone and neither Burroughs nor Fernie were certain where they were.

From the position of the moon Vaux suspected that they were

heading away from Arras towards Doullens. If so they had run off the edge of his map. Vaux was about to voice this suspicion when they all saw German half-tracks approaching from the opposite direction. They drove on past and in the gloom the Germans did not realise they had just encountered a lost British tank. At least their position was now clear. 'The Germans were going towards Arras, we, therefore, were going away from Arras. And, of course, we couldn't turn round, and we couldn't join them, so we just had to keep going. But we knew the locality and we thought if we turned right in about four or five miles at Beaumetz-les-Loges we could work our way round to Vimy from there.'

It was like a fireworks display. Everyone seemed to be shooting off Very pistols at once. It was impossible to tell which were British and which were German. Sometimes in the light of the flares figures could be seen. Germans flitting between the trees on the other side of the river, Royal Norfolks crouched low, scuttling between their battered positions in and around the old cement works, carrying ammunition or food. Burning flares were reflected in the still water of the River Escaut. Once they lit up another wave of assault boats. They didn't last long. That was followed by an angry barrage of intense German mortar fire. The noise was incredible. Heavy fire seemed to be coming from behind as well, British artillery concentrated on an area over to the right. There had been mortar bombs all day and they had not stopped when night fell. A lot of the section had been wounded by shrapnel. Some walked off, some were carried off by stretcher-bearers, some were dead. The firing lessened in intensity. Ernie Leggett looked up to where a full moon rose in a peaceful sky. A single green flare shot up to the right and the moonlight on the water was dappled green. Then it started again. There would be no sleep tonight.

Martin McLane and his men were woken at midnight. A request for support had come in. Apparently they were hard pressed down on the riverbank where the Germans had been attacking all day. There were rumours of a breakthrough between the Norfolks and the Lancashire Fusiliers. Wearily the Durhams got their things together and hauled heavy packs on to tired shoulders and then trudged away again downhill in the bright moonlight towards the river. Nervous anticipation of a possible counter-attack with fixed bayonets was dulled by fatigue. In the end they waited while a fierce artillery barrage hit the riverfront ahead of them. Then a report came back. If there had been any German penetration, it wasn't there now. They were stood down again and crawled off back to the lines and a few more hours' sleep.

The moon was high in the sky when Peter Vaux reached Beaumetz and what it revealed caused his heart to sink like a stone. A small German unit of some half-tracks and a lorry had turned left towards Vimy by mistake and an officer was reversing them back on to the main road. He was obviously very angry. Vaux didn't know what to do next. But his driver, Corporal Burroughs, took control. He changed down a gear and at a steady twelve miles an hour crashed into the back of the lorry. The men inside all shouted. The officer said something angry in German. But he cleared the half-tracks out of the way, and waved Burroughs on and through. Their luck had held. Their tanks had no obvious markings and nobody had realised that they weren't a German tank trying to barge its way through a traffic jam.

Vaux was astonished. He thought, My father's war was never anything like this. I can't think what's going to happen next. He asked the major what they should do now. 'Keep going,' he replied. When they got to Doullens they came across a German canteen. 'There were military police in the road directing all the traffic round to the right – the way they wanted to go. No traffic was being directed to the left.' They turned left. The road was blocked by a tank and some men. Someone fired a pistol at them but they were through and then they continued up the hill out of Doullens towards Amiens, thinking, We'll get to Amiens. They can't be there. The French will be there.

The tank suddenly stopped dead and slewed into the ditch at the side of the road. The solid rubber tyre on one of the bogey wheels had unwound itself and everything had seized up. They were stuck. Burroughs and Vaux jumped out with crowbars to try to unjam the rubber from the bracket, and as they did so they heard a tank rattling up the road behind them. Since they had no ammunition there was nothing they could do. They were caught. And then the German tank stopped about a hundred yards away with its engine running. It didn't move. It stayed there. Frantically they cleared the rubber out of the bracket. They could barely believe their luck. They started the engine and then they were away, clattering and banging up the hill with their loose track. And no one was following them.

A few miles farther and over the ridge and there was the light of a huge fire in the sky in front. It could only be Amiens: the whole town must be ablaze. 'It just didn't seem a sensible place to go.' Everything was different now. There was no way back to Petit-Vimy and no obvious way forward. Burroughs pointed out that the petrol was getting really low. They had been fighting all day and now they had driven a long way too. There was only about an eighth of a tank left. After a brief discussion they decided to head for Domart, one of the nearby villages where they had been billeted a few weeks before. Perhaps there they could find some friends and some petrol. They turned off the main road and approached the village cautiously. There were German vehicles parked in the main square, their crews in a nearby café. With its loose track clanking and grinding, the British tank drove straight past them.

Burroughs said the petrol gauge was reading empty. They turned west on to minor roads, reached Franqueville and stopped in an orchard. The tank was spluttering. They pulled up under a bank, more or less hidden, then took the guns out and scattered the bits. Vaux smashed the radio, Burroughs opened the engine cover and smashed the carburettor and anything else that would break. Satisfied that their vehicle wouldn't be any good to anyone any more, the three men took their food and the tank's compass and broke into an empty house. It was like one of the villages Vaux had been scouting only the previous day, completely deserted. They collapsed with exhaustion.

As Peter Vaux slept, Churchill was dictating memos and letters until late into the night. He was still at work at two o'clock on the morning of 22 May. After a few hours' sleep he rose and flew once again to Paris. There he met Prime Minister Reynaud and was impressed by the new French Commander-in-Chief, General Maxime Weygand, who spoke in determined tones of counter-attacks and final victory. This was language more to Churchill's liking than the despondent French phone messages of the last few days. That evening, back in London, he gave his War Cabinet an upbeat account of plans for the British and French armies to move towards each other and cut the German invasion force in half. It was called the Weygand Plan. But Churchill also continued to monitor preparations for a possible evacuation of the British Army.

In London Special Branch officers were calling at the homes of some of Britain's leading right-wingers. Sir Oswald Mosley was arrested along with two hundred other members of the British Union of Fascists. Under new regulations, rushed through Parliament, the authorities could now intern anyone they considered 'sympathetic' to the enemy.

When Peter Vaux woke on the morning of 22 May the sun was up and it was already hot. Looking nervously out of the window, he could see German troops driving past. Upstairs, the major had found a child's atlas and as they studied it their position became horribly clear. The Germans had evidently speared through the French lines on a narrow front and were heading towards the coast. The British Expeditionary Force must be very nearly cut off from the French in the south. Their little tank must have travelled almost the whole way through the German lines from north to south, because if Amiens was still on fire the front line should be there or not far beyond. And that was where hope lay. Looking at the map, and trying to think like German generals, they reckoned that the advancing Panzers would be using the River Somme to protect their left flank. The three Englishmen were only a few miles' walk from the Somme. If they could just get there and then get across, they ought to find French troops on the other side. They found a basket and packed the food in it. Each of them had his pistol. Vaux also carried a pair of binoculars and the compass from the tank.

Vaux's reading of the situation was accurate. For the Germans the assault on the Escaut, though pressed with fierce determination, was no more than another holding operation. Their main attack had been delivered against the French farther south. On 20 May, the day before Vaux's regiment had attacked near Arras, General Guderian's tanks had seized Amiens and Abbeville farther west. As Vaux and his fellow fugitives had slept, the spearhead of the German Army had already reached the salt marshes at Noyelles on the coast. The British Expeditionary Force was cut off.

Chapter 4

22–26 May

Once again the sun was high and hot. Some of the men that Ernie Leggett had shot the previous day were still lying where they had fallen. The litter of destruction lay all over both banks of the River Escaut, and in the hot sun the smell of death was upsetting the defenders of the cement factory. They were utterly exhausted and yet nervously alert to every sound. They had begun to wonder whether they were imagining movements in the bushes.

Today had been easy. Occasional shelling, occasional bombs. Sniper fire if anyone was fool enough to move into the open. But so far no major attack. Had they given up? Or could they be slipping across the river farther up, round the flanks of the thinly spread clusters of British soldiers?

There were only four of Leggett's section left on the second floor. They dreaded the thought of being cut off from the rest of the company, the thought of Germans with bayonets fixed coming up the back stairs. They could see pretty well to the right from where they were by the balcony and it all looked safe. But how many people had survived the night over on their left? To look out that way and behind the factory they had to get across to the windows on the other side of the floor some sixty feet away. There was nobody over on that side of the building to give them reassurance. Finally the lance-corporal said, 'Ernie, nip across and see if the bastards are infiltrating on our left flank.'

Leggett put down his rifle and, crouching low, set off across the room. He hit the ceiling, then he heard the bang and then he hit the floor. The mortar bomb had come through one of the holes in the roof and exploded on the concrete beneath him. He couldn't feel his legs. A pool of blood was spreading across the floor. His blood. He felt weak and numb and very sleepy. He thought, Well, this is it, and his mind drifted and vividly he saw his family sitting in front of the fire in their chairs and then his mother at the door of their little Norfolk house and the postman bringing a telegram and his mother's face going pale. And he saw his church and the east window with the crossed keys in a circle with the silver crossing the gold. His good-luck charm. And then he was back in Belgium and he thought, well, so much for the cross-keys of St Peter.

The two privates ran over, pulling out their field dressings. They ripped off Leggett's trousers and tried to conceal their horror at the size of the wound in his groin. If it had severed the artery he was dead, no question. Still, they got all their field dressings together and 'they bunged one into the wound at the back, pushed it up, put another in the wound at the front and they tied the other two on the outside. Then they got a piece of rope and tied a tourniquet.' They picked Leggett up and carried him downstairs. They put him on a bench in a little outhouse.

A few minutes later Leggett came to, and realised he was alone. Mortar shells were landing near by and he could hear machinegun fire rattling against the metal hoppers on the factory's upper storey. He decided to try to get back to Headquarters, which was only about 120 yards away. He tried to stand and immediately fell over. He would have to crawl. A railway line provided some cover. He was naked from the waist down apart from a pair of blood-soaked underpants. As he crawled he could hear bullets ricocheting off the tracks to his left. He remembered Sergeant Gristock patiently explaining that if you kept your head down a railway line was high enough to protect you. He remembered Barclay's words in the forest: 'Now more than ever your training will stand you in good stead. Keep your heads down and spirits high.' Another bullet whined overhead. He thought, I suppose they don't know I'm wounded. I suppose they think I'm just another soldier trying to get away.

He was hauling himself by his fingers, with his legs dragging uselessly. Soon his fingernails were broken away. His underpants were ripped off by the rough stones and his shirt had gone. He was practically naked and bleeding heavily once again as the field dressings worked loose. And as he crawled, inch by agonising inch, the bombardment intensified. An explosion threw up a shower of earth, covering his back. He rested, he prayed, he crawled another couple of yards. 'Still numb, not painful, numb. Fortunately I hadn't broken any bones. Another explosion and I was covered up with earth again.' The third blast was very close. 'I felt all the earth coming on top of me. And I remember being covered up, trying to get out, and I couldn't. And I involuntarily said, "Please help me". And I must have passed out because the next thing I felt was my wrists being pulled. And I looked up into the faces of two men who I knew well, "Chum" Woodrow and "Bunt" Bloxham. They were both clarinet players in the band. And they said, "Bloody hell, it's Ernie". And they pulled me out, laid me down, and I heard, I don't know which one it was, but one said to the other, "Bloody hell he's had it".'

Leggett was put on a stretcher, lifted up and laid on the ramp of a fifteen-hundredweight truck, with the white painted crossed keys of the 2nd Division right by his head. The truck set off, bumping noisily over the cobbles. He was semi-conscious. After a few miles he was taken down. A figure knelt beside him. A medical officer. He must be a doctor because he had a big hypodermic needle in his hand. He was putting the needle into a container, and then he withdrew it and he squirted it to get the excess off, carefully measuring the dose. Beside him was a nurse wearing a huge white headdress. She must be French or Belgian. And then – nothing.

As the French Army crumbled, there were only two questions that really mattered: 'Will Britain survive?' and 'What will America do?' The answer to both involved ships.

It was a week since President Roosevelt had rejected Churchill's first request for the loan of the fifty old American destroyers. The Prime Minister's next move was an aggressive, even brutal cable that played unrelentingly on all of Washington's anxieties about the balance of naval power. Swearing that he would never himself consent to surrender, Churchill made it clear that those who followed him might have no choice:

> If members of the present Administration were finished and others came in to parley amid the ruins, you must not be blind to the fact that the sole remaining bargaining counter with Germany would be the Fleet, and, if this country was left by the United States to its fate, no one would have the right to blame those then responsible if they made the best terms they could for the surviving inhabitants. Excuse me, Mr President, putting this nightmare bluntly.

Churchill was telling Roosevelt to send help now or face the prospect of the Royal Navy in German hands. This disturbing possibility was already being considered in America. James Pierrepoint Moffat was a senior diplomat. A prudent man, he knew that America needed a contingency plan in case the worst should happen in Europe. On 21 May Moffat wrote in his diary: 'the main type of problem to be decided is to what degree we can help the Allies and to what degree we must conserve our own inherent strength for our own defensive purposes . . . we have to face the possibility that there may be a complete German victory . . . What this would mean in relation to the British fleet is the crux of the problem for ourselves.'

Roosevelt reacted to Churchill's alarming cable, but not in the way that its author had hoped. Instead of sending American ships to join the Royal Navy, the President began plotting to bring the Royal Navy under American control.

Roosevelt began with Canada, America's northern neighbour and a pillar of the British Empire. As she had done in 1914, Canada had already sent every available battalion and every available ship to help the British cause. But in Ottawa, Prime Minister William Lyon Mackenzie King was watching the situation with apocalyptic images running through his mind.

In truth the apocalypse was never far from King's thoughts. A devout Christian and keen Bible-reader and spiritualist, he filled his diary with observations about his prayers, dreams and visions – most of which focused on his keen sense of living in a world trembling on the edge of the abyss: 'Germany has got into the hands of humans possessed of the devil. They are controlling, for the time being, the affairs of men.' On 22 May he woke expecting the worst: 'Read morning paper, greatly fearing it contained mention of landing of Germans on British coast.' What the North American papers did contain that morning were headlines like 'Germans Smash to Channel Ports'.

The next day, 23 May, President Roosevelt had a scheduled meeting with Canadian diplomat Hugh Keenleyside. Ostensibly it was to discuss some detail of the arms industry. In fact, as Keenleyside immediately reported to his Prime Minister, Roosevelt's true purpose was to suggest an extraordinary diplomatic gambit – a secret meeting between himself and King. According to Keenleyside's account: 'the object of the proposed meeting would be to discuss "certain possible eventualities which could not possibly be mentioned aloud" for fear of laying the speaker open to the charge of being a "defeatist". [The President] added that if I would mention to the P.M. the words "British Fleet" Mr. King would understand the lines along which the President's mind was working.'

King was shocked. The President of the United States was inviting him to discuss the consequences of the defeat of Britain, before that defeat had taken place and without telling Winston

Churchill, the political leader of the Empire in which King fervently believed.

On 24 May, a meeting of the Canadian Cabinet was interrupted by a telephone call from Cordell Hull, the American Secretary of State. He wanted to speak to King in person and immediately. '[He] asked me if I could send someone at once to Washington, someone in whom I had the fullest confidence and could trust in every way, to come and have a talk with him and another person higher up. There were some things that the latter wished me to know.'

In 1940 global power was measured in ships. To get to any part of the British Empire an enemy had first to get past the British fleet. Since Nelson's time, nobody had. In May the Royal Navy was the largest fleet on the oceans. It guarded an even more imposing merchant navy of more than 4,000 ships totalling 21 million tons; 2,500 British flagged ships would be at sea on any one day. And they needed to be. Britain was dependent on them. It produced enough food to feed only half its population and had reserves to last only a few months. All oil and most other industrial raw materials were also imported.

Britain's enemies knew that this was her Achilles' heel. Stop the ships and the British would starve. During the Great War Germany had developed the submarine for this specific purpose, and in 1917 had come very close to success. But they had not quite defeated the Royal Navy.

Britain still put enormous faith in its senior service and naval men were proud of this trust. The ships were manned by professionals with a training that was thorough and very tough. Iain Nethercott was a recent product of this system. He had moved to Essex from Scotland when his father, a major with the Argyll and Sutherland Highlanders, had been sent to guard the docks at Purfleet against rioting dockers. A grammar school boy, Nethercott did a spell at

Lloyd's of London but he didn't enjoy it so in 1938, at seventeen years old, he joined up under the accelerated promotion scheme.

Discipline was violent and arbitrary. Once Nethercott was given twelve cuts of the cane: someone had stuck a cigarette in his hand and run off just as the 'crusher' (naval policeman) came in. Every morning the boys climbed a mast 140 feet high. There were no safety nets and Nethercott's first sight of death was when a fellow trainee lost his balance at the top. But the boys got a good general education as well as learning seamanship – how to sail boats, use ropes, tie knots and splices, swab decks and master every detail of naval gunnery. In the end they were proud to be in the Navy.

On board ship conditions remained spartan: 'You just had a broadside mess, that was a wooden table and a wooden stool to sit on and hammock hooks – that was all for your hammocks. No heating, we had no water on tap, you had to go and pump up a bucket of water on the iron deck, and you had three wash places for about 140 men. Wash bowls. No baths, no showers, nothing like that. And it was hard.'

The nation was proud of the Navy, but over the last twenty years it had not wanted to spend much money on it. Many of its ships were near obsolete – too slow, inadequately protected with armour, and armed with old guns with antique fire control systems. They would be fine until they came up against one of the enemy's more modern vessels. As yet Germany had few of these but those that she did have were very powerful. And, just as before, she had her U-boats – sleek, underwater killers.

To Britain's relief, interwar naval limitation treaties had kept all the world's fleets small, and thus Britain's proportionally large. But with imperial and trade interests stretching from Singapore to the Suez Canal, Britain needed more ships. She had to maintain forces in the China Seas, the Mediterranean and the North Sea. She had to have a home battle fleet to protect the coast and engage the enemy. She had at once to blockade Germany and protect her own convoys. In May 1940 the Royal Navy was doing all this, but only just. The fleet was at less than half its World War I strength. The China station and the Mediterranean command had been reduced to the bare minimum. The Dominions had sent what ships they could. But the blockade and convoy patrols were sustained by converted passenger liners painted grey and armed with short-range guns of Boer War vintage. Trawlers and drifters were pressed into service for minesweeping and anti-submarine patrols. Above all there was a desperate shortage of the all-purpose small warship, the destroyer. In 1918 there had been 488 of them. In 1939 there were 201.

But the Navy was not short of courage. It bristled with Captains full of do-or-die Nelsonian daring. Captains like Roope of the destroyer *Glowworm* who had rammed the heavy cruiser *Admiral Hipper* in April before blowing up. Unlike the Army or, for the most part, the Air Force, the Navy had been fighting since the beginning of the war. Since early April it had been engaged in a fierce, bloody and muddled war in the ice and snow of the Norwegian fjords. In late May a huge naval force was still committed there. In Norway the Fleet Air Arm had lost 60 per cent of its planes but, in sinking the cruiser *Königsberg* in Bergen harbour with Skua dive-bombers, it had accounted for the first capital ship ever to be destroyed from the air. A German cruiser and another battleship had been torpedoed by British submarines. And at Narvik, in northern Norway, five British destroyers had fought like tigers, sinking two German destroyers, six supply ships and severely damaging five more destroyers. One of the British ships engaged that day, the *Hotspur*, had been Iain Nethercott's first ship after training. Now Nethercott was an anti-aircraft gunner on another destroyer, HMS *Keith*, a flotilla leader on the Dover Patrol.

London seemed utterly bizarre. People were just carrying on as normal. Only two days earlier, Denis Wissler had landed at Northolt in a De Havilland 89 transport, but already he felt so much better. Rest was a wonderful thing. On this burning hot afternoon he had taken a stroll from his parents' home in Blackheath through Greenwich Park to the river. The city was strangely complacent. There were boys playing cricket on the heath. Eighteen months before he'd been doing the same.

Wissler knew how a hot sunny day could suddenly be changed into a horror of blast and burning ruin. How would these people react? He wondered what was going on back in France. Knots of people, clustered round newspaper placards which announced that the Germans were advancing on Boulogne, were talking nervously. There was a mood of subdued gloom. Quite a lot of people seemed to have started carrying gas masks. He wondered if the ground crew had got to Boulogne before the Germans. They had his kit on their lorries. He didn't expect to see any of that again.

There was a slight swell but nothing to worry about. 'Action stations,' ordered the captain. 'Get your cork life-jacket on,' advised the leading seaman gunlayer, Bob Dunbar. Poised by the port two-pounder pom-pom of HMS *Keith*, Iain Nethercott was peering up at the sky above. With all this noise going on you had to see the planes coming. But all he could see was seagulls. The air was the worry because the four 4.7-inch guns wouldn't elevate high enough to take on planes. Nethercott's gun and the other two-pounder were the only anti-aircraft defence.

His Majesty's destroyers *Keith* and *Vimy* slid through the deep-water channel towards Boulogne harbour. Off the port bow four French destroyers were shelling the hills north of Boulogne. Looking through binoculars, Nethercott could see German tanks, motorcyclists and infantry advancing in rushes from one bit of cover to the next.

On the port side, as they approached, they could see Welsh Guards exchanging fire with the Germans on the slopes. The Welsh were clearly fighting hard, but Nethercott was horrified by the chaos that was revealed as the ship reached the Quai Chanzy: 'As we tied up it was just absolute confusion on the jetty. There was a trainload of wounded that had been unloaded there and they'd just put the stretchers on the jetty. And there was this great horde of British soldiers charging around drunk out of their bloody minds. And fighting and trampling all over these wounded and God only knows what. And of course as soon as we tied up they rushed us and tried to get on board.' The captain ordered the torpedo men to fix bayonets and drive the troops back to the jetty. 'They were standing around in groups yelling and shouting and some begging for mercy and God knows what.' They were 'base details', hastily called-up labourers and stevedores, mostly unarmed and untrained.

As the gangways were cleared the medics did their best to get the wounded on board. The whole area was under sporadic fire and some of the wounded were killed on their stretchers. Some of the sniping seemed to be coming from hotels over the river and Nethercott was soon picking out targets for his two-pounder and too busy to pay much heed to the mob.

Farther across the harbour Irish Guards were engaged in a battle with invisible Germans hidden among the warehouses. Towards the sea Nethercott could see French troops pushing cars into the harbour. British civilians dashed towards the destroyers and shouted to the sailors, pleading to be taken aboard. They were directed towards the bridge. After about half an hour the brigadier commanding the Guards came on board to liaise with Dover. A party was sent ashore to bring in the body of the four-ring captain who had led a demolition party sent over the day before. Still there were no orders to evacuate. The *Keith* continued to wait. The sailors felt distinctly vulnerable tied up to the quay.

Before polio struck in the 1920s, Franklin Delano Roosevelt was lean, athletic, confident and very good-looking. The disease had left him crippled, but there remained something of the youthful charmer about the man. Political associates and rivals alike marvelled at his ability to win people over. He inspired trust, a very useful quality to find in a politician and one that the two-term President had frequently exploited. During a run on the banks at the height of the Depression, Roosevelt had closed them all for a few days and then gone on national radio to declare, simply and calmly, that the problem had now been solved and that people should return their money. Millions of Americans did exactly that and the crisis passed.

Although many felt drawn to him, few ever claimed to know their President intimately. He was guarded, enigmatic. There was idealism there, a sense of history too. But, unlike Churchill, Roosevelt did not usually favour elaborate language, nor did he wear his heart on his sleeve.

By late May 1940, the normally phlegmatic Roosevelt was very anxious. Personally he despised Hitler and wanted to do everything he could to keep Britain and France in the war. But most Americans wanted no active part in another European conflict. Roosevelt had already pushed America's strict neutrality laws to the limit by selling the Allies thousands of tons of military supplies. Going further and offering direct military assistance, such as the old destroyers coveted by Churchill, was politically impossible. Congress and the press would not stand for it. His many enemies would call such an act 'reckless meddling in a foreign war'. 'A waste of national assets' too, since, in all probability, any ships sent over the Atlantic in early June would soon end up as part of Hitler's navy. Such a blunder could cost him the upcoming election.

Roosevelt didn't need Churchill's crude cable to remind him that the Royal Navy might soon be in German hands. American thinking on the subject was epitomised in a cable from diplomat George Messersmith during the last week of May: 'There are, therefore, so far as we are concerned, only two safe places for

75

the British and French fleets – at the bottom of the sea or in our own hands.'

Secretary of the Interior Harold Ickes had been discussing the same problem with his President. He confided to his diary that Roosevelt was very worried about a possible German peace offer that would secure the Royal Navy for Hitler. Such an offer would, perhaps, come attached to a threat to bomb British cities flat until the precious fleet was handed over. With the British navy at his disposal, Hitler would be able to dominate the world's trade routes, pursue his interests in South America and forge a grand alliance with the Japanese. 'There is no doubt in my mind that this country is in the most critical situation since we won our independence,' wrote Ickes.

Desperate times called for desperate measures. Hence Roosevelt's unprecedented secret approach to Canada. If Britain was to fall America needed some means of bringing Iain Nethercott and the rest of the Royal Navy over the Atlantic, perhaps to serve some new political entity made up of America and the remains of the British Empire.

Early in the afternoon of 23 May, Admiral Bertram Ramsay stole a few moments to write to his wife: 'Things are so desperately serious . . . I have now been entrusted with "What is to happen". No bed for any of us last night and probably not for many nights. I'm so sleepy I can hardly keep my eyes open, and we are all the same . . . We've been on the telephone to everyone from the P.M. downwards, and the situation only becomes more & more difficult from hour to hour . . .'

Ramsay had been told to plan the rescue of the BEF. His team had already lifted several thousand base personnel out of France and Belgium, but their ships were attracting more attention from the Luftwaffe every day. He shuddered to think what would happen if they really had to implement Operation Dynamo, their full-scale evacuation plan. He thought of a young Scottish Wren called Daphne Lumsden in his cipher office. Her husband, Graham, was a lieutenant on the destroyer HMS *Keith*, and here she was sitting in the tunnels under Dover Castle transcribing signals from the ships at sea. Everyone could see that she was dreading the moment when she would get bad news about her husband's own ship. The destroyers of the Dover Patrol were supposed to be daring but what they had been called upon to do recently was to say the least unusual. Yesterday they had ferried a brigade of Welsh and Irish Guards into Boulogne in an effort to hold the port. They had not heard from them and so this morning he had sent the *Keith*, Graham Lumsden and all, to find out whether they were still holding the port. They were, but only just. Now he was waiting for London to tell him whether to bring the troops home again.

He sighed and went back to his letter: 'It's having to order ships to do things and go places where one knows they are going to get bombed to blazes and to send troops into what I know to be an inferno . . .' From the window of his office, cut deep into the cliff, he could hear the explosions around Boulogne.

Sweat was seeping down Iain Nethercott's back. By four o'clock in the afternoon Boulogne harbour was hotter than hell. Sunlight reflected from HMS *Keith*'s metal superstructure as her sailors toiled under tin helmets and inside lamby coats and cork life-jackets. The destroyer was still tied up to the Quai Chanzy alongside HMS *Vimy*. German fire had been more subdued after the two ships' opening salvos, but grey-uniformed soldiers were still edging steadily closer. Nethercott had just opened up on some troops he'd seen creeping on to the jetty along the riverside. No order to evacuate had been issued, and for the moment the Guards Brigade was holding the Germans on the fringes of the town at either side of the port. Its commander was still on board the *Keith*, in conference with Nethercott's captain. The ship's radio was now the only means of communication with England.

Suddenly a Fieseler Storch reconnaissance plane circled the harbour, then about a dozen Junkers 88 bombers flew over hotly pursued by British fighters. The Storch dropped a flare and within seconds, thirty or so Stuka dive-bombers swooped down out of the sun, heading straight for the Quai Chanzy. At that moment a swarm of enemy tanks and infantry poured over the hill across the river, directly above the hotels that lined the far bank, firing as they came. Nethercott found himself staring at them. A shout brought him round and his two-pounder gun swung upward to meet the more immediate threat from above. As the Stukas came whining down on the two vulnerable destroyers, Nethercott tugged on the trigger. One line of Stukas swerved away, and then the gun jammed solid. A bomb hit the jetty alongside, killing two sailors and showering the decks with lumps of concrete. The port pom-pom and the ship's Lewis machineguns all crackled away in metallic harmony.

Nethercott hammered the back of the breech of his starboard gun with a mallet but it wouldn't shift on to the retractor screws. They lifted the top off: there was a shell jammed crossways. 'Bugger these canvas belts!' A loader went running below for the ordnance artificer. It was his job to deal with things like this – whether the ship was under attack or not. Another bomb exploded in the water port-side, covering Nethercott's crew in sticky, foul-smelling mud. Temporarily deprived of their two-pounder, the sailors broke out the gun-deck rifles and started to exchange fire with the advancing German infantry across the river.

A mortar opened up from behind some warehouses to the starboard side in the port area. Nethercott had never come across a mortar before. But, then again, very little of his last few hours' work had been covered in naval training. Not fighting off panicking British troops. Not shooting at tanks. And certainly not sitting tied up at a quayside while some Guards officer tried to get London to tell him whether they could all go home now, and half the German Air Force used your ship for target practice.

The first mortar bomb hit the jetty. The next exploded a few yards closer to the ship. The crew watched, transfixed by this unfamiliar creeping menace. 'Then one fell right on the iron deck about twelve feet away and it made a big hole in the steel decking and covered us with splinters. And in my life jacket I looked like a bloody porcupine! Down one side all these slivers of steel had landed – I got some in the shoulder too – and my tin hat was clanging and banging and got dents all over it. But anyway, I think the troops must have had a go then and put them out of action because we didn't get any more after that, thank God. I mean, the next one would have been right on our gun deck.'

The ordnance artificer and his mate came clambering up to the gun deck carrying spanners and wrenches. Bullets were whistling everywhere, but the two men calmly stripped the breech of the gun, chewing tobacco, looking for all the world as if they were doing monthly maintenance back in Portsmouth. By the time they shouted to Bob Dunbar and Nethercott to try the gun again the Stukas had pulled away and the German ground fire was falling around them again. Nethercott swung the gun on to the warehouses and away it went, firing almost a round a second towards what he thought was a machinegun position.

A few seconds later the gun suddenly swerved off target

> I yelled out to Bob that I was off target and when I looked he'd got no head, his head was clean off his shoulder, he was just there and he'd been cut off right across his body with a chunk of tank shell or something pretty big.
>
> And of course in the Navy, it's automatic with gunnery drill, I was number two, he was number one. So the number two moves up to number one and number three moves up to my position on the gun. So of course I got out of the seat and I went round and I thought oh my God, the deck was covered in blood, pouring out.

Nethercott pulled what was left of Dunbar out of his harness and took his place, shouting to the lads to get the body clear. Number three was already on the ring sight. 'Gun ready!' The deck was swimming in blood and the loaders threw down sand to stop them slipping. That was in the gunnery drill too. Smearing the grip with sand, Nethercott swung the gun back across to the warehouses, yelling at the nearby Guards to get their heads down.

As Nethercott shot up the harbour's edge he heard someone shout out, 'The captain's dead.' Captain Simson had been shot by a sniper. His first lieutenant was already wounded in the leg. Suddenly Nethercott felt the ship move. Looking up he saw the *Vimy* passing slowly by, stern first. Her captain was dead too, lying over the edge of his shattered bridge with half his face missing. Then the *Keith* snapped her mooring wires and was also under way, edging out stern first. Orders to evacuate had finally arrived, only seconds before the current onslaught. The navigating lieutenant, Graham Lumsden, was trying to direct her by peering through a porthole. Whenever he stuck his head out to get a view, bullets ricocheted off the metal surround. The *Keith* backed out slowly, her guns blazing, her decks covered in dead and wounded men.

As they reached open water they signalled to Captain 'Crazy' Comber on HMS *Whitshed* that, following the death of Captain Simson, he was now in charge of the destroyer flotilla. *Whitshed* and *Venomous* came forward to take the place of *Vimy* and *Keith* and pick up the Guards. Nethercott watched as *Venomous* fired her main 4.7-inch guns directly at a row of large houses and brought the walls of two hotels down on top of a German tank. Another tank took a direct hit from a naval shell and flipped over backwards. Yes, a destroyer could be a pretty useful anti-tank weapon, Nethercott thought.

As Nethercott's ship found open water, the survivors began to clear the decks and the bridge of bodies. Many of the Army stretcher cases had been killed where they lay. Dead soldiers they took home. Dead sailors, as was traditional, were relieved of their identity tags, had a spent shell placed between their legs, and were carefully sewn into their hammocks. The last stitch was passed through their noses to be sure that they were dead. Nethercott and his friends searched for Bob Dunbar's head but they couldn't find it.

At sunset the two battered destroyers stopped off the Varne light-ship. Both had huge gashes in their superstructures. Sand and carbolic had not entirely removed the smell of blood. The crew bowed their heads and for a few seconds heard nothing but the calling of seabirds. Then the first lieutenant read the prayers and the shrouded sailors were slipped quietly into the grey water of the English Channel.

All at once Nethercott felt desperately tired, so tired he could hardly move. He went down below. Eventually the sick bay 'tiffy' found time for him, took off the lamby coat, cleaned his wounds and put a dressing on. He said, 'You'll be all right.' Nethercott said, 'Yeah, that's fine, do I get anything out of it?' The 'tiffy' said, 'Yeah, the Coxswain's handing out rum.' Nethercott had never been given navy rum. He was still nineteen and the handout began at twenty. But rules could sometimes be ignored, even in His Majesty's Navy. 'The Coxswain was walking round with a rum jar and a big mug and he saw me sitting there and I got a big mug full of neat rum. That was the first time I'd drunk that much rum and it knocked me out practically, I couldn't even get up on the fo'c'sle when we were coming into Dover harbour.'

A dramatic afternoon, mostly spent in the Upper War Room at the Admiralty. It began with the news that the Germans were in Boulogne, that the BEF could not break through southwards to join up with the French, and that they only had two days food left. It seemed all but certain that our army would have to retire precipitously and try to embark, under Herculean difficulties, for England. Then the PM spoke on the telephone to Reynaud and Weygand. The latter claimed that the French had recaptured Amiens and Peronne. If true the news is stupendous, although the position of the BEF still remains critical and they will have to fight their way southwards against heavy odds.

Jock Colville's diary, 23 May

In the signals room Daphne Lumsden had learned that HMS *Keith* had left Boulogne with serious damage and casualties among the officers. Later someone arrived to say that the *Keith* was back and that Graham, her husband, was alive and sent his love. She relaxed a little, but she was so busy that she hardly had time to take in the relief. Graham had to leave for Chatham to get the boat repaired again and was not even able to come ashore for half an hour.

There were constant signals from Boulogne and on the whole things were going OK. At about half past eight in the evening *Whitshed* and *Vimiera* came out with Guards embarked. Other Dover destroyers, *Wild Swan*, *Venomous* and *Venetia*, followed them in. *Venetia* was damaged and backed out but the others evacuated more troops at about 9.30 p.m. *Windsor* brought out yet more soldiers at about 11 p.m. Finally and tentatively, in the middle of the night, *Vimiera* went back and managed to pick up 1,400 more men. The next day the undamaged destroyers were switched to Calais, where reinforcements had been brought in on 23 May. The warships bombarded German positions under constant bombing. *Wessex* was sunk and both *Vimiera* and *Burza* were damaged.

It was a favourite Churchillian maxim that a small moment of aggression could bring an unexpected reward, and so it had proved with the counter-attack at Arras. Surprised and temporarily thrown into a panic, General Rommel's Panzer Division imagined itself assailed by a much larger force. The division had suffered 378 casualties that day, by far its heaviest losses of the campaign to date, and the shock of the moment had confirmed its respect for the fighting qualities of the British Army. The German staff officers had always worried about the flanks of their fast-advancing armour. And they got more jittery the farther they advanced. The strike at

Arras confirmed their fears. Their precious tanks were now poised to move into difficult marshy country near the coast to attack defended obstacles. They could be cut off in there by another flank attack at any moment. On Friday, 24 May the Panzers were halted by the Führer's direct orders on the line of the Aa canal while infantry support caught up and the gains of the past week were properly consolidated.

Air Marshal Göring had insisted that it was pointless risking the tanks near the coast anyway – his Luftwaffe would now take care of the British as they sat with their backs to the English Channel. They made a perfect, concentrated target for the kind of air warfare Germany had made her own. The already depleted German tank force could be conserved for its next priority, the push south towards Paris and the final defeat of the French.

Friday, 24 May was Empire Day, and King George VI broadcast to the nation: 'let no one be mistaken, it is no mere territorial conquest that our enemies are seeking. It is the overthrow, complete and final, of this Empire and of everything for which it stands, and after that the conquest of the world.' He called for a national day of prayer that Sunday.

The Anglo-French alliance was beginning to crack. On 25 May Paul Reynaud sent Churchill an angry cable. He complained about the British Army's sudden withdrawal from Arras and its failure to carry out its part of General Weygand's grand counter-attack. Reynaud apologised when it became clear that Amiens was still in German hands and that the French Army had failed to carry out its part of the plan as well.

Churchill was also angry. Infuriated by what he thought was a supine attitude in the Army, he wrote to his Chief of Staff, General Ismay, 'if one side fights and the other does not, the war is apt to become somewhat unequal'. General Gort had warned that he might have to retreat to the coast. It had seemed to Churchill far too early for such thoughts, but preparations had been put in train, nevertheless.

Admiral Ramsay had drawn together a strong force of destroyers, trawlers and ferries, but a mass evacuation under air bombardment had never been attempted before. No one knew how many men could be brought home before the Germans overran the entire coastline. Ramsay's best estimate was that he had until 28 May and might bring off 45,000. And no one knew how many of the precious destroyers would be lost in the process.

Alexander Cadogan, Permanent Under-Secretary for Foreign Affairs, returned from another exhausting day in Whitehall and wrote in his diary: 'just as gloomy as usual . . . everything is complete confusion: no communications and no one knows what is going on except that everything's as black as black'. Joseph Kennedy saw Cadogan's boss, Lord Halifax, and then cabled to Washington: 'the situation, according to the people who know, is very grim'.

Grim indeed: the French Army was in tatters; Italy was poised to enter the war on the German side, so threatening the British position in the Mediterranean and Suez Canal; the Americans were unable and unwilling to intervene. Outside a small circle in London, few knew the true scale of the looming disaster. But rumours were circulating. The Ministry of Information had people out in the streets and the pubs listening in to conversations. They reported disquiet, confusion and bewilderment in the nation.

Sunday, the day of prayer. The King and Queen went to Westminster Abbey. Crowds of people stood outside and heard the service relayed on loudspeakers. Denis Wissler and his parents walked to their church in Blackheath. It rained steadily.

Pray for all who serve in the Allied forces by sea and land and air
Pray for peoples invaded and oppressed; for the wounded and for
  prisoners
Remember before God the fallen, and those who mourn their loss.

Annie McLane took her baby to kneel in her pew in Newcastle. Peter Vaux's father and mother went to church in Devon. They had just received a telegram: their son was reported 'missing'.

O Eternal Lord God, who alone spreadest out the heavens and rulest the raging of the sea: Be pleased to receive into Thy protection those who in this time of war go down to the sea in ships and occupy their business in great waters.

Iain Nethercott's family prayed for him in Ilford.

O Lord, let Thy mercy be shewed upon us;
As we do put our trust in Thee

In Clippesby, Norfolk, Ernie Leggett's parents prayed for their son under the crossed keys of St Peter.

Oh God the Father of heaven;
Have mercy upon us.

At a few minutes before seven that evening the Admiralty order to implement Operation Dynamo was sent to Dover.

Chapter 5

26–27 May

By the weekend Churchill's War Cabinet was cracking too. The cause was the prospect of an Anglo-French approach to the Italian dictator, Benito Mussolini. On Saturday, 25 May the French had suggested such a move, 'with a view to exploring the possibilities of a friendly settlement'. The diplomatic circuit buzzed with reports that, if Mussolini intervened, Hitler would be prepared to stop the war. In return he would want German-speaking territory in France returned to the Reich, some small British colonial concessions and the understanding that, with France cowed and disarmed, he would be given a free hand in central Europe and the East.

A short war followed by a peace conference and a redrawing of borders and treaties. The nineteenth-century way. Better than another draining epic like the Great War, better than another mountain of corpses and the already creaking Empire pushed into complete bankruptcy.

Foreign Secretary Lord Halifax was Britain's senior diplomat. It was his duty to explore any idea that might get his nation off the hook. If the terms were reasonable then a peace deal was better than fighting a ruinous and unwinnable war. After all, Hitler had said for years that he regarded the British Empire and the British Fleet as foundations of the international order.

Churchill was instinctively sceptical. At 9 a.m. on Sunday, 26 May, during the first War Cabinet meeting of the day, he announced that he was 'opposed to any negotiations which might lead to a derogation of our rights and power'.

Paul Reynaud was in London. Churchill discussed the Italian idea with him over lunch and then, at another War Cabinet meeting, again urged caution. But Halifax expressed interest in the suggestion. Another meeting with Reynaud was followed by the third War Cabinet of the day at 5 p.m. By now Churchill was becoming exasperated: 'We must take care not to be forced into a weak position in which we went to Signor Mussolini and invited him to go to Herr Hitler and ask him to treat us nicely. We must not get tangled in a position of that kind before we had been involved in any serious fighting.'

Churchill argued that Britain should do nothing until after the coming evacuation, a huge gamble. A diplomatic initiative might save the Army and prevent the aerial onslaught that most expected Hitler to unleash upon the British people.

Halifax, cool and rational, now spoke up. He said that he was in favour of asking France to try out the 'possibilities of European equilibrium'. Churchill had spoken about the impossibility of dealing with Hitler and the crushing terms he would impose on Britain. Halifax disagreed. Picking his words with exquisite care, he widened the gap between himself and the Prime Minister. According to the Cabinet minutes 'he [Halifax] was not quite convinced that the Prime Minister's diagnosis was correct and that it was in Herr Hitler's interest to insist on outrageous terms'.

For the first time since Churchill assembled his government, the atmosphere in the Cabinet room crackled with the tension of open disagreement. And this was no academic discussion. On the question of negotiation or defiance hung the fate of the Army in France, the future independence of the British state, Hitler's mastery of Europe and, in all probability, the lives of every man and woman in the room.

Churchill was under pressure. He could not risk a full-scale row with Halifax, the second most powerful man in his government, the man who commanded much loyalty on the Conservative benches. He played for time, saying that he was happy for some kind of secret approach to be made to Mussolini. But he added that 'Herr Hitler thought that he had the whip hand. The only thing to do was to show him that he could not conquer this country.' The conversation moved to a different subject, but the argument was far from settled.

The Permanent Under-Secretary for Foreign Affairs, Alexander Cadogan, attended the meeting. Halifax was his immediate superior. Cadogan was almost certainly expressing his master's attitudes to the Prime Minister when he summed up the Cabinet conversation later that evening in his diary: 'WSC too rambling and romantic and sentimental and temperamental.'

When Ernie Leggett woke he was alone, inside some sort of lorry, being driven along some sort of road. Eventually the lorry stopped. Leggett could hear noises: engines letting off steam and engines shunting. The sound of a marshalling yard, he thought. They were going to France to fight the Germans. They'd been travelling all the way from Gibraltar with his leopardskin and drum. No, that was weeks and weeks ago. He'd already fought them. Killed a lot of them too. With the Bren gun. He slept some more. He dreamed of Clippesby. It was dark in the church. There was rain pounding on the roof. He woke and he was being carried and could look up and see wires and telegraph poles and the sky. When he next looked around he was in a railway carriage, with racks for stretchers where the seats should be. His bandages were changed. A nurse came with food and water and a smile and she held his hand and then a doctor gave him another injection and he went back to sleep. The next time he woke he was still on the train. Stopped. Then travelling. He had lost track of time and he had no idea where he was. Just the train and the injections and his hand being held. For days, maybe.

Eventually Leggett was carried to another ambulance. This time there were four stretchers, two either side. He was seeing things a bit more clearly now. Feeling them too, as the morphine began to wear off and the banging and crashing of the ambulance began to take hold. It was a rough journey and with every jolt his swollen legs and groin felt worse. But he was alive and he still had his balls. In one of his first conscious acts he'd felt down under the dressing and checked.

The back doors opened and he was carried across a road, and then the crisp footsteps went dull. Sand. He was put down on the sand. There were smells. First the sea – it was definitely sea air. Then smoke, fumes. The stench of burning oil. Cordite too. 'Where am I?' 'This is Dunkirk. You'll be taken home from here. There's a hospital ship going back to England.' Sandy steps came closer. 'The ship isn't going to be here for some hours. They need to wait till high tide for deep water. We'll put you up in the dunes. You'll be safe there.'

The smoke dimmed the sun at times. As he lay there he heard wave after wave of planes coming over and bombs dropping and anti-aircraft fire, and shells from the warships offshore whistled overhead. 'I was a wee bit frightened. Because I couldn't walk and I was at the mercy of whatever happened, I just couldn't get away, I'd have had to take it regardless. But other than that I was in a state of mind with the morphine hitting me, I just couldn't care less.'

Paul Richey was not exactly feeling well but in a lucid moment he persuaded his American nurse to take dictation of a letter home. She was a pacifist but had come over to Europe to do what she could. First in Finland, then in France. Paul was beginning to miss his family. He missed Page Huidekoper too, their American lodger who worked with those awful Kennedys. From Paris Paul sent a telegram to the American embassy in London: 'Bullet in neck removed doing very well – American Hospital'.

On 26 May Richey was sitting up in bed, a week after his operation, and beginning to feel much better. Sergeant Soper burst in, followed by 'Johnny' Walker, 'Boy' Mould, 'Prosser' Hanks, 'Stratters' Stratton and 'Killy' Kilmartin – almost all of the boys from No. 1 Squadron, all relieved and on their way home to England. They talked about the last battle, in which Paul had been shot down – there had not been much action since. They were going back to England to form a fighter school under their squadron leader, 'Bull' Halahan, to try to pass on their experience in combat to untried pilots. Paul would be able to join them soon.

'Hiker's knock', they called it in the north-east: glazed expression, slavering at the mouth, snot running down from the nose and the man not knowing or caring what he looked like, just wandering on, arms swinging loosely. Martin McLane had seen it before, on cross-country runs and training marches.

There were quite a few like that now: 'knocked', 'knocked' to buggery.

It was 2 a.m. somewhere between Armentières and Merville. No trains, no lorries, no idea where the next position was. Stupid bloody disorder.

Some of the men were losing heart. At the last skirmish a corporal had thrown his 'Boyes' anti-tank rifle into a ditch after watching another of its little shells rebound from a tank. McLane had made him pick it up. Someone else had used it later to knock a sniper out of a church tower. Only thing it was good for.

'Boyes' rifle was right. They felt like boys against men. The Germans would shoot their automatic rifles while McLane's troops pinged back one shot at a time. The Germans seemed to have artillery at their beck and call while the Durhams hadn't heard a British shell land for days. And then there were the Stukas and the tanks.

It almost made McLane weep to see the state of his lads. Crack

troops they were. They'd trained hard for war. They were proud
of the regiment and its history and sure they could do what their
fathers had done in 1914: stopped the Germans in their tracks.

The British Army, the finest infantry in the world, all those
battle honours on the flags at church parade. How could they lose?
They couldn't, they wouldn't. McLane spat, wiped the corner of
his mouth, and took another step along the cobbled road.

'We can't call him "Boss-Eye" anymore,' someone said, 'let's call
him "Hawk-Eye" instead.' Ken Lee was standing outside the mess
when he heard the other pilots discussing his nickname. A hawk.
He liked that. A predator swooping down from above. And the
eye part? Well, hadn't he already proved himself the best spotter of
enemy planes in the squadron? Waggling his wings and leading the
others towards their prey time and time again. Yes, a good name for
a fighter pilot. And far better than being teased about his drooping
right eyelid.

The first battle had been one mad rush. Lee had glimpsed the
bomber formation through a gap in the cloud, a few thousand feet
above the climbing Hurricanes. Fifty or so, all with the neat little
crosses painted on the wings, just sitting there waiting to be attacked.
He'd pushed the throttle so far forward that he'd almost broken
through the restraining wire put in by the ground crew to protect
their beloved engines from over-eager pilots. Engage sights, release
the gun safety catch, close to three hundred yards and fire. He'd
wasted a little ammunition by holding the button down too long
as he admired the damage his eight Browning machineguns were
doing to the rear end of the bomber. He wouldn't do that again.

They'd seen no German fighters that day, and hardly any in
the days that followed. The bombers would shoot back, but to
little effect. Then things had changed. There were Messerschmitts
everywhere now.

Lee was part of the RAF Volunteer Reserve. It was a great

way to get free flying lessons. 501 had been mobilised when war was declared, had trained in England and were then posted to France on 10 May. For a while life had been good. In between the fighting, there were loud evenings in the bars. There were some real characters too: 'Lofty' Dafforn, who was six foot three, 'Jammy' Paine, 'Ginger' Lacey – all great pilots, all great comrades. 501 was friendly, but it had an edge of competition too. Everyone wanted the highest score.

Lee and Flight Lieutenant Johnny 'Gibby' Gibson had known each other for only a couple of weeks but they were already great friends. 'He seemed to be a little man but he was absolutely irrepressible and he liked to have a jar.' Gibson was a newly trained pilot who'd come out just after the real fighting started on 10 May. He'd been trained on biplanes and had never even fired the guns of a Hurricane before his first combat sortie. But, unlike some of the other newcomers, Gibson handled himself brilliantly. It was obvious to the rest that, like Ken Lee, he was a natural fighter pilot and a natural leader. Soon both men were made flight leaders. They had a private competition going. Whoever got the most kills and was shot down the least would be the winner.

501 was caught up in the general retreat. In fourteen days Lee and Gibson had to move airfields five times. When they evacuated Boos, near Rouen, in a tearing hurry, nobody remembered to tell Gibson, who was resting in a hotel after his first bale-out. The Germans were already in the village when Gibson ran out of the back door. A fisherman rowed him over the River Seine. When he finally found Lee and the others at the new base his first words were: 'You abandoned me, you buggers.'

Martin McLane was trudging along the road from Calonne to Saint Floris. It was a country lane punctuated by farmsteads with the little river a short distance to their right and meadows to the left. The day had begun grey and muggy. Now there was a steady light rain falling.

At least they had found something to eat. They had taken some food from one of many abandoned farmhouses and boiled it up.

Bombers had been passing overhead all day. None of the bombs had come their way, but they were not far from the fighting on the ground. Every so often they heard shouting in the distance and periodic bursts of small-arms fire. Most of the time there was the shuddering thud of shelling too. Sometimes they saw shells landing. It sounded as if a series of attacks and counter-attacks was going on close by.

A short way beyond St Floris they ran into other members of their battalion. It was 'C' Company, or rather what was left of 'C' Company. 'I found the storeman called Rutherford walking across the field picking up the rifles of the fallen. And all around was blood and the debris of a bayonet attack. By then they'd lifted up some of the wounded, but there were dead people lying there, both Germans and British, all over the place. When you see the blood and the mess and the gore after a bayonet attack, nasty. They had driven them back to the line of the railway.'

He was looking at the bodies of two Manchester machine-gunners. Their faces were horribly contorted. McLane picked up a dead German's rifle and found about thirty rounds of ammunition in the former owner's pouches. He had given his own rifle to a soldier who had none, but he preferred to have something a bit more powerful than his revolver. He was feeling very subdued. Some of the bodies he had just seen were men he'd played rugby with a few weeks earlier.

Before long they were marching again. Half a mile farther on they were shot at by a single machinegun. They fell flat and peered across the fields to their left. McLane picked out a figure in the hayloft of a barn. He was just about to shoot when his rifle was deflected by the company sergeant-major, 'It might be a Frenchman.' 'It's a bloody German,' said McLane, 'he's sighting the gun on us.' It was still raining. They filed off cautiously and a mile or two later reached St Venant, the small town that the battalion was now supposed to hold. 'D' Company was sent on farther to the right while the other companies dug in in the fields in front of the town. McLane had been told that the Berkshire Regiment was to his right but there was no sign of them. He found himself next to a farmhouse. The owner was still inside. Rather than throw the Frenchman out, the Durhams, still obeying the considerate edicts of the General Staff, borrowed spades and dug slit trenches in the field beside the building. The ground was very wet and the trenches quickly filled with water.

McLane went to check the approaches to their position. He found a small humpbacked bridge over a little canal. As he walked along the road towards company headquarters, the Germans started shelling. He saw the company commander, Lieutenant Gregson, another rugby player, coming towards him. Gregson asked him what he was doing and McLane replied that he was checking the positions of the other companies and the fields of fire. As the officer walked off the shelling got more intense and McLane saw him go down. He ran after him. Gregson was twisting and moaning in agony.

> He was on the bottom lying in a bit of a ditch and he had a big lump of shrapnel stuck in the base of his spine. I grabbed a hold of it to pull it out of his back. And it was red hot, you couldn't touch it, it was burning his back as well as my hand. And he was taking his pistol out to shoot himself, because he must have been in terrific pain. Right in the base of the spine and into his thighs. And there was nothing I could do for him other than to get stretcher bearers. But during the shelling there was no one to be seen, so I ran along the 200 yards to the company headquarters.

By the time the stretcher-bearers came, Gregson was unconscious. Sergeant-Major Metcalfe gave McLane a cup of tea and told him that he was now second-in-command of the company. As he left, the stretcher-bearers came by carrying the lieutenant on a gate. They looked across, shook their heads and gave him a thumbs-down sign. McLane went back to his men. By now it was dark.

A message came through from battalion headquarters ordering

him to send out a patrol. McLane got together Sergeant Donaldson and three of his troublemakers, the toughest men he had, including Whitely, the battalion boxing champion. He told them to keep their heads down. Two hours later they came back soaking wet with staring eyes: 'The whole bloody German army's out there. They've got tanks. They've got artillery and they're just taking it easy. They're in a village this side of the canal and they've lit bonfires. Look at them buggers eating, we're starving, they've bonfires going and we cannot strike a light.' McLane sent a runner to Headquarters with the message that the German armour was already on the British side of the La Bassée canal. Then they spent a damp and uncomfortable night, waiting.

The rain dripping steadily off the leaves had begun to trickle down the back of Peter Vaux's neck. It was early Sunday afternoon and the three soldiers were hiding in the woods above l'Etoile, a small town on the northern bank of the River Somme. They had got down to the river in one night on a bearing from the compass they had taken from the tank. They had quite a lot of bully beef and biscuits in a wicker basket they had found in the house in Franqueville. The night journey had been frightening but uneventful. Only once had they to run for cover when some dogs started barking fiercely as they skirted the last village. As they approached the Somme they had pulled away uphill and found a barn to pass the night in. Then they crossed the road, scrambled up a very steep slope, and found themselves in this wood.

This was their third day in the wood, hiding by day, trying to explore during the short nights. They were dirty, unshaven, tired of bully beef, and now they were pretty wet too, although they were glad that they had brought their overcoats from the tank. They were getting more and more nervous. The main road bridge down in l'Etoile was strongly fortified and the place was full of Germans. They should have guessed that. And with the French not far away on the other side of the Somme, the Germans were in a high state of alert. It was going to be very difficult to get across the river unless there was some sort of distraction. Their best hope was if some kind of attack was mounted by the Allied troops on the far side. From this high position they had hoped to see something happen, but so far nothing had.

At least the pouring rain would keep people at home. The trouble with this place was that it was too close to the edge of town, an obvious place to take the dog for a Sunday afternoon walk. The cemetery was only just below. They would move away tonight and see if they could find a better and quieter spot farther along the ridge. They huddled closer to the trunk of a huge oak tree that gave them some protection against the rain.

Hugh Keenleyside was a middle-aged Canadian diplomat more used to discussing details of immigration and trade policy than playing the secret agent. As Ottawa's chosen envoy to Washington, Keenleyside had been ushered into the White House by a side entrance. Inside he had met President Roosevelt and Cordell Hull, Secretary of State, for the confidential discussion the two Americans had requested. Keenleyside then left immediately for home. Evidently excited by his new role in life, he wrote up his account of his meeting in a schoolboy code. Roosevelt became 'Mr Robert', Churchill, 'Mr Clark', and so on. In equally cryptic language, Keenleyside entitled his document 'Report of a discussion of possible eventualities'.

Keenleyside's Prime Minister, Mackenzie King, normally took Sundays very seriously. He would rarely work, preferring to devote the Sabbath to private thought and Bible study. But on 26 May his devotional reverie was punctured by the arrival of Keenleyside's document. The 'possible eventualities' it discussed were enough to plunge King into depression.

The paper began: 'Facing an air superiority of about 5 to 1 it is unlikely that the United Kingdom can withstand such an assault for many weeks.' Roosevelt, the paper explained, feared that Britain would soon succumb to the temptation of a soft peace: 'Such a decision, he feels, would mean not only the temporary extinction of civilization in western Europe but its permanent destruction throughout the world.'

This was a long way beyond normal diplomatic language – the American President obviously shared Mackenzie King's darkest fears. King had already filled his diary with a sense of humanity poised on the brink of the abyss. His dreams, which he would describe most mornings, were frequently filled by visions drawn from the more bloodthirsty chapters of the Old Testament and the Book of Revelation.

'I question if ever in the history of the world, a message came picturing possibilities more appalling than those communications revealed,' King wrote the following day.

> The President and Mr Hull were doubtful if England would be able to bear up under attack, and the President has it from what he believes good authority from Germany that Hitler may make an offer of settlement based on . . . the turning over of the fleet to the Germans . . . The President wanted me to line up the Dominions to bring concerted pressure to bear on England not to yield to making of any soft peace even though it might mean destruction of England comparable to that of Poland, Holland and Belgium; the killing of those who had refused to make the peace, but to have her fleet make its base at different outlying ports away from Europe and send the King to Bermuda.

Washington knew that once peace talks began the Royal Navy would be Britain's only bargaining chip. America's leaders were now desperate to keep that fleet out of German hands – even if that meant Britain being bombed flat. Roosevelt wanted to draw up a plan for the evacuation of the Navy to Canada and other outposts of the British Commonwealth. He had told Keenleyside that the idea of Hitler controlling both the British and the French fleets meant, quite simply, the 'end of hope' and that Germany and Japan would together dominate the world in a grand totalitarian alliance.

Referring to the chance of urgent American aid to Britain, Roosevelt had also spoken to Keenleyside about problems with US public opinion. 'Opinion in the republic is changing but not with sufficient rapidity to make effective aid possible,' the Canadian reported to his Prime Minister.

For King the real sting came at the end. Roosevelt wanted him to approach Churchill and raise the prospect of sending the fleet to the New World. King's diary records his distress:

> For a moment it seemed to me that the U.S. was seeking to save itself at the expense of Britain. That it was an appeal to the selfishness of the Dominions at the expense of the British Isles . . . I instinctively revolted against such a thought . . . I would rather die than do aught to save ourselves or any part of this continent at the expense of Britain.

As the last week in May began, King and his top diplomats considered how best they should respond to Washington and what, if anything, they should tell Churchill of the American President's ideas.

Peter Vaux peered through the leaves. Everything seemed quiet. They were clear of the town now and they had an unrestricted view from here out over open country. He edged forward into the long grass, put his binoculars to his eyes and surveyed the wide riverscape before him. The valley of the Somme was quite steep on either side where well-wooded hills rose from the river. At points the river seemed to split confusingly into several channels, and there were great pools either side of the main stream. He could see Germans on the long bridge on the outskirts of the town. There seemed to be no other dry way across. Wait – just below them and to their left there was a railway bridge. No, two. The second had a train on it, hanging dramatically over bombed rails. Suddenly he heard a plane. There it was, flying down the river. A German spotter plane. He wriggled back a bit towards the trees. What was that glinting on the other side of the river? They were armoured cars. Definitely French armoured cars. 'Look at this! I think something is about to happen.' The others crawled forward towards him.

Something did happen. There was a sudden rustling in the trees and out sprang a German officer with a Luger pistol balanced in his hand. They had been taken completely by surprise. 'Stand up,' he said in English. They stood; there was nothing else to do. The German took the pistol from the driver. He took the pistol from the major. They had lanyards on them and he wound the lanyards around his wrist. Then he looked at Vaux and saw the binoculars hanging from his neck. He snatched them but overlooked the pistol on Vaux's belt. 'Go, go, go, get up.' Vaux assessed his chances against this man. From the colour of his shoulder flashes, Vaux realised he was in the artillery, a lieutenant like himself. His boots were highly polished and he had a little silver eagle on his chest. He looked very fit and rather formidable.

The three prisoners shambled off along the edge of the wood at the top of the hill. Burroughs led, Vaux followed, Major Fernie and the German were side by side. They were deliberately dawdling. The German said, 'Go on, go on, go, *schnell, schnell.*' Burroughs speeded up, Vaux did not, and as the German swept forward, the major hung back and then dived into the bushes. The German turned and fired a shot at him. Vaux got his pistol out and fired a shot at the German. He missed.

But he turned his attention to me now because I was the one who'd got a gun. And he ran towards me shooting and I was shooting back. And I shot four shots without hitting him. The fifth shot, when he was still some distance away went right into his chest and to my astonishment he kept on running, he kept on shooting, he kept on shouting. He was shouting for help. And he came right up to me and leant against me and pushed his pistol into my stomach, and I now know about Luger pistols, you can tell when they're empty and it wasn't empty. There's a lever which comes up on top when it's empty, and it wasn't up, it was down. The pistol still had at least one shot in it and I had one shot left too. And I put it into him and he fell down. Dead. Because I hit him in the left chest.

They all three turned and ran down the hill through the long grass as fast as they could. They practically fell over the bank at the bottom, scrambled across the road, dived behind some walls and ran down a grassy track towards the nearest wood. At the bottom of the hill, they came upon some ruined buildings. Behind a broken wall they lay in the grass, panting.

There was a rusty metal cross leaning against a window. The ruins must have been some sort of priory, medieval, heavily overgrown now and deep in nettles. The walls were built out of dressed white stone. Rather beautiful where the stonework emerged from the ivy. The largest structure was a circular tower, and Vaux walked round the outside of it towards an archway. 'Here, look at this!' Burroughs whispered. Major Fernie and Vaux went over to where he was standing. The wall was covered with graffiti. Names cut into the soft white stone. Most of them were German. Fortunately they were dated 1916. Inside there was an area that was dry and concealed from view. That would be their hiding place.

Creeping out again to explore the access to their den, they looked nervously at a farm house about two hundred yards away. Behind it was an old barn that seemed to have quite a few people in it. They just had to hope the people in it never went into these ruins. It didn't look as if they did. The few paths were overgrown with brambles and ferns. Anyway, they could hardly move again now. The German had been shouting for help. He obviously had friends in the woods. They must have found him by now and they would be searching for his murderers.

Vaux was beginning to feel very peculiar. He had an awful sense of guilt about the strong, smart and brave man he had just killed. He was having great difficulty getting the German's face out of his head. It was stupid. If he had not killed him they would all be prisoners now, or he would be dead himself. As he went over the details of the scene he realised they were in even worse trouble. 'We had left all the food in the basket at the edge of the wood.' The food, their coats, two pistols and the binoculars.

The Hotel du Sauvage at Cassel was perched on one of the few hills on the Flanders plain. On the fine morning of Monday, 27 May a little group of English officers walked round the village and admired the view. They could hear the sound of artillery to the south where 2 Division had been thrown in to try to stem the advance of the German Panzers. The hotel had holes in the roof and walls but the piles of debris had been swept neatly aside. Last night General Adam had received the order from Lord Gort to prepare the Dunkirk area for defence and evacuation.

He had come to Cassel to organise concerted action with the French. At 7 a.m. General Fagalde arrived from Dunkirk, and together the two agreed that Fagalde's troops would hold the river Aa and the western part of the canal as far as Bergues. The British would be responsible for the twenty-five miles from Bergues to Nieuport. Non-essential vehicles would not be allowed inside the perimeter. The Frenchman remarked that for the last three days his men had held the Germans easily because their tanks had been withdrawn from the fight. What were the Germans up to? Perhaps their armour was being saved for a major attack south towards Paris. Or perhaps not. If the Panzers came back the two generals wondered how long their perimeter defences could keep them out.

The bombardment to the south grew louder. At 7.30 a.m. other French generals arrived. A representative of Weygand urged an attack from Gravelines to recapture Calais. His colleagues nodded politely but did nothing to implement the measure. Suddenly shells began to land all around the hotel. The generals concluded their meeting and the British party hurried to their car. As he left, General Adam could look down and see where for two days 2 Division had held the southern flank of the corridor along which the BEF was retreating towards Dunkirk. 1 Division would be on its way to the perimeter line by now. He was glad he was not down there near St Venant or on the La Bassée canal. If those tanks came back, he wouldn't give much for their chances.

At St Venant the shelling had started before dawn and by first light Martin McLane's men were ready for action. The smoke ahead probably concealed advancing German infantry. McLane was confident that the little canal in front of him gave him some protection from vehicles, but far from sure about his right flank. The forward platoons were entrenched in open fields and looked very exposed. The Durhams had very little ammunition and he had told them to hold fire until they could make their shots count. He took position at the corner of the farm. About eight he heard tanks moving in the distance. The worst they could do was spray fire from the far bank of the canal. But what about his right flank?

McLane walked a few yards to the road behind the farm – the point he had nominated company headquarters – and peered into the distance to his right. One of his platoon came running back in obvious panic. 'Fitch of the platoon has been killed!' 'So? Get back to your position!' McLane stood at the corner of the barn and began to pick off advancing German infantry with his German rifle.

Soon, there were others running back from the forward positions. Up came Sergeant-Major Metcalfe with his stretcher-bearers and runners. 'What's happened?' 'A full scale attack,' McLane replied. Men were staggering back wounded now. 'You do a counter attack.' 'What with?' asked McLane. Yesterday afternoon every man had been placed along the dangerously extended front. They had no reserve. 'There's only you and me and these lads here to go on the attack with.' Metcalfe seemed to give up the pretence. 'Oh, forget it,' he said.

Over on the right McLane could see men running away. He

couldn't yet see tanks but he suspected they were out there somewhere and responsible for all this panic. A private came back to the
road wounded in the groin with blood squirting down his trouser
legs and more blood oozing out from under the webbing at his
ankles. At first glance McLane knew he was going to die. His face
was already bleached white, the blood loss too severe for battlefield
first aid. 'Sergeant Major, help me,' he implored. 'There's nothing
I can do, son.'

There were several other badly wounded men looking for treatment, but there were no facilities. No one even had field dressings
any more. Metcalfe was sending up Very lights, the SOS signal, but
he wasn't getting any response. No supporting fire, nothing.

McLane and some of his men were sheltering behind a hedge.
He could see the Germans only a hundred or so yards away and
advancing. They were spraying the hedge with fire from automatic weapons, and the Durhams were taking still more casualties.
McLane used his last German bullet, threw down his rifle and pulled
out his revolver. Metcalfe said, 'What are we going to do?' 'Give
the order, every man for himself.' 'I can't do that.' 'Then I'll do
it,' said McLane, and he turned to the rest of the lads and shouted,
'When I say "Every man for himself" get into that field and run,
then when I shout, "Get Down", you drop. Right . . . "Every man
for himself!"'

Two or three men were shot before they got clear of the hedge,
but most of them had made forty yards when McLane yelled, 'Get
down!' They were hidden in the sharp, green corn stalks. McLane
still had to shout above the gunfire: 'Now listen to me, lads, listen,
and do as I say. When I say "now crawl", crawl to your right,
when I say "get up", get up, and when I say "get down", get
down like a shot. "Now crawl."' He crawled until they had gone
far enough for there to be some hope that the Germans had lost
track of their position. 'Run!' He launched himself forward and
ran, heart pounding, flattening corn. There was a crackle of fire.
He heard someone fall with a cry. 'Get down!' They dived. 'Now,
crawl!' But Whitely, just to his left, was not moving. McLane

crawled back to him. Whitely smiled through obvious pain. 'Sergeant Major, leave us. I'm badly hit. I've had it.' McLane looked at the bullet holes across his stomach and nodded. He patted his shoulder and turned away. There was no time to say goodbye. 'Right lads, run!'

At the far end of the field they found a gap in the hedge, rolled down a bank the other side and almost landed on a platoon of Vickers machinegunners sitting by their lorry in the lane. McLane exploded. 'We've been screaming for help over there! We sent up Very lights. Didn't you see them? What the fuck are you bastards doing loitering here?' The machinegunners jumped into their lorry and drove off. 'Don't go that way!' McLane yelled after them. 'You'll drive straight into them!' But they were gone. 'What do we do now, Martin?' asked Metcalfe. It's come to something when the company sergeant-major's using your Christian name, thought McLane. Aloud, he said, 'There's only one thing to do. Make away from the fight.'

Across the next field a line of willows announced the Lys canal. Metcalfe sank to his knees on the towpath. 'Oh Christ, that's me buggered, I can't swim.' McLane looked at him. The man was shattered. Of the other eight, five also said they couldn't swim. McLane looked across the water: there were barges moored on the other side. He took his pack and webbing off and dived in. The canal had sheer concrete walls but he hauled himself up by a rope on to a barge. A few yards down he found a boat. There was no sign of any oars and no time to look so McLane lay on his stomach in the bottom and paddled across with his arms. The nine Durhams piled into the boat and paddled themselves over. More men had appeared on the other bank now, and McLane pushed the boat back to them. It was only then he realised he'd left his pack on the far bank. Annie's photo, lost.

On the far side of the canal they plunged into the forest of Nieppe. McLane had a pocket compass and he led them on a bearing north-east. Where they emerged another infantry unit was preparing defensive positions. McLane was soaking wet and his companions also looked filthy and shattered. Walker and 'Dusty' Miller were wounded.

The infantry officer was aggressive and sceptical: 'What are you doing? What are you running away for?' McLane and Metcalfe tried to explain but he wouldn't listen. 'Disgraceful! Disgraceful! You will be punished for this,' he thundered. 'Get these wounded men seen to. And you lot, you get in that barn. Get your clothes off. Get them dried. You're in my unit now!'

Martin McLane and his Prime Minister were both fighting rear-guard actions on 27 May.

Churchill began the day complaining to his War Cabinet that 'The United States had given us practically no help in this war, and now that they saw how great was the danger, their attitude was that they wanted to keep everything which could help us for their own defence.' This did not surprise anyone in the room. No one in London yet knew that Roosevelt was talking to the Canadians about Britain's imminent defeat, but it had become very clear very quickly that Churchill's early predictions of massive American aid had been over-optimistic.

Next before the War Cabinet was a Chiefs of Staff report on the relative air strengths of Britain and Germany. It calculated a four to one advantage in Hitler's favour. Churchill questioned the figures. Air Marshal Richard Price, Vice-Chief of the Air Staff, put forward some new tables, recalculating the German advantage at only about three to one. This was about as encouraging as the morning got.

The Army surrounded with its back to the sea, the bad air ratios, the lack of support from Washington. You did not have to be a defeatist or even an appeaser to feel, on 27 May, that the war had been all but lost. This was, after all, what just about every well-informed person was saying in every capital city in the world.

That afternoon the War Cabinet returned to the possibility of an approach to Mussolini so that the Italian might broker a peace deal.

Once again Halifax and Churchill disagreed. The Prime Minister said he was 'increasingly oppressed with the futility of the suggested approach to Signor Mussolini', fearing it would 'ruin the integrity of our fighting position in this country'. 'Let us not be dragged down with France . . .' he urged with increasing passion. 'At the moment our prestige in Europe is very low. The only way we can get it back is by showing the world that Germany has not beaten us . . . Let us therefore avoid being dragged down the slippery slope with France. The whole of this manoeuvre is intended to get us so deeply involved in negotiations that we shall be unable to turn back.' He concluded that 'The approach proposed is not only futile, but involves us in deadly danger.'

Halifax then spoke of 'certain rather profound differences of points of view'. The chilly and careful official minutes do little justice to a moment that shook everyone present. The civil servants describe Halifax as saying: 'In the discussions the previous day he [Halifax] had asked the Prime Minister whether, if he was satisfied that matters vital to the independence of this country were unaffected, he would be prepared to discuss terms.' The previous day, Halifax had thought that Churchill had an open mind. Now it seemed to him that the Prime Minister was saying that there could be no deal at any price.

Then Halifax made his decisive contribution:

> The Prime Minister has said that two or three months will show whether we are able to stand up against the air attack. This means that the future of the country turns on whether the enemy's bombs happen to hit our aircraft factories. I am prepared to take that risk if our independence is at stake; but if it is not at stake I would think it right to accept an offer which would save the country from avoidable disaster.

Avoidable disaster. The words echoed around the Cabinet Room. The Foreign Secretary, the man who commanded the loyalty of much of the Conservative party, thought that the Prime Minister was leading the nation into an 'avoidable disaster'.

Immediately after the meeting Halifax told Cadogan, 'I can't work with Winston any longer.' Later he wrote in his diary:

> We had a long and rather confused discussion about, nominally, the approach to Italy, but also largely about general policy in the event of things going really badly in France. I thought Winston talked the most frightful rot, also Greenwood, and after bearing it for some time I said exactly what I thought of them, adding that if that was really their view, and if it came to the point, our ways must separate. Winston, surprised and mellowed, and, when I repeated the same thing in the garden, was full of apologies and affection. But it does drive me to despair when he works himself into a passion of emotion when he ought to make his brain think and reason.

Thinking and reasoning had led Halifax to conclude that the military position was hopeless and that if a peace deal could be obtained which guaranteed Britain's independence then it should be taken.

The argument that Monday afternoon went to the heart of the differences between the two men. All Churchill's instincts were to fight on and see what might happen, believing that a show of defiance could change everything. In language that doubtless made Halifax wince, Churchill told the War Cabinet that he would rather go down fighting than be enslaved to Germany. But Halifax did not see the world, or this war, in such dramatic terms. Diplomacy normally offers a middle way: a concession here, a trade-off there.

But Churchill understood something that Halifax did not. Hitler was not a nineteenth-century statesman and this war was not about redrafting treaties or adjusting the balance of power. It was something else, something outside either man's experience. It was a war of ideology, of enslavement, and even, perhaps, of annihilation.

In these last hours before Dunkirk, Britain's leaders were as close to caving in as they ever came. Had Halifax been sitting in Churchill's chair, as he so nearly was, then some kind of peace deal might well have been attempted. Whether the nation would have accepted it is a different question. But deprived of firm, confident leadership, and faced with disaster in France and the likelihood of terror bombing, many would surely have accepted the judgment of their government.

But Halifax was not sitting in Churchill's chair. And strangely, surprisingly, out of the mouth of the embattled Prime Minister, a kind of script for the Battle of Britain began to emerge. Instead of accepting the logic of defeat, Britain would rearm, regroup and remotivate herself. From her island fortress she would spit defiance, her sailors would deter invasion and her pilots would claw the Luftwaffe out of the skies. Even though her cities might be flattened she would put up such a glorious show of resistance that the rest of the world, and especially America, would realise that she was worth supporting.

Such an epic scenario, in these last dismal days of May, must have seemed to some of Churchill's colleagues like the worst kind of wishful thinking. But it was all the war policy the Prime Minister had to offer. Somehow, and quickly, Churchill would have to find the will and the words to persuade his Cabinet, and the rest of the British people, to act out their parts in the script.

But first he had to get his army home.

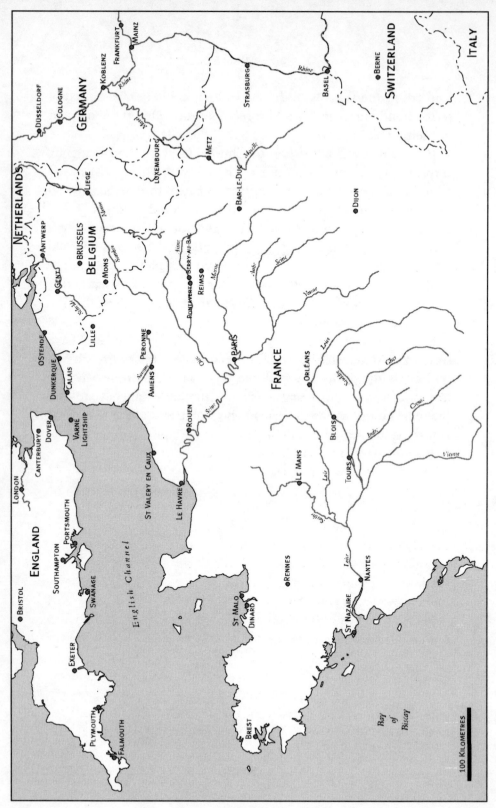

Map 2   North West Europe

Chapter 6

28 May–1 June

As HMS *Keith* steamed out of Chatham docks, Iain Nethercott went up to the deck. The dark estuary water was crowded with tugs and barges and all sorts of smaller craft, all making for Sheerness. For the last few days everyone had been working flat out as the ship was patched up after its gun battle with the German Army at Boulogne. There had been no time to repaint and the destroyer was now pockmarked with red lead. Still, most of the holes had been filled and Nethercott's two-pounder gun had been replaced with a newer model with steel retractor clips and articulated ammunition belts instead of the useless old canvas ones. They also had some additional anti-aircraft defence, an old three-inch gun and a couple of extra Lewis machineguns with brand new 'hostilities only' ratings to fire them.

They also had a new captain, Captain Berthon. They anchored at Sheerness and Berthon cleared the lower deck, read the Articles of War and introduced himself to the crew. 'As you know, we're going across to Dunkirk,' he said. Nethercott didn't know. Well, that's bloody nice, he thought, I've just got out of one spot of bother and now here comes another one.

As they joined the traffic from the Thames the sailors looked about them, astonished: 'everywhere you could see there was trawlers and long lines of motor boats that they'd dragged up from the Thames being towed across with an unhappy looking sailor stuck in each one'. They were all heading out along what Admiral Ramsay's planners called 'Route Y', first towards Ostend and then turning south down through the narrow sandbanks of the 'North Channel', through what the sailors called the Zuydecoote pass and in towards the Dunkirk beaches. As they came in close to the coast, the *Keith* found itself in the now familiar position of being shelled by German artillery.

For much of the time Iain Nethercott and his shipmates were shooting back at the Germans north of Dunkirk. Then, when the inevitable dive-bombers came, their role changed. Poorly armed as HMS *Keith* was against aircraft, she was better equipped than almost every other ship off Dunkirk, and her captain had been ordered to keep the Stukas away from the more vulnerable troop-carriers. Nethercott blasted away at everything that came close with his new gun, but he had no idea if he ever hit anything.

It was another odd situation. Here they were off one of the longest beaches in Europe. But instead of holidaymakers, the expanses of sand were covered with lines of little black dots. Some of the boats that had been towed over from England were going back and forth to the beaches and ferrying little parties of soldiers to the bigger boats – mostly requisitioned trawlers and drifters and rusty old barges that were standing out in the deeper water.

Meanwhile, at what was left of Dunkirk harbour, destroyers, passenger ferries and pleasure cruisers were going in to pick up larger groups of troops. The docks had already been destroyed by the Luftwaffe, but someone had worked out that it was possible to bring ships in alongside the narrow, sinuous East Mole that stretched out almost a mile into the sea. To everyone's relief, thick drifting smoke from a burning oil refinery next to the harbour stopped the circling Stuka pilots picking out the ships loading from the mole. They could only dive down and attack when they were farther out to sea. This, at least, gave the captains a chance to manoeuvre out of the way of the falling bombs.

Through his binoculars, Nethercott watched the ships as they headed home, their decks now covered with the same little black dots he'd seen waiting on the beaches. Some passed close to the *Keith*. He waved; the dots waved back. The whole thing seemed completely mad. Away from the smoke it was sunny and bright. And there they all were, the remains of the British Army, looking for all the world like day-trippers out on a sixpenny cruise, but with dive-bombers for company. Nethercott was amazed at the number of near-misses; it seemed dozens of bombs were exploding in the water, sending great harmless spouts of it up and over the ships as they turned first one way and then another. Whether it was good seamanship, bad bombing or plain old divine intervention, it was clear that a lot of people were getting away. But only just.

In London on 28 May bad news broke before dawn. At four o'clock in the morning the Belgian government capitulated, adding another name to the list of nations conquered by Hitler's armies. At the 11.30 a.m. War Cabinet, Churchill announced that the terms of the Belgian armistice gave the German Army free passage to the coast north of Dunkirk, further exposing the British and French forces retreating to that port.

The first day's evacuation figures were not encouraging. Only about eight thousand soldiers had been rescued on 27 May. But the morning reports from the air marshals raised the Prime Minister's spirits. During the previous day's fighting above and around Dunkirk, the RAF had claimed over fifty German aircraft for the loss of only twelve of their own. And, for the first time, substantial numbers of the latest fighter type had been thrown into the fray – the Spitfire. By all accounts it had performed very well.

It was impossible to confirm such figures. Postwar calculations point to a more even score. Nevertheless, it seemed clear to the Prime Minister and his Chiefs of Staff that the nearer German planes got to Britain, the easier they were to shoot down. And on

28 May Churchill was the last person to question a morale-boosting statistic. He seized on the RAF's performance, building references to their three-or-four-to-one 'clawing-down rate' into all his major meetings and speeches over the next few days.

The War Cabinet discussed the Belgian surrender. Then the Minister of Information, Alfred Duff Cooper, read out an ominous report from the Press Censorship Bureau. The Bureau was a shadowy body whose function went some way beyond telling the press what they could and couldn't print. They also organised random phone-tapping and private letter-opening to find out what ordinary Britons were thinking. And, according to such sources, ordinary Britons were very uneasy. What rankled the most was the lack of honest information. People wanted to know the full facts about the fate of their army. The Press Censorship Bureau's report called for 'a frank statement of the desperate situation of the BEF' in order to protect public confidence in the government. Churchill decided to make an immediate statement to the House of Commons.

Within hours the Prime Minister was on his feet in front of a grim-faced audience of MPs. He spoke of the grave position of the BEF and said that 'the House should prepare itself for hard and heavy tidings'. His prediction of only fifteen days before, of 'blood, toil, tears and sweat', was coming painfully true, painfully quickly. And although the Prime Minister finished his short statement with the promise that the nation would move 'through disaster and through grief to the ultimate defeat of our enemies', few in his audience were left in any doubt that disaster and grief aplenty, rather than the defeat of any enemies, would be filling up the days to follow.

The Prime Minister walked away from the House of Commons in a sombre mood. The War Cabinet would reconvene at 4 p.m., and he knew that once again the possibility of a negotiated peace would be on the agenda. For two days now he had struggled to resist the logic of Halifax's position. He knew that Attlee and Greenwood, the two Labour members of his War Cabinet, were with him, leaving Neville Chamberlain vacillating somewhere between himself and Halifax. If he could hold Chamberlain then perhaps all would be well. If not, then the two senior Conservatives in his government might lead their party against him in the name of making the best out of a losing war, especially if the Dunkirk evacuation went badly wrong.

Everything hinged on those men on the beaches.

Ernie Leggett heard feet approaching through the sand. Standing over him were two stretcher-bearers and a nurse. She was English. She said, 'We're going to take you on board ship now. You're going home.' They lifted him up. He could hear their feet on the sand. Then stone. Then they were walking along wood. He could hear their footsteps. Then they were walking on metal. They put him down on the deck of a ship. It was painted white.

There were bombs falling and explosions. They sounded very close. A white ship must stand out a mile. A medical officer was moving from stretcher to stretcher. He had a syringe. Leggett saw the doctor bending over him and then, once again, he went out like a light.

Leggett woke and his head was clear. There were seagulls crying. He could still hear the waves. He was on the tarmac in the sunshine with the smell of melting tar. 'Along came a Salvation Army nurse with a trolley and she gave me a lovely hot mug of tea and a cigarette.' Leggett asked, 'Where am I?' She said, 'Newhaven, dear.'

He was lifted on to an ambulance. There were already two wounded men on stretchers to either side. He was last on and placed in the gangway. It was a bumpy ride. The morphine had worn off and Leggett felt excruciating pain, especially in his back. Every time the ambulance shook, all five injured men winced or cried out. The ambulance was driving slowly to minimise their discomfort but the journey seemed to take for ever.

Finally it drew up outside the Royal Sussex Hospital. The steps to the entrance were lined with doctors and nurses, and they all clapped and cheered and welcomed the soldiers home and promised to look after them. At long last Leggett felt safe and secure. And he even murmured out loud, 'Thank God I'm home.'

The War Cabinet sat down together at four o'clock in the afternoon. Churchill began by stating very firmly that the French were trying to get Britain to join them on the 'slippery slope' of negotiation. Halifax countered by saying that, of course, Britain should fight to the death for its independence but that, if independence could be guaranteed, then there might be certain concessions that could be made to secure peace. He pointed out that the current terms might well be better than those available in a few months' time.

Churchill focused again on the likely effect on national morale of any move towards mediation. Reading from a prepared draft, he sketched out how he feared a negotiation would go. Britain would sit at the table, the terms presented would be unacceptable and then: 'When, at this point, we got up to leave the Conference-table, we should find that all the forces of resolution which were now at our disposal would have vanished.'

Churchill went on. 'Signor Mussolini, if he came in as mediator, would take his whack out of us. It was impossible to imagine that Herr Hitler would be so foolish as to let us continue our re-armament. In effect, his terms would put us completely at his mercy.' Chamberlain and the others listened. Halifax said he could not understand why Churchill thought mediation was so wrong. At this point Chamberlain intervened. Influenced, perhaps, by Churchill's description of the likely peace negotiations (and perhaps also thinking of his own humiliating experiences of negotiating with Hitler), Chamberlain declared that going for mediation now 'involved a considerable gamble'. It was not exactly a ringing endorsement of Churchill's position, but it was enough.

Churchill spoke again, declaring grandly and, to Halifax, no doubt, gratingly that 'nations which went down fighting rose again, but those which surrendered tamely were finished'. Halifax said for the record that nothing in what he had proposed 'could even remotely be described as ultimate capitulation'.

Churchill had won only a temporary reprieve, a chance to try it his way for a little longer. Chamberlain had said that the moment was not right for an appeal for mediation. Perhaps another moment would be. If Dunkirk was a disaster then talk of mediation would inevitably recur.

Within an hour there was an extraordinary meeting in the Prime Minister's office in Parliament. With Halifax and Chamberlain absent, Churchill met and addressed his wider Cabinet for the first time. Over thirty people were crammed into the small room. They had already been impressed by their new leader's hard work and attention to detail. Nevertheless, Churchill's audience that evening included several men who mistrusted his judgment. Many had served Chamberlain and some had been Churchill's sworn enemies during his long years out of office.

They were treated to a vintage performance, bristling with passion and belligerence but starkly honest about the situation in Europe. Churchill spoke about Dunkirk and the state of the army. He said that saving fifty thousand should be possible but that he hoped to save more. A hundred thousand would be 'magnificent'. He spoke of the likely fall of France and the coming Battle of Britain. He defended his refusal to pursue mediation and he reinforced his warning that a peace deal now would soon mean rule by a British Fascist like Sir Oswald Mosley.

Warming to his theme, Churchill elaborated on his vision of the coming months, the one that had begun to form during the punishing War Cabinet arguments of the past few days. He spoke of the RAF's 'clawing-down rate', of the people's endurance under fire and of how America would be sure to respond to a great show of heroic resistance from across the Atlantic. He concluded: '. . . if this long island story of ours is to end at last, let it end only when each one of us lies choking in his own blood upon the ground'.

He was greeted by a wave of approval, the stamping of feet and the slapping of his back. Minister for Economic Warfare Hugh Dalton called the speech 'magnificent'. He walked up to the Prime Minister and said, 'you ought to get that cartoon of Low showing us all rolling up our sleeves, and frame it'.

'All Behind You, Winston', David Low's drawing had been called. It had shown a Cabinet, a Parliament and a nation marching firmly in step behind their resolute cigar-chewing leader. That evening in Westminster the cartoon was beginning to come to life. Churchill had managed to touch all of the most important figures in British politics with a first-hand sense of his own determination. And how the ministers had warmed to his message. All was not lost after all. Some of them felt light-headed with excitement. Within a few hours all political London knew about the meeting and about the way the Cabinet had risen and acclaimed its leader. Britain had found her chieftain. They had felt like characters in some Shakespeare history play. Yes, they had been just like the soldiers around Henry V.

Later in his life Churchill modestly described himself as the agent of a natural force of resistance that ran throughout the land. But that cannot stand as the sole explanation for the peculiar chemistry of this moment. During these last few days of May, with the Army about to be lost and Britain's only allies falling headlong out of the war, with the Americans on the sidelines and international opinion convinced that Hitler was unstoppable, Churchill *was* the force of resistance.

The British people were a lot more fragile at this time than they would later remember – hence the phone-taps and the letter-openings and the intense official concern about morale. Without the hope and inspiration that began to flow from the top,

David Low, 'All Behind You, Winston', *Evening Standard*, 14 May 1940

Front Row: Winston Churchill, Ernest Bevin; second row: Clement Attlee,
Herbert Morrison (with glasses); third row: Neville Chamberlain, Arthur Greenwood,
Lord Halifax, Archibald Sinclair. Anthony Eden (with moustache)
is at the far right of the third row

Bob Doe of 234 Squadron with Spitfire 'D for Doe' and ground crew

Spitfires photographed from a German reconnaissance plane

Pilots of 501 Squadron at Hawkinge: Ken Lee (seated centre) is talking to Johnny Gibson

Pilots of 85 Squadron 'B' Flight with Dickey Lee in the centre

HMT *Lancastria* sinking, photographed from HMS *Highlander*.
The dots on the upturned hull are passengers attempting to escape

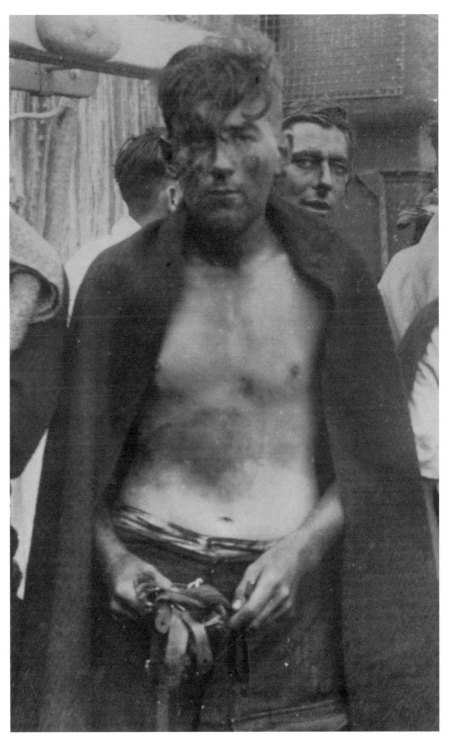

A survivor from the *Lancastria* aboard HMS *Highlander*

Dorniers with Beachy Head behind them on their way to bomb Kenley aerodrome
on 18 August 1940

A Stuka dive-bomber, forced down on Ham Manor golf course,
near Arundel, Sussex, with members of the local Home Guard

Issued by the Ministry of Information in co-operation with the War Office and the Ministry of Home Security.

If the

INVADER

comes

WHAT TO DO — AND HOW TO DO IT

THE Germans threaten to invade Great Britain. If they do so they will be driven out by our Navy, our Army and our Air Force. Yet the ordinary men and women of the civilian population will also have their part to play. Hitler's invasions of Poland, Holland and Belgium were greatly helped by the fact that the civilian population was taken by surprise. They did not know what to do when the moment came. *You must not be taken by surprise.* This leaflet tells you what general line you should take. More detailed instructions will be given you when the danger comes nearer. Meanwhile, read these instructions carefully and be prepared to carry them out.

I

When Holland and Belgium were invaded, the civilian population fled from their homes. They crowded on the roads, in cars, in carts, on bicycles and on foot, and so helped the enemy by preventing their own armies from advancing against the invaders. You must not allow that to happen here. Your first rule, therefore, is :—

(1) IF THE GERMANS COME, BY PARACHUTE, AEROPLANE OR SHIP, YOU MUST REMAIN WHERE YOU ARE. THE ORDER IS " STAY PUT ".

If the Commander in Chief decides that the place where you live must be evacuated, he will tell you when and how to leave. Until you receive such orders you must remain where you are. If you run away, you will be exposed to far greater danger because you will be machine-gunned from the air as were civilians in Holland and Belgium, and you will also block the roads by which our own armies will advance to turn the Germans out.

II

There is another method which the Germans adopt in their invasion. They make use of the civilian population in order to create confusion and panic. They spread false rumours and issue false instructions. In order to prevent this, you should obey the second rule, which is as follows :—

(2) DO NOT BELIEVE RUMOURS AND DO NOT SPREAD THEM. WHEN YOU RECEIVE AN ORDER, MAKE QUITE SURE THAT IT IS A TRUE ORDER AND NOT A FAKED ORDER. MOST OF YOU KNOW YOUR POLICEMEN AND YOUR A.R.P. WARDENS BY SIGHT, YOU CAN TRUST THEM. IF YOU KEEP YOUR HEADS, YOU CAN ALSO TELL WHETHER A MILITARY OFFICER IS REALLY BRITISH OR ONLY PRETENDING TO BE SO. IF IN DOUBT ASK THE POLICE-MAN OR THE A.R.P. WARDEN. USE YOUR COMMON SENSE.

The front page of a leaflet issued by the Ministry of Information in June 1940

One of a series of Home Office posters preparing for the possible
invasion of Britain

then the draining logic of appeasement might well have taken root once again.

Coming only three weeks into his government, three weeks of constant crisis and exhaustion, Churchill's rebuttal of the peace moves of late May was a determining moment in world history. For a few precious days he had managed to hold the brakes on the 'slippery slope' down which the world was careering towards Nazi victory in World War II.

As Churchill was addressing his ministers, Martin McLane was approaching Dunkirk. He had been walking all day, mostly through pouring rain. He had lost track of time. The officer who had threatened to report him had left without a word whilst McLane and his men were sleeping off their ordeal at St Venant. They had woken and wandered off, looking for information. He remembered the moment when he learned where he was going. He had climbed a hill and a wide view had opened up all round him. It was breathtaking. There was a huge rainbow and all the roads were glistening with lorries, their windscreens shining in the rays of sunlight that broke through the dark rain-clouds overhead. It had also been a moment of revelation. They couldn't all be running away, could they?

Some tired British infantry were shambling past with the dazed look in their eyes of men who had recently seen action. He ran over to their officer: 'Sir, can you tell me what's going on? I've got some men here and we're lost.' The officer replied, 'Don't you know, Sergeant Major? We've got to make for Dunkirk. We've got to be evacuated, if possible.' The words were still ringing in McLane's head hours later. The British Army that he loved had been beaten and were going to be evacuated. He had been so dumbfounded that he had only just remembered to salute.

They walked down the hill and followed the crowds. Near a town called Poperinge the nightmare began. Lorries were burning by the roadside. A column had been halted by bombing and the drivers were abandoning and burning any undamaged vehicles. Then the lorries gave way to horses, a long line of French horse-drawn transport. But they had been bombed too. There were dead men on the top of the bank and piles of injured horses struggling to stand up. Bewildered Algerian drivers were going round with rifles, finishing off their wounded animals. Some were in tears. And the smoke from the burning lorries hung over everything. That is what hell is like, McLane thought. On and on and always people shouting, 'Get a move on, get a move on. That way! Keep moving!'

For some miles now they had been trudging past abandoned transport vehicles. Nobody had set these on fire. Their loads lay scattered about around them. When they first saw them, McLane and his men searched for hard-tack biscuits because they were very hungry. At one point they saw a crashed Hurricane and went to see if they could help the pilot. But the nose of the plane was buried deep in the ground. As they got nearer Dunkirk more and more equipment was lying beside the road. Eventually they could walk only in single file. They stumbled on over two canal bridges and finally they came out on the dunes and looked down on the beach.

Even in the evening it was an amazing sight. White sand stretched out for miles in both directions and blue-grey water lapped at the flat beach more than a hundred yards away. 'Perfect for a nice game of beach cricket,' someone said. But there were dead soldiers and more abandoned vehicles scattered around where the holidaymakers should have been, and all the seafront buildings had been bombed. Vast numbers of troops were huddled in the dunes and queues of soldiers were snaking out over the sand.

Wednesday, 29 May saw an all-out effort by both sides. It began badly for the evacuation forces. In the small hours the destroyer

Wakeful was sunk by a small German E-boat and the *Grafton* went the same way at the hands of a U-boat which had slipped through the cordon of British submarines that were guarding the flanks of the evacuation lanes. The weather was poor with low cloud and the first German air raid did not get under way until half-past three in the afternoon. Two destroyers, the *Mackay* and *Montrose,* collided trying to avoid the bombs. Both were badly damaged but somehow stayed afloat.

German fighters strafed the beaches too, seemingly unmolested by the RAF. The lines of little black dots would break and scatter as the Messerschmitts flew low over the top of them. Finally, just after 6 p.m., a sudden raid caught the mole crowded with ships. This time the smoke from the burning refinery did not save them.

Fifteen British and four French ships were sunk that day. But never for one moment was there a pause in the evacuation. In fact practice was making it more efficient. Around 17,800 men had been brought off on 28 May, but 47,310 were lifted on 29 May.

Frightened by their losses, the Admiralty told Ramsay to withdraw eight of his most modern destroyers, leaving him only fifteen. It now looked as if the beaches were the main hope of escape. Concentrating warships by the mole was just inviting air attack. But there were not enough small boats to go in and out of the breaking waves. Nothing like enough. That evening a call went out on the BBC appealing for pleasure craft and their civilian crews.

Thursday, 30 May was flat calm with a deep sea fog. Divine intervention yet again. The *Keith* was hardly troubled by the Luftwaffe all day long and the evacuation went very smoothly. The main harbour entrance was still open, the mole was being used again and the beaches filled with men waiting for the growing number of small boats to pick them up. That day 53,823 were successfully brought home.

At the end of the day *Keith* was pressed into troop-carrying service herself. She picked up a full load of several hundred troops from the mole and carried them across the Channel by night. Iain Nethercott was impressed by the men he saw marching down the mole with all their weapons and kit. 'The problem was that once we got them on board, the minute they sort of hit our deck, they collapsed. And they'd got such complete faith that they'd made it and all they had to do was sit there now and get back to Dover for their nice shrimp tea.'

On 31 May the *Keith* was sent back again, this time with orders to pick up Admiral Wake-Walker, who was in charge of all the ships off Dunkirk, and with him to try to marshal the other, smaller ships lifting men off the beaches. On the way in, Nethercott was struck by the sight of a large German observation balloon high in the air over Nieuport. 'What's the bloody RAF doing?' he said. 'There's two men sitting up there in a basket, must have been up there for days, surely they should have shot it down by now, but no one did, it was there the whole bloomin' time directing their fire.'

There were still bodies floating in the water from where the *Wakeful* had been sunk two days before. *Keith* bombarded some German artillery positions: 'We put one gun out of action, silenced it, but as we silenced it about three more opened up. And we had to get out of it quick because they were straddling us right in this narrow channel.'

The previous day's miraculous fog had now burnt off and the Luftwaffe was back. Nethercott could see the beaches being strafed again. 'It was the German fighters that were the trouble, not so much the bombers. They flew level with the beach and went up and down, up and down.' Through binoculars he watched the soldiers scatter, diving into holes that they had dug in the sand. When the planes pulled away they would come out again.

The beaches were black with men and every now and again they'd made a little pier of lorries and things, and they were

sitting on them waiting . . . Because the tide goes up and
down quite a lot, you had to evacuate them when the tide
was right. And there was other places where the men were
standing in a long line right out to the water. And the leading
ones had been standing there for hours waiting for one boat
to come in and the minute it got there they all hung on to
the side, all on one side and tipped the bloody boat over.

Near the beaches Nethercott saw French and Belgian fishing boats
with civilian crews. The water was crowded with small boats now,
and many of them were no longer simply ferrying soldiers out to
the Navy but setting off for home themselves. All around him
were little ships with soldiers crammed on the decks. People yelled
from one to another in all kinds of languages. Smaller ships, harder
to bomb, thought Nethercott. And that day, despite the renewed
bombing, just over 68,000 men were carried to England.

Nethercott's gaze was pulled away as the *Keith* suddenly gained
speed and began to weave. He knew what that meant. 'There they
are again!' someone shouted. Nethercott leapt to his seat and trained
the two-pounder up towards the sun, its repeated fire drowning out
the now familiar shriek of a diving Stuka. A line of four appeared
over the port side. He tried to follow the leading plane:

> The skipper was flinging the ship around at full speed, about
> 35 knots, and of course I had to swing my gun right round
> to follow the bastard down, because you've got to hit them
> right in front on the nose when they're coming towards
> you. And before I knew it I'd shot all of our bloody wireless
> aerials away. Leaving poor old Commander Wake-Walker
> out of communication with Dover. I got a bollocking from
> the First Lieutenant but I said, 'Well, you know, sir, it's a
> choice of whether you want the wireless aerials re-strung or
> a thousand pound bomb on the bridge.'

At the edge of the beach McLane found a fifteen-hundredweight truck. One of his men said the tyres were puncture-proof. Having nothing better to do, McLane started firing his revolver at them to see if it was true. It was. But just as he had proved this to his satisfaction, a Frenchman came out of a little building and angrily told them to leave his lorry alone.

They surveyed the beach. There were queues of men, and at their head little boats were picking up soldiers ten at a time and taking them out to some bigger boats in the misty distance. It would take for ever to get all these men off the beach. They walked on towards Dunkirk itself. Eventually they were intercepted by a military policeman. He directed them up a road towards a huge pile of earth and rubble where a lot of soldiers were sitting. He was told that there they would be put into groups, taken on to the port and put on a ship from there. This seemed like a better idea, so they clambered up the mound. From up there they had a fine view. They could see that the huge billows of black smoke they had been walking towards for miles came from the port area – probably some oil installation on fire. The place was being bombed even as they watched. At first there were just bombers. Then there was a cheer as a squadron of British fighters tore in. Now there were planes going down in flames, leaving their own trails of smoke.

At this point a Humber staff car pulled up and a smartly dressed officer got out. 'He hasn't done any fighting,' someone remarked. 'Any men from the 2nd division here,' he shouted, 'come forward!' This was it. They were going back to fight. McLane had been expecting it. He got up and went forward and his men followed him. Another officer, obviously very senior and obviously very frightened, got out of the car and then drew his pistol and pointed it at McLane. 'Now you men follow me,' he said, 'and don't you dare run away.'

McLane was livid: 'Don't you dare insult men of the Durham Light Infantry, sir! We know what we're here for! We know what you want! How dare you threaten a man of the Durhams, sir, put your pistol away.' The officer took his name. McLane said, 'Don't you worry, sir, I don't have to ask your name. I know what unit you belong to from your vehicle and I'll report you when I get back to England for daring to threaten to shoot men who knew they were going forward to do some more fighting.' The officer ordered them to follow, got in his car and led them away from Bray Dunes and back into the country.

At the outer canal bridge they were handed over to a major of the Cameron Highlanders. He had been expecting rather more men. McLane suggested trying to get some from the road and went off to do so. He pulled out over a hundred volunteers from the troops coming into Dunkirk and requisitioned a large number of Bren guns, ammunition and grenades. They took up defensive positions on the side of the canal.

The next morning the Camerons got orders to withdraw and they took McLane and his men with them. They had been allocated a place on a boat and they marched back towards Zuydecoote. It was hot, and as they reached the dunes the smell of death was all around them. They saw bodies decomposing in the heat of the sun. Hands and legs were showing through the sand where it had shifted away from a body in a shallow grave.

When it got dark Corporal Burroughs and Lieutenant Vaux crawled up the hill through the long grass to try to retrieve their basket of food. It had gone, and they could hear German voices in the wood. They crept down again and discussed how to cross the River Somme. They explored towards the farm but there were always too many people about and there seemed to be no concealed route down towards the river. As they skulked around the ruined abbey the next day, a little girl wandered towards them. She came straight up to their hiding place. 'Sshh!' said Peter, putting his finger to his lips. The little girl smiled. 'Sshh' she replied, imitating him.

They had to get away. That night they tried the opposite direction, away from the farm. Straight away they hit boggy ground, a network of little streams and treacherous meadows where they sank to their knees in mud. 'It was ghastly and we were hungry and exhausted and cold and it rained and it was dark and from time to time we saw Germans and heard German voices. We sloshed about in these marshes and we couldn't get anywhere near the river.'

The next day the little girl came back. 'Sshh!' she said, and gave them a basket with bread and some cheese. She said that it came from the German officer's room in the farm. 'Sshh!' they said emphatically. Vaux wandered around nervously, looking for any path they might have missed and thinking about that German officer. There was a stream blocking the obvious route south and no way across. When he came back he found Corporal Burroughs carving his name in the darkest recess of their hideout. 'What are you doing that for?' 'Why not? Everyone else has done it.' It was true. There were names and little pictures and lovers' hearts and all kinds of things carved into the old grey stone. Perhaps some of them had been fugitives too, Germans caught behind the lines, dreaming hungrily of home and of breakfast.

The next night they tried again. Whenever they got anywhere near the river they met German patrols. They were exhausted. Instead of going back to the abbey they went on to a barn with hay in it and slept there. In the night Burroughs woke Vaux. The officer was alarmed, thinking there was someone coming. 'What is it?' But Burroughs was just upset. He said, 'That German soldier sir, when we were in the tank. I keep dreaming about that German soldier, how dreadful it must have been for him when our bullets were chasing him up and down the road.' He knew now how it felt to be hunted.

Next morning the major said, 'I don't know, we may have to give ourselves up.' The corporal said, 'Not me, sir,' and Vaux agreed: 'Not while I have a gun.' At that moment they were surprised by a little man in a beret with spectacles and a black moustache. He spoke in English. 'It's all right. Don't be frightened, I'm a Belgian. My name is Monsieur Gilis. I know who you are, I know you're here. I'm with a large group of refugees in the farm and they've made me their leader. They all know you're here. They know you've killed a German officer. There are notices up warning everybody that there are three British "Franc-tireurs" at large who have shot a German officer and they're wanted for murder. And the notice goes on to say anybody who helps them will be shot. You've got to get away from here.'

'Well, we've been trying,' they all said at once. 'Have you been in the marshes?' the Belgian asked. 'You look as though you have.' To their assent he replied, 'Well that's no good, there's only one place you can get across the river here and that's on hard ground by the railway bridge. There's hard ground on either side and you can get over there, but there are Germans about.' 'However will we get down there?' asked Vaux. Gilis replied: 'I will bring some civilian clothes and one of you should come with me and we'll go down there in daylight and I will show you the way to where you can swim over the river. We have no time because you can't rely on the silence of the refugees for very long.'

Later that day he came back and brought some food, apples and a loaf of bread. Also some peasant clothing and a pair of pliers. Vaux, ever the reconnaissance officer, got dressed and with M. Gilis set off towards the river. They had agreed on a cover story: the children relied on milk from the cows, the Germans had broken the fences, the cows had escaped. So they were going to mend the fences; that was why they had the pliers. As they went down towards the river they cut through any barbed wire they encountered. They passed three German outposts. Gilis, who was a commercial translator, spoke fluent German and he told their tale to each one and they went on almost to the river bend below the railway bridges. There they ran into a machinegun commanded by a large sergeant.

'What are you doing here?' he demanded. Gilis told the story once again. The sergeant said, 'I don't believe a word of it. Let's have a look at your identity card.' Gilis produced his identity card, all perfectly in order. Then the German turned to Vaux. 'Show me yours.'

The Belgian was superb. He turned on him like a tiger. He said, 'You are a revolting race. Here is this boy, only speaks Flemish, parents killed by your horrible aeroplanes, walked all the way from Belgium and you ask him for an identity card!' The German suddenly looked quite shattered. He said, 'Go on, go on, get away.'

They left. Vaux's heart had missed several beats. He marvelled at the Belgian's courage. As they got close to the farm he asked him why he was helping them. 'I am an old soldier. I fought them in the first war. I was taken prisoner. I know how it feels.' Vaux already felt very humble. He dropped the conversation.

Back in the barn Vaux changed back into military uniform. It was safer should they be caught, but not much. That night the three British soldiers crept slowly and quietly down the path that Vaux had taken with M. Gilis towards the riverbank. There was no sign of the German sergeant but there were patrols up and down the towpath. They waited and watched and worked out that there was a ten-minute gap between sentries.

They took off all their clothes and tied them up in a bundle with the compass in the middle of it. Major Fernie took charge of this. The corporal said that he couldn't swim very well so Vaux, younger and fitter than the major, said that he would help him across. The three men quietly lowered themselves into the water. It seemed harmless enough in the dark, and the opposite bank looked so close. But the river was running fast after the recent rain and there were strong currents under the surface.

The three soldiers were light-headed with exhaustion. They had eaten practically nothing for five days. After a few strokes Vaux realised that Burroughs was in trouble. 'He choked and bubbled and disappeared and bobbed up.' Vaux swam back. 'I grabbed him by the arms and tried to pull him but we were naked except for pants, and human bodies in water are slippery and his arms slipped from my hands.'

Vaux dived under the water, his hands searching frantically

in the cold, dark water for any sign of Corporal Burroughs. He no longer cared if a German sentry heard the splashing. Burroughs was his driver, his corporal, his responsibility. But he had gone.

> I didn't grip tight enough. I failed to take him across to the other side. It has haunted me for the rest of my life. The Major did get across but he has no recollection of getting out of that river at all, though he did, and got the clothes out. And I don't remember getting out of that river but somehow I found myself on the far bank. And I crawled up and I shouted out to the Major but there was no answer.

Vaux was alone. He staggered up the hill barefoot into a French roadblock, and was taken to their headquarters. There was the major wearing his uniform. He'd left the other uniforms behind, having given Vaux and Burroughs up for dead.

Martin McLane was sitting on the sand with the Cameron Highlanders when in the crowd he caught sight of a face he knew – his own platoon runner. He'd been attached to another company after the battalion split up. McLane shouted to him and he shouted back. 'You've got to take your men back to Brigade Headquarters.' McLane said, 'Away lads,' took his men from the Durhams and left the Cameron Highlanders behind. They trudged off after the runner to where brigade headquarters had been set up by the quartermaster of the Royal Berkshires. He said, 'Sergeant Major, I've got a rotten job for you. You are to find volunteers to make up a section of men to form a platoon with two other sections I have got here already and then you've got to go back to the last canal and hold the bridge toward Zuydecoote to the last man. There's a lorry over here that I'll give you.'

On the bridge was a large artillery piece with one round in the breech. The gun would be the first thing the Germans hit when they came. McLane tried to work out how to fire it from a distance by using some rope. Then he found an igniter set to blow the bridge up. It had wires attached and underneath the bridge were huge yard-long slabs of amatol explosive ready to blow. He drove a Thorneycroft workshop lorry on to the bridge and wedged it against the railings and left just a narrow gap. There were still men coming through as the British perimeter positions thinned out. Once again McLane took from them any Bren guns he could get hold of and had the men dig in round the bridge. Later he was visited by a brigadier, who ordered him to let British troops over but to direct French troops farther along towards Dunkirk.

While McLane's section was resting, one of them came to him and told him that he had overheard some of the other soldiers planning to clear off as soon as it got dark. They didn't see why everybody else should get off and they should have to stay and fight to the last man. McLane put some of his own men on the bridge as sentries and ordered all the rest of his improvised platoon to join him in the yard behind a farmhouse next to the bridge. One of their sergeants was in his blanket, claiming to be ill, and McLane kicked him out of bed too. When he had the platoon assembled, McLane said, 'Right, I want your name, rank and serial number. I'm going to list them because there's shit falling around, and if anyone gets hit I want to be able to let your families know what's happened to you.' They fell in and McLane wrote all their details in a little pocket-book.

Then he stood back from them and said, 'Now you buggers. If any of you disappear from this bridge tonight the first thing I'll do is inform your next of kin that you're a coward in the face of the enemy and then I'll inform your regiment so they can record the fact that you disappeared from a position you've been told you have to defend to the last round, last man.'

Several soldiers brought their rifles down and pointed them at McLane. His own men pointed their rifles back. The Durhams were outnumbered. McLane shouted, 'Stand to attention. Put your rifles up! Stand to attention!' They obeyed. He said, 'Right now, don't anyone leave this bridge tonight because what I've told you will be passed on as I've said. Right, fall out.'

Churchill, having just quelled a different kind of mutiny, wrote a 'Strictly Confidential' memo to Cabinet ministers and senior officials on the morning of 29 May. 'In these dark days the Prime Minister would be grateful if all his colleagues in the Government, as well as high officials, would maintain a high morale in their circles; not minimising the gravity of events, but showing confidence in our ability and inflexible resolve to continue the war till we have broken the will of the enemy . . .'

Churchill was well aware that the international press had been writing about defeatism in London and splits in his Cabinet. He was aware too that Ambassador Kennedy was still sending back to Washington a very bleak account of Britain's immediate prospects. And if he needed reminding about the importance of Britain's image in America, then he had only to listen to his chief arms buyer.

Arthur Purvis was in charge of purchasing weapons in America. He was in Washington at the end of May trying to persuade senior officials to release US military stocks for immediate sale to Britain and France. Some supplies were sold after General George Marshall, American Chief of Staff, agreed to declare them 'surplus' to US needs. But the biggest prizes, especially the fifty 'mothballed' destroyers, seemed as far away as ever. Henry Morgenthau, the Secretary of the Treasury and a key ally of President Roosevelt, told Purvis that 'the President has decided that it would be impossible at this time to obtain from Congress a modification of the Law which at present prevents the sale to belligerents of existing United States Army and Navy stocks . . .'

In private, Morgenthau, a passionate anti-Nazi, had told Purvis that he and his Prime Minister were attempting the impossible. A glance at the daily papers could have told Purvis the same. The aviator Charles Lindbergh, perhaps the most celebrated and famous American of his generation, was attracting tens of thousands to 'America First' rallies. The Catholic Church was strongly against intervention in foreign wars. The German-American Bund was marching in support of Hitler. Street-corner anti-Semites harangued passers-by in the cities of the East Coast.

Such forces were far from dominant in the spring of 1940 but their existence meant that anyone in America who wanted to confront Hitler had vocal enemies all around them. And this was an election year. Powerful interest groups might swing the vote one way or another. No one in Washington was going to make an historic foreign policy shift without studying the opinion polls very carefully.

And fear persisted that aid to Britain would be wasted because the British were about to lose the war. Harold Ickes, Roosevelt's Secretary for the Interior, wrote in his diary that Churchill had inherited 'an empire which was practically in articulo mortis'. Roosevelt had said as much to the Canadian envoy, Hugh Keenleyside, during his secret visit to the White House, and Keenleyside had told his Prime Minister, Mackenzie King.

During the last few days of May, King and his Foreign Office discussed their problem. Roosevelt wanted him to press Churchill on the fate of the British fleet. But the Canadians, like many before them, couldn't quite decide what kind of a game the American President was playing. He seemed to expect peace talks to begin any day and he was clearly terrified that, as a result, Hitler would soon be in command of the world's greatest navy. So he wanted Churchill to send the fleet – Britain's only real bargaining chip – overseas, even if that meant punitive air raids from the Nazis. Mackenzie King, who dreamed nightly of such horrors, could foresee a terrible, exterminating air attack laying waste his imperial motherland.

Canadian diplomats in Washington fed back to Ottawa what they could glean of America's intentions. The Canadian legation predicted that Britain's defeat would mean a huge shake-up in North American relations. King could foresee pressure to join the two countries together in a continental alliance against

Germany and Japan, with the remains of the Royal Navy as its international teeth.

But how to raise such a question with Churchill? King would have to find a way to sweeten the message. In a cable of 31 May he chose to present the American request as an opportunity for Britain to win support in Washington, and thereby boost its chances of winning substantial aid. Without saying that anyone on his side of the Atlantic expected Britain to lose the war, King explained that a theoretical commitment to sending the fleet abroad in the event of defeat would make Washington more willing to help.

King, not one to downplay his contribution to world history, wrote of his cable to Churchill that 'it may well be the most significant of any message that has, thus far, crossed the ocean since the beginning of this war'.

Then he waited uncomfortably for Churchill's response.

'My God! Look at that!' shouted Iain Nethercott. It was 8 a.m. on 1 June and HMS *Keith* was lying three-quarters of a mile off Bray Dunes, north of Dunkirk. The air to the east was filled with layer upon layer of German aircraft, bombers banked up and swarms of fighters riding high above them. It was the biggest raid so far. The crewmen put their well-polished aircraft-spotting talents to work: Heinkel 111s, Junkers 88s and, of course, Stukas. 'Just look at them bloody Stukas!' The anti-aircraft gunners watched as about sixty dive-bombers peeled off towards the evacuation fleet, now swollen with the thousands of small civilian boats that had responded to the appeal for help.

The destroyer was now tearing through the sea at full speed, but they were in a narrow part of the deep-water channel and there was limited space in which to weave. Four lines of Stukas attacked from different directions. There were just too many of them. Nethercott picked a line out to port and brought the gun to bear, pumping shells at the planes. 'And I just suddenly saw this

Stuka appearing over the bridge – it seemed to be almost touching it – and this great big bloody yellow bomb fell from its clamps. It was a thousand-pounder. He dropped it. We were moving to starboard and he dropped it down the port side. It didn't land on us but it blew a part of the port side in, it fractured all the rivets and that.'

The *Keith* slowed down and started to ship water. This is how it starts, Nethercott thought. He'd seen it many times over the last few days. The first hit, the ship half paralysed and the rest of them all swooping down to finish you off. He kept firing away. Then another Stuka put a bomb right under the stern. 'When a ship gets hit anywhere under the stern on its rudders you can't do anything, you just go round in circles.'

The *Keith* circled slowly, beginning to tip sideways. Captain Berthon called the *St Abbs*, an Admiralty tug, to come alongside and dropped anchor. First on the scene was a speedboat, MTB 102, which took off the admiral and some of his staff. But the Luftwaffe hadn't finished with them yet. The next bomb landed right by the three-inch gun, cut through to the engine room and blew up there, killing everyone inside and blowing the ship's sides out.

'She really started to settle then and took a terrific list to starboard and the coxswain was standing up on the signal deck with his bosun's pipe screaming out, "Abandon ship!" The *St Abbs* came alongside and its crew took the wounded aboard. Nethercott and the other gun crews stayed behind to keep firing.

> Then I saw the *Basilisk* sinking over on our starboard side, then the *Skipjack* went, she was a sloop. Ships were sinking all around us, everywhere you could see destroyers going down with this terrific attack. And as she started to really lurch I couldn't get the gun elevated properly, but we hung on because when the bombers had gone these fighter planes came down and they started strafing anyone in the water or on the decks. And while I'm watching I saw the *St Abbs* with all the survivors including our Captain. She hadn't got very far and they got a bomb right down her funnel. The

whole bloody lot went sky high. They were all in the water again, well those that got blown over the side. And already in the water you'd got survivors from five or six ships. Some were soldiers. And great big pools of black oil. They were all floundering around in the oil screaming and yelling.

The *Keith* wasn't going to last much longer. There were two badly wounded men on the deck. Nethercott and the rest of his crew climbed down from their gun position and started to throw any spare timber they could find over the side. Then they cut a 'Carley' life-raft clear, threw that in from the side of the ship now closest to the water and managed to lower two of the wounded men into it. The ship was lurching right over now. Nethercott said to his crew, 'Come on, let's go. There's nothing we can do now.'

The men jumped into the water. It felt very cold. They had no idea where to go, but with his cork life-jacket on Nethercott was confident that he wouldn't sink. So he hung on to the side of the Carley raft with the wounded men inside it and paddled slowly away from the sinking destroyer.

He had swum only a few yards when he heard more planes and looked up to see two Messerschmitt 109s swooping down straight at them. Machinegun bullets slashed through the water and straight across the top of the raft, killing the two wounded sailors in an instant. Nethercott tried to dive to his right but the cork jacket kept him afloat. He managed to force his head under but his feet were sticking up in the air. He was just thinking that he must look a bit like a duck when a bullet went right through his knee.

The raft seemed to have gone. He couldn't kick his leg. He felt very weak. He lay back and floated. Then he passed out. Some time later he awoke, still trembling with the shock and the cold. He couldn't feel his injured leg at all now.

> I was on me own then and I thought, 'Well I don't know, I'm probably going to die.' And I had a long talk with my God.

He floated around for a long time, passing in and out of conscious-
ness, and then he found himself drifting towards a merchant ship
that had been bombed and had run aground on a sandbank. He
could read her name, *Clan McCallister*. He could see about a dozen
survivors up on the deck. 'My God, that's Captain Berthon. How
the hell did he make it?' Soon she was rearing above him, forty foot
of sheer metal. But there was a rope ladder. Nethercott clung to it
as he drifted by. Then someone on the deck above spotted him.
They came down the ladder and tied a line around his waist and
hauled: 'they dragged me all up the side with limpets cutting into
me and God knows what, which added to my problems'.

On the upper deck Captain Berthon asked where he was
wounded. Nethercott said, 'I've got a bullet in my leg I think.'
There was a lot of blood there. The captain said, 'Oh that's just
a scratch. It's gone right through.' They put a dressing on.

> There was a bloke there and he said, there's some stuff in
> the galley. I said, I'm terribly thirsty, dying for a drink. So he
> said 'well we found some big tins of pears' and they opened
> up these tins and gave me one with all the juice and that.
> Cor! put real life into me. And while I'm drinking this lot
> there was an old cement barge from Tilbury Docks that came
> alongside with soldiers on it but no sailors. So the skipper
> said come alongside and we all got aboard her and Captain
> Berthon took over because they were heading the wrong way
> anyway, they were heading up towards Holland I think.

Several hours, and many more tins of pears, later, the Tilbury
cement barge made its way into Dover harbour. Nethercott was
laid out on the jetty.

> I'd got no proper uniform on and they thought I was a
> soldier. And I was sent to some hospital at the back there
> in Kent where they just bound me up and kept me in for
> about three days and then sent a naval ambulance to take
> me to Gillingham Naval Hospital. Of all places, the worst
> place in the world that was. There was me thinking I was

going to have a lovely period of time in a civilian hospital with these pretty nurses and I landed up in Gillingham with these monkey-faced sods in the Navy. You know the sick bay 'tiffies' they were the cruellest men out.

Martin McLane had been relieved at his bridge by a party of French marines. The whole perimeter was held by French troops now. He was driven through the smoking ruins of Dunkirk town to the port, where he walked to the base of the mole. Looking out to sea, he could see the results of the intense air attacks of 1 June. McLane and his men queued up and waited. A little naval cutter came along and an officer with a megaphone stood up and shouted: 'You'll have to go back on the beaches, nine out of twelve ships have been sunk. We'll try our best to get you off tomorrow.'

At the same moment shells started to fall. One hit the granite section of the mole that was nearest the shore and exploded in the middle of a group of French troops who, like McLane, had been waiting for a ship that wasn't coming.

> I've seen some ghastly sights but there was a pile of men in exactly the same state as them horses. They were all mown down. Blokes on the bottom with legs off, dead, others piled up moaning, a bloke stuck in the middle with his jugular vein cut and he's breathing and the blood's squirting from him. We were so shocked we shot off there on to the sand and left them. But we came back to do what we could for them.

McLane headed back to the relative shelter of the dunes, sick to his stomach, and settled down for another night on the beach.

Chapter 7

1–10 June

During the morning of 1 June, in Operation Dynamo's cipher room under Dover Castle, Daphne Lumsden received the message that she had been dreading: 'HMS *Keith* sunk by enemy bombing. There is no news of any survivors.' She took it through to the admiral, feeling strangely detached, just carrying on with her job. Maybe he had got away again. Maybe. It didn't sound very good, though. Usually the messages were upbeat. If there were many survivors then they would have said so.

Lumsden was kept busy. That afternoon she went down to the harbour. Boats were coming in constantly and soldiers were clambering off, most of them hollow-eyed and bedraggled. A lot of them were French; she had not seen that before.

Someone touched her arm. She turned. A petty officer was standing beside her dressed half in naval uniform and half in a blanket. 'Excuse me but are you Mrs Lumsden?' he asked. 'Yes.' 'I'm from the *Keith*. I just wanted to say that I saw Lieutenant Lumsden. I saw him in the water after the ship was sunk and he was swimming strongly. He might have made it.' She waited at the harbour, watching the ships for a while, and then she went back to her digs to sleep. She had to sleep whatever happened because she would be on duty again tonight.

When she woke there was still no definite news about Graham.

It was dusk when she returned to work. Operations were frantic now because Admiral Ramsay had decided so many ships had been lost that he must suspend daylight operations. As things stood this night would be the last chance to get men home. Lumsden knew that they'd already evacuated far more than the admiral had ever dreamed possible. But it was a bitter kind of a victory and no one felt much like celebrating.

She was still working when she heard someone at the door asking whether she was there. 'Yes, here I am,' she said, and turned, hardly daring to hope. The man's face was smeared in oil. He was wearing a French naval sweater. 'Don't you recognise me, Daphne?' he asked. She ran across the room and hugged him.

Martin McLane and the men still with him expected to be captured soon. They dozed and talked about whether they should surrender to the Germans, who, they were sure, were already in the outskirts of Dunkirk. McLane was thinking about Annie again. He'd tried to keep those kinds of thoughts at bay over the past week, but now, lying in the sand and unable to sleep properly, they all crowded their way into his head. She would want him a prisoner of war rather than a corpse. McLane smiled as he imagined the parcels she would organise. She'd probably get half the street to contribute.

At first light on 2 June they went looking for food. At the top of the beach they found five British Army ambulances painted white with big red crosses all over them. They thought there might still be tea and sugar inside for the wounded men. But when they opened the doors a hideous stench came out. All the men in all the ambulances had been killed several days ago. The roofs were completely riddled with large-calibre bullet holes, bullets from Messerschmitts like those that had been flying up and down the beaches. McLane had already seen some men driven half mad with them, running about trying to shoot them down with rifles and revolvers. They left in a hurry and went down to the wet sand near the water's edge. There were no planes; the German pilots were probably still in bed. For a long time they sat there. They could still see the ambulances but tried to avoid looking.

McLane walked along the beach. It was very still and quiet and there were no boats to be seen anywhere near. But just under the surface of the water there were dead bodies floating. Others were being moved by the waves back and forth along the shoreline, all mixed up with the seaweed in undignified black and green and khaki bundles. Everywhere there was abandoned equipment. Anti-aircraft guns and Lewis guns lay around, hurriedly disabled by their departing crews. He could have done with some of those back at St Venant. What a waste. For a while he slept again in the dunes. Then the group went hunting for food again.

As it began to grow dark they returned to the mole. All day they had heard the sound of ground fighting in the town. The French were obviously still hanging on, but the end could not be far away now. The occasional shell hit the beach. Not many targets left here, thought McLane. They were dangerous if you were close by, but the sand absorbed a lot of the explosive power. There were clusters of French and British soldiers waiting in cover near the road that led out to the mole. McLane stopped and spoke to them. Most thought that the last boats had come and gone. But then a naval officer appeared and urged them all along the road. They ran.

If they were going home, McLane wanted it done properly. 'I made them carry all their equipment, their ammunition, their rifles and even the Bren Gun. We didn't abandon anything.' As they reached the base of the mole a destroyer came into view through the gloom and the smoke. Two hundred yards farther and they could see that it had jagged shrapnel holes all down the side. An officer shouted through a megaphone from the bridge: 'On as quick as you can! Jump, lads. Jump!' McLane jumped. He wouldn't be needing those parcels after all.

The boat was only about half full. 'It pulled out and a bomber came along and it dropped bombs that straddled the back of the boat which lifted up and the water came over but we got away all right.' Then they fell asleep.

It was dark when they arrived in Dover and they were sent into a floodlit shed where women were handing out sandwiches, apples and tea. They ate like savages. Then some guardsmen led them to a carriage on a train and told them to stay there. The train pulled out into the dawn. 'We didn't know where we were going so we just scribbled little notes out and flung them out at stations as we passed.' The crowd on the platform were offering to post messages. McLane found a luggage label under his seat. He wrote a note to Annie on it and pushed it out through the window.

Despite the loss of many valuable warships, the evacuation had been a fantastic success. Over a third of a million men had been brought out from directly under the guns and the bomb-sights of the enemy. Only about thirty thousand of the rearguard, almost entirely French, had been captured. The Royal Navy had performed with all the courage and dedication expected, and the RAF, for the first time flying in large numbers and directly controlled from Britain, had successfully engaged large formations of German planes.

Churchill's faith in the fighting qualities of his people had, it seemed, been vindicated. Senior military figures and civil servants congratulated each other, hardly believing what had been achieved during the past week. The danger had not gone away – next would come the air raids and then, perhaps, an invasion – but for the moment any new talk of peace in the Cabinet Room seemed inconceivable. The war would go on and it would be fought Churchill's way.

Senior Foreign Office official Alexander Cadogan still complained that his Prime Minister was 'theatrically bulldoggish'.

But Number 10 secretary John Martin concluded that all left his presence as braver men. Churchill's infectious courage had a ruthless side. He told the War Cabinet that Britain should use any method to defend its shores. According to the minutes, 'the Prime Minister thought that we should not hesitate to contaminate our beaches with gas if this course would be to our advantage. We had the right to do what we liked with our own territory.'

Gas, troop transport, anti-tank weapons, the reinstatement of officers' leather shoulder straps; the Prime Minister pursued his officials and Chiefs of Staff with daily (and, frequently, with nightly) suggestions and demands for information. But most of them loved him all the more for it. 'Despite the odds against us, he made us believe that we could actually win,' says Marian Holmes. '. . . he was asked just after Dunkirk, in that moment of enormous peril, if our paintings from the National Gallery should be sent to Canada for safety. And he said, "no, no they should be hidden in caves and cellars. We are going to beat them."'

Annie McLane was standing outside her home in Addison Street, Heaton. It was time for the post. She and her friends had stood outside like this for days, and each day some of them had got notes from their husbands and some had got telegrams with bad news. But she had had nothing. She was beginning to lose heart.

Here he was now, the postman. He was coming down the street, waving his arms and holding something up in the air, and he was coming straight towards her: 'Mrs McLane! He's all right! He's all right, Mrs McLane!' He handed her a luggage label with her address on it in Martin's handwriting. The neighbours gathered round. Some of them were crying too. She turned the label over: 'Dear Sweetheart, I am back in Blighty safe and sound. This is all I could raise in the way of writing material. Letter later. Love from Mac. XXXX Baby XX.'

Churchill had been working on a speech he planned to deliver to the House of Commons and then broadcast to the world. Its theme was the deeper significance of the Dunkirk evacuation and the likely events of the coming months. It was his chance to articulate the vision of the coming months that had been forming in his mind during the fraught War Cabinet meetings in the days before Dunkirk.

He did not normally employ speechwriters. He would pace and mutter and sometimes grimace and then the phrases would all come at a rush. Given the cigar and the lisp and the occasionally absent false teeth, secretaries like Marian Holmes had to listen very carefully:

> Now he could be a bit cross, but he would never let one go off duty without a word of encouragement. He'd say, 'Your work is very good, very fine, thank you very much'. Speeches we often did in shorthand because we did them in relays. And somehow he found that better. But normally we would do things and give them to him immediately to initial, because very rarely did he need to correct anything.

High on Churchill's agenda was a desire to praise the RAF. Returning soldiers had been heard complaining about the lack of British fighter cover. Accounts reached Whitehall of pilots being abused and threatened in pubs and out on the streets. In fact the RAF had been very active during the evacuation, but not always visibly so. They had not prevented the Luftwaffe from bombing ships and men but they had seriously blunted those attacks. According to the statistics that reached Churchill, 262 German planes had been shot down. In a speech delivered to a crowded House of Commons on the afternoon of 4 June he embellished the figures even more.

> This struggle was protracted and fierce ... The enemy was hurled back by the retreating British and French troops. He was so roughly handled that he did not harry their departure

seriously. The Royal Air Force engaged the main strength of the German Air Force, and inflicted upon them losses of at least four to one; and the Navy, using nearly 1,000 ships of all kinds, carried over 335,000 men, French and British, out of the jaws of death and shame, to their native land and to the tasks which lie immediately ahead. We must be very careful not to assign to this deliverance the attributes of a victory. Wars are not won by evacuations. But there was a victory inside this deliverance, which should be noted. It was gained by the Air Force.

The speech, broadcast within a few hours, was most people's first chance to hear the full details of Dunkirk. There had already been colourful accounts, in print and on the radio, of the small boats and their brave crews of tugmen, fishermen, sea scouts and the like. But hearing Churchill's description of the scene was different. So, too, after months of disappointment and humiliation, was hearing ringing praise for their own armed forces. The Germans were widely believed to be particularly dominant in air power. Reports from the Spanish Civil War and more recently from Poland, France and the Low Countries had all reinforced this idea. But now here was Churchill saying that the RAF could beat them.

When we consider how much greater would be our advantage in defending the air above this Island against an overseas attack, I must say that I find in these facts a sure basis upon which practical and reassuring thoughts may rest. I will pay my tribute to these young airmen. The great French Army was very largely, for the time being, cast back and disturbed by the onrush of a few thousands of armoured vehicles. May it not also be that the cause of civilisation itself will be defended by the skill and devotion of a few thousand airmen? There never has been, I suppose, in all the world, in all the history of war, such an opportunity for youth. The Knights of the Round Table, the Crusaders, all fall back into the past – not only distant but prosaic; these young men, going forth every morn to guard their native land and all that we stand for, holding in their hands these instruments of colossal and shattering power, of whom it may be said that:

'Every morn brought forth a noble chance
And every chance brought forth a noble knight',

deserve our gratitude, as do all the brave men who, in so
many ways and on so many occasions, are ready, and continue
ready, to give life and all for their native land.

His audience was used to rhetoric. This was a time of church
sermons and public meetings. But never before had so many people
heard language like this directed at them in their own homes, and
in almost every home at the same moment. Few would ever forget
the experience. Hope and heroics were being offered to a nation
starved of both, and offered in the rousing language of Shakespeare
and the King James Bible. Churchill, with his ornate phraseology
and his instinctive feel for the totems of Britain's glorious past,
began to make his listeners feel a part of history themselves.

I have, myself, full confidence that if all do their duty, if
nothing is neglected, and if the best arrangements are made,
as they are being made, we shall prove ourselves once again
able to defend our Island home, to ride out the storm of war,
and to outlive the menace of tyranny, if necessary for years,
if necessary alone. At any rate, that is what we are going to
try to do. That is the resolve of His Majesty's Government
– every man of them. That is the will of Parliament and the
nation. The British Empire and the French Republic, linked
together in their cause and in their need, will defend to the
death their native soil, aiding each other like good comrades
to the utmost of their strength. Even though large tracts of
Europe and many old and famous States have fallen or may
fall into the grip of the Gestapo and all the odious apparatus
of Nazi rule, we shall not flag or fail. We shall go on to the
end, we shall fight in France, we shall fight on the seas and
oceans, we shall fight with growing confidence and growing
strength in the air, we shall defend our Island, whatever the
cost may be, we shall fight on the beaches, we shall fight on
the landing grounds, we shall fight in the fields and in the
streets, we shall fight in the hills; we shall never surrender.

146

Like the sight of a battered destroyer surging up out of the darkness when all idea of rescue had been abandoned, Churchill's words lifted his audience and made them dare to hope again. Across the country and across the world, millions of listeners felt for the first time something of the thrill, something of the elating rush of confidence, that had swept through the Cabinet members in the Prime Minister's parliamentary office a week earlier.

The British people were not stupid. They knew that Hitler was winning the war, that the German military was awesomely well equipped and well trained and that most of western Europe had fallen to the storm troopers and the secret policemen. Prague, Warsaw, Oslo, Brussels, Antwerp and Amsterdam were already darkened by occupation and soon, no doubt, Paris would follow. Did the same fate await Canterbury, Manchester, Aberdeen? That would be the obvious, the logical, end. If so, then a moment would come to shrug and make the best of a bad time in a bad world, like millions of other Europeans. But suddenly, and with a force and a language that seemed to spring from an ancient wellspring of resolve, here was Winston Churchill saying that there could be a different ending to the story.

Omdurman and Mafeking, Tonypandy and the Dardanelles; as a Liberal Home Secretary and a Tory imperialist; through wars and strikes and the rise and fall of governments, Churchill had been part of British life for as long as most people could remember. The parents and some of the grandparents of the soldiers and sailors at Dunkirk had served under him. Good old Winston, a man from a lost world with his Edwardian clothes and top hats, his brandy and his funny old cigars. For much of the 1930s he'd been a bit of a joke – going on and on with his big red face about India and the Empire and always calling for more battleships and warplanes and wanting to fight Germany all over again.

And as he slipped towards a dyspeptic, disappointed old age, out of favour and out of office, he was remembered – often unfairly – for sending troops to Welsh mining villages and men to die on the beaches of Gallipoli. 'A gung-ho sort of a bastard,' thought Iain Nethercott; 'a bit of a bull at a gate,' Peter Vaux's colonel had said. And yet none of that mattered now. Some scowled and grumbled by their radio sets, but not enough to make any kind of a difference. He was their leader, obviously he was – their leader in this vast, terrifying but also now somehow rather thrilling enterprise. On 28 May Churchill had won his ministers and outflanked the peacemakers in the War Cabinet. On 4 June he won his people.

Praise poured into Downing Street. 'Worth 1,000 guns and the speech of 1,000 years,' wrote Colonel Josiah Wedgwood. Vita Sackville-West wrote to her husband, MP Harold Nicolson, Parliamentary Secretary at the Ministry of Information: 'Even repeated by the announcer it sent shivers (not of fear) down my spine. I think that one of the reasons why one is stirred by his Elizabethan phrases is that one feels the whole massive backing of power and resolve behind them, like a great fortress.'

Churchill's speech was thrilling. Edith Heap, Winifred Butler and lots of other WAAFs were listening in the mess at RAF Debden in Essex, and their eyes all lit up. During the broadcast they nodded silent but vigorous agreement and at the end they cheered.

They had especially admired the bit about the RAF. They both had boyfriends in 17 Squadron and they knew just how hard the RAF had been fighting over France. All through Dunkirk, the boys had been flying sorties over the beaches. Some days Heap would get a call from Jerrard Jefferies or Butler from Richard Whittaker to let them know that they were still alive, and how they were getting on. They had been told how Ken Manger had been shot down into the sea and had had a fist fight with an Army officer who didn't want to let him on his boat. Manger had got back to England on a destroyer and been back up in the air over Dunkirk the next morning. They had seen 85 Squadron come back in bits and pieces, absolutely shattered, to reform at Debden. But some of their best pilots, like Dickey Lee, had transferred straight away to another active squadron to carry on fighting. Lee had been shot down once over Dunkirk too.

The RAF deserved all the praise they got from Churchill, and, heavens, it had been a speech to put fire in the belly! The two WAAFs marched straight off to practise on the .303 rifle down on the range. Best to be as well prepared as possible.

Before the war Edith Heap had lived for horses. She would still have been show jumping if Hitler had not intervened. Her father had died in 1933 when she was fifteen, and after that she had shuffled between her mother and her married sisters when she was not on an equestrian course or performing in a show. Heap was practical and well organised, but she had a streak of adventure in her too. She'd been taken up in a Gypsy Moth a few times by her brother-in-law at the local flying club and found it completely thrilling. So, when the war began, she'd joined the Women's Auxiliary Air Force as soon as she could, leaving behind her favourite horse, Mouse, at Nun Monkton near York with her eldest sister.

Heap signed up as a Motor Transport (MT) driver for four years. The examining doctor did not notice that she was completely deaf in her right ear. She reported to RAF Yeadon near Leeds and quickly made a friend of another driver, Winifred Butler. In October, eight women, including Butler, were posted to Debden in Essex. Butler arranged a swap so that Heap could go there too. After a journey that took all day they were picked up in pouring rain from Audley End station and driven to the base. With another WAAF they were allotted a house in airmen's married quarters. It was damp and icy cold but within a week they'd made a home of it.

They didn't know what to do with the WAAFs in the RAF. Half the men didn't want them there at all, thinking they would distract the pilots and then crack up under attack. At first they spent a lot of time in the cookhouse or scrubbing the lino-leum floor, but the motor transport officer was one of those who believed the women could be useful and soon put a stop to this misuse of their time. Instead they were introduced to the Albion 2.5 tonner with a crash gearbox. They had a few minutes' coaching in a dual-control lorry with a sergeant who kicked Heap on the shin for resting her foot on the clutch. Then they were away with much grating of gears and stalling of engines. After that they drove everything from 'Queen Marys' to staff cars, the sanitary lorry, the coal lorry. They backed mobile field kitchens down the narrow road to the cookhouse so that ground crews could be fed in the middle of the night.

Best of all were the tractors. Butler and Heap both fell in love with them. They got the knack of swing-starting them and loved tearing around the base doing all kinds of jobs. At night they laid the flare-path to help their Blenheim pilots land, placing a mobile 'chance light' at each end of the landing path and marking the track with little paraffin 'goosenecks'.

Within a few weeks Heap and Butler were driving to the base at Martlesham with spares. The pair of them were soon known as 'the Kids' to the pilots, mostly ex-public school boys no older than themselves. Sometimes they took the Humber Snipe down to Filton near Bristol with damaged stern frames from Blenheims. There were no signposts so one of them had to read the map while the other drove. Their days were filled with driving and maintenance, with drill, PT and gas practice. They fenced and played hockey against the men. The house sergeant had an eagle eye for dust and ruled with a rod of iron. They queued for insipid food at the mess and joked about the RAF's endless diet of baked beans. There were films projected on to the wall of the old hangar and second-rate travelling variety shows put on by the military entertainment agency, ENSA. But very soon they felt that they were contributing something useful to the war effort. Some of the older male officers still had their doubts about how the WAAFs would behave under fire, but for now they were forced to admit that the women were a useful addition to the team.

Many of his listeners were so transported by the 'Never Surrender' passage that they failed to notice the politically significant final lines of Churchill's speech.

> . . . we will never surrender. And even if, which I do not for a moment believe, this island or a large part of it were subjugated and starving, then our Empire beyond the seas, armed and guarded by the British Fleet, would carry on the struggle, until, in God's good time, the New World, with all its power and might, steps forth to the rescue and the liberation of the old.

In Ottawa, Canadian Prime Minister Mackenzie King took note of Churchill's closing remark. He had been anxiously awaiting London's response to his cable about the fate of the Royal Navy, sent almost a week before. It seemed as if this section of the speech had been drafted with his message in mind. That at least was what King's staff believed: 'When Skelton came over to my office he was filled with delight. Said that Keenleyside had come into his room with eyes blazing, so pleased to see what he recognised at once as the result of the information we had imparted.'

In Washington Harold Ickes, Roosevelt's Secretary of the Interior, reacted in the same way. 'It was a great speech. He really served notice that the British fleet, whatever might happen, would not be surrendered to Hitler.'

But the following day a 'Most Secret and Personal' cable went from London to Ottawa. It was not what the Canadians had expected. 'British situation vastly improved by miraculous evacuation of BEF,' wrote Churchill.

> . . . we must be careful not to let Americans view too complacently prospect of a British collapse, out of which they would get the British fleet and the guardianship of the British Empire, minus Great Britain. If United States

were in the war and England conquered locally, it would be natural that events should follow line you describe [i.e. the promise of a transfer of the Navy to the Dominions]. But if America continued neutral, and we were overpowered, I cannot tell what policy might be adopted by a pro-German administration such as would undoubtedly be set up.

Although President is our best friend, no practical help has been forthcoming from the United States as yet. We have not expected them to send military aid, but they have not even sent any worthy contribution in destroyers or planes . . . Any pressure which you can supply in this direction would be invaluable.

King was perplexed. At the climax of his great speech Churchill had clearly stated that if Britain were occupied then the war would be continued from overseas with the Royal Navy at the heart of it. This was exactly what Washington had wanted to hear. And yet now, in his cable, Churchill was reverting to an aggressive attitude towards the Americans and even asking King to use the threat of German control of the fleet as a lever to get immediate help from Roosevelt. King sent his envoy, Hugh Keenleyside, on another mission to the White House to explain the problem to President Roosevelt.

Churchill told the British ambassador in Washington, Lord Lothian, to drive home the same point: America should not assume that it would pick up the Royal Navy if it stood by and watched Britain fall. Churchill told his ambassador to tell the Americans that 'If we go down then Hitler has a very good chance of conquering the world.'

Churchill tried in person, cabling Roosevelt in desperate terms: 'Nothing is so important as for us to have the thirty or forty old destroyers you have already had reconditioned . . . The next six months are vital. If while we have to guard the East Coast against invasion a new heavy German–Italian submarine attack is launched against our commerce, the strain may be beyond our resources; and the ocean traffic by which we live may be strangled. Not a day should be lost.'

The destroyers were the key. The Navy needed them desperately, and they would also show the world that Roosevelt was throwing America's resources behind the British. But the President continued to rebut all such requests. He could not send such a force outside American control, breaking the spirit if not the letter of America's neutrality laws, unless he had firm domestic political backing. And to get that he needed pledges from Churchill about the fate of the Royal Navy should Britain be occupied or brought to a 'soft peace'. If he sent the destroyers to Britain and they were then 'inherited' by Hitler's grateful admirals, Roosevelt would most likely be driven out of office.

But, despite what he had said on 4 June, Churchill would not make any such explicit pledge on the future of his fleet. He feared that even talking about the possibility of defeat and naval evacuation would trigger exactly the kind of defeatist attitudes that he had been struggling for weeks to resist. The old American destroyers featured in a series of ill-tempered exchanges across the Atlantic, but the result was stalemate.

Through the winter and spring, Edith Heap and Winifred Butler got to know the pilots based at Debden very well. They met them when they delivered things to dispersal and they met them at the various social events. On her twenty-first birthday in late November 1939, Heap had bought a car, a little maroon Jaguar. At least, it had been maroon. When she brought it to the base it had to go straight into the workshop and came out camouflaged in ugly green and brown stripes. The car improved life and gave Heap real status on the base. She and Butler could go to Cambridge when they wanted. Sometimes she lent it to the aircrew so that they could go to London. As they spent more time with the pilots, and particularly their respective boyfriends, 'Jeffers' and 'Whitters', they used it to go out to dinner and to films.

Jerrard Jefferies was quite a catch, tall and deadly handsome, with jet-black hair with a silver streak in it. Everyone envied Heap. Richard Whittaker was handsome too, cheerful and friendly. There were regular dances in the airmen's mess, and every Sunday night they would be invited to a dance at the sergeants' mess. Both they and the boys were very shy at first. Some of them had only just left boarding schools and had hardly ever been let out alone with the opposite sex. It was exciting and headily romantic and the slightest gesture seemed vastly significant. As they got to know one another there was endless flirting and a lot of chat. When Dickey Lee turned up with 85 Squadron, most of the WAAFs just gasped. He was unbelievably handsome and, boy, could he fly an aeroplane. He gave a certain added *frisson* to the job of removing the field kitchen from 'B' Flight's dispersal.

One day, as Heap drove up in her tractor, one of the pilots threw something and the engine stopped. At first she was alarmed, and then the pilots laughed and she was furious. 'What's your name?' she demanded of the culprit. 'Denis,' he replied a little sheepishly. 'Right Denis, you can start it again yourself,' she said, pointing to the crank handle.

Two days after Churchill's speech came the dreadful day. They had been to Martlesham and soon after they got back Heap was called to the phone in the guardroom. It was Jefferies. Richard Whittaker had been shot down over France and he was dead.

Martin McLane got off the train near Aldershot and marched to a tented camp. He was feeling rather groggy and dazed. Twenty of them were put into a bell-tent and they lay down and went to sleep. Some time the next day they woke to the sound of a military band. They went to see what was going on and recognised a Durham Light Infantryman they knew playing in the band. Bob Bulmer went to speak to him and came back with some money. So they all went for a drink. Four pints later and feeling very much better they went back to the tent, where the lad they had left guarding the equipment was in the middle of a heated argument with a Canadian sergeant-major. The Canadian announced that he wanted their Bren guns. McLane retorted, 'You're not getting the Bren guns, they are Durham Light Infantry weapons now. We carried them home and you're not getting them. You can bugger off.' The sergeant came back with a Canadian officer who said, 'I'm sorry but we've got to have the guns. They're very short of weapons for the defence of Dover and the invasion's imminent. We need all the weapons and ammunition you've got.' McLane, shamefaced, handed them over.

Despite the stirring words of 4 June, some Conservative MPs were still uneasy. As usual, the majority of the cheers for Churchill had come from the Labour side of the House. Outside, Whitehall was being sandbagged, and there was a sense that the war was coming very close. Many expected Germans to invade or land by parachute at any moment. MP Harold Nicolson and Vita Sackville-West were both carrying poison pills so that they could commit suicide before they were captured.

On 6 June Churchill received a final audit of the French campaign. The BEF had lost or abandoned 475 tanks, 38,000 other vehicles, 1,000 heavy guns, 12,000 motorcycles, tens of thousands of machineguns, rifles and small arms, and countless rounds of ammunition. Of the 38 British destroyers employed during the evacuation, 6 were sunk and 26 damaged by bombs, shells and collisions. Of 46 troop-ships and other large vessels, 9 were sunk and 11 damaged.

Air Vice-Marshal Dowding then reported the ominous state of his fighter squadrons and tried to prevent any more being sent to fight in France. The only good news came from the Ministry of Air Production, where Churchill's friend Lord Beaverbrook was boosting the production and repair of planes to record levels.

Stimulated by the evident national peril, workers were at their machines around the clock.

As the German Army launched their attack southward towards Paris, the British government was still busy eavesdropping on its citizens. Jock Colville wrote on 6 June: 'Interesting censorship report on public opinion, as shown in letters. There is no frenzied fury against the Germans but much cold and reasoned hatred. . . . There is no sign of bad morale, and little wish for peace at any price, but it is noteworthy that discouraged and defeatist women outnumber men by two to one.'

Churchill struggled to counter the idea that Britain could now only fight a defensive war. To his Chief of Staff, General Ismay, he wrote: 'The completely defensive habit of mind, which has ruined the French, must not be allowed to ruin all our initiative.' He suggested setting up small raiding parties to tie the Germans down along the long coastlines of Norway and western Europe. 'How wonderful it would be if the Germans could be made to wonder where they were going to be struck next instead of forcing us to try to wall in the Island and roof it over. An effort must be made to shake off the mental and moral prostration to the will and initiative of the enemy from which we suffer.' He demanded 'a reign of terror', 'butcher and bolt' tactics and 'a trail of German corpses'.

Meanwhile Churchill was under constant pressure from Reynaud in France to send more fighters. On June 7 the War Cabinet sent a cable to Paris detailing the extent of their continued air support of the Allied armies fighting near the Somme, and ending with a new gesture: 'To-morrow it is proposed by amalgamating three fighter squadrons, to send two additional fighter squadrons at full strength to be based in France.'

Denis Wissler had been back at work for a fortnight, but half of that had been leave; 85 Squadron was now in reserve, resting and rebuilding at Debden in Essex under a new CO, Peter Townsend. Half the squadron's pilots had been lost in France and the replacements had to be trained. After only seven terrifying days in action, Wissler was now considered fully operational. The pilots eased back into flying, trying to learn landmarks that would help them find the airfield and then dodging in and out of clouds to test their recognition of the patchwork landscape of Essex and Suffolk. The first night they had had a reunion party and talked late into the night. On Wednesday evening they listened to one of their surviving aces, Patrick 'Woody' Woods-Scawen, broadcasting on the radio about 85 Squadron's experiences in France. On Thursday they did some practice dogfighting and, in the evening, a practice dispersal of the Hurricanes to the farthest extremities of the airfield.

One evening a young WAAF driving a tractor came along to take away the field kitchen. She was rather pretty and Wissler thought it might be fun to make her stop and talk. He grabbed a handful of sand and threw it at her tractor's fan belt to make her engine stall. She had never seen this trick before, but just as Wissler and the others were enjoying her confusion she had become rather impressively angry. He felt very embarrassed when she made him restart the tractor and he tried to apologise.

The WAAFs had not been in France and they were an intriguing feature of life at Debden. Wissler and his fellow pilots were already comparing notes about them. He wondered what this tractor driver was called, but since his attempt to effect an introduction had not gone well he thought he'd wait for a better moment.

The squadron took a flight of six planes to Martlesham Heath near Ipswich. They spent the day sitting in the sun at readiness and then flew back to Debden. War was bearable when it was like this, and there was every prospect that this pleasant respite might last a few weeks. As they flew back they saw dozens of British bombers on their way to Germany. They got back to the news that two of the new pilots had crashed their Hurricanes and both had been killed.

On Saturday, 8 June Wissler received the most terrible shock. After lunch Squadron Leader Townsend sent for him and told him that 17 Squadron was going back to France and had asked 85 Squadron to give them two operational pilots. He was very sorry but Wissler would have to go. His companion would be Count Manfred Czernin, the son of an Austrian diplomat, but raised by his mother and schooled in England. Like Wissler, he had joined 85 just before the German offensive.

The two victims realised that Townsend was sacrificing the least experienced of his operational pilots and the implication was not lost on them. They wangled two hours in London and Wissler had dinner alone at the Trocadero. He got absolutely sozzled and had to be put to bed at Kenley airbase. At 3.30 a.m. the next morning the wing commander ran a cold bath and woke Wissler with some Alka-Seltzer. He took off with the count and soon they were both completely lost, landing and asking for directions four times *en route* to Le Mans. Finally they reached their new base at five in the afternoon. 17 Squadron had arrived the day before and had hardly had time to settle in. The pilots were sleeping in tents in the woods near their planes.

Wissler was thrown straight back into the familiar chaos of air warfare over France. He flew two patrols, both over two hours long, without so much as sighting an enemy plane. He looked down on Le Havre where the oil storage tanks were burning. The great column of smoke was awe-inspiring, and the centre of the fire glowed red.

The Hurricane shuddered as it fired and as always Ken Lee noticed a check in the airspeed. The attack drill was familiar by now. You see them, hopefully before they see you, you lower your seat, to give you as much protection as possible, you switch on the guns, then the Aldis sight, fitting in the calibration of the aircraft you're attacking. You close for the kill. Like a hawk, just like a hawk, swooping down, watching the target get bigger and bigger inside the sight, then, when the wings with the little crosses fit neatly into the slot, you fire. That would be three hundred yards. 'We were trained time and time again to think of a circle about three feet wide and at three hundred yards all your eight guns were firing straight through that little circle.' But if you really wanted to do serious damage then another hundred yards or so closer was the thing to try.

If he was on target bits would fly off the Dornier or the Heinkel, or else glycol or petrol would come streaming out. 'And of course it's always very satisfactory when the rear gunner stops firing because you've protected yourself there to some extent.'

Back at base and everybody was always talking at once. 'Did you see mine? Did you see it go down? There was one that just burst into flames, did you see it?' Everyone trying to get confirmation from the others of anything that he'd done.

> The perfect fighter squadron was a bunch of comrades who had a similar background and all wanted to fly. You could rely completely on one another to cover you in all kinds of situations and they wouldn't steal your girlfriend when you were away flying and they were back on the base.

501 was a squadron like that and Ken Lee was proud to be a member of it. Proud too of his score, five confirmed by the end of May. His friendly rival, Johnny Gibson, had exactly the same statistics.

> We were all rather proud of ourselves, I think we had in those few weeks about 45 confirmed victories. You can't just say you shot somebody down, you've got to have somebody else to confirm that they saw it go down, or get confirmation from the ground forces. And during that time we lost about eight or ten killed, which was out of an average strength of eighteen.

Rather a high percentage. But one or two of them weren't long standing members of the squadron, they'd come in and in the next couple of days they'd be gone. Well I suppose one reaction is that I'm jolly glad it wasn't me. But I mean if it's a really close friend it would affect you particularly, but if it is just somebody in the other flight who you didn't know particularly well you'd just sort of think 'hard bloody luck.'

'Hawk-eye' Lee was still performing the role of 'arse-end Charlie', weaving behind the rest of his flight, looking out and around for the enemy. 'And when I heard the others say, "well we hope Hawk-eye's doing the rear cover today" I felt proud of myself.'

Lee never saw the plane that first shot him down. It could have been a lucky shot from one of the Heinkel bombers he was chasing into some cloud over the River Seine or, more likely, it could have been a cannon shell from a lone Me109 that had evaded his celebrated eyesight.

There was a loud bang, a pain in his leg and all of a sudden none of his controls would work any more. 'So when I came out of this cloud, diving pretty swiftly, I decided to jump out. But I was going so fast that the wind just blew me back in again.' Fortunately for its pilot, the doomed Hurricane began to slew from side to side and Lee half fell and half pushed himself out of the cockpit.

His hand reached for the parachute release handle. 'And then there was this huge forest below me and when I got down to about four or five thousand feet I heard bullets going past. The French on the ground were shooting at me coming down in this parachute and I could hear them going "Parachutiste! Parachutiste!" So, I took my identity card out of my pocket and said "Je suis Anglais" as loud as I could.'

Lee crashed down into the top of a tree and bounced into the lower branches and then landed on the ground. The French were all apologies. A huge unshaven Corsican hugged him and planted a kiss on his cheek. As he travelled back to his base, Lee asked himself if he had been scared. The honest answer was no, he'd been too busy trying to get out of the plane. 'It was instinct, if you can't do anything about it and can't control the situation where you are then you get out and start again.' Now all he wanted was to get back to his friends and have a drink in the mess. Wait until they heard about the Corsican.

Paul Richey was feeling better. French friends came to visit him. The lovely Vicomtesse d'Origny took him out to lunch. More and more French wounded were coming in, and on 5 June Richey asked to become an out-patient, staying with a friend at the American embassy and passing the day at the Racing Club in the Bois de Boulogne. Walking on the Champs Elysées he met 'Cobber' Kain who had stayed behind temporarily when the squadron flew home. Kain told him that his score was now seventeen, but he seemed quiet, nervous and preoccupied. He kept breaking matches between his fingers.

On Monday, 9 June, with the Germans reputedly twenty-five miles away at Mantes-la-Jolie, Richey decided that it was time to leave Paris. He'd become friends with a well-informed American journalist called Larry LeSueur. LeSueur worked for CBS and was a friend of Bill Shirer, whose reports from the forward German columns were holding the attention of the world. LeSueur told Richey that he expected to see him in London soon. CBS was already discussing how it would cover the invasion of Britain.

He added that the remains of the RAF in France were now based at Blois. Richey said his farewells and went to get on a train, but the stations for the south were besieged by Parisians trying to get out of their city. Instead he got a lift with some RAF policemen, who were also fleeing Paris. The roads were a continuous jam of refugees. The police truck dropped him off near Blois, where he found what was left of the Battle and Blenheim light bomber squadrons. No. 103 Squadron's commander had lost almost all of his pilots. His bitterness was directed chiefly at the French Army, which had failed to destroy the bridges that his pilots had then been sent to attack.

The Blenheim pilots of No. 12 Squadron had a strange air of detachment that became explicable when Richey learned that they had lost twenty-six complete crews of three and only six of the original squadron pilots were still alive. Richey knew that many of these men had been lost because of the lack of effective fighter cover, but the bomber pilots acknowledged the practical difficulties. It was not always the fighters who had missed the rendezvous; they had got lost, too. It all came down to intelligence and guidance and control. Next time they fought it was vital that they should know where they were, where their friends were, and where the enemy was.

From Blois, Richey got a lift back to Chateaudun, where the rest of No. 1 Squadron had gathered. Only three of the original pilots were still there, trying to teach the new intake how to fight. He spent a couple of days with them, catching up on what was happening, but then they were sent down to Nantes and he took a plane back to England.

It was raining as he lifted off from the bomb-pitted airfield, casually counting the burned-out French and British planes. His neck still burned with pain as he strained it to look out of the window. As he flew over Normandy he could see through the storm clouds the columns of refugeees choking the roads and the pillars of smoke that rose from many of the towns and villages. Richey dozed; his wound still made him very tired. He woke over England and looked down on South Coast villages where smoke trailed from cottage chimneys. And what was that? He suddenly felt sick with anger and disgust. By God, they were playing cricket. These smug, complacent Englishmen behind their twenty miles of sea were playing cricket while half an hour away by plane everything was carnage and rubble. The heartless, stupid fools. A few bombs would do them good!

Chapter 8

10–16 June

'. . . until, in God's good time, the New World, with all its power and might, steps forth to the rescue and the liberation of the old.'

In the drawing room of an elegant town house on New York's East 82nd Street, a young journalist called Whitelaw Reid sat by the radio with an old family friend. The friend was better placed than most to comment on what the British Prime Minister had said. He was Herbert Hoover, President Roosevelt's immediate predecessor. Hoover sat quietly for a moment. Then he announced to his companion that the words were fine indeed, but that Britain was finished.

Whitelaw Reid was used to the company of presidents. They came with the family business: publishing newspapers. Reid had been born, so everyone said, with ink in his veins. In fact two currents had flowed together to make his family's name and fortune – one of ink, the other of gold. His grandfather, also called Whitelaw, had been a famous journalist. He'd reported the Battle of Gettysburg and he'd edited the *New York Herald Tribune,* one of the most influential newspapers in the country and a pillar of the Republican Party. By 1872 Reid was the newspaper's owner.

A few years later he married an heiress, the daughter of a California Gold Rush tycoon. Money that had come from selling shovels to miners on the West Coast found its way into publishing and property on the East. By the turn of the century, the Reid family lived in high style. It owned a castle and country estate in upstate New York, a private summer camp in the Adirondack mountains, a couple of fine houses in New York City, and much more besides.

Within a few years Reid was running for office. He was the defeated Republican vice-presidential candidate of 1892. In 1905 he was offered the plum job of ambassador to Britain. He mixed with politicians and princes until he died in England in 1912, a victim of asthma and the London smog. By then his son Ogden was managing the newspaper, aided by his energetic and talented wife, Helen Rogers Reid. She had been a leading suffragette and, although now married into a Republican family, she was also a great friend of Eleanor Roosevelt, the wife of the future Democratic President.

Whitelaw Reid had been born into this world in 1913, six months after the death of the grandfather from whom he took his name. As a child he was taken into the big city to wander the floors of the *Herald Tribune*. He slid down the poles that connected the press room to a vast floor below where the great shining rolls of white paper were laid on to the presses. At four years old he wrote to the editor, who also happened to be his father, to complain about the treatment of horses in the streets of New York. Even then he must have sensed that his family was powerful. The morning after he posted the letter he looked out at the streets, expecting something to have been done about the poor horses.

There were ponies to race and mountains to climb. There was sailing, ice-skating and canoeing and, back in New York, there were parties and receptions and dinners. Visiting European royalty, American Cabinet ministers, famous writers and artists – they would all come to the larger of the family's two New

York homes opposite St Patrick's Cathedral on Madison Avenue. And always there was talking. Politics and journalism, politics and journalism, at all hours of the day and night.

Reid graduated from Yale in 1936, sporty, gregarious and good-looking. He sailed across the Atlantic with some of his university friends. They were young Americans, they had lifetimes of opportunity before them, and here they were out seeing the world. But the world was turning colder. They visited Germany; it was unfriendly and sinister. They had to have an escort. His friends fed the policeman tinned peaches down in the cabin, diverting his attention whilst Reid shinned up the mast to take some forbidden photographs of the Kiel Canal. They could all have been arrested.

Back home Reid's parents wanted him to learn the basics of their trade. He was taught to set type by hand – at the Rochester Athenaeum and Mechanics Institute, side by side with the men and women who were going to work for him. He learned to operate a Linotype machine; he worked on the composing-room floor.

On that June afternoon, sitting listening to Hoover's low opinion of Britain's chances in the war, Reid thought that it was fortunate his friend Dorothy Thompson wasn't there with them. She would have told Hoover exactly what she thought. Thompson was a columnist on the *Tribune*. Spiky and passionate, hers was one of the clearest and strongest voices raised against fascism in America. For months now she had been urging more aid for Britain and France, even suggesting that one day soon America might have to fight Hitler too.

From the *Tribune*'s postbag, and from the conversations at the family dinner table, Reid knew that the American people were far from ready for such a step. His mother's powerful friends were always discussing which way the Republicans should go at the next election. They would have to select a candidate soon to run against Roosevelt. The *Tribune* and those who ran it were certainly not isolationists. But a lot of powerful people in the party were, especially those from the Midwest, where ties to Britain didn't feel so strong.

Reid's mother had already seen one of her soirées disrupted by arguments about this subject. It had been a dinner in honour of British ambassador Lord Lothian, and she had invited two possible presidential candidates, Wendell Willkie and Robert Taft. Talk had soon turned to American aid to Britain. Taft had said very angrily that there were no votes to be had in a foreign war. He'd even banged the table. Whitelaw Reid had been there too and saw that his mother was not at all impressed with Senator Taft.

Reid wasn't sure about any of this. But he knew one thing: if Hoover was right and Britain was about to fall, then this had to be the biggest story in the world and he wanted to cover it. He'd just switched from typesetting to reporting, all part of his training in the newspaper game. He had better move fast before the Germans got to England first. The ink in his bloodstream began to flow a little faster. Perhaps the paper's London bureau could use a little help?

The argument around Whitelaw Reid's mother's dinner table was being duplicated throughout the Republican Party. Roosevelt had no idea which way his opponents in the November election were going to jump. Harold Ickes, Roosevelt's Secretary of the Interior, wrote in his diary about the great danger facing America: '. . . and yet the politicians continue to play politics. Apparently the Republicans will be willing to go completely isolationist if they think that they will win the election.'

On 10 June Italy declared war on Britain and France, placing a large and modern naval force at Hitler's disposal. The British-controlled island of Malta was bombed for the first time early the following morning. It was easy to feel contempt for this last-minute entry

into the war, but in London contempt was mixed with panic. Anti-Italian riots broke out. There was a large community of emigrant Italians in the city, centred on Soho. Many were restaurateurs whose windows were broken and staff threatened. Old Papa Bertorelli put up a notice in his window reminding the mob that all of his three sons were serving in the British Army. Churchill ordered the internment of all Italian subjects in Britain and by the next day the government was ready to seize '1,500 desperate characters'.

The French government had left Paris and Churchill flew to meet them with an escort of twelve Hurricanes. The British party landed at Briare and was taken to a nearby château. After Churchill had attempted a rallying speech, General Weygand, whose aggression had so impressed the British in May, coldly informed the conference that he now held out no hope of halting the German advance. He had no reserves and the trickle of troops and fighter planes still coming from England was quite insufficient to make any difference. Churchill spoke of fighting in the ruins of Paris and the French froze.

Weygand demanded that every British fighter should be sent to France. Churchill said that was impossible. He proposed a plan to hold Brittany and supply it from England. He suggested guerrilla warfare. He promised that if France could hold on for a few more months then Britain, armed with new American weapons, would come to her rescue. 'Machines will one day beat machines,' he predicted. But these were all pipe dreams and most of the British delegation knew it. The French, it became clear, were poised to ask for an armistice.

Returning home, Churchill flew, like Denis Wissler, over the smoking ruins of Le Havre. He appealed by telephone to Roosevelt. 'If there is anything you can say publicly or privately to the French, now is the time.' During the evening Churchill learned of the plight of the 51st Highland Division. They had been deployed close to the French coast and were cut off when the Germans broke through near Abbeville. Dieppe had been bombed and the Navy judged evacuation there impracticable. The division was ordered to retreat to Le Havre. An advanced guard made it but the main bulk was cut off by German armour and trapped at the little port of St Valéry-en-Caux. British destroyers sent to look for them came under fire from German positions on the cliffs. An evacuation was attempted during the night of 11 June with 67 merchant ships and 140 small craft, but there was to be no repeat of Dunkirk. At Veules, four miles away, some 4,000 British and French troops were rescued. But 6,000 men from one of the Army's best fighting units were taken prisoner. The most 'brutal disaster' of the war, Churchill told Jock Colville.

At midnight Reynaud rang from France. The line was so bad that Churchill could not understand what he was saying. Eventually he learned that the government had retreated to Tours and that Reynaud wanted to see him the next afternoon. Churchill landed in a thunderstorm. The airfield had been bombed and there was no sign of any representative of the French government. Seeing some French airmen, Churchill got out of the plane. 'He said, in his best French, that his name was Churchill, that he was Prime Minister of Great Britain, and that he would be grateful for a "*voiture*".' They were lent a car and drove to Tours. Nobody at the Prefecture took the slightest notice of them. Eventually a staff officer spotted them and took them to a nearby restaurant.

Finally Reynaud arrived and said that his government needed a firm assurance of massive and immediate aid from Roosevelt in order to continue. Failing this, he wanted to know what Britain's attitude would be to a French appeal for an armistice. Britain would fight on, Churchill said. In emphasising his point, he drove his cigar into the antique desk at which they were sitting, causing a deep burn. His delegation trudged around the garden and returned home. The next day the Germans marched into Paris. On the following day, 15 June, Churchill cabled the Prime Ministers of Canada, New Zealand, Australia and South Africa. He told them, 'I personally believe that the spectacle of the fierce struggle and carnage in our Island will draw the United States into the war.'

That evening Jock Colville joined Churchill for dinner at Chequers, the British Prime Minister's official country retreat. There were old friends present and Churchill could relax:

> Dinner began lugubriously, W. [Churchill] eating fast and greedily, his face almost in his plate . . . champagne and brandy and cigars did their work and we soon became talkative, even garrulous. Winston, in order to cheer himself and us up, read aloud the messages he had received from the Dominions and the replies he had sent to them and to Roosevelt. 'The war is bound to become a bloody one for us now,' he said, 'but I hope our people will stand up to bombing . . .'

Much of Churchill's talk now was about the consequences of French surrender. The thought that Hitler might soon have the French Navy to add to the Italian preoccupied him. Later that evening in the Chequers rose garden, Colville was told by his master:

> 'Tell them [the French] . . . that if they let us have their fleet we shall never forget, but that if they surrender without consulting us we shall never forgive. We shall blacken their name for a thousand years!' Then, half afraid that I might take him seriously, he added: 'Don't, of course, do that just yet.'
> He was in high spirits, repeating poetry, dilating on the drama of the present situation . . . and spasmodically murmuring 'Bang, Bang, Bang, goes the farmer's gun, run rabbit, run rabbit, run, run run'. About 1 a.m. Winston came in from the garden and we all stood in the central hall while the great man lay on the sofa, puffed his cigar, discoursed on the building up of our fighter strength, and told one or two dirty stories. Finally saying 'Goodnight, my children', he went to bed at 1.30.

Whitelaw Reid took the Pan Am 'clipper' to Lisbon. On board

he met Ben Robertson. Robertson was a journalist too, but his newspaper, and his background, were very different from Reid's.

Robertson came from Clemson, among the red hills and cotton fields of South Carolina, and his easy Southern charm was one of the qualities that had already taken him a long way in journalism. Another was his feeling of being an outsider – a small-town Southerner with a powerful sense of his own culture and its rights and wrongs. At school in Clemson he had played piano with the Jungaleers dance band, worked as a writer on the *Tiger* magazine and edited *Taps*. He was a natural writer, was awarded a degree in journalism from the University of Missouri, travelled restlessly and wrote. He had worked for many newspapers in Chicago and New York, and Australia and Hawaii. All the way he was dazzled by the smarter and richer people that he met. He did not feel their equal in the way that Reid might have done. Robertson observed them with the detachment of a foreigner. This same flair landed him the mission to report on how the English were taking defeat.

Robertson talked to Reid enthusiastically about the new paper that he was writing for, a left-leaning tabloid called *PM*. It didn't sound as if it would compete for readers with the *Herald Tribune*. *PM*'s founder, the idealistic publisher Ralph Ingersoll, had launched his paper on a clear mission to speak up for the underdog: 'We are against people who push other people around, just for the fun of pushing, whether they exist in this country or abroad.' Robertson was an idealist and these were sentiments he could endorse.

On the long journey Reid and Robertson talked and got on well. Reid, who was equally comfortable in the company of politicians and printers, found Robertson jovial, slightly plump, easy-going. Robertson was older than Reid – in his mid-thirties. Neither of them liked Hitler much, but neither was sure that they would make it to London before he did. The Germans looked invincible, and if they could hop over the sea with bombers and parachutes then the British would surely go the way of the French. *PM*'s first few editions had been full of great picture stories about the German army, their brand-new tanks and their fanatical troops, and lurid artists' impressions of storm troopers in speedboats whizzing across the Channel, the skies over Britain dark with bombers.

The seaplane stopped at Bermuda and then flew on to the Azores. Robertson had never been in a plane at night before over the sea and he did not much like the idea of taking his clothes off and sleeping, just in case anything happened. Reid quickly fell asleep. They landed at Horta and Reid filed a telegram while the plane refuelled. Robertson watched the locals. He was already chain-smoking.

A Dutch ship took Peter Vaux back to England. On the way across the English Channel the captain talked about how his country was lost and how awful it was not knowing where his family was. Vaux boarded her at Cherbourg, only a few days before the Germans took the port, and landed at Weymouth. Dorset seemed unruffled by war. From the window of the train to London, Vaux could see church fêtes and picnics. The countryside was very green despite the unusually hot spring weather. It was a strange contrast to the place he had just left.

Vaux had to report to the War Office for debriefing. He had managed to get a replacement uniform from a depot before he left France so he was in battledress, which made him feel better because just about everybody else was wearing a uniform of some kind. Everyone was rushing about and there was a great deal of tension and the occasional short temper.

Then Vaux went on leave back to his family home at Paignton in Devon, close to the beach. His parents told him about Churchill's speech. They were nervous but determined. Vaux's father asked if Peter could get him a pistol. In the evening Vaux walked with his mother by the sea. It was calm and beautiful and there was little sign of war except that the beach was guarded by an elderly gentleman with a shotgun wearing an armband labelled 'LDV' – Local Defence Volunteers.

Before he rejoined the regiment, Vaux went to meet Corporal Burroughs's family at their farm near Newent in Gloucestershire. He couldn't write to them; he had to see them. Again and again he had gone through in his mind the circumstances of those days and that awful night. What they should have done. What he should have done.

When he got to the farm he was ushered in by Burroughs's father, Charles. The whole family was gathered there in the parlour. A lot of them, it seemed. And they were all looking at him. So he told the story from beginning to end and they all listened in complete silence. And when he finished there was still silence. Then slowly the farmer shifted in his seat and said, 'All right lad, everything was done that could be done. Don't blame yourself.' The tension broke. Vaux was so relieved that tears sprang to his eyes. It was a wonderful thing for a father to say. He felt that if Mr Burroughs had said anything else he would have broken down.

He found what was left of his regiment camped at a racecourse in Hampshire called Tweaseldown. The men were there, but for the moment there were no tanks. They had been told that they would be supplied with new tanks just as soon as the factory had built them. There was no telling how long that might be.

It was good to see people again and to swap stories, but there were so many old friends missing. Five of his own troop of twenty had been killed and there were letters to write to bereaved relatives. There was one man, officially missing, he could not track down. He had been a dispatch rider and Vaux had hardly seen him after the beginning of May, although he was theoretically part of Vaux's command. The dispatch riders were always busy elsewhere. In peacetime he and Vaux had competed together in motorcycle trials, representing the regiment. Vaux was very fond of him. After considerable effort, Vaux eventually found him in a lunatic asylum in Sussex.

He went to the hospital and there he was, sitting up in bed looking perfectly well. The two men were delighted to see each

other and they talked for a while and Vaux answered all the man's
questions about the regiment and about who had survived and
who had been killed. Then the man said:

> 'shall I tell you what happened to me in France sir?' And I
> said, please do. 'Well' he said 'I was on my motorcycle doing
> a job for the colonel and I was at a crossroads in a village and
> there were masses of refugees there, there was quite a traffic
> jam. And the Germans came over and they bombed it, and it
> was a dreadful scene and I was blown off my motorcycle and
> I found myself beside a little boy of about five and he'd had
> his legs blown off. And he was blinded in one eye and he
> was in terrible pain and I took him in my arms and I could
> see he was dying and I took out my revolver and I shot him
> sir. I did do right didn't I?' I said, 'Yes, you did do right, I
> would have done the same'. And we talked of other things,
> and then he said, 'shall I tell you what happened to me in
> France sir?' and he did it again all the way through. And then
> the nurse came in and she said, 'you must leave him now'.
> And I said, 'does he do that all the time?' She said, 'he never
> stops. Over and over and over again he tells that story. And
> I don't know whether we'll ever be able to cure him.'

At the Waldorf Astoria Hotel in New York, a party was held to
celebrate the German victories in Europe. The host was Gerhardt
Westrick, a leading Nazi business lawyer and an executive in
the German branch of America's International Telephone and
Telegraph Corporation. Westrick had been sent to New York
to make discreet contacts with top businessmen. He took a house
in fashionable Scarsdale and regularly entertained at the Waldorf
and other grand hotels. Executives from Ford, General Motors
and several oil corporations were in his circle.

Gerhardt Westrick's acquaintances were not necessarily pro-
Nazi; they were just sensible businessmen and most had large

German subsidiaries. Whatever Churchill had been saying on the radio, it felt as if the war was all but over. Here was a business-minded Nazi urging American industry to retain its profitable ties with Europe. It didn't take a genius to work out that having warm relations with the newly enlarged Reich was likely to be very good for company profits.

Just below the surface a propaganda war was raging. British officials and agents tried to get the press on their side. Whitelaw Reid's family, like other powerful press people, were gently pressured to investigate men like Westrick. He had, it transpired, an artificial leg, the result of a British World War I shell. But he had not registered this fact when he applied for his American driving permit. This minor infringement was blown up by pro-British columnists like Walter Winchell and the German was eventually forced to leave the country.

But the propaganda flowed both ways. Even Ben Robertson's strongly anti-Nazi *PM* newspaper reported in mid-June that Congressmen were very concerned about the existence of a shadowy 'British Fifth Column' that was trying to drag naïve Americans into another European war. Isolationists in Congress were quoted as saying that the big banks had made a lot of money by acting on Britain's behalf during World War I and were out to do the same again. To most American readers the phrase 'big banks' was a simple code for 'Jewish financiers', an attempt to play on an anti-Semitism that still barred Jews from many American golf clubs and boardrooms.

When Joe Kennedy had taken Page Huidekoper to work for him in London, he had promised her father that if it should ever get dangerous for her to be in England then he would send her home. Now was the time. He broke the news to Page over breakfast in front of her friends so that she couldn't argue. Kennedy was sending his own children home too. The reason was obvious enough. He was telling people that the Germans would be in London within weeks. They had all the American newspapers spread out in front of them. 'Nazis March Through Paris' was the dominant headline. The usual picture stories about German super-troops were now supplemented by maps and diagrams showing Hitler's possible strategy for the invasion of Britain and the respective naval forces, adding the French and Italian fleets to the German.

Although she missed her parents, Page desperately wanted to stay. It seemed silly but she felt like a Londoner, and she wanted to share in whatever the city was about to go through. As she walked to the embassy for her last day at work she wondered whether she was looking at these familiar streets for the last time. She tried to imagine the sky over Grosvenor Square dotted with bombers, like the drawings in some of the papers, and all of the grand old houses in ruins. If she was ever able to come back, would these walls still be standing? And all her British friends. Would they be arrested? Would they be dead? She would miss the Richey family. Paul was back from France now, but he still looked very sick. Page could well imagine him volunteering to go up and fight again weeks before he should. And then what? Only the other day in Chelsea she had seen a young woman dressed in black, walking slowly, eyes downcast. Her husband had flown a bomber in France.

There were long queues of people besieging the embassy. It had been like this for days, so many people desperate to get out of Britain. There were Jews who had been chased from country to country by the Nazis. A good number of well-off society people had suddenly decided to spend the summer abroad, and various artists and writers had remembered engagements in New York. She was going to take one of the treasured places on one of the last boats out and she didn't even want to go.

When Ben Robertson and Whitelaw Reid reached Lisbon they found everything in chaos. Paris had fallen and the Germans were already at Bordeaux. Portugal was full of refugees trying to get to

America, to Algeria, to Brazil, to the Belgian Congo. Pan Am had cancelled the extension of their journey to London because of the danger of air attack now that the Germans controlled most of France. Getting to Britain was not going to be easy and both journalists were even more worried now that Hitler might get there first. Reid arranged passage on a little Portuguese freighter that was heading for Gibraltar. From there he would join a convoy for Britain. Robertson preferred to stay and try his luck with the airlines.

After innumerable visits and cables to ticket agents, consuls, air attachés and ambassadors, Joseph Kennedy's staff in London finally got Robertson a place on a plane. It was a big Douglas airliner that had flown from Amsterdam before the crew had escaped in it to England just ahead of the Germans. Now it was flying home some shipwrecked sailors, some displaced military personnel and anyone with the influence or money to get on board. Robertson fully expected to be shot down in transit. He kept his eye on the Dutch radio operator for any sign of stress in the crew, but the flight was unmolested by the Luftwaffe fighters he kept imagining every time he looked out of the window.

Robertson's first impressions of England were not favourable. While he waited for the customs officer to clear him through, he watched glum-looking airmen tending beds of roses and making tea. Everything seemed impossibly casual. They're going to be defeated and they know it, he thought. The journey to London confirmed his fears. The train was comfortable, the passengers read newspapers without a sign of agitation. 'Didn't they know the Germans were just beyond the English Channel?'

London was different. Here at last was evidence of war. On arrival at the Waldorf Hotel in the Aldwych he was given a gas mask. But he had no idea how to use it. The blackout came as a shock to an American fresh from the bright lights. How would he know when the bombers were coming? What did an air-raid siren sound like? The next morning he took a long walk through central London. Soldiers were stretching barbed wire along streets, sandbagging buildings, digging trenches in the parks. Everywhere he saw feverish activity. Old men and teenage boys were drilling in courtyards. The streets were full of soldiers from Canada and New Zealand. In Westminster Abbey the tomb of Queen Elizabeth was buried beneath sandbags. The Elgin Marbles were no longer on display in the British Museum but had been stored in a secret bunker somewhere. In St Paul's, leaflets had been printed with a prayer he'd never heard at church in South Carolina: 'A prayer for protection against air-raids'. He sat down in front of his typewriter to file his first report.

Bob Doe was one of the young 'knights of the air' that Churchill had eulogised in his recent speech. Men like Doe would soon have to face up to the best that the famous German Air Force could throw at them. But Doe wished he had never joined the RAF. It was plain that he just wasn't good enough, and he was convinced that he would be shot down in his first fight. That's what happened to inexperienced pilots, or so everyone said in the mess. If they made it through the first few hours in the air with Messerschmitt 109s for company then they were very, very lucky.

Doe had already had two narrow escapes. His squadron was about to be equipped with the lumbering old Fairey Battles. A flying coffin, that thing was. Fortunately the Air Ministry had thought twice about this and they had got Spitfires instead. The second brush with death was when they were all on stand-by to be deployed forward from Leconfield in Yorkshire and sent to cover Dunkirk. Almost every other fighter squadron in the RAF had done a stint there but the evacuation ended just before they were due to go.

The truth was that Bob Doe had always felt a bit second-rate. He was an only child and had a difficult relationship with his mother. He didn't start school until he was over seven and he was picked on by some of the rougher types. He left as soon as he could at the age of fourteen.

He became an office boy with the *News of the World*. He fancied the Air Force but he didn't have the right kind of smart background for a pilot or the technical skills for a ground-crew trade. Then he heard about the volunteer reserve scheme. They would pay you to learn to fly. Doe signed up. He did about seventy hours flying and he loved it. One day he walked into the Air Ministry in Whitehall and said he was ready to be a fighter pilot now. When the interviewers learned that he had left school at fourteen and hadn't passed any exams, their faces formed studied frowns. But eventually he found himself in front of an untidy old man with a kindly face who talked to him for half an hour in a friendly way. The man explained that because he lacked an education he would have to sit a special exam at the Ministry. 'I'll tell you what,' the old man said, taking a book out of a drawer, and marking a particular paragraph, 'learn that by heart.' Doe learned the paragraph and returned the book and when he sat the exam he found that he had been given the answer to the only difficult question.

The RAF was putting all its efforts into bombers, so Doe was trained as a bomber pilot on twin-engine Ansons. In November 1939 he was posted to the new 234 Squadron forming at Leconfield. The pilots arrived by train at Hull station and were taken out to the airfield by lorry. They asked the driver what sort of squadron it was but he didn't know. At the mess they met the CO and the two flight commanders but they didn't know either.

When they went down to the hangars the next morning they found that they were equipped with two basic training aircraft of Great War vintage. In December some Blenheims came and went. In February two Fairey Battles arrived.

But then, in March, a Spitfire landed and taxied over to their hangar and the pilots strolled across to take a look at it. They stroked its sleek sides. They took turns to sit in it. For Doe it was love at first sight. He thought it was the most beautiful creature he had ever seen. It had a very small cockpit. Doe's broad shoulders touched each side and his head was about a quarter of an inch away from the canopy on top. But he liked the sensation of filling up the cockpit. He felt as if he had become a part of the machine. It was not him sitting in an aeroplane, he was the aeroplane. To the delight of the pilots, fifteen more Spitfires appeared and suddenly they were a fighter squadron.

Soon he was flying one. The pilots were talked through the technique and off they went. They were told to be very careful when taxiing because the brakes were sensitive and if applied too roughly would tip the plane on to its nose. And they were warned about the hand-operated undercarriage which meant that they had to change hands on the stick as they took off. Doe was very careful. He taxied out cautiously, his right hand on the stick, his left hand on the throttle, easing it forward ever so gently. Then left hand to the stick and right hand to the pump as the fighter took to the air, 'and then all of a sudden, this tremendous power suddenly seemed to go through the aeroplane and you were up and away before you knew it, and it was the most wonderful feeling – having got the undercarriage up, you were part of the air. You were a bird in the air . . . this thing flew. You didn't have to think about turning, you did turn, it just automatically went.'

Then came gunnery practice. Each pilot was allowed twenty rounds and told to fire at the North Sea. Even a self-styled second-rater like Bob Doe could hardly miss that. German fighters would be a bit more tricky.

Chapter 9

16–20 June

On the morning of 16 June Jock Colville brought Churchill a telegram from Bordeaux as he was 'lying in his bed, looking just like a rather nice pig, clad in a silk vest'. The French government had just asked its ally for permission to conclude a separate peace. The 10 a.m. War Cabinet agreed to release the French to do this, on the condition that they immediately send their fleet to British ports.

But before the French were told about this decision, another idea intervened. General Charles de Gaulle was in London on an extraordinary mission. He was a tank commander, and one of very few French officers who had impressed Churchill. Over lunch he outlined a plan that struck Churchill as an idea of genius. He suggested that the only way to save the situation was to make England and France one country. The concept seemed to offer miraculous hope of prolonged French resistance. Immediately, the two men drafted a declaration of union. De Gaulle managed to call up Reynaud in Bordeaux on the phone. He approved. The War Cabinet approved too. By 4.30 p.m. the finished document was dispatched to France in de Gaulle's hand. Churchill was to meet Reynaud to sign it the next day. Somebody thought to tell the King about what was being done to his Empire. Plans were made to fly the French flag from government buildings. Churchill boarded a train for France.

Then the bubble burst as phone call followed phone call from Bordeaux. First there was a ministerial crisis. Churchill's train was stopped. Then Reynaud resigned. Then Pétain took over the government. Finally, late the same evening, Pétain asked the Germans for an armistice.

In all the confusion and excitement one crucial detail had not been communicated to the new French government. Churchill believed that he had extracted a promise to send the French fleet to Britain as a condition of any armistice. But this stipulation had not been understood in France. The French fleet didn't move.

The 17 Squadron pilots were convinced that fifth columnists were informing the Germans of their every move. Each time they took off Morse code started up on the radio and each night, when the Germans bombed the airfield, there seemed to be Very lights guiding them in. The smoke was still over Le Havre. On Wednesday, 12 June, Denis Wissler's flight had caught four Heinkel 111s bombing the ships evacuating troops from the port. The Hurricanes swooped down out of the sun in the classic pounce. Wissler's section attacked first, and as he fired he saw smoke pour out of the starboard engine of the German bomber. He made two more attacks and all four bombers were shot down without loss. He had opened his account at last.

By now he was back in the disordered rhythm of air fighting over France, with the added hazard that much of the fighting was over the front lines. The German anti-aircraft fire was dense and terrifying, and his Hurricane would come back peppered with holes. Some days were peaceful, usually when it rained. But on others it was just total confusion. One day after Wissler landed, another pilot, Harold 'Birdy' Bird-Wilson, told him that he had shot a Messerschmitt 109 off his tail. Wissler had never even seen it.

The place was falling apart around them. The station canteen staff had already run for it, leaving all the supplies behind. Wissler took off for Dinard in Brittany with a thousand cigarettes tucked away in the cockpit. The pilots went out for dinner in the evening and Wissler met an attractive French girl called Irène. Sunday, 16 June was another wonderfully grey day of bad weather and no flying, and after five hours at readiness Wissler took Irène out to dinner again. She offered to wash his dirty clothes – true love at last. He wrote in his diary: 'Oh God I do wish this war would end.' At least the next day was his day off.

It did not turn out quite as he had expected. He had arranged to see Irène again, but in the event he didn't even have time to say goodbye to her. The news came through at lunch-time on Monday, 17 June that the French had given up and that they all had to leave immediately. They flew to Jersey airport and found themselves in the middle of a huge party with much French wine and brandy being drunk. Some time about midnight someone announced to great cheers that the Russians had changed sides and declared war against Hitler, but they had hardly begun toasting their new allies when they were persuaded that the rumour wasn't true.

The next morning Wissler was seriously hung over and far from keen on flying. Just as his turn on stand-by was coming to an end the squadron was scrambled to patrol over Cherbourg. Down below it looked as if another evacuation was taking place. They were ordered to fly back to Guernsey and were met by another wonderful rumour: tomorrow they were bound for England. 'Oh I hope it is true,' wrote Wissler.

It was. At four o'clock in the afternoon they landed at Tangmere and then flew on to Debden. The mess that night was overflowing with champagne and relief. 'Whoopee, back in England again.'

Ships and fleets loomed large in Churchill's mind. On 17 June he sent an angry cable to Weygand and Pétain: 'I wish to repeat my profound conviction that the illustrious Marshal Pétain and the famous General Weygand, our comrades in two great wars against the Germans, will not injure their ally by delivering over to the enemy the fine French fleet. Such an act would scarify their names for a thousand years of history.'

RAF squadrons and British troops were withdrawn as quickly as possible. It was widely assumed that the French had given up immediately, although in fact fighting continued until the Armistice had been ratified and signed a week later. On 16 and 17 June there were frantic evacuations of British and Canadian units from St Malo and Brest. Much equipment was left behind when the evacuation was terminated, although it turned out that another whole day might have been used. Meanwhile an estimated forty to sixty thousand British troops converged on Nantes on the River Loire. Evacuation from St-Nazaire, the adjacent port at the mouth of the river, began on 16 June. About thirteen thousand men with stores and transport were evacuated on 16 June, and although the Luftwaffe attacked the shipping at anchor in Quiberon Bay only the liner *Franconia* was damaged. Ships were sent across as they became available. The liner *Lancastria*, fresh back from the evacuation of Norway, was immediately ordered to France. Such was the hurry that the captain was refused permission to discharge his surplus oil.

By the night of 16 June about ten thousand soldiers and RAF ground crew were encamped on an airfield just outside St-Nazaire. One of them was 'Oscar' Cornish, an instrument-maker with 98 Squadron, the support squadron for the Fairey Battle bombers in France. They had heard about Dunkirk but they never imagined that the whole of France was collapsing. On 15 June their remaining aircraft were flown out and in the evening the men were packed into lorries and driven to St-Nazaire. There had been no ships at the port so they were diverted to the half-finished airfield. Early on 17 June they marched to the docks, boarded a ferry and were transferred to the *Lancastria*. They were almost the first to arrive and were sent down to the cargo hold. For a while Cornish watched the boarding and tried to get some food, but each time he got close to being served the air-raid warning sounded and the hatch was slammed down. By midday the ship was absolutely packed. In the end he went back to the hold to get some sleep. Most of his mates had done the same.

The largest ships off St-Nazaire were the *Lancastria* and another liner, the *Oronsay*, each of 17,000 tons. They and some smaller merchant ships were protected by destroyers and anti-submarine trawlers. By midday the *Lancastria* was crammed to capacity. At least five thousand servicemen were on board along with a few British and Belgian civilians. She then waited for the other ships to be filled so that they could all sail in convoy. Fighter cover was being provided but it was intermittent and just before 2 p.m. the *Oronsay* was hit on the bridge by a bomb. The captain of the *Lancastria* was getting increasingly worried, but all he could do was get the ship's lifeboats ready, just in case, and wait. The Admiralty was too scared of submarines to allow the liner to travel alone. At 3.45 the air-raid alarm sounded and very soon afterwards the *Lancastria* was hit.

Deep inside the ship there was a roar and everything went black. Oscar Cornish thought he had gone blind. He could smell burning. Then he saw a faint shaft of light and groped his way towards it. The light was filtering down from the hold's loading hatch. He found that ropes had been dropped down and people were attempting to climb up. As he thought about the climb two people lost their grip and fell. He climbed up one of the vacant ropes. All around him men were screaming out for help.

There were only two thousand lifejackets on board. Most of the lifeboats were tipped over in the panic to lower them from the ship's rapidly tilting sides. The improvised timber staircase from the hold broke under the rush of men trying to use it, and so most of those down there never had the chance to get out. Many men lucky enough to find one of the hard cork lifejackets died when they jumped forty feet into the water and had their necks broken by the lifejackets on impact; 1,407 tons of oil spilled from the ship's deep tank and spread across the surface of the sea. Calcium flares broke off the rafts and drifted on to the oil and it caught fire. Meanwhile the air attack continued. Hurricanes of No.1 Squadron were back on the scene, but the air raid kept most other ships from getting anywhere near the *Lancastria*.

A sailor helped Oscar Cornish up at the top, told him the ship was sinking, and directed him to the bows. He was shocked to find that he was naked apart from his socks. The blast had blown his clothes off. When he made the deck the bows were already under water. He just waded in and started to swim. By sheer luck he missed the oil and spotted one of the lifeboats. He was hauled aboard in time to see the ship's last moments. It had turned on its side and the hull was lined with soldiers who could not swim and had no lifejackets. As the ship went down, some of the men were singing 'Abide with Me'.

The anti-submarine trawler *Cambridgeshire* rushed to the scene, followed by the destroyer *Highlander*. Both had to cut their engines as they got close, for fear of killing survivors in the water with their propellers. Other ships were slower to respond. The *Lancastria* was a long way out in deep water close to rocky cliffs. Many small French ships put out but it took time to reach the survivors and the estuary was still under air attack.

George Dakin, assistant canteen manager on HMS *Highlander*, was passing shells to the destroyer's forward gun. Standing on a table with his head through a hatch, he also watched *Lancastria* sink. They launched boats, let down scrambling nets and pulled in all they could. Many had swallowed or inhaled oil and, despite their best efforts, died on board. They saved a baby girl. Dakin's friend Frank Clements pulled her out of the water when she slipped from her mother's arms. They transferred the survivors to the *Oronsay*. In the evening they sewed the remaining bodies into hammocks, held a brief service and committed them to the deep. 'Each plunge made me think, "somebody's husband, brother or boy friend".'

It was a catastrophe, far greater than any other single disaster in the war thus far, with at least two thousand and probably many more dead. When Churchill heard the news he decided that it had to be kept secret. Ministry of Information reports on national morale were speaking of gloom and apprehension; this might be one disaster too many. As the survivors reached Plymouth they were herded out of sight whilst other troops in full kit were marched out to the cheers of the waiting crowds and the photographers. When the journalists went away the bedraggled survivors were loaded on to trains and buses and sent on their various ways.

Lord Halifax had not mentioned peace or mediation in the War Cabinet since the arguments of late May. But on 17 June, the day that news of the French armistice broke, a conversation with Halifax's deputy 'Rab' Butler left the Swedish Minister in London, Björn Prytz, with the strong impression that the British Foreign Office was ready to talk peace. That evening Prytz reported the conversation in a telegram to his government in neutral Stockholm:

> . . . Mr Butler's official attitude will for the present be that the war should continue, but he must be certain that no opportunity should be missed of compromise if reasonable conditions could be agreed, and no diehards would be allowed to stand in the way. He was called in to Lord Halifax and came out with a message for me that common sense and not bravado would dictate the British Government's policy.

The battle between common sense and bravado is exactly what Halifax thought he had been fighting in the War Cabinet. Within hours, Swedish diplomats were talking to their German contacts about what seemed like a serious split in the British government and a real chance of negotiating an end to the war.

Churchill made another speech, written as a clarion call to rally the nation after the shocking news that the French were asking for an armistice. He spoke in the Commons, dismissing the idea that the Germans could launch a successful invasion, even with Italian help, while the Royal Navy still had ships to guard the Channel. Then, anticipating an air battle to come, he stressed the value of home advantage to the RAF and predicted confidently that the courage of the British people would withstand bombing: 'I do not at all underrate the severity of the ordeal that lies before us, but I believe our countrymen will show themselves capable of standing up to it, like the brave men of Barcelona.'

He spoke on, building to a resounding conclusion:

> What General Weygand called the 'Battle of France' is over. I expect that the battle of Britain is about to begin. Upon this battle depends the survival of Christian civilisation. Upon it depends our own British life and the long continuity of our institutions and our Empire. The whole fury and might of the enemy must very soon be turned upon us. Hitler knows that he will have to break us in this island or lose the war. If we can stand up to him, all Europe may be free, and the life of the world may move forward into broad, sunlit uplands; but if we fail then the whole world, including the United States, and all that we have known or cared for, will sink into the abyss of a new dark age made more sinister, and perhaps more prolonged, by the lights of a perverted science. Let us therefore brace ourselves to our duty and so bear ourselves that if the British Commonwealth and Empire lasts for a thousand years, men will still say, 'This was their finest hour.'

Churchill probably first learned about Butler's conversation through security monitoring. But he learned more when the British ambassador in Stockholm was questioned about it by the bemused Swedes. They could not square what Butler seemed to be telling them with Churchill's words on the radio. Neither could Churchill. The Prime Minister soon had all the telegrams before him and asked Halifax to investigate, writing that 'Butler held odd language to the Swedish Minister and certainly the Swede derived a strong impression of defeatism . . . any suspicion of lukewarmness in Butler will certainly subject us to further annoyance of this kind'.

After a political career that was haunted by this moment, Butler went to his grave denying Prytz's account of their meeting. He claimed that the Swede had misunderstood and misquoted him. If this had been an attempt at a private peace initiative then it had been sadly bungled. A loyal servant of the old regime, and an old enemy of Churchill, Butler immediately offered his resignation. But he was kept in place and there were no more embarrassing conversations with foreign diplomats. Nevertheless, the whole murky episode suggested that if things went badly there were those in London who might yet move swiftly to seize the 'common sense' option.

'. . . the whole world, including the United States . . .' As usual the peroration had been designed for foreign as well as for domestic ears.

Canadians had been at war with the United States in 1814 and Irish-American raiders had troubled the Ontario militia as recently as 1870. The members of Mackenzie King's Cabinet had all grown up with stories about brave redcoats driving the Yankees back across the Niagara. Most English-speaking Canadians were proud of their position in the world: a foundation stone of the British Empire but self-governing and independent, loyal to their King out of choice not compulsion. And wary of their powerful southern neighbours.

But all of that seemed to be changing. By mid-June Ottawa was awash with talk of the new political and defence arrangements that would be necessary if, or perhaps when, Britain fell. 'My heart aches for the people in the British Isles,' wrote King, but the Canadian Prime Minister was also growing impatient with London's refusal to take his advice. He had hoped that Churchill, half American himself, might understand the delicate situation he was in. And yet whenever he suggested a gesture from London on the future of the British fleet all he received back from Downing Street were unhelpful strictures about pressing America to hand over their old destroyers. But America was not going to do this without a guarantee about the future of the fleet.

King was having almost daily meetings with America's man in Canada, James Moffat. They talked about the new relationship Canada might soon need with Washington. It was decided that Canadian military representatives would travel south, ostensibly to meet the British arms buyer Arthur Purvis. Once in the city they would hold secret meetings with the highest American military officials.

In a letter to his uncle, James Moffat wrote:

> there is a great deal of thinking going on in relation to North American defence. There is very little public talk on the subject, and I think that any tendency to public expression at this juncture will be discouraged on the ground that its major premise is the continuation of reverses to the Allies in Europe. Even to discuss such a contingency seems to the average Canadian a form of defeatism which if cabled or written back to England might in its present state of mind be discouraging ... Do not think, however, that although the subject is publicly taboo, it is not in people's minds.

Churchill, unaware of all this activity, cabled his ambassador in Washington. He instructed him to press once more for the fifty destroyers but on no account to be drawn into any talk about pledges on the future of the fleet:

. . . I don't think words count for much now. Too much attention should not be paid to eddies of United States opinion. Only force of events can govern them . . . We have really not had any help worth speaking of from the United States so far. We know President is our friend, but it is no use trying to dance attendance upon Republican and Democratic conventions. What really matters is whether Hitler is master of Britain in three months or not. I think not. But this is a matter which cannot be argued beforehand. Your mood should be bland and phlegmatic. No one is downhearted here.

When he came out of hospital Iain Nethercott was given fourteen days' survivor's leave. He was sore and very tired and felt like a human pin-cushion. Bits of a Messerschmitt bullet had been cut out of his leg, his mementos of Dunkirk. Other scars on his shoulder and back reminded him of the shoot-out in Boulogne. He went home to Essex to discover that his father had joined the Local Defence Volunteers and was masterminding the defence of Colchester from the local pub. He was bought a number of drinks on the strength of his war stories and his scars. They had a lot of faith in the Navy, did these people in the pub. The Navy and Winston Churchill. And the more they drank the more faith they seemed to have.

Nethercott returned to Chatham barracks to find the place in turmoil. They had about a hundred rifles and four ancient three-inch anti-aircraft guns. The gunnery school was in charge and they were teaching sailors how to throw hand grenades. Unfortunately there were no hand grenades available, so all the sailors lined up out on the football field and used large stones instead, pretending to bite the pin out, and flinging them as far as they could.

Nethercott was used to farce in the Navy so it did not surprise him when Old Bill was called up from retirement. Old Bill was a tank, built at Chatham and manned by sailors at the Battle of Cambrai in 1917. Since then it had stood by the parade ground. Now they tried to get it going again. They worked on the engine and eventually it burst into life in a cloud of blue smoke. Amid cheers, it was driven up the colonnade to the main gate and there it waited for the German Army. Nethercott thought it was typical of the naval mind to think that the Germans would come straight through the front gate to face a vintage tank and a thousand sailors armed with pebbles.

Nethercott had trouble sleeping. He couldn't forget how he had felt drifting by that life-raft with his injured friends inside and the fighter sweeping down on them all. Then the mad splashing of the bullets in the water and suddenly being all sleepy, bleeding comfortably into the sea, alone with his God. In his mind everything was getting mixed up: Boulogne, Dunkirk, tanks shooting at ships, ships shooting at planes, the men on the beaches, the men in the pub, brave as lions all of them, brave as Old Bill, brave as Winston bloody Churchill. Bravery wasn't the problem – the problem was all the tanks and the fighters and all those machinegun bullets making the water boil and splutter.

Did any of them stand a chance?

Drinking was part of Churchill's public personality, along with the tall hats and bow ties, the cigars and two-fingered salutes. There would be champagne, wine and brandy with most meals and then a weak whisky and soda to carry around later. Visitors expected it, especially American ones. But was he a drunk, as Ambassador Kennedy frequently suggested to Washington? No. None of his staff, his ministers or his generals ever saw him lose self-control or that relentless attention to detail. But alcohol was required; it was his fuel. 'I have taken more out of alcohol than alcohol has taken out of me,' he would say. It was hard to imagine all that drive and panache, all those big ideas and expansive phrases that had to be written down and acted upon immediately, without the champagne, the wine and the whisky.

Marian Holmes never saw her employer drunk. 'He never drank

to the point that he wasn't clear minded, ever. I never saw it even on celebratory occasions . . . He drank with food, that was the point, and there's all the difference in the world, because he was a very good trencherman.'

Churchill was leading a nation armed with pebbles and pitchforks. And the belligerence he inspired and came to symbolise was sometimes based on not much more than pub talk, Dutch courage, bravado. But whether you were dining at Chequers, or drinking in a pub with the Colchester volunteers, in June 1940 it helped to have a glass in your hand if you wanted to believe that Britain could win this war.

The sober editors of the world's press did not think that it could. Under the headline 'Peace Moves Heard in London and Berlin', Ben Robertson's paper, PM, reported that 'Britain fears not only the force of German bombers but what effect a Blitzkrieg would have on her own appeasers who might seize the opening to make peace as Marshal Pétain's government did . . . Britons fearful of a sell out remember that Neville Chamberlain, guiding genius of the Munich appeasement, is still a member of Churchill's cabinet.'

To drive home the point the paper printed a diagram showing that the Italian, German and French fleets added together almost equalled the total strength of the embattled Royal Navy. Analysts in New York concluded that Germany planned to make one more demonstration of her military prowess by crushing the Royal Air Force in the hope that the British would then rid themselves of Churchill and make a sensible peace.

Whitelaw Reid wasn't sure which of his rivals would get to London first, journalist Ben Robertson or Nazi dictator Adolf Hitler, but he knew that it wouldn't be him. Choosing a maritime route had not turned out to be a very smart move. He had come by sea before, as part of his great Atlantic sailboat expedition back in 1936. But that was before U-boats and eight-knot convoys that seemed to be routed somewhere via southern Ireland. It took Reid eleven tedious days to get from Gibraltar to England. What made it worse was that there was every possibility of being torpedoed *en route*.

To Reid's relief Bristol was still in British hands when they finally docked. He got straight down to being a journalist. When the customs official had finished with him, Reid asked the man how he thought the war would go. He assured Reid that all would be well and then told him how he had been teaching his daughter to fit a broom handle into the end of a beer bottle and how to break off the end. 'Any bloody Nazi comes in my house, he's going to get that right in the face!'

Some of their leader's aggression had rubbed off on these people. Or was it the other way around? Had Churchill spoken with the voice of the customs man or the customs man with the voice of Churchill? Either way, broken bottles on broomsticks suggested that the British would fight. Good. But it didn't mean that they would win.

Reid travelled east and met more broomstick people. He bought an MG so that he could explore this fools' paradise. Maybe it was because he was American, but everyone wanted to tell him that they would fight on the beaches, just like Mr. Churchill had said they would. They even seemed to be glad that the French, or the 'Frogs' as they always called them, were no longer around to get in the way. The idea that they might not have the means to defend themselves, or that they were facing an efficient and resourceful war machine, did not seem to trouble anyone very much.

In London they were taking war more seriously. Reid saw the gas cleansing stations and the barrage balloons. The city had a gloomy charm. He was impressed by the little slits through which the traffic lights glowed, by the chatter and buzz coming from the blacked-out cafés and bars, by the sandbags and the searchlights. He met up with Ben Robertson again. He had just been to Plymouth and described camouflaged factories, anti-tank obstacles on golf courses, the name-plates removed from railway stations and everywhere people getting ready to resist an invasion. Both men agreed that it was one hell of a story.

Robertson's first colour piece had just been published in *PM*. It was about London in the spring. Moody, maybe a little too sentimental, but it was how he was beginning to feel. 'People seem suddenly to realise what London means to them.' He wrote about lazy days in the parks and flower-beds and Speaker's Corner and day trips to Brighton. 'The people are yearning to be commanded . . . they want to be sure they are doing something . . . The earnestness and vigour of the common people's effort . . . has stirred the admiration of the remaining Americans.'

But back in New York *PM* also reported continued support for isolationism. One story described how angry New Yorkers tore down a 'Stop Hitler Now' banner in Queens. A review of the other American papers and their letter columns showed a large majority in favour of keeping out of the European war – as did *PM*'s straw poll of New York workmen. From Kansas City came a story about thousands turning out to cheer Charles Lindbergh and his latest peace and isolation speech. Telephone calls and letters to the local paper ran ten to one in Lindbergh's favour. Many called for him to run for President.

PM hated the Nazis, but its columnists in late June could find little cause for hope. 'Keeping enemy nerves twitching has long been a feature of German strategy. It still is. British sang-froid will be severely tested these next few weeks. The Nazi blockade, unhappily, has an excellent chance of success.'

Peter Vaux had returned from leave and was now part of a newly equipped tank battalion, with machines fresh off one of the Ministry of War's production lines. Sitting near East Grinstead with their fifty tanks on trains waiting to be transported to wherever the invader might strike, Vaux's unit was the only modern armoured force in the country.

He was still the reconnaissance officer, but instead of Vimy Ridge and Arras he was now scouting out potential battlefields in places like Brighton and Hastings. 'I felt that it was an extraordinary thing to be going into these villages and imagining that Germans may well be coming over the crest of the next hill.'

The crews and their equipment had to be deployed in villages close to the tanks. Vaux had to requisition all kinds of things. An orchard to hide some lorries in, a barn for workshops, bedrooms for the men. Most people were helpful, but not all. It was easy enough to find places for the men and the NCOs to stay. The inhabitants of the ordinary-looking terraced houses were pleased to take them in. But once Vaux moved on to the farmers and the bigger landowners, their reaction was sometimes very different. Hostile even. Owners of Tudor manors grumbled when told to put their furniture in the loft and make room for the Army. 'One man who owned his own pub wanted to have nothing to do with us. And another man who'd built a nice house said, "What's the good? Look what they've done in France . . . You lot won't hold them up. They'll be in here in no time. I don't want my house spoiled."'

It wasn't just pebbles and broomsticks. Unknown to most of its people, there was one area of modern warfare in which Britain had a world lead: the detection and direction of aircraft. This was something that none of Hitler's previous opponents had possessed, a way to see the enemy coming, a way to bring defending fighters into battle at the right place, in the right numbers and at the right time. Nurtured during the cash-starved 1930s by a dedicated group of scientists and RAF officers, Britain's fighter control system would soon be tested to the limit.

First warning of a raid was provided by a chain of top-secret

Radio Direction Finding (RDF) stations strung out along the eastern and southern coasts. RDF could detect all but the lowest-flying aircraft, but its effectiveness varied according to the height and the size of the raid. If the enemy were flying at 20,000 feet, they would be spotted a hundred miles away, giving about twenty minutes' warning. If they flew lower, then the warning period was shorter.

British aircraft were fitted with an IFF device (Identification Friend or Foe) which blipped in a distinctive manner on the RDF screen. Several features of the system still needed improvement. Calculating the size of an enemy force from the appearance and behaviour of the echo was very difficult. Even the most proficient operators sometimes had to guess.

Fighter Command was divided into groups. No. 11 group covered London, Essex, Kent and Surrey. To the north was No. 12 and to the west No. 10. Each group was subdivided into sectors, protected by a main sector station. The squadrons were assigned in varying numbers to each sector.

These first warnings were passed by phone to the filter room at Fighter Command Headquarters in Stanmore, just north of London. Stanmore checked that the radar contact was hostile and passed its position to the relevant group. As it went on the board at Group, a WAAF 'teller' there would phone the plots through to the sector stations. Once a raid crossed the coast then responsibility for tracking it passed to the Observer Corps. Hundreds of pairs of eyes strained skyward for the first sighting of an expected raid. The observer posts were linked by secure land-lines to the group and sector HQs and would immediately phone through their estimate of the size, height and direction of the enemy force. Cloud cover could obscure the view, and then the observers would try to use sound instead, but the results were much less reliable. At group headquarters and at the sector stations the movements of the raids would then be plotted by the WAAFs and followed by the controllers.

Group HQ decided which sectors were affected by a raid and

sent them orders about how many aircraft should take off. Once the fighters were airborne then the sector controller was responsible for guiding them to the target and for bringing them home. His deputies were in direct touch by radio with the fighters of his squadrons. They kept track of their own squadrons by means of 'Pip Squeak', a device that automatically switched on the high-frequency transmitter in the aircraft for fourteen seconds in every minute. This transmission enabled each sector station to follow the progress of four fighter units, each broadcasting every quarter of a minute. Knowing the course of the bombers and the course of the fighters, the deputy controllers on the ground could work out a vector or course on which the fighters would intercept the enemy.

By late June the controllers, plotters and pilots who were practising guided air interceptions knew that the course of the war would depend on how well the system worked when the real bombers came.

The commanding officer summoned the Debden MT drivers and asked if any of them wanted to become 'plotters'. Nobody knew what plotters were and nobody wanted to stop being a driver. The first few WAAFs he asked gave him a resounding 'no', and the CO, frustrated, sent them all away to think about it. Edith Heap and Winifred Butler had been curious about plotting and absolutely hated being sent from Debden to nearby Duxford. After a fortnight they rang Bill, their flight sergeant, and asked if they could come back and plot.

The first consequence of their decision was that they were made to sign the Official Secrets Act. They suddenly realised that what they would be doing was something hush-hush, important, influential, something they could not discuss even with the other WAAFs. The magic letters RDF were revealed to them. Through science, they were told, Britain had a means of knowing what the enemy was doing, long before he got near. They held the secret. Nobody else must know. Among the station personnel the plotters were soon regarded as an exclusive clique.

The station operations room was surrounded by earthworks like a Roman fort. The roof was reinforced concrete and was level with the top of the bank. For the first time, Heap and Butler stepped through its reinforced steel door and entered a world of wires and sockets, headphones and plugs. It seemed to buzz with electricity. The control room was like a small amphitheatre with a balcony so that the controller could survey the movements on the floor below. Underneath was a large table covered with a grid map of England, extending west to Portsmouth and north to the Wash, marked 1 to 10 along the bottom, and 1 to 10 up the side. It had four phone points at the top and four at the bottom, and was tilted towards the controller's balcony.

The Observer Corps gave the plotters practice runs, phoning in with pretend sightings, and, now and again, with the offer of a date. They practised intensively. It was routine work, but it required concentration and accuracy. Heap would leave the operations room exhausted and drenched in sweat. Eventually the controller selected the positions for each WAAF in each watch. Heap was to be RDF1, sitting bottom right of the table, and Butler RDF2 at the top right. Each plotter was responsible for part of the map. As RDF1 Heap received the first information, coming from the 'teller' in the 11 Group operations room at Uxbridge, about any enemy movements. Her sector of the map included France, ran west to Beachy Head and north to Chelmsford. Further north was Butler territory, further west another WAAF's, but it was Edith Heap's privilege to monitor the first news.

On the wall was a plotting clock divided into five-minute triangles, coloured red, blue and yellow. When first warning of a raid was phoned through, it was given a code number (H5, say), an estimated size (40+), a height expressed in 'angels' (thousands of feet) and a pair of co-ordinates. Heap would take a triangular wooden block, select letters and numbers from a tray and make up the height and size on the block. She would fix a little flag on top showing the raid number. Then she would place it on the board at the grid reference she had been given. Next to it she placed a plastic arrow showing the direction of the raid. The arrow was coloured (yellow, say) to match the five-minute segment of time on the clock when news of the raid had first come through. Every five minutes the block would be moved forward and a new arrow placed on the table. After fifteen minutes, when the clock reached yellow again, the first plot would be removed from the table. By then the raid's position should have been plotted in red and blue and yellow again, so that it was constantly traced with three plots showing the course that it had followed. When it moved west of Beachy Head or north of Chelmsford, it became the responsibility of the WAAF in charge of that area of the map.

In the gallery upstairs the controller watched developments on the table. Next to him sat two more WAAFs. One plotted the progress of British fighter squadrons (drawn from the neighbouring direction-finding room in which the Pip Squeak signals from British planes were monitored). The other plotted the bombers as shown on the big map below. With reference to these two maps the controller issued 'vectors' to the squadrons: he gave them courses expressed as compass bearings on which to find the enemy. When busy, deputy controllers would help him and speak to the pilots in the air. A large speaker fixed to the wall broadcast what the pilots themselves were saying. The rule in the operations room was silence. The women spoke only when spoken to.

There were four watches. Heap and Butler were in 'B' watch. They worked four hours on, four hours off, with eight hours on every third night followed by eight hours off. They had twenty-four hours' leave occasionally and forty-eight hours once a month. This became an unalterable routine. That and baked beans for every meal.

Chapter 10

20 June–11 July

After flicking through the works of William Shakespeare, Jock Colville found the quote he had been looking for in *Henry VI*, Part 3.

> *'Tis better using France than trusting France.*
> *Let us be back'd with God, and with the seas,*
> *Which he hath giv'n for fence impregnable,*
> *And with their helps only defend ourselves.*
> *In them and in ourselves our safety lies.*

Churchill said it was very fine. Perhaps he'd use it in a speech, but without the insulting line about the French. It didn't make much difference, thought Colville. Worse things were being said about France around Churchill's dinner table every evening now that the details of their armistice had percolated back to London. The release of captured German pilots was the most hurtful thing. Reynaud had promised to send them to Britain. But after he fell they were handed straight back to the Luftwaffe. Soon, no doubt, those same men would be dropping bombs on Whitehall. Then there was the destiny of the French Navy. Its commander, Admiral Darlan, had told the British ambassador that his fine battleships and cruisers would never fall into Hitler's hands: 'As long as I can issue orders, you have nothing to fear.'

But could he be relied upon? Could any of them be relied upon now that they were Germany's latest vassal state? 'There is a good deal of Anglophobia in France and Algeria,' wrote Colville. 'There is a good deal more Francophobia in England. Such is the fate of the *Entente Cordiale*.'

Churchill's commanders in the Mediterranean told him that the Armistice left them very exposed. Once-friendly French bases were strung along the North African coastline. Now they were out of bounds, officially neutral and potentially hostile. The Mediterranean trade route was abandoned. The distance from Britain to Suez thus increased from 3,000 to 13,000 nautical miles and the distance to India from 6,000 to 11,000. The Royal Navy was left with only three friendly Mediterranean ports. Gibraltar controlled the Atlantic entrance, Alexandria controlled the Suez Canal, and Malta allowed British submarines to threaten the supply routes to Italian North Africa. But Malta was uncomfortably close to the Italian Air Force in Sicily.

Keeping Malta and Alexandria supplied became another commitment for an already overstretched Navy. With no more French bases and the Italian Navy menacing on every side, the Admiralty judged the position untenable. On 17 June it had circulated a memo recommending 'the withdrawal of the Eastern Mediterranean Fleet to Gibraltar as soon as it is apparent that French control of the Western Mediterranean is about to be lost to us'. Churchill disagreed. If the fleet retreated from Alexandria then Britain's whole position in the Middle East would collapse. The Prime Minister formally vetoed the proposal to withdraw on 23 June.

The balance of naval power in the Mediterranean had been based upon the combined power of the British and French fleets against the Italian. Without the French fleet the British were seriously outnumbered in all classes of vessel except the battleship – and even the British battleships were old and slow. If Mussolini's force were to be augmented by the powerful French Navy then the position in the Mediterranean would be utterly hopeless. Could the British hold Gibraltar and bottle up these hostile fleets in the Mediterranean? Would fascist Spain come into the war and launch an assault from the land? What if Gibraltar fell or was blockaded and bypassed? Then would come a challenge in home waters. Not since the Battle of Trafalgar had Britain faced an enemy that could seriously threaten its command of the seas. But now in London and Washington there arose the spectre of a vast armada, German, Italian and French, with squadrons of dive-bombers circling above, sailing forth to contest the English Channel. Could Britain's 'fence impregnable' stand up to that?

Sam Patience loved the sea. He had been brought up in the small village of Avoch on the Black Isle between Inverness and Cromarty on the north-east coast of Scotland. He went to the little village school until he was thirteen, and then he went to sea in his father's fishing boat. He was the youngest of seven sons. The life was hard and simple and dominated by strict Calvinist discipline. Every Sunday night at 9 p.m. they took the Book. 'No gas, no electric, although we had good food, fresh fish which my mother bartered with local farmers for vegetables. But I still marvel now how my mother brought us up. When we sat down at dinner my young sister and I were the two youngest and we had to stand over where there was a sink; there wasn't enough room at the table.'

The sea was like a magnet to him. He spent more time at the harbour than he did in school, digging up lugworms and wading in the water. The most exciting ships were the big transatlantic liners, and Sam Patience dreamed of steering one. He would never be an officer, he knew that. But to steer a liner across the great oceans . . .

He began his nautical career rolling cigarettes for his brothers, and although he quickly moved up the ladder of seniority he soon decided that fishing was not for him. He couldn't see any future in it. In this part of Scotland the eldest son inherited the fishing boat. Many young fishermen joined the Royal Naval Reserve for the six-pound 'bounty'. Since the Navy paid the fare down to Portsmouth there was nothing to lose. Patience did his six months' training and, on the way back home, stopped in London and signed up with the New Zealand Shipping Line.

During the 1938 Munich crisis he was called up for a few days. Then he sailed off again to New Zealand, to Arabia, to the Red Sea and the Black. That was his life and he loved it. But it ended all too soon. He was called up again in August 1939, sent to Chatham and then put straight on to the 29,150-ton battleship *Resolution*, built in 1916. It was like going back in time. The ship was a creaking old tub run by officers who would have felt at home in a different century. Under all circumstances the men were to be in their hammocks by 10 p.m. Petty infringements of the dress code were severely punished. Patience was given seven days' punishment for complaining that the potatoes were burnt. He half expected the cat-o'-nine-tails.

Resolution's first wartime job was to take Britain's gold reserves to Canada. Patience was part of a human chain loading gold bars into the shell room with a watchful marine guard standing behind every fifth man. They did three runs to Canada, through the freezing winter, taking out gold and bringing back Canadian troops. Then they were sent to Norway. Patience was directed through a steel hatch and down five ladders to the magazine room where the cordite charges which propelled the shells were stored. He got out of this dangerous spot because you had to wear felt slippers so as not to cause a spark and they had no slippers big enough for his size-twelve feet. So they put him on the deck below in the shell room. He worked the machine that lifted the five-foot-long fifteen-inch shells into the hoisting cage. Then he sent them on their journey up to the huge guns high above, hoping to God that the ship would not be hit, because if it was then there wasn't much hope for the lads below the cordite on the bottom decks.

Off northern Norway a bomb did hit the *Resolution*, exploding in the marine band's mess deck. Another eight feet and it would have gone straight into the magazine. They had been bombed so often in Norway that when they got back to Scapa Flow the rifling on the barrels of the anti-aircraft guns had worn out. Then they were rushed down to Gibraltar, part of what was called 'Force H'. They were joined by the aircraft carrier *Ark Royal* and two other battleships. One was the mighty *Hood*, the pride of the British fleet. The ship was alive with rumour. Some said they were here to stop the Spanish joining Hitler and seizing Gibraltar. Others talked about a secret mission somewhere in North Africa.

Churchill's admirals, generals and air marshals asked each other the same question over and over again: what was Hitler going to do? The Admiralty believed the German fleet was stronger than it really was. They didn't know how much damage they had already done to the Germans with their own submarines, destroyers and dive-bombers. But they were fully aware of their own weaknesses. By the end of June half of the entire British destroyer force was on anti-invasion duty. The problem was that of the 202 destroyers available at the outbreak of war only 74 were now out of the dockyard.

Even so, looked at rationally, it should not be difficult to defeat an invasion. The Germans had only a small surface fleet and no experience of amphibious warfare. Surely they would not risk crossing the English Channel with a huge army until the Royal Navy had been neutralised? That might happen if the Luftwaffe won complete control of the air, but even after that a prudent war leader might take a few weeks to bomb all of Britain's home naval bases.

Another possibility was a mixture of air power and the sudden deployment of a German fleet swollen with ships gathered from Italy and France. But this would be a breathtaking gamble. If just a couple of British warships could get in and amongst the invasion fleet they would wreak havoc. Just sailing close to barges laden with troops at 20 knots or so would send most of them to the bottom of the English Channel.

Perhaps they would come by parachute, seize airfields and be supplied by transport planes? But the logistical problems would be immense, and no one knew of any German plane that could carry heavy armour. Peter Vaux's tanks would make short work of unsupported parachutists. But what if the parachutists landed in support of a smaller surprise naval force that could seize a working port and bring in heavy supplies that way? Surely surviving Royal Naval warships would pound the transports to pieces. But maybe the Channel could be filled with German mines and patrolling U-boats? Maybe, unless, if, if, if . . .

While speculation continued it was prudent to prepare for the worst. And such preparations served another purpose. 'He [Churchill] emphasised that the great invasion scare . . . is keeping every man and woman tuned to a high pitch of readiness. He does not wish the scare to abate therefore, and although personally he doubts whether invasion is a serious menace he intends to give that impression, and to talk about long and dangerous vigils etc.,' wrote Colville.

Hitler's army was very keen on invading in 1940, but his navy was much less optimistic. Nevertheless, plans were prepared and logistical preparations put in train. The Führer's own attitude seemed to vary. It is likely that he hoped that the threat of invasion combined with an overwhelming display of air power would be enough to secure the peace deal he desired.

With a measure of hindsight the real danger becomes clear. Not an invasion in the summer of 1940 but the destruction of Britain's air and naval power, leaving the country exposed to an increasingly effective U-boat blockade and remorseless bombing. Britain's starving population, driven from their burning cities, would then either demand an end to war or else face an invasion in the spring of 1941. In the meantime Churchill might fall and be replaced with someone willing to reach a commonsense deal.

Writing from inside Number 10, and entirely without the benefit of hindsight, Colville could see the way things might go. 'The big aerial onslaught is expected daily now, followed perhaps by a peace offensive rather than by an invasion.'

Churchill did not want such speculation made public. The bulk of the British people were psychologically prepared to fight an invasion, and it was important to keep them watching the skies for parachutists dressed as nuns. But a forced peace, rather than Panzers in Sussex villages, was the most likely way Britain might lose the war in 1940. Either way, whether the end came through invasion or political collapse, the most important thing, the only important thing, was to preserve both the RAF and the Royal Navy. 'Winston . . . is contemplating violent action against French ships in African ports,' wrote Colville on 28 June.

When the aircraft carrier *Ark Royal* steamed back from Norway, morale was at the bottom of the North Sea. She made it around Northern Ireland and all the way south to Gibraltar without any problems, but Petty Officer Dickie Rolph's gloomy mood did not dissipate. 'There didn't seem to be anything that could save us at the end of June 1940. Nothing at all.' Rolph was a navigator in the Fleet Air Arm, flying in one of the Skua dive-bombers that had taken 60 per cent casualties over Norway. So many friends dead. It had begun in glory when he as navigator and his pilot, Eric Monk, had helped sink the *Königsberg* in Bergen harbour – the first capital ship ever to be destroyed by dive-bombing. But almost every mission since then had gone savagely wrong. The aircraft carrier *Glorious* sunk and practically everybody on her gone too. And that last mission to try to sink the *Scharnhorst* – that had been a shambles to remember. So many friends dead. He had never been so terrified in his life.

Now they were off to North Africa. From freezing Norway to the blazing Mediterranean and God knew what they would be asked to do there.

Whitelaw Reid could imagine the headline straight away: 'English anglers find the right bait, to catch a Panzer'. There they were, right in front of him, British soldiers on anti-tank training popping up out of ditches and casting a charge of explosives on to the roof of a dummy German tank by use of – yes – a kind of modified trout-fishing pole. This had to be the best one yet.

He couldn't write the story anyway. The British censor wouldn't allow those kinds of details to leave the country. They didn't want to tip off the Wehrmacht that their mighty armoured divisions were about to be fly-fished to oblivion. They should be more worried about Americans laughing at them.

He was feeling like a proper war reporter now. He'd been up to Scotland and interviewed Polish soldiers dreaming of a return to Krakow and Lodz. He'd been in London with his aunt, Lady Ward, who was organising private relief parcels from America. He'd met Anthony Eden, Lord Beaverbrook and even Mrs Churchill at one of his aunt's lunch parties, and throughout it all he'd kept up a steady stream of articles for the *Herald Tribune*. There were five of them in the bureau. The paper had printed a great photograph of them all with their tin hats and gas mask cases.

Reid's new friend Ben Robertson was also sending back stories every day. He tended to avoid high politics and military strategy. Instead he wrote about the little details of everyday life that made these British people seem touchingly ordinary.

Robertson had been brought up to think of Britain as a slightly sinister, bloodthirsty place with drunken aristocrats at one extreme and filthy slums at the other, its people united by little more than pride in the bayonet and the battleship. But most of those he met and wrote about were not like that at all. In Dover in early

July, Robertson painted one of his favoured scenes of small-town defiance:

> Waves broke against Dover beach with unbroken tempo. The Union Jack fluttered above Dover Castle on the white chalk cliffs. Back in town housefolk tended their carefully kept gardens and merchants tried to carry on with what was left of Dover's one-time business . . . People in the streets were friendly. The thunder of the battle for Calais had reached them across the Channel and Dover boys had risked their lives in flimsy boats to rescue the BEF from Dunkirk.

Robertson's editor, Ralph Ingersoll, was doubting Britain's resolve. On 28 June he wrote, 'Twilight hangs heavy over the British Isles. The anxiety of the world produces rumours, rumours that England may sue for peace . . . These stories, born of the grim proximity of death that stares England in the face, may be nothing but rumours. Yet one wonders.'

It was essential to do something savage and decisive. Churchill decided to seize, neutralise or destroy the French Navy. It was the only sure way to keep it out of German hands. Such an action would also send a signal to Roosevelt. The Americans were infuriating Churchill with their demands for a pledge on the future of the Royal Navy. All they could think about was what would happen when Britain lost. Churchill needed to make them think about how they might help Britain win or, at least, how they might help him survive an anxious summer.

The Admiralty called the anti-French operations 'disagreeable and difficult' in a cable to the Mediterranean admirals. But it also urged them: 'be relentless'. Sam Patience, Dickie Rolph and the rest of Force H sailed from Gibraltar at 1700 hours on 2 July with two destroyer flotillas screening them. The sailors had not been told where they were going. In the small hours a signal arrived from the Admiralty giving the text of the ultimatum to be delivered to Admiral Gensoul at Mers-el-Kébir, the military port of Oran in French North Africa . The choices offered were stark: join the British, sail to a British or West Indian port, scuttle, or be attacked by the formidable arsenal on board the British warships. Captain 'Dutchy' Holland of the *Ark Royal*, who knew some of the French officers at Oran, was sent forward in the *Foxhound* to negotiate.

Meanwhile, at dead of night in Portsmouth and Plymouth, armed parties boarded and seized two French battleships, four cruisers, some submarines, eight destroyers and two hundred smaller vessels. Only on the submarine *Surcouf* was there a fight, resulting in the death of two British officers and a rating.

At dawn in Alexandria Sir Andrew Cunningham's fleet pointed their guns at a French battleship, four cruisers and their escorts, while he tried to persuade them to disarm. Eventually they did. A squadron was sent to prevent the French ships in the West Indies from making any attempt to leave.

On 3 July the French sailors at Oran awoke to the distant presence of a British battle fleet, its threatening grey silhouettes just visible on the horizon. On board HMS *Resolution*, the captain told Sam Patience over the Tannoy why the Royal Navy had sailed through the night to menace its former allies. The French fleet was going over to the Germans, he said, and it had to be stopped. Most of the sailors had a low opinion of the French and were less troubled than their officers by the prospect of firing guns at them. The aircrews on HMS *Ark Royal* were briefed. Swordfish bi-planes were to lay mines in the harbour entrance and spot for the battleships. The more modern Skuas were to protect them. Dickie Rolph's mother was French and he had been to Oran in 1935. They had played the French Foreign Legion at football and lost. The French had been wonderfully hospitable and they had had a great time. The idea of attacking the place was horrific. 'I'm sorry, Dickie, but you've got to go,' he was told.

Negotiations lasted all day. Captain Holland shuttled back and forth into the harbour to negotiate with Admiral Gensoul. On his second visit he could see that the French ships were at action stations. Messages flew between Oran and Toulon, Toulon and Bordeaux. Other messages went between Force H and London. At first it seemed as if the French might comply, then cables from Toulon were intercepted which suggested that reinforcements were coming to confront the British force. There was little trust on either side for the negotiators to draw upon. Admiral Gensoul swore that he would never hand over his fleet to the Germans, but he was also adamant that Britain did not have the right to tell the French Navy what to do with its ships at gunpoint. In France Gensoul's commander-in-chief was shocked that London did not respect his word and seemed to be threatening France with war.

Both of Britain's Mediterranean admirals were prepared to accept the word of honour of their French colleagues. They attempted to persuade their political masters to change their minds, and not to force them into a course of action that they felt to be deeply dishonourable.

But Churchill was long past the point of trust as far as France was concerned and, as every inconclusive minute dragged past, fears grew in London that German U-boats might arrive. 'Settle this matter quickly,' Force H was told. Finally, when it seemed apparent that the French force would not comply with the British terms, Captain Holland was recalled.

At 5.54 p.m., from a range of 17,500 yards, HMS *Hood* opened fire, followed by HMS *Valiant* and *Resolution*. Each ship fired twelve salvos; 144 fifteen-inch shells, each weighing three-quarters of a ton, shrieked through the air and exploded in the harbour. As they passed over the cruiser HMS *Arethusa*, ahead of the battleships, each shell sounded like an express train passing through a tunnel. The first salvo fell short, the second hit the breakwater, showering French decks with concrete. The third hit the *Bretagne*'s magazine and the explosion caused an enormous cloud to rise over the harbour. Ten minutes later the battleship capsized with the loss of 1,012 lives. The same salvo hit the destroyer *Mogador* and blew off her stern. *Provence* got five hundred yards before she was hit and a serious fire broke out. *Dunkerque* was hit by three shells but kept firing six of her eight guns until her electrical power failed. The *Strasbourg* moved fast. Ripping away the bollards to which she was moored, she pulled clear just in time to avoid another incoming salvo. Five destroyers pulled away with her. *Strasbourg*'s movement was reported by a spotting Swordfish but discounted by Admiral Somerville. She pulled out of harbour just as he retired to avoid the increasingly accurate shore batteries. By the time *Hood* gave chase, it was too late.

Sam Patience had been at action stations for hours. Reprieved from the shell room, he was manning an anti-aircraft gun. All day he had been sitting in his anti-flash jacket in the incredible burning heat. His gun crew were playing 'ukkers' to while away the time. Suddenly the giant ludo board leaped into the air as *Resolution*'s guns opened up and the whole ship shook. *Hood* and *Valiant* were firing their guns too. Patience could hardly believe the noise. It was one of the most concentrated big-gun broadsides in history and the result was not a battle, it was a massacre.

From above, Dickie Rolph could see the shelling, but its effects were soon obscured by the great black cloud that rose from the *Bretagne* and covered the whole harbour. What a way to die. For a while he couldn't see a thing until through the smoke he picked out French Curtiss fighters engaged in an uneven dogfight with another flight of Skuas. Two British planes were trailing smoke as they fled. Behind, the *Ark Royal* was signalling frantically for its planes to return, and as they turned Rolph glimpsed the *Strasbourg* nosing her way out of the smoke in the direction of the *Ark Royal*.

The French did their best to return fire, chiefly with coastal batteries, and coloured plumes of spray erupted around the British ships, straddling *Arethusa*. In the ten-minute engagement, the Royal Navy killed more Frenchmen – over 1,250 – than they had killed Germans in any single action in the war thus far. The Prime Minister had spoken of his desire to seize the initiative in this war, to 'butcher and bolt'. But no one could have imagined that Frenchmen would be the first to be butchered.

''Tis better using France than trusting France,' Colville had quoted half in fun a few days before. It looked as if Shakespeare's jibe was now government policy. Colville spent the evening with Sir John Dill, Vice Chief of the Imperial General Staff, who 'said that he had never seen anything comparable: the two nations who were fighting for civilization had turned and rent each other while the barbarians sat back and laughed'. At 11.30 p.m. there was a meeting of the Chiefs of Staff. Churchill told Admiral Pound 'that he did not see how we could avoid being at war with France tomorrow'. A warning was sent by the Admiralty to all flag officers to that effect. Indeed, that night Admiral Darlan signalled to his remaining ships to prepare for war with Britain, but Pétain and the Council of Ministers calmed his outraged belligerence.

Attacks on French ships continued for several more days with mixed success. Within a week, the better part of the French Navy had either been seized or put out of action. But of the four modern French capital ships that so alarmed the Admiralty, only one, *Dunkerque*, was badly damaged, while another, *Strasbourg*, had escaped to France. Of the other two, *Richelieu* was attacked and slightly damaged in Dakar, West Africa, and the unfinished *Jean Bart* was left stranded in Casablanca.

In Parliament Churchill explained his dilemma. 'It is with sincere sorrow that I must now announce to the House the measures which we have felt bound to take . . .', he began. He listed French betrayals, especially the handing back of captured pilots to the Luftwaffe, he explained his fear that the French ships might fall into German hands. He set out the terms that had been offered to the French, told of the negotiations and the final attack. He concluded, 'I leave the judgement of our actions, with confidence, to Parliament. I leave it to the nation, and I leave it to the United States. I leave it to the world and to history.'

There was no optimistic conclusion on this solemn occasion but, once again, the political sting in Churchill's speech lay in its tail.

The action we have already taken should be, in itself, sufficient to dispose, once and for all, of the lies and rumours which have been so industriously spread by German propaganda and Fifth Column activities that we have the slightest intention of entering into negotiations in any form and through any channel with the German and Italian governments. We shall, on the contrary, prosecute the war with the utmost vigour by all the means that are open to us until the righteous purposes for which we entered upon it have been fulfilled.

For the first time Churchill was enthusiastically cheered from all sides of the House. According to Harold Nicolson, 'The House is first saddened by this odious attack but is fortified by Winston's speech. The grand finale ends in an ovation with Winston sitting there with tears pouring down his cheeks.'

The brutality at Oran was just what North America had been waiting for. In Ottawa Mackenzie King shared his pleasure with the American envoy, James Moffat, and wrote, 'I really think . . . that Britain is justified in seeing that the French fleet was destroyed before it got into the hands of Germany.' Roosevelt's Interior Secretary, Harold Ickes, agreed: 'I feel very happy about it . . . The effect on the morale of the English must be very great indeed. I admire the boldness of Churchill.' The British ambassador, Lord Lothian, sent a note to Roosevelt: 'You will see that Winston Churchill has taken the action in regard to the French fleet which we discussed and you approved.'

In New York, Ralph Ingersoll, the editor of *PM*, no longer doubted Britain's resolve: 'England gave the world today an answer to the question: who gets the French Fleet? . . . I want to record what a deep satisfaction it was to me to read the news that someone stood up to Adolf Hitler, taking dangerous toys away from him . . . When an allied officer gives an ultimatum . . . and it isn't a bluff, that's news.' The paper published a cartoon showing Chamberlain's furled umbrella, the hated symbol of appeasement, abandoned at the quayside as the Royal Navy steamed out to battle. Ingersoll concluded: 'I am for sending supplies to England as long as it's governed by a Churchill who will fight.'

Ken Lee was beginning to enjoy life as a pilot. Since he had been shipped back to Devon with his arm in bandages after the French gave up, life had improved considerably. The squadron was re-forming, which meant rest and leave and light duties. He spent as much time as possible in London, feeling that life owed him some fun after France.

They would meet round Piccadilly Circus and stay the night at the Regent Palace Hotel on the corner. Since the Canadians had invaded London the place had become known as the Canadian Riding School, but Canadians were not the only boys to get riding lessons there. Up the side streets were clusters of cafés, restaurants and bars. The pitch-black pavements were thronged round Piccadilly and Soho. As Lee stumbled up Denman Street he was bumping from body to body. 'Sorry! my dear.' 'Did you see the streamlines on that one?' Then a yellow glare as he opened the door of Chez Moi and an overwhelming wave of sound and excitement.

Chez Moi was a favourite with the fighter squadrons. A cartoonist worked there and the walls were covered with caricatures of pilots. Someone was playing jazz on the piano. He saw the gang from the squadron as he came down the stairs, and a woman turned round and looked at him. 'Good God there's Kenny Lee, had his wicked way with me when I was still at school.' 'Peggy, how are you darling? She's exaggerating, of course.' He pushed his way to the bar to buy pink gins for them all. He would spend most of the evening explaining that innocent grope away, but given luck the night would end with more than a grope. Pilots were glamorous in London and there were single women in the downstairs bar of the Riding School who, if not exactly easy meat, did not take much charming by a man wearing wings. A double room was only seventeen shillings a night. You needed something to relieve the stress – pretty soon the serious work would begin again. You could never tell which ride might be your last. 'Your round I think, Johnny.'

Conversation turned to flying and to the usual moans about the superannuated ground staff and controllers on the base at Middle Wallop. Some of these 'penguins' were sticklers about things like dressing for dinner, but most of them hadn't left the ground for years. 'Hey, Ken, what's the definition of a penguin?' 'Don't know.' 'A bird that flaps but can't fly.' 'They sent me on some mad flap the other day. Searched through the clouds for hours and never saw a thing.' 'Trouble is, when they should be plotting the fuckers, all they can think about is fucking the plotters!'

A time to be ruthless, sometimes needlessly. Four thousand Italian men had been interned within days of Italy's declaration of war. At the beginning of the war the Austrian and German community in Britain, some fifteen to twenty thousand people, had been swollen by sixty thousand refugees, mostly Jews or left-wing opponents of the Nazis. After 25 June all 'C'-class German and Austrian men in the country were rounded up and sent through transit camps to the Isle of Man. 'C'-class aliens were those judged least harmful. The 'A's and 'B's were already behind barbed wire. The plan was to send them in batches from the Isle of Man to Canada. On 2 July the liner *Arandora Star*, carrying 1,500 German and Italian internees, was torpedoed and sunk off Ireland; 714 of them died. It soon became clear that not all of those who drowned had been Nazis or fascists. Far from it. Such aliens as were still at large, often because they were engaged in vital research for the war effort, were forbidden to own cars, bicycles or maps and were put under curfew.

A twenty-mile-wide 'Defence Zone' stretching from Rye to

the Wash could be visited only by permit. On 3 July all beaches from Brighton to Selsey Bill were closed to the public. On dark nights nervous Local Defence Volunteers would take pot shots at tipsy motorists who failed to stop at the flash of their torches. There were frantic hunts for fifth columnists whose signals had been spotted by innumerable civilians with 'Fifth Column fever'. Very few were found, a frustration that left the hunting posses even more convinced of the devilish cunning of the Nazi spies and their secret aiders and abettors. The very few real agents who were caught and hanged were anything but cunning. When a woman masquerading as a landscape painter was caught cutting military telephone wires on the Isle of Wight she was sentenced to death, later commuted to fourteen years.

A schoolmaster was thrown into jail for teaching 'defeatist' theory to his pupils. One man was put in prison for saying in public that 'it will be a good thing when the British Empire is finished'. Fines were introduced for spreading alarm and despondency. Duff Cooper's Ministry of Information was so zealous in its attempts to gauge the public mood that 'Cooper's Snoopers' were denounced in the press. 'Careless Talk Costs Lives' posters were on the walls in every public place. There were also posters demonstrating the uniforms of German parachutists, although everyone knew that these were of no use if the devious Hun was disguised as a nun.

Virtually all known or suspected British fascists had now been picked up and imprisoned, among the 1,769 British subjects under detention without trial. Leading fascists were in Brixton Prison with their wives in Holloway. Jock Colville recorded that, on 29 June, 'In reply to a request from the P.M., the Home Secretary sent a list of 150 "prominent people" whom he had arrested. Of the first three on the list two, Lady Mosley and Geo Pitt-Rivers, were cousins of the Churchills – a fact which piqued Winston and caused much merriment amongst his children!'

Debden was nothing like the Canadian Riding School. For one thing the WAAFs took their unwritten orders not to distract the pilots very seriously at first. The pilots too thought hard before developing serious relationships with these women. These weren't Soho floozies, these were the sort who had accents like their own mothers and sisters, the sort they might marry.

There were exceptions to the rule. One of Edith Heap's friends had a superb figure and wheat-coloured hair and was quite stunning. She had a knack of pinching everybody's boyfriend. Heap only found out how later on. The Senior WAAF officer, Petters, married the station adjutant, Flight Lieutenant Disney. She resigned when she became pregnant, to the disappointment of all the WAAFs, who liked her. Heap liked Disney, too – even though he made her furious by calling her 'Uriah' after the nauseating character invented by Charles Dickens.

She did not see much of Jerrard Jefferies during those long days when the fighter pilots got up before dawn and were on duty until nightfall after ten. Then he was posted as a flight lieutenant to take charge of a new Czechoslovakian squadron, 310, based at Duxford – not far away, but far enough. She saw even less of him. And he never wrote.

Denis Wissler knew something about sex: twice he had visited brothels in France, egged on by more experienced colleagues. Now back at Debden, he looked with distant longing at Bridget Anderson, a general's daughter who was the telephonist and clerk at 'B' Flight's dispersal hut in the woods. But the days were so very long that there wasn't much chance to take anyone out. The powers that be seemed to be trying to find out just how much they could take. At readiness until 10.30 at night and then up at 3 a.m. every day. Mostly they were practising: finding landmarks; locating suitable fields for emergency landings; formation flying; new attacks worked out in France; practice scrambles; practice dogfights; dusk and dawn take-offs and landings; navigating. They got very tired of seeing the dawn break.

Sometimes on evenings off the mess got rather wild. They would tussle drunkenly at 'high cockalorum', riding around on each other's shoulders and jousting with rolled-up newspapers; one evening ended in mass 'debaggings', the forced removal of a chosen victim's trousers. That sort of thing was tolerated as good for team morale. And they were a real gang now: 'Birdy', Alf Bayne, Geoff Pittman, 'Pip' Stevens, Pete Dawbarn, Dave Leary and the others. Squadron Leader Ralph MacDougall would get as pissed as a fart with the rest of them given half a chance. But they rarely got half a chance. If you had to get up at 3. a.m. then a beer between landing at 10.30 p.m. and bed at eleven was about the limit. One Sunday Wissler did get down to the party in the sergeants' mess and took the opportunity to tell Bridget how he felt about her. She was very polite, but he got the feeling that she wasn't quite as keen as he was. And perhaps she was a bit too posh.

Dickey Lee had turned up again, limping from the wound he had picked up at Dunkirk and still off flying. He had just received a second medal for Dunkirk to go with his Distinguished Flying Cross (DFC) from France. Ken Manger from 17 Squadron also got a DFC for Dunkirk, where he had shot down three planes before coming down himself into the sea, but it was no consolation for the death of his best friend, Richard Whittaker. Wissler took two days' leave to celebrate twin anniversaries, that of joining the RAF a year ago on 10 July and his twentieth birthday the day after. He was looking forward to seeing his parents again. The late nights made it difficult to phone them as often as he should.

Bob Doe's 234 Squadron moved from Yorkshire down to St Eval in Cornwall, where they were just about the only fighter squadron in that corner of England. Geoffrey Gout was rich and had a sports car. He was very pleasant. There were two friendly Australians too, but Doe wasn't really close to the other pilots. He still felt a bit out of things, and he was still convinced that he was never going to make the grade. Doe's squadron was expected to mount night patrols over Plymouth and then cover coastal convoys during the day. When they weren't doing night patrols they were at readiness until half an hour after last light and again from half an hour before first light. It was exhausting. One night Geoffrey – the rich one – crashed and was killed. Nobody ever found out why.

Lack of sleep made simple things like landing difficult. One night Doe felt too tired to circle the aerodrome as he should have done and just brought the plane straight down. It was a risk but it worked, and he taxied gingerly away from where he knew they were digging a new runway. He stopped and switched off and thought, Oh, thank God, I'm home. At that moment the whole plane tilted slowly sideways. Doe had parked with his wheel on the rim of a ditch and it slowly slid in. There was only minor damage but Doe got thoroughly 'bollocked' by the squadron leader.

Paul Richey was out of the fighting. A medical board had decided that he was unfit to fly and had insisted that he take a month's sick leave. Actually he was glad. He was feeling rather strange and disorientated. Sudden noises would have him diving for cover, which could get a bit embarrassing. He could not get used to the absence of real bombs and rubble and carnage. Worst of all, the sight of an aeroplane made him feel physically sick. He took a train down to Devon and spent the month with his wife, Teresa. He slept a lot. Often he would wake up, eyes staring, in a sweat, gripping the controls of an imaginary Hurricane.

General Freyberg, Commander of the New Zealand Forces, was enjoying an unpredictable evening with Churchill. It had begun with the greeting 'I am tired; you're tired; we're all tired! Let's have some bubbly'. Churchill was full of enquiries and enthusiasm, but you could never tell what he was going to say next, or whether he meant it. To Freyberg's horror, Churchill proposed bringing Australian and New Zealand convoys through the Mediterranean. Then the Prime Minister asked him whether he thought the Germans would attempt an invasion. Freyberg replied that he believed an invasion would not succeed, but that with all resources concentrated in the south east of England there was a grave danger of losing Egypt to the Italians. Churchill seemed not to react to this retort, or to Freyberg's alarm at the idea of his Anzacs running the gauntlet of Italian submarines, bombers and battleships. But as he left, Churchill confided, 'You do not think they will attempt an invasion. Neither do I – but you must not say so.'

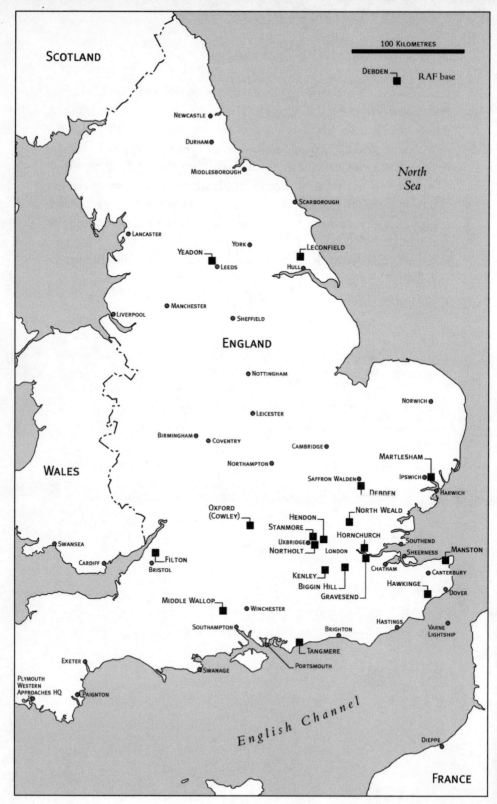

Map 3   Battle of Britain: Fighter Command Bases and Luftwaffe Targets

Chapter 11

16 July–15 August

On 16 July Hitler ordered preparations for an invasion to begin, but he still hoped that the British would come to terms. In a speech to the Reichstag, he issued what he called his Final Appeal to Reason: 'A great Empire will be destroyed, an Empire which it was never my intention to destroy or even to harm . . . I consider myself in a position to make this appeal since I am not the vanquished begging favours, but the victor speaking in the name of reason.' The response from London was instantaneous and crude. A *Daily Express* journalist, Sefton Delmer, announced on BBC radio: 'Let me tell you what we here in Britain think of this appeal of yours to what you are pleased to call our reason and common sense. Herr Führer and Reichskanzler, we hurl it right back at you, right in your evil smelling teeth . . .'

CBS correspondent Bill Shirer was inside German radio head-quarters with officers from the High Command. They, like many Germans, believed that the war was effectively over. When they heard the BBC ridiculing their Führer's words they said that the British were crazy.

After four weeks sitting in his garden in Devon, Paul Richey felt ready to go back to war. When they examined him for a second time, the RAF medical board disagreed. They said he needed three more months on the ground. How would he feel about being a fighter controller? It would be good for the pilots to be guided by someone who knew what it felt like to go into battle. Richey took a short course to master the current state of the system. He was impressed.

And so Paul Richey, fighter pilot, temporarily grounded, became Paul Richey, 'penguin'. He was posted to RAF Middle Wallop in Hampshire, a sector station in No. 10 Group, whose principal concerns were the western naval stations and ports – Southampton, Portsmouth, Plymouth, Bristol, Cardiff and Milford Haven.

The war in the air had been quiet since Dunkirk, with only sporadic attacks on British ships in the Channel and the southern and eastern ports. Then, in mid-July, just after the BBC's discourteous rejection of their Führer's reasonable terms, the Luftwaffe began to attack in force.

Slow-moving coastal convoys were the first target. They sailed within easy reach of the new German bases in Holland, Belgium and France. Dive-bombers were sent to hit the ships whilst Me 109s circled above waiting for the British fighters.

The RAF tried to defend the convoys, for the first time using radar to vector pilots on to enemy formations. Often things did not work out. Radar contacts sometimes proved to be friendly planes that had neglected to switch on their IFF beacons. Some of this delicate equipment malfunctioned in the wet weather. It was impossible to tell whether the radar echo represented dive-bombers or fighters. It was the Stukas which the RAF wanted, but their squadrons sometimes found themselves engaging large formations of German fighters on a 'free hunt'. If that happened then the dive-bombers would get through. But the main problem was timing. By the time the Spitfires and Hurricanes were scrambled the damage to the convoy had sometimes been done and the raiders were returning home. So squadrons were brought to smaller stations nearer the coast.

17 Squadron at Debden was one of them. Each day they flew to the sector's forward base at Martlesham Heath near the sea. Denis Wissler returned from leave to the news that 'A' Flight had just shot down five unguarded bombers. Things really were hotting up. But it was not always so easy to catch the Germans. Usually the pilots saw very little of them. Once or twice the convoy had been bombed before they even got there.

One day a team of American journalists from *Life* magazine came to Debden. They wanted a formation flying show. After a day patrolling over convoys the pilots produced a display that they thought looked as tired as they felt. But the Americans were an uncritical lot. Besides, they were still excited by what they had seen earlier in the day. Dickey Lee, eager to prove his combat readiness though still limping from his latest wound, had excelled himself in a display of trick flying. He flipped his plane over on its back so close to the ground that he came back with hay wrapped round the aerial. The Americans were open-mouthed.

Pilots were in the news a lot. The handsome Austrian flying with 17 Squadron, Count Manfred Czernin, had just been interviewed in the *Daily Sketch* about the number of his kills, his glamorous countess, his Italian villas and his dog. Czernin was not the most reticent of men. His fellow pilots read the upbeat propaganda piece with hoots of laughter and then, tongue in cheek, wrote an open letter to the paper to express their concern at Czernin's excessive humility: 'In fairness to our fellow pilot we should tell you that his bag of Nazi planes to date is eighteen not eight. He's such a modest bloke we think it our duty to let you know this.'

The weather remained indifferent and there was a lot of waiting about 'at readiness', tedious, nerve-racking and tiring. The weather was humid and unsettled with rain and thick, low cloud. It made it difficult to find the enemy and it made it difficult to fly home, especially since the return flight was often done at dusk. There were highlights: a nice dinner with Bridget Anderson at the Red Lion near Duxford; a victory over a sulky Harry Britton in a practice dogfight; a memorably drunken party when Squadron Leader MacDougall was replaced. Wissler didn't like the look of his new CO: Cedric Williams, fresh from Air Ministry Intelligence with strong ideas about making head-on attacks on enemy planes.

The convoys that Wissler helped to escort round the coasts of Norfolk, Suffolk and Essex moved slowly on to the Straits of Dover. There they were at their most vulnerable, within twenty miles of a hostile shore. Convoy CW8 passed westward through the Straits on 25 July. That day five ships were sunk by dive-bombing, and later the two escorting destroyers and four more merchant ships were damaged. The next day the survivors were attacked by fast German E-boats armed with torpedoes and three more ships were sunk. Only eleven of the convoy's twenty-one original vessels made it past Dungeness.

On Monday, 29 July Denis Wissler was woken at 4.30 a.m. and staggered out of the dispersal hut with Alf Bayne and Birdy, all rubbing bleary eyes and pulling on their flying jackets. He felt relatively fresh. Yesterday had been more or less a day off. He walked over to his Hurricane, where the ground crew had been turning over the engine to warm it up. He grabbed his parachute and climbed into the cockpit. The squadron left Debden for Martlesham Heath at dawn. Blue Section, consisting of Bayne, Bird-Wilson and Wissler, carried out one uneventful patrol in the morning but were up again after lunch. At 3.10 they were ordered to intercept a coastal raid, X17, an unidentified aircraft. The radar plots were good and they soon identified a Heinkel 111 at 4,000 feet below them, moving in and out of some cloud.

They gave chase in line astern. Quickly overhauling the medium bomber, Bayne led them in on a frontal attack out of the sun, followed by a second from astern. It was three against one, and the German bomber had no chance. As Wissler lined up for his second attack the Heinkel's undercarriage dropped and the bomb-aimer jettisoned his bombs into the sea. Pieces of metal were falling off and oil was spurting out of the engines, splashing over the fighters as they flew past. But the rear gunner still had some fight in him. As Wissler closed from behind, lazy puffs lobbed towards him and seemed suddenly to accelerate and tear towards and then past his cockpit. He pressed the firing button for two or three seconds and then pressed it again. Each move from his thumb sent three or four hundred bullets into the stricken plane. The rear gunner stopped firing and Wissler watched his prey sink slowly down towards the water and then level out. Was it trying to play dead and escape low down? He turned for one more attack. This time the plane went into the water and the circling British pilots watched as three men clambered out and tried to inflate a little boat. There were normally five in the crew of a Heinkel.

As they reached land again over Kent, Bayne called up coastal forces to send out a boat to pick up the Germans. Birdy and Denis talked about how awful it must feel to be splashing about in the Channel as night fell. The three pilots put in a joint claim for one conclusive kill. Wissler had hit German planes before, but this was only the second time one had definitely gone down, and the first in England. Maybe he wasn't quite in Dickey Lee's class, but he felt he was slowly becoming a proper fighter pilot. And it felt very, very good.

Despite some successful interceptions, coastal convoy losses were alarming. At the end of July the Admiralty declared that heavy ships should not operate in daylight south of the Wash. The next westbound convoy passed Dover on 7 August. It was attacked by E-boats and lost three ships to their torpedoes. The next day it spread out over eleven miles and the air attacks began. This time the Stukas were met by Hurricanes and driven away.

The convoys were made smaller and defended more heavily. New 'Hunt'-class destroyers, with better anti-aircraft defences, replaced the older ones. Ships with barrage balloons guarded the flanks; anti-submarine trawlers and armed motor launches joined the defending escort. The Germans, meanwhile, were building giant gun batteries at Cap Gris Nez. Their completion was delayed by British bombing, but on 12 August they began to shell Dover and ships passing through the Straits.

All this action drew the press corps to the coast. On 14 July BBC correspondent Charles Gardner broadcast an excited live commentary on the fighting over the sea. This was judged distasteful and he was told not to do it again, but it alerted the Americans to the virtues of the viewpoint. In early August Ben Robertson got a call from Helen Kirkpatrick of the *Chicago Daily News*, suggesting that they travel down together with Virginia Cowles of the *New York Herald Tribune*. Ambassador Kennedy phoned to express his concern but the Americans went anyway. They booked into the Grand Hotel and registered with the Chief Constable. Over half of Dover's pre-war population had already left. British press liaison people showed them the medieval caves that were now being used as long-term shelters. Chalk dust filled the air and the people were coughing and didn't look very healthy. But some of them had moved furniture in and recreated their homes, right down to flowers on the table.

The next day the sun was shining and the Americans took a taxi to Shakespeare Cliff, perched between Dover and Folkestone, where some British journalists had already established a viewpoint. It was very thrilling. At the first drone of engines they all jumped into a ditch, but the planes were too high to see clearly and the distant bangs told them little. Later they saw some German bombers on their way home, the first time Robertson had seen any. British fighters chased them out to sea. The sight and the sound were disjointed. Planes shot past each other and a second or so later the tinny rattling sound of machinegun fire reached the spectators on the cliff. A German plane fell into the sea; there was no parachute.

The British journalists cheered heartily but Robertson wasn't sure how to react. He had just seen someone die. 'For some German boy that was his last tour of duty,' he wrote later that evening.

Next morning they decided to walk, carrying large picnic baskets. They had just passed the King Lear pub at the foot of the cliff when they heard the Germans coming. They started bombing Folkestone harbour and then one of them turned towards Dover and headed straight for a barrage balloon floating high above. Anti-aircraft fire burst around the raider; German bullets whizzed past the balloon. Some impacted near the journalists, who promptly ran back down the hill and into the pub.

As the days went by the Americans got used to the pace of life on the cliff, the droning of bees and the smell of dry grass waving in the coastal breeze. Rounds of beer and lemonade would come up from the pub; someone would quote from a sonnet or put a record on the wind-up gramophone. They would lie there on their backs, Helen, Ben and Virginia, watching gulls soaring against the blue sky and philosophising about freedom or the insignificance of the individual in war. Then suddenly there would be the drone of engines or the urgent siren from down in the harbour and their tin hats would be on and they would crouch watching, or pointing cameras. The anti-aircraft guns made the ground shudder. For a few minutes there would be the most extraordinary noise and then it would end again just as suddenly.

Someone would get up, dust themselves down, and suggest that maybe another round was in order. Off they would stroll to the King Lear, returning with trays of ginger-beer shandy. They could not get over the strange sensation that they 'could be in the midst of life one moment, in death another', spectators in the sunshine, watching other people fight and die. Like paying customers at the Roman Colosseum, one of them had said.

They were paying to watch Ken Lee and his gang in 501 Squadron, in the thick of the battles over Dover. 501's pilots slept in their new base at Gravesend and then every morning flew their Hurricanes down to Hawkinge near the coast. There they would land and disperse around the perimeter. It was a large grass field with no proper runways. There were four small tents where the pilots sat waiting for something to happen, writing letters, reading the papers, playing cards.

A girlfriend had given Lee a little 'Jiminy Cricket' doll as a kind of good-luck charm. Lee made sure he always had it in the cockpit, just as he always liked to take a leak against the tailwheel of his plane before he took off. One of the many little superstitions that the pilots had developed. And, to be honest, you needed a pee before going into combat – you just did.

Their tactics had not changed – they still flew the standard 'number one' attack and the old 'Vic' formations. It was the only thing that the new pilots were capable of. But by now most of them had their guns set to converge closer than the recommended three hundred yards.

They were frequently on stand-by until dusk. Sometimes they slept in the tents. Three or four times a day the 'scramble' call would come. One of the others was teaching Lee and his friend Johnny Gibson how to play bridge. They'd put their cards down carefully with the intention of finishing the rubber later on, and all run for their planes. Minutes later they would be climbing, hungry for height, always worried that the Me 109s were already up above them. The fighter controller would come on the RT: 'Blue Leader, Blue Leader, Vector 120, Angels 15.' 'You'd see black in the distance and you'd be climbing and climbing and climbing all the time pressing on. You'd try to judge the curve, you're climbing to come round behind them. You go in and squirt off your guns and hope bits will fall off and when you've used all your ammunition you just pull out and go back and get some more.'

The world's press saw Lee get his first Stuka. A great cloud of them were dive-bombing Dover harbour and some ships out to sea. 'There the buggers are. Tally Ho!' Lee dived down and straight through the Dover flak, which should have stopped once the Hurricanes came into view but as usual didn't. 'Flaming onions!'– not an expletive but a kind of anti-aircraft shell. Bright orange flashes all around, the acrid smell of cordite somehow penetrating Lee's cockpit.

And now there are Stukas everywhere. Up close the large planes with the odd-shaped wings look duck-like and defenceless. A rear gunner shoots away with a pair of machineguns. Soon sort him out. Then eight Brownings all pour fire into the pilot and the engine. Manoeuvre closer now to finish the bastard off for good. Press the button and what sounds like rattling peas on the cliffs is a tearing roar in the ears of the sweating, panting pilot, and then the Stuka just begins to fall apart and plunges down into the sea, taking both the bastards with it. 'Got you, got you!' A cheer from the cliffs that Lee can't hear. The Stukas have dropped their bombs and are running for home. 501's two Polish pilots are following them to France as usual. Maniacs, both of them, but God can they fly. Call up Gibson on the RT: 'Did you get one? By the way, three no trumps doubled! See you back at base.'

On the ground is a new pilot, Sergeant Howarth, with his plane full of holes. He's shaking. 'I just looked down into the cockpit to switch my guns on and when I looked up you'd all gone. I never saw anything hit me at all.' They laugh and pick up the cards. Where's Gibbo? Gibson rings in later from Dover to suggest that someone else plays his hand. He's been fished out of the water again.

A man called Sylvester was one of 501's best pilots. He liked to get in nice and close, with the result that he took more than his fair share of punishment. He'd been shot down so often in France that, under his seat, he carried a special escape kit including a razor and a clean shirt. Back then he always seemed to land in the grounds of some château, and he would come back a couple of days later with a huge grin on his face, having been wined and dined by some beautiful aristocrat, or so he always said.

One day Lee lent Sylvester his Hurricane, Jiminy Cricket and all. But he never saw the doll, the plane or the pilot again. Sylvester went down during one of those fights over Dover, lost somewhere in the sea. This time there were no pretty ladies, no nice meals and no need for a clean shirt. Silly bugger – he should have pissed on the tailwheel. You had to laugh.

After a few days there was quite a party on Shakespeare Cliff and at the Grand Hotel. News had soon spread that this was where the action was. You could watch the convoys being dive-bombed and see the Germans hit the Channel ports. Since all this drew the British fighters in, it was also the best place to catch the action in the air. Veteran journalists were there: Art Menken was filming for the cinema newsreels; Jimmy Sheean scribbled tortured prose. Ed Murrow or Eric Severeid came to broadcast for CBS. They met English journalists too. Ben Robertson was most impressed by Hilde Marchant of the *Daily Express*. Robertson thought that the tiny redhead was herself 'a sort of Spitfire attached to the ground'.

One day in early August the skies were dark with German planes. From their various holes in the ground the Americans watched in awe. Then they were equally impressed at the sight of half a dozen Hurricanes darting towards the middle of the swarm.

The siren warned Dover. Jimmy Sheean said, 'We'll see the time come when it will warn Baltimore and Washington.' Sheean was still pessimistic. All his life he had distrusted and disliked British imperialism. The events of 1938 had 'strengthened these feelings to the point of bitterness'. He could not see how these hordes of planes could lose, and he was watching the Royal Navy being driven back from Dover in both directions. Convoys crept through by night now, if they came through at all. And the Germans had begun to shell Dover too. You could see the flashes from the huge batteries on the other side of the Channel. Count to six, seven, eight, then shells would start landing all over the place. Jimmy Sheean was used to supporting the losing side. He had done it in Spain and Finland. 'How come my side is always firing at planes with rifles?' he asked. What was important was that he referred to 'my side'.

In a way Britain's weakness was appealing. Seeing old men with pitchforks defending cliffs and watching Ken Lee and five mates take on the German Air Force all made it easier to accept that the old Empire was an underdog now, was a good cause. And those Spitfires and Hurricanes were at last striking back at fascism. Remembering the transformation of his opinions at Dover, Sheean later wrote, 'The flash of the Spitfire's wing, then, through the misty glare of the summer sky, was the first flash of a sharpened sword.' Gradually, as they watched the fighting in the air over Dover, the American journalists were becoming more and more pro-British.

Like most vaguely progressive or left-wing Americans in the 1930s, Ben Robertson had thought of Britain as an imperial overlord, ruling the waves with its navy and shooting down Indian protestors with its soldiers. Now, increasingly, he saw it as a democracy just like America, filled with people with the same names and faces as those he had grown up with. Yes, Sheean was right, this was 'our side'. Robertson saw the pilots above him, charging the phalanxes of the enemy, and had a moment of revelation. He watched their sacrifice and it illuminated history for him. He no longer felt afraid because he now had a sense of belonging to a cause, and that made survival unimportant and death valuable. He now knew what he was standing for:

> I was for freedom. It was as simple as that. I realised the good that often can come from death. We were where we were and we had what we had because a whole line of our people had been willing to die. I understood Valley Forge and Gettysburg at Dover.

233

Whitelaw Reid was sometimes in Dover too. Like Ben Robertson, he was hugely impressed by what he saw. Reid was now certain that all possible help should immediately be sent from America. He wanted to replace these splendid people's fishing poles and broken bottles with anti-tank guns and hand grenades.

In New York the family newspaper took an ever more explicitly pro-British line. The *Herald Tribune* was a barometer of opinion in the Republican Party. A few months before there had been talk around the Reid dinner table of running an avowedly isolationist candidate against Roosevelt in November. But now the paper turned decisively against isolationism. 'There still seem to be people in the U.S. incapable of understanding how much there is which hangs upon the defence of this last bulwark of the free and democratic world,' thundered an editorial in early August. It concluded by pressing Roosevelt to send Britain the fifty moth-balled destroyers as soon as possible.

Churchill was kept fully briefed about American opinion. After the good publicity that followed Oran and the battles over Dover, he again pressed Roosevelt in passionate terms about Britain's need for destroyers:

> Destroyers are frightfully vulnerable to Air bombing and yet they must be held in the Air bombing area to prevent sea-borne invasion. We could not keep up the present rate of casualties for long, and if we cannot get a substantial reinforcement, the whole fate of the war may be decided by this minor and easily remediable factor. I cannot understand why, with the position as it is, you do not send me at least 50 or 60 of your oldest destroyers ... Mr President, with great respect I must tell you that in the long history of the world this is a thing to do now.

Roosevelt's personal envoy, William Donovan, came to London. He was given the best possible access to everyone in government, the military and the royal family. He was wined, dined and kept well out of the way of the official American representative in Britain, Joe Kennedy. In August Donovan reported to Roosevelt that the British were in a better state than previous American assessments had suggested.

Roosevelt considered his position and looked at the opinion polls. This was the most difficult foreign policy decision of his career. If he got it wrong and overstated America's appetite to aid Britain then he could kiss goodbye to re-election. From Ottawa, Canadian Prime Minister Mackenzie King picked up every rumour of the intense debate in Washington about the destroyer deal. It was, King wrote, 'a terrible misfortune for the allies that this election is as late as November'.

Harold Ickes attended a Cabinet meeting in the White House. The destroyers were discussed in detail: 'Churchill has . . . been begging for help from the President . . . I was glad to discover that the President and Cabinet, generally, were much more sympathetic to the proposition of sending some of these destroyers to England if possible.'

Roosevelt discussed the terms and promises that America needed in return. To evade the Neutrality Act he needed to be able to say that sending these ships abroad added to the security of the United States. Leasing some British bases in Newfoundland and the West Indies would help. But the President also still needed a promise that if Britain fell then the Royal Navy, American destroyers and all, would sail across the Atlantic. And this was a promise that Churchill seemed unable to give.

There would have to be a fudge, a form of words agreed that the British could present one way and the Americans another. In Downing Street Jock Colville saw Churchill grow 'nervous and irritable' as he struggled with the complexities of the deal: 'The President has sent a message to the effect that he can persuade Congress to let us have our fifty destroyers if we give him an assurance, not necessarily for publication, that we will not allow the British Fleet to be scuttled or surrendered, and if we sell or lease to the U.S. naval and air bases in all British possessions from Newfoundland southwards (this rather smacks of Russia's demands on Finland).'

Churchill consulted his War Cabinet. They thought that America was driving a hard bargain. But Churchill called it a 'long step towards coming into the war on our side. To sell Destroyers to a belligerent was certainly not a neutral action . . . the effect of the proposal as a whole on Germany would, he thought, be immense.'

Soon all was prepared. In a prearranged and pre-drafted exchange of letters, Churchill would vaguely reaffirm his desire to fight on, whatever happened to Britain. Then the bases would be transferred. Then the destroyers would be sent. Churchill would present all these messages and exchanges as if each were a separate manifestation of transatlantic goodwill. Roosevelt would present it as a package deal, and one that added to America's security. Roosevelt's version would be a lot nearer the truth. The Washington press corps was told to expect the announcement of a major foreign policy initiative. But there was one more element that he had to put into place. Something that Winston Churchill must not know about until it was too late for him to stop it. Once again the White House summoned the Canadians to a secret meeting.

On his day off Denis Wissler attended Pilot Officer Harry Britton's funeral in the churchyard at Wimbish. A week or so before they had been practising dogfights together. Nobody knew why he had crashed. He'd left the formation after circling RAF Debden and had gone back with something wrong. The rest of them had flown on to Martlesham. When they got home they learned that Britton had stalled in a turn and down he had come. No chance to jump. It could have been any of them. Wissler hated funerals. Looking at the faces around him, it was clear that they all did. The awful slow march with the coffin to the chapel. Death was close enough without having to go through formal introductions like these. Thank God it's over. Quick march straight to the bar, several stiff drinks and in the evening Cambridge and a curry.

The next day was Sunday, 11 August. The pilots sensed that something big was happening. First they changed groups. They were now under the orders of Air Vice-Marshal Sir Keith Park of 11 Group, the defenders of the south-east corner of Britain, the front-line boys. Before they had time to digest this a big battle developed – much bigger than anything they had seen so far. 'B' Flight made Martlesham Heath in thirty minutes flat but arrived too late. 'A' Flight had already shot down three raiders, but Ken Manger DFC had been lost, last seen chasing some bombers fifty miles out to sea. The pilots were subdued. It would have taken some of the joy out of the regular Sunday night party even if it had not already been cancelled by Operations because there were so many raids on the board.

On Monday, 12 August the station photographer came to visit 17 Squadron. The pilots had their pictures taken as a group and each alone with his machine. Denis stood with 'V', 'V for D', as he called it. He always felt a bit silly posing for pictures, owing to his slightly crowded teeth. He did his normal half-smile with the lips closed.

The pilots did not know it, but they were approaching 'Eagle Day', 13 August, the start of an intense Luftwaffe campaign to destroy them and the entire Royal Air Force. Hitler's air chief, Hermann Göring, had a plan: bomb the RAF's bases into ruins; wreck as many planes on the ground as possible; pounce on any British fighters that made it into the air with a superior number of Messerschmitt 109 and 110 fighters. It was a tried and tested approach. It had worked in Poland, Belgium, Holland and France. 'The defence of Southern England will last four days and the Royal Air Force four weeks. We can guarantee invasion for the Führer within a month,' Göring told his commanders.

But the RAF was led by a cagey and skilful man who had spent four years preparing for just this battle against just this enemy. Air Vice-Marshal Hugh Dowding had learnt from the mistakes of Hitler's earlier opponents. He made sure that large numbers of his precious fighters were kept safely out of Göring's reach, either based on distant stations or widely dispersed along the fringes of his airfields, some inside individual blast-proof pens. And Dowding, unlike the defenders of Poland and France, did not have to commit himself to one great do-or-die air battle to try to save an invaded nation. All he had to do was keep Fighter Command in the war. Shooting down German planes would be part of this, but it wasn't his overwhelming priority. If necessary he would avoid combat, especially if the odds did not look very encouraging. He would feed his squadrons into the battle with great care and great economy. This meant that on almost every occasion the British pilots would find themselves seriously outnumbered, but it also meant that Dowding never staked a decisive proportion of his own force on one single action.

Then there was radar and the Fighter Control network that Dowding had conscientiously built, supervised and trained. It bought him time. Keith Park's all-important 11 Group could scramble its fighters and bring them into battle at a moment and a place of their choosing. The radar and Observer Corps plots could also warn RAF bases that bombers were heading their way.

The Luftwaffe first underestimated the value of radar and then overestimated British ingenuity. On the eve of Eagle Day the Luftwaffe hit the southern radar stations hard. Its crews reported them destroyed, but German signals intelligence detected them still working later the same day. They assumed that the British had done what they would have done and protected the important scientific equipment in underground bunkers. So the attacks tailed off and the system did not come under the kind of sustained pressure that Dowding had feared and expected. In fact the radar operations rooms, like the station ops rooms, were overground and vulnerable in the extreme.

Göring's great day of the Eagle did not go as planned. Bombers with fighter escort were sent to a variety of targets, but almost every attack was intercepted. Some got through, doing serious damage to Southampton and RAF Coastal Command airfields along the southern coast. Thirty-nine German planes did not make it back to France. Only fifteen British fighters were lost.

Bob Doe's 234 Squadron was brought forward from Cornwall to Middle Wallop on 14 August. They had come to replace 238 Squadron; 238 had experienced the worst of the previous day's fighting, losing five pilots, and was considered to be in urgent need of a rest. Doe's squadron landed on the grass and parked their Spitfires away from the hangars. That was lucky because the hangars were bombed thirty minutes later. Two of the squadron's pilots never reappeared in Middle Wallop. The rest could only assume that they weren't able to face what was coming.

It wasn't a very encouraging start for the young fliers. But they did not have long to think about the prospect ahead. On 15 August they were scrambled. Not one of them had been in combat before.

Paul Richey, in the Middle Wallop ops room, issued his orders. 'Tango squadron patrol Swanage, Angels 15.' He had seen the new squadron fly in the day before and he didn't give them much of a chance against the Luftwaffe. Richey felt his shirt begin to dampen with sweat, as it had done when he had faced the 109s and 110s. The exultation and terror of it all were still part of him – wheeling and diving, firing and screaming out at the top of his lungs. The raid coming in was laid out on the plotting table, estimated at two hundred plus. Under his breath Richey said a prayer for the boys in 234.

As he began to taxi, Bob Doe was convinced that he was going to die. He already knew that he was the worst pilot in the squadron. He hated flying upside down and he couldn't do aerobatics to save his life. And how could he shoot at a moving target without practising on something more mobile than the North Sea? He could feel his throat tighten and dry.

234 Squadron took off and formed up in line astern of the flight lieutenant in four tight Vics. The inexperienced pilots concentrated hard on keeping in station. They reached 15,000 feet, and as there was nothing to be seen they patrolled, flying up- and down-sun. Doe craned his neck round to look behind. He could see nothing. He was completely blinded by the bright light. This isn't too clever, he thought. He went through what he had been telling himself again. This is not an aeroplane, it's a flying gunsight. Concentrate on that little orange dot in the centre of the screen. Once more they wheeled round from down-sun to up-sun, and then again, around and around, waiting for something to happen.

'Where's Yellow Section?' 'They've disappeared.' 'Christ, look over there!'

Richey heard the conversation with alarm. There must be something he could do. He was about to tell them to climb and then he heard: 'Bandits four o'clock low, hundreds of them!' 'Tallyho!' 'Wake up, Doe, follow me!'

For an instant Doe had been stunned by the sight of more than a hundred aeroplanes with little black crosses on them. He never really understood what happened next. For one thing he became very still and very cool. With involuntary precision, he wheeled after his section leader and found himself right behind a Messerschmitt 110. He fired a first burst from a distance and nothing happened. So much for his accuracy! But the German didn't seem to have noticed. Accelerating hard, he pulled closer, much closer, and opened fire again. In a few seconds the 110 flopped on to its back and dived, trailing smoke, all the way down into the sea. Doe followed it down, staring astonished as it hit the water. Had somebody else shot at it? He looked round. There was no one else there. He said under his breath: 'At least you didn't make a fool of yourself.'

Doe pulled up and away from the water. The sudden movement saved his life. Another Me 110 shot straight past him. Doe heard the echo of its cannon. 'My God, he must have been shooting at me!' Doe accelerated again and with a series of simple, accurate manoeuvres he placed his orange gunsight smack over the two-engined German fighter. Smoke came out of one engine, then flames. Then it, too, fell away and plunged into the English Channel. The sky was empty and so were his magazines. He turned towards the coast.

Back at Middle Wallop, Doe went to bed very early, in a kind of daze. He just lay there and thought. It was obvious that he could fly a bit after all, obvious too that the Spitfire had a combination of speed and quick, responsive control that could put it just where a decent pilot wanted it to be. But Doe was still critical of his own performance. 'I hadn't seen any enemy aircraft until they'd been right on top of me. I hadn't known what was happening in the air around me. I was utterly blind. I should have been shot down by the second plane. It was purely through luck that I wasn't.' How to avoid being shot down, that was the thing. He felt that if he could work out how to do that then he might even become good at this fighter pilot business. He turned over and fell asleep.

The squadron learned some lessons too. It turned out that one of Yellow Section, a New Zealander, had been shot down and killed. The others were missing. After that, the squadron took off as a loose 'gaggle' rather than a fixed formation and positioned themselves wherever they wanted. In Doe's case this was invariably below the leader, looking over him to wherever he thought the danger might come from. He formed a partnership with Sergeant Harker, flying as they had seen the Germans do, abreast of each other and about two hundred yards apart. Doe worked out a plan for seeing something in the air: 'it was not as easy as you would think. You normally saw something about ten to twenty degrees off the point at which you would be looking for it. There's a sort of fraction of movement, which sort of catches your eye. And that's when you first see them.'

Thursday 15 August, Bob Doe's first day in combat, was another good day for Fighter Command. It lost 35 planes but shot down 76 of its assailants. British officials claimed 180. The following day's newspapers trumpeted a great victory. The Luftwaffe also claimed 15 August as a triumph, saying it had shot down 100 British fighters and destroyed many more on the ground. The Germans had hit some Fighter Command bases on that day, especially Hawkinge and Lympne, but damaged only a handful of planes there.

RAF Debden's forward base at Martlesham Heath airfield was bombed too; 17 Squadron's Red and Green sections took off but were still climbing hard when the Germans arrived. Flight Lieutenant Harper was shot down but baled out wounded. Several thousand-pound bombs left the airfield a sorry sight, but it had been repaired by morning.

Bob Doe's system worked. On 16 August he shot down a Messerschmitt 109 and two days later another.

Churchill was elated by the exaggerated accounts of the RAF's initial victories. This was the battle he had hoped for, the moment when the world would see that Hitler could be confronted and beaten. On 16 August he visited the Uxbridge Command Centre of 11 Group to watch the battle unfold. He saw serious-faced WAAFs push wave after wave of German bombers across the plotting table, and he saw each one engaged by one of Keith Park's fighter squadrons. The Prime Minister was impressed by the professionalism of the control system. And he was intensely moved as he imagined the courage of the men sent up to harry and confront the far larger numbers of German raiders. As he was driven away he coined a phrase that would soon ring around the world: 'Never in the field of human conflict has so much been owed by so many to so few.'

The small border town of Ogdensburg is about fifty miles south of Ottawa on the American side of the St Lawrence River. President Roosevelt and Canadian Prime Minister Mackenzie King held a two-day meeting there on 17 and 18 August.

The meeting with King was to seal a two-month-long secret dialogue between the Canadian and American military. It produced a defence pact, the first such agreement between a dominion of the British Empire and a foreign power, and one that London knew nothing about. The pact established a Permanent Joint Defence Board for North America. From now on America and Canada would share some aspects of continental defence, including control of the British fleet if it ever came across the Atlantic.

The Joint Defence Board was designed to give Roosevelt political cover in Washington. He could now say to Congress that he had a mechanism for taking control of the British Navy. Once this was added to Churchill's fudged promise about sending that navy to Canada, then all the intrigues of the past few months began to make sense. Taken together with the promise of British bases, they allowed Roosevelt to make a strong case for sending the destroyers.

This was political manoeuvring of the utmost skill and finesse. The President knew that he faced huge legal and constitutional problems in getting the destroyers to Britain. The Neutrality Act stood in his way. So did another law forbidding the sale of weapons that were needed to defend America. Roosevelt's Attorney-General was jumping through hoops to find gaps in the legislation. It was said that the legality of the whole action hung on the placement of a single comma. Roosevelt feared an argument in Congress. He told his secretary, Grace Tully, that 'Congress is going to raise hell about this but even another day's delay may mean the end of civilization'. The military pact with Canada was part of Roosevelt's strategy to survive the coming storm.

But when the news about the destroyers did break, there was no storm. Calls to the White House were heavily in favour of the deal. Some newspapers complained, as did the America First

Committee, but in Washington the deal was allowed to slip through almost unopposed. Something had changed. Maybe it was all those articles about Hurricanes over the Dover cliffs, or maybe it was a sense that Britain was now fighting hard and had a real chance. For whatever reason, nobody thought it worth making much of a fuss about Roosevelt's constitutional sharp practice. What had seemed politically impossible in May was now acceptable and accepted.

It was, in fact, what Churchill had always predicted. A show of British defiance had led to an American change of heart. But that did not stop the British Prime Minister fuming about the behaviour of the Canadians. He sent King a sharp note which hinted that the Canadian was letting Britain down: 'I am deeply interested in the arrangements you are making for Canada and America's mutual defence. Here again there may be two opinions on some of the points mentioned. Supposing Mr. Hitler cannot invade us and his Air Force begins to blench under the strain all these transactions will be judged in a mood different to that prevailing while the issue still hangs in the balance.'

Churchill was irritated by the sight of Canada slipping into a new relationship with the United States, but King's actions had done him a huge favour. Ogdensburg meant destroyers. For the first time the world would see that America was beginning to throw its resources behind Britain. The fifty old ships were physical proof of it.

King certainly felt he had done well for Canada, for Britain and for the world: 'Morgenthau [US Treasury Secretary] said at dinner to Moffat that he really believed the turn in the tide of the war would date from the Ogdensburg meeting of the President and myself, and the defence agreement reached as a result thereof.'

King was right. The political intrigues in which he'd been involved were as important to Britain's long-term survival as the air battles being fought out in the skies over southern England. Without the RAF, Britain would lose the war or be forced into a humiliating peace. But without long-term American support much the same thing would happen, if not in 1940 then soon thereafter.

Chapter 12

16–20 August

Bess Walder liked to sit on the wall of her house in Kentish Town, North London, and watch the firemen drilling in the school playground next door. Both she and her brother Louis used to go to the school, but it had closed down and had been taken over by the Auxiliary Fire Service. The part-time firemen had old London taxis to carry their equipment, so the playground was now full of black cabs pulling heavily laden trailers. They looked very silly really. She was friendly with one of the firemen, a teenager called Jim. He would come and talk to her when they weren't too busy. He had applied to join the RAF and would be going away in a few weeks.

Bess was fifteen and might be going away herself soon. It was clear that things were getting very serious. First the council workmen had taken down the railings from in front of the house to have them melted down to build battleships or something. Bess's dog Mick loved that – it meant there was nothing to keep him in now. Then her mother had collected together half the pots and pans from the kitchen and given them to the war effort. Next the whole family spent a day filling sandbags and hauling them up against the house. And now at the corner of the street there was a barrage balloon tethered to the ground with a guard of women from the Auxiliary Territorial Service, looking so glamorous. Guarding the factory, she supposed. Shouldn't mention that – Careless Talk Costs Lives! Bess wanted to be a Wren. She had always wanted to go to sea.

The Great War had turned Bess Walder's father into a socialist. He mistrusted politicians and generals and didn't want what he called the 'ruling classes' to drag him and his family into another disaster like that again. But he had also read *Mein Kampf*. He had a translation of it in the house and he had read some of it to his daughter to show her just how wicked and dangerous this man Hitler was. Sometimes in the evening there were noisy political discussions in the sitting-room between her parents and their friends. Bess listened in from the upstairs landing. Some of the visitors didn't really approve of Mr Churchill, but that didn't matter now because, whatever else, he was a fighter and the country had to fight Hitler. He was a dictator and a 'Nazi'. The way they said that word made her think it was the nastiest name you could ever call anyone.

Her parents knew all about bombing too. They had taken a big interest in the Spanish Civil War when the wrong side had won and the German planes had helped them. Now they had burned down Rotterdam and it was said that 25,000 people had died in the flames. Next it would be London. The Walder family obeyed the air-raid instructions. They put tape on all the widows so that they did not shatter and they had rugs ready to seal the doors against gas. For a shelter they had the cellar in the school next door.

Bernard Walder watched his teenage daughter sitting on the school wall flirting with that young fireman. What kind of world had he brought them into? Bess and Louis were precious to him. He had to protect them. For weeks he and his wife Rosina had been talking about evacuation. They hated the thought of parting with their children, but if London became an inferno, if London was to be bombed to smouldering, rat-infested ruins, or occupied by Nazis . . .

The Walders decided to apply for a scheme to send children to

Canada. Rosina Walder was quite upset. Her hand shook on the breakfast teapot when she told them the news. Without thinking, both of them shouted, 'Wonderful, when can we go?' To Bess, Canada meant America and America meant movie studios and movie stars. Louis, only nine and so less practical than his big sister, imagined he might see real cowboys and Indians!

The German High Command believed that it was winning the Battle of Britain. Luftwaffe intelligence calculated that the RAF had begun July with 900 modern fighters. Based on reports from their fighter and bomber crews, the Germans believed that 770 RAF fighters had been destroyed since that date. Intelligence from Britain suggested that only about 300 replacements had been manufactured in that time, leaving total Fighter Command strength on the evening of 16 August at a vulnerable-looking 430. Assuming a normal 70 per cent serviceability rate, this left only about 300 combat-ready fighters to defend the entire British Isles. On 16 August another 92 British fighters were claimed – leaving the RAF, by 17 August, with barely 200 planes left to face the Luftwaffe's 2,200 serviceable fighters and bombers, and so almost beaten.

But German intelligence was badly mistaken. Fighter Command had actually begun July with only 800 fighters but since then the force had steadily grown. Only 300 planes had been lost since 1 July, not the 770 the Germans believed. Meanwhile Lord Beaverbrook's factories had produced over 700 new fighters, not the 300 the Germans believed. And so Fighter Command had 1,100 front-line aircraft on 16 August, with over 800 of them ready for action, and not the 200 the Germans believed. More than 280 other British fighters were safely hidden away in reserve ready for immediate use.

Nevertheless, the Luftwaffe aircrews awoke optimistically on 18 August – the day of their greatest attack yet on the RAF, the day when many hoped they would finish off their enemy for good.

It started quietly enough. In the Debden operations room the last act of the midnight watch had been to guide a section of 257 Squadron, who were patrolling a convoy off Essex, on to a lone Dornier 17 at 7.30 a.m. They pursued the reconnaissance plane for ages as it dived low, but in the end it escaped, to everyone's great disappointment. Then nothing. Edith Heap was just about to go off duty when her headphones suddenly crackled into life: 'Hello Kiwi, hello Kiwi. Hostile 3, 40+, Angels 20, WR 91, 32. Hostile 4, 50+, Angels 15, WR 92, 09. Hostile 5, 50+, Angels 20, WR 94, 16.' Fay Swaine had come in and was helping Edith make up the blocks to the figures she was noting down. Heap still had not got used to how weird and amazing all this was. It was as if, through her headphones, she could hear the Germans taking off in France.

Within half an hour Fighter Command HQ was issuing plots on six separate raids with an estimated total strength of 350. Just before one o'clock Debden's 17 Squadron were scrambled to patrol between Canterbury and Margate.

Lord Willoughby de Broke was 11 Group controller. Debden was one of his seven sector stations. He gave the orders to send the squadrons up and then it was the sector controller's job to lead them to the enemy. De Broke had to think fast, especially when so many raids were coming in at once. Every minute's delay meant 2,000 feet of altitude to the fighters. But if you sent them up in reaction to a spoof raid, then you wasted time and petrol and the boys might be back down refuelling when the real attacks came in. Fighter controlling could be a fine art, a game of feint and parry. But not today – today looked like a day for sledgehammers. Willoughby de Broke soon had every available squadron in the air and vectored towards the incoming raiders.

Not every plane was sent up to fight. Fighter Command's sector stations at Kenley and Biggin Hill sent any unserviceable fighters that could still make it into the air on a 'survival scramble', getting the precious aircraft out of the way of the raids that were making straight for their home bases.

The Hurricanes of 501 Squadron were on their way home from Hawkinge to Gravesend. It was supposed to be their afternoon off. Since there was little prospect of action, Ken 'Hawk-eye' Lee was leading his flight instead of weaving behind the whole squadron on the lookout as he normally did. Today a couple of newcomers were getting some practice at this. 'I had six aircraft in front of me and I was in the box with two aircraft following either side of me and one behind and then the eleventh and twelfth aircraft were doing the weaving.' They were halfway to Gravesend when their controller came on the RT. 'We've got a very big raid coming in, vector 90, patrol Canterbury, Angels 20.'

They turned into the climb, moving up and up and up. They reached 17,000 feet, still climbing and still mentally readjusting between a day off and this unusual midair alert. The weavers never saw a thing. A single German fighter swooped down out of the sun and in one devastating pass picked off both of them. Then down went the man behind Lee and, before he even fully understood that he was under attack, Lee too felt his plane begin to fall apart around him. He'd just become an unknowing and unwilling participant in one of the greatest single air-to-air exploits of the entire war, the work of Oberleutnant Gerhard Schöpfel of the Luftwaffe's fighter Geschwader 26.

> The first thing I knew there was a bang on the back and my leg shot up in the air. A bullet had hit me in the back of the leg. And immediately there was smoke and flames coming out from underneath the main tank.

On Dover's Shakespeare Cliff, Ben Robertson watched a large formation of German bombers pass overhead at about one o'clock.

249

The anti-aircraft batteries opened up with an awesome noise, but they had no noticeable effect on the imposing echelons above. A little later he heard bombs exploding inland.

Denis Wissler was away from 17 Squadron on leave in London. The pilots were tired and they had been taking leave in rotation. He was just settling in to listen to the one o'clock news when the BBC abruptly ceased broadcasting. The Hatfield transmitter had been switched off to prevent the Germans using it as a beacon. Wissler wondered what was going on with mixed feelings. If something big was on he should be with the squadron.

Wissler's comrades reached their Canterbury–Margate patrol line by about 1.30 p.m. without seeing anything of the enemy. About a quarter of an hour later they saw a few Messerschmitt 109s passing overhead, heading back for France, and then suddenly huge numbers of bombers were visible below them just to the south, streaming towards Dover. 'Tally ho,' called Squadron Leader Williams, and dived to the attack. Back in Debden the plotters were listening. But Williams was alone. The rest of the squadron had disappeared.

Their necks craned back and their cameras pointed at the sky, the Americans watched as Williams's solitary Hurricane dived towards some sixty German bombers, now back over Dover on their way home. Another Hurricane fell from the sky in flames – there was no parachute. Above the bombers the weaving vapour trails suggested a battle between fighters. It was hazy and distant and things were difficult to see. But they saw the lone Hurricane tear right into the bomber formation and they saw a Dornier catch fire and limp low over the sea. Then they saw the same Hurricane set upon by three German fighters and dive and twist and roll just above the waves, until eventually they all stood and cheered its escape. And suddenly, like magic, the skies were empty again and the show was over for a while.

Edith Heap heard the fighting over Dover. The atmosphere in the room was strained. She picked up Williams's 'Tally ho' on the loudspeaker and then seconds later heard Blue and Green sections being attacked by fighters. When Williams got back on the RT after his sea-level encounter with the three 109s he was furious; his Hurricane was full of holes and questions were being raised about the conduct of some of the pilots. Still, at least most of them seemed to be safe; only one, a new pilot on his first mission, was missing.

High over northern Kent, Ken Lee's plane was out of control and on fire. The last time Lee had jumped was back in France when he had nearly been killed by his own tailplane. This time he rolled the doomed Hurricane on to its back, pushed the stick forward, undid his belt, took out his stopwatch, pushed himself out, set his stopwatch, and jumped. Something held him back; he had forgotten to unplug the oxygen line. He yanked it free. Now he was in free fall.

Lee had planned what to do next, because only the night before he had heard that the Germans had started shooting pilots escaping by parachute. It might only be a rumour, but he wasn't going to put it to the test. Lee knew that with a parachute a body falls at only about 1,000 feet per minute. From where he was that would mean nearly 17 minutes in the air. But without a parachute a person takes about six seconds to fall a thousand feet. That was the way for him: 10,000 feet in 60 seconds, down and out of danger.

But no one had ever taught the pilots how to free-fall and Lee soon found himself twisting head over heels in horrible disarray whilst he waited for his stopwatch to register a minute. He yanked the ripcord and the parachute opened from between his legs. Luckily they didn't get tangled up in it. He wafted gently down, dizzy but relieved, and landed in a cornfield near Whitstable. Suddenly 'an old chap jumped up from the corn with a military cap on and a gun which apparently he'd captured in Gallipoli himself from the Turks'. Lee's boot was soggy with his own blood. His back had been peppered with fragments of explosive bullet so his shirt was also bloodstained. It was a hot day and they were bound for base so he wasn't in uniform. The old man didn't believe him when he said he was British, and marched him off at gunpoint. Then some soldiers of the London Irish arrived. Their officer accepted Lee's story, shook him warmly by the hand and took him to the local golf club bar for a refresher.

The bombers were getting through all over the place. The important sector stations at Kenley and Biggin Hill were both hit, although Biggin Hill suffered only slight damage and two killed. Kenley was visited at treetop level by a specialist low-flying Luftwaffe unit. It was supposed to be a surprise raid but the Observer Corps spotted them coming. Three of the nine Dorniers fell to the base's anti-aircraft defences but the rest left huge holes all over the airfield. The Luftwaffe followed up with a high-level raid on the same target. A hundred bombs hit Kenley. The station headquarters, the sick bay and three of the four hangars were destroyed. Nine people were killed and four fighters were destroyed on the ground. But within minutes of the attack, despite the many fires and unexploded bombs, the base was able to receive, refuel and rearm fighters stationed there.

Down at the coast hundreds of bombers and dive-bombers overwhelmed the Fleet Air Arm base at Ford and the RAF Coastal Command station at Thorney Island. The radar station at Poling was also hit, as was another naval airbase at Gosport. All along the coastline near the Solent clouds of black smoke drifted from shattered barracks, hangars and fuel tanks.

The Spitfires of Bob Doe's 234 Squadron came to the defence of the South Coast. Today Doe was Red 2 in 'A' Flight. On his plane, marked 'D' for Doe, the ground crew had painted 'A' Flight's insignia, a Spitfire superimposed on a broken swastika. They were scrambled just after lunch and vectored to Portsmouth, where some German fighters were playing shoot-down-the-barrage-balloon and clearing a path for nearby dive-bombers.

Doe picked out a target. The Messerschmitt saw him coming and peeled away. But Doe was developing into a persistent hunter of German warplanes. He flung his fighter into a power dive and followed his prey from 12,000 feet all the way down to sea level somewhere near the Isle of Wight. The German pilot tried to throw him off but Doe was not to be thrown. Slowly and precisely, he manoeuvred his flying gunsight on to its target. It wasn't exactly getting easy – it would never be that – but Doe felt as though he was now truly flying his plane, making it react to his will, rather than trying to keep up with everything that was happening all around him. This game was about concentration and focus and that little orange circle that now had the disintegrating Messerschmitt right in the middle of it.

Deflection shooting – the true fighter pilot's instinct for firing just a little bit ahead of the target, sending the bullet stream to where it will be rather than where it is. To Doe that part seemed to come without thought.

He was out over the sea now, heading for France, and the Germans ahead of him were desperate to get home. He glimpsed a new target, another 109. He was low over the water but taking no evasive action, just relying on his lead to get him to France. He was probably low on fuel, maybe already damaged. Doe gained on him slowly, firing occasional bursts, and then finally caught up. The Messerschmitt slowed and its canopy flew away. Doe drew level with the German about thirty yards away. He was a big man with blond hair and a round face, the first enemy Doe had seen close up. 'His engine had stopped, his hood had come off, his wheels had come down, and the thing was falling to pieces, and I saw him . . . I couldn't, I couldn't shoot him in that condition.'

Doe watched the German plane glide into the sea. This blond man would still need a lot of luck to survive. Doe turned his plane around and emptied his magazines into the water. He would tell the intelligence officer that he had run out of ammunition. It was almost true.

Jock Colville had taken a break from Number 10 to visit his cousin near the coast. He had a ringside seat for the attack on Thorney Island: '"There they are", exclaimed Moyra, and shading our eyes to escape the glare of this August day we saw not far in front of us about twenty machines engaged in a fight. Soon a German bomber came hurtling down with smoke pouring from its tail and we lost sight of it behind the trees . . . Out of the melee came a dive-bomber, hovered like a bird of prey and then sped steeply down on Thorney Island. There were vast explosions as another and then another followed . . .'

But Thorney Island? Gosport? Ford? Fighter Command's senior officers could hardly believe their luck. Why were the Germans hitting places like that? Did they think they were Fighter Command stations? They did, or rather they were not sure. Dowding had a firm policy of sending up planes to drive away each and every reconnaissance flight detected, with the result that Göring's planners had to make do with inferior high-level photographs of British airbases. From over 25,000 feet they all looked much the same. And so, on 18 August, hundreds of planes were sent against peripheral airfields. Above Thorney Island fifteen out of twenty-eight attacking Stukas were damaged or destroyed. Göring was sending high-quality pilots to die over low-quality targets.

Late in the afternoon another big raid loomed. 'Calling Kiwi, hello Kiwi, Hostile 1, 40+, Angels 20, WR 92, 41; Hostile 2, 40+, Angels 20, WR 86, 33; Hostile 3, 50+, Angels 15, WR 96, 37.' Edith Heap was hearing the first radar reports from 11 Group at Uxbridge and frantically filling blocks. Upstairs, the controller was speaking on the phone with Uxbridge, receiving orders to deploy his squadrons. 'Yes, sir. Scramble 85 Squadron. Tell them to patrol Canterbury Angels 20. Bring 257 to readiness.' The plots on the board were moving north from Calais and converging. Outside they could hear the roar of 85 Squadron's planes leaving Debden. The raid continued to move north. 'It's coming our way. Tell 85 to orbit.' When would they turn east? The raid could be aimed at Martlesham, but their own airfield, Debden, was a more likely target for so many planes. 'Bring 17 Squadron to readiness again.' They were waiting at Martlesham now. Then the Germans did turn east. 'It looks like North Weald.' 'Good, we'll have a reception committee. Where are 85? Order them to intercept. Aim them at Chelmsford.' Two squadrons were already harrying the Germans, but they were still going for their target.

Another raid came on to the board, this one heading straight for Kent. But the old northern plot was Debden's main problem. By 5.35 it was over Malden. Three fighter squadrons, including Debden's own 85 Squadron, were now waiting south of Chelmsford, and 257 Squadron was closing from the north. The radio crackled into life as battle was joined over the Essex coastline.

The worst thing was the screaming. Men from the base, men from 85 or 17, men who had been chatting and joking with you a few hours before, you could hear them cry out when they were hit. And if they were caught in a burning cockpit, well, that was just hideous to listen to. Sometimes the WAAFs would shout 'Look out' in reaction to an attack, although they knew that no one could hear them, or 'Please jump, please jump, oh God, please jump' when they heard that one of their planes was going down.

The cloud was getting thicker all the time. 'Tally ho from Wagon leader.' 'They're turning away!' A great cheer rang out. 'Tally ho from 257.' They were waiting for the voices of 85's pilots. 'Red 2's hit.' 'There's a parachute.' 'Townsend's got one.' Peter Townsend. Heap knew him well, the dashing young leader of 85. Dickey Lee was up there too in that mêlée over the sea off Kent.

Total confusion now as they listened to the babble of voices, scarcely able to breathe. 'Marshall's pulling out.' 'What the hell's he doing there? It's his afternoon off.' 'Hemingway's hit.' 'He's going down.' 'Has he got out?' 'Blue leader break off, you haven't enough fuel. Blue leader, turn round. That's an order.' Townsend's voice, angry, concerned too. Blue leader? That was Dickey Lee. What was he doing?

Near Dover Whitelaw Reid came upon a family stretched out in their garden enjoying the late afternoon sun. As planes roared overhead, the adults entertained themselves with the latest novels. Their children scampered around playing bows and arrows. Suddenly there was the shriek of power dives. High in the clouds, a few miles to one side, bursts of gunfire started to crackle. As novels were cast aside, the family took to its heels – but not for shelter. Snatching up pairs of field glasses, the members ran to the highest nearby hill to watch the action from a better viewpoint. After the raid, in which bombs fell indiscriminately about the countryside, an old man leaned over his fence and said to Reid indignantly, 'It's all wrong, this is, the way the Germans are bombing the little churches and the little pubs.' When the American looked suitably shocked, he added with a smile, 'It's all right; they didn't get the pub.'

Reid typed out his story for the *Herald Tribune*. 'Nazi Raids Fail To Upset British. South Coast Villagers Run Not to Shelters but to Hills to see Dogfights.'

At Debden the controller talked the planes home. Half an hour later the fighters were landing in ones and twos. News came through that Paddy Hemingway had been rescued by a boat sent from the Clacton lightship. But Dickey Lee did not come back. He was last seen by Townsend thirty miles north-east of Margate, pursuing three German fighters out to sea. He had not responded to Townsend's orders to return. Edith Heap knew that Lee had been in a funny mood the day before. He'd recently lost a very close friend and was obviously beginning to take this war very personally. Heap had seen that happen before. She could imagine him charging off after those Me 109s, not really caring about being outnumbered or low on fuel. For a while they all hoped, but as night fell and there was still no news the WAAFs and aircrew realised that RAF Debden had lost its best and most-loved pilot.

The intense air battles of 18 August ended with 69 Luftwaffe aircraft destroyed; 27 damaged German planes made it back to France. In all 94 German aircrew were killed, 25 were wounded and 40 were taken prisoner. Their opponent's losses were smaller: 31 British fighter planes were destroyed, 11 RAF pilots died and

19 were wounded. As a result of the bombing the British side lost a further 8 fighters on the ground along with 51 military personnel; 13 British civilians also died, the result of stray or misdirected bombs.

The Battle of Britain was about the survival of RAF Fighter Command. On this day it lost 39 fighters in the air and on the ground. But pilots were more precious than planes. Downed German pilots went to prison camps; downed British ones went to hospital or sometimes straight back into action. On 18 August the RAF lost 11, and in return had either killed or captured 134 of the Luftwaffe's best aircrew.

At the time neither side knew the true state of their enemy. The RAF's exaggerated claim of 140 German kills was broadcast around the world as proof of another great victory. Although shaken by the unexpected RAF resistance, the Luftwaffe High Command, which claimed 147 kills, was still convinced that it was grinding Fighter Command down.

The Fighter Command bases that were worst hit, Kenley and Biggin Hill, managed to patch themselves up and remain in the battle. The fact that only eight fighters were lost on the ground was entirely due to the early warnings that came from radar and the Observer Corps. It did not necessarily feel like this to the exhausted men and women of Fighter Command, as they looked out over their smouldering bases or mourned the loss of another comrade, but the RAF was winning.

   ... Never in the field of human conflict was so much owed
   by so many to so few.

On a sultry 20 August an overcrowded House of Commons nodded and murmured their approval of Churchill's description of the RAF's resistance. In the same speech he perfectly described this new kind of war as 'a conflict of strategy, of organisation, of technical apparatus, of science, mechanics and morale'.

But the political highlight of this speech was an announcement that many in his audience feared might never come: progress with the Americans. Jock Colville described the scene:

> It was less oratory than usual and the point of chief interest to the House was the account of the bargain with America about the lease of air-bases in the West Indies (he did not divulge what we hoped to get as a quid pro quo) . . . The PM ended by comparing Anglo-American co-operation (will it one day be unity?) to the Missouri river and saying 'Let it roll on!' I drove back with him in the car and he sang 'Ole Man River' (out of tune) the whole way back to Downing Street.

Colville misremembered the river. It was the Mississippi that Churchill had been talking and singing about, a happy symbol of Anglo-American co-operation flowing in full flood, flowing on together 'to broader lands and better days'. Colville knew that the bases were part of an elaborate deal that would soon bring the much-requested destroyers across the Atlantic. Last-minute niggles over the precise wording of the notes that would be exchanged held up the full announcement of the deal for another two weeks, but by mid August Churchill knew that his ships were finally coming in, and knew too that a new attitude towards Britain in the United States was largely responsible.

And so it was fitting that he should invite Whitelaw Reid to lunch. Reid could hardly believe it when the message arrived. He put on his best suit and went along to Downing Street, where he found Churchill, his wife and eighteen-year-old daughter, Mary, awaiting him. He got the full treatment, a proper official luncheon with various secretaries and generals popping in and out bringing reports and documents for the great man to read or sign. Maybe it was the champagne, or maybe Churchill's flattering remarks about his mother and the work of the *Herald Tribune*, but the event quite went to the young American's head. He even asked Mary Churchill out on a date, cycling in Hyde Park the following week. She said that she would love to, but he never got back to her about it.

Later he wrote: 'Dear Mr. Churchill, I must send you a brief though belated note of thanks for your delightful luncheon at 10 Downing Street last week. The tribute you paid the work of the *Herald Tribune* was most heartening and should inspire it to even greater heights. I only hope it can succeed in inspiring those destroyers! . . . May your Mississippi roll on until it floods the nation!'

In mid-July Hitler had given his navy two months to complete preparations for the invasion of Britain, code-named Operation Sealion. As the Battle of Britain progressed, Hitler kept postponing a decision about it. Throughout this time he was receiving contradictory advice and giving contradictory orders. His army High Command, still heady with the confidence of repeated victory, kept talking of Sealion as a kind of glorified river crossing. But Hitler's admirals knew that the Channel wasn't a river – or, if it was, then it was a particularly treacherous one with savage tides and sandbanks, sudden bad weather and dozens of formidable British warships sailing upon it. No place for the collection of two thousand river barges, pleasure craft, tugs and lightly armed trawlers that was being assembled in the Channel ports.

Even as they gathered their forces on the coast, pulling in ships from all over western Europe and severely dislocating the economy of the Rhineland, the German Navy advised their Führer that it was a very dangerous scheme. Without total air superiority it would be insane; with total air superiority there was a serious risk while the Royal Navy had anything like a half-decent force still afloat. Friedrich-Karl von Plehwe, one of the naval planners, felt that 'The intervention of the British fleet was almost too terrible to contemplate.'

Hitler told some of his confidants that he planned to invade and told others that it was all a big political bluff meant to intimidate the British into surrender. Churchill always judged that there was no significant invasion threat in the summer of 1940, or at least he did in private. In fact he was sufficiently confident on 23 August to order a substantial armoured force to leave Britain to reinforce the British Army in Egypt.

The senior naval officers in the Mediterranean had opposed the attack on the French to a man, and its consequences for them were serious. They were now utterly isolated, with no friendly base between Gibraltar and Alexandria except for Malta. The immediate priority was to attempt to reinforce Malta, which might be attacked at any moment from Libya or Sicily. The island was being bombed, and its only air defence was three obsolete Gloucester Gladiator biplanes that had been assembled from kits found abandoned there and immediately christened 'Faith', 'Hope' and 'Charity'. The island was needed as a base for offensive operations by submarines and aircraft. If convoys could not be kept running to supply Malta with food and munitions the islanders would starve. Without Malta the Mediterranean would truly become what the Italians already called it, '*Mare nostrum*'.

After the Oran operation Force H sailed into the Mediterranean on a three-day manoeuvre intended to divert Italian attention away from a convoy evacuating women and children from Malta. Another mission in early August flew a squadron of Hurricanes to Malta while diversionary attacks were launched on Italian airfields. On both occasions the ships were bombed from altitude. The defending Skuas could fly only up to 13,000 feet and the Italians were operating much higher. Again and again ships were straddled by towering plumes of spray as bombs fell all around them. The old and slow ships were particularly vulnerable. A near-miss shaved the side of HMS *Resolution* and shrapnel penetrated all four screens of one of the anti-aircraft guns and hit the deck-head behind the crew. Sam Patience thought the ship was going over. But it didn't. They seemed to be leading a charmed life.

The admirals thought so too. If such a ship were hit it was likely to sink quickly in deep water with the loss of a thousand lives. Admiral Cunningham warned the Admiralty that if he engaged the Italians 'there is considerable risk of losing an old battleship'. Cunningham asked for one or two more ships with equal range to their Italian rivals and an aircraft carrier with some effective modern fighters on board. He was outnumbered 7 heavy cruisers to none, 12 light cruisers to 9, 59 destroyers to 25 and 98 submarines to 24.

At the end of August Cunningham was given his reinforcements, the new armoured carrier *Illustrious*, the modernised battleship *Valiant* and the anti-aircraft cruisers *Coventry* and *Calcutta*. *Illustrious*, *Valiant* and *Coventry* had radar. After the usual diversionary attacks and feints, Malta was reprovisioned under heavy bombing and Cunningham's reinforcements got through. *Resolution* was considered too slow to risk and stayed put in Gibraltar harbour.

Chapter 13

20 August–4 September

On Ground Subjects: Results above average, and good all round.

On flying: Above average, keen and quick to learn. Should make a good squadron pilot.

On qualities as officer: Keen on his job, but is young in ways and appearance. Will be useful with more experience.

Confidential assessment of Pilot Officer Denis Heathcote Wissler

Denis Wissler was recalled early from leave on 19 August. He flew back in a Hurricane that had been down in London for an inspection, dodging the thick cloud that was giving everyone at Debden a much-needed respite. His own plane was not going to be ready until the morning, so he caught up with the gossip in the mess. The whisper was that faced with some two hundred enemy aircraft the day before, some of 17 Squadron's pilots had not hung around to fight. One in particular had been blamed and was to be posted.

Wissler fell asleep in a comfortable bed for once, thinking about courage. To be posted – imagine! Even the word had a dreadful ring of finality and failure about it. No good, washed up, yellow. The poor bastard. It sounded like a kind of death sentence: the worst thing that could happen, short of being killed or badly burned. Or maybe it was even worse than that. But, Jesus, you could understand why people might decide to keep away from trouble now and again. Perhaps pretend to hear a bit of engine trouble, or maybe even think they did hear it, or else shoot off all their ammo into the air and then head home. Understand it, yes, but not do it, please not ever do it.

As Wissler flew down to Tangmere the next day it was still cloudy, and when he could he kept nervously looking around for enemy planes. He wouldn't stand much chance on his own. At least there was one thing to be said for being over the coast: finding the place wasn't difficult; there it was, nestling between the South Downs and the sea. You could easily see the great cross of the runways despite the fake hedges that had been painted on to the airfield to confuse enemy bomb-aimers. As he closed, Wissler began to pick out details. The last time he had flown into Tangmere was in June, returning from France. Then, despite the freshly camouflaged buildings, it had seemed like a safe haven from the war. Now it was in the front line. The hangars were obliterated, just piles of bricks and twisted girders, looking like some of the French ones had. He remembered the daily pasting they had taken from the bombers at Lille. As he landed, he expected to have to dodge bomb craters, and he did, but he found that they had all been freshly filled with rubble.

As he was helped out of the cockpit, Wissler congratulated the ground crew on the repairs. They explained that the place had been pounded by Stukas. All four hangars had been hit and all the buildings around the square, including the officers' mess, the workshops, stores, sick quarters and pumping station. But the telephone lines had been repaired, new runways defined on the grass, and in all essentials the place was still working. He found the other pilots in cheerful mood at dispersal, and 'B' Flight's green wooden hut with glass windows was a massive improvement on the old shack at Debden. But it was true that one of 'A' Flight's officers had left in disgrace.

There were other anxieties too. On 18 August 'Taffy' Griffiths had been forced down at Manston, the much-bombed forward base right on the coast near Ramsgate. It looked to be in a terrible state, and whilst he was waiting around his Hurricane had been destroyed in a strafing attack. If all the bases got that kind of treatment, then pretty soon there wouldn't be anywhere much for Fighter Command to fly from.

The pilots had arranged a surprise for their loquacious Austrian comrade, Count Czernin. They all lined up outside the dispersal hut and awarded him a specially engraved silver medal, the 'line-shooter's medal', in recognition of his services to self-glorification.

Wednesday, 21 August was still cloudy and activity was limited to chasing intruders. Wissler's Blue Section only managed to glimpse one enemy aircraft flitting between clouds, but Green and Yellow sections were luckier and each of them succeeded in bringing down a bomber. Birdy, now a section leader flying Green 1, saw his Junkers 88 force-land on the very tip of Selsey Bill. When they returned, his section went off in one of the squadron cars to take a look at it. He came back in triumph bearing the tailplane and a machinegun as souvenirs, but he was furious that an intelligence officer had refused to let him see the German pilot in Chichester prison. He had wanted to make him surrender his pistol. The others laughed and pointed out that German pilots were probably not allowed to take their own firearms inside His Majesty's prisons. Shrugging off their teasing, Birdy proudly nailed the tailplane to the 'B' Flight dispersal hut. Next day he had an emblem painted on his cockpit door – three vengeful swords flying towards an alarmed-looking eagle balanced on a swastika.

They were all tired but on the whole morale was still pretty good. Sometimes, when you were a bit tetchy, it was easy to see other people's mistakes or accidents as signs that they were not whole-heartedly committed to the fight. You had to avoid that thought, like you avoided mentioning the dead. They all believed in this war, that was clear, and they all desperately wanted to see Hitler beaten. But most of them were also sustained by the simple determination not to be thought of by the others, or by themselves, as cowards. Wissler was increasingly conscious that he hadn't shot down as many planes as some of them. There was a lot of luck involved in that. They could think him a poor shot if they must, but they would never call him a coward.

So much, so many, so few. The air campaign over southern England in August 1940 was one of the most decisive military engagements in history. On it rested the fate of Europe, if not the world. If the Luftwaffe could grind the RAF down, then Britain would be defenceless against bombing, her factories, her cities and her navy exposed to Hitler's will. Without Fighter Command Britain might starve, might be invaded or might suffer a collapse of its resolution to carry on the war.

And yet compared to any other battle of equal importance the numbers engaged were minute. On 21 August Fighter Command had 1,377 fighter pilots at its disposal. On a particularly tough day perhaps 15 or 20 would be killed and about the same number wounded. Add in the ground crew and even the civilians, and total daily casualties would rarely rise above 150.

This did not mean it was easy. For everyone employed at the increasingly battered fighter stations, the last ten days of August were horribly difficult. The Germans had eventually worked out which were the key bases. The raids came in more often and had larger numbers of fighters guarding them. And hit-and-run solo attackers suddenly appeared overhead, giving only seconds to run for a shelter or pull on a tin hat. And the pilots were tired, shatteringly tired after two weeks of 'readiness' and three, four or five scrambles a day.

But Dowding's system kept on working because behind 'the

few' stood the many. Fighter Command was at the apex of a giant pyramid of supply, maintenance and repair that stretched back across the whole of the country and sucked tens of thousands of civilians into the Battle of Britain.

Some of the least-glamorous, but by no means the least-important, members of the system were the men who patched up the phone lines. A great part of the Luftwaffe's success in France had been their ability to disrupt their enemy's communications. Nobody knew what anyone else was doing; fuel and ammunition were not ordered or did not get through. Units acted on their own, in the dark. In these circumstances their conviction and will to fight quickly seeped away.

Dowding had gone to great lengths to ensure that this fate would not engulf Fighter Command. This was what radar, Pip Squeak, IFF and all the other gadgetry was all about. And there was the Defence Teleprinter Network, installed just before the war. Teleprinter lines relayed combat reports, intelligence reports, requirements for replacements of pilots and aircraft and damage assessments. Each of Dowding's main sector stations depended on a huge network of buried telephone and teleprinter lines. Field repair was the responsibility of the Post Office War Group, headed by Mr H. R. Harbottle. Harbottle directed the efforts of the Defence Telecommunications Control organisation with its regional branches across the country. If the German attacks on the sector stations were to be successful they had to smash up the cables faster than Harbottle's men could repair or reroute them.

A quick report on the 18 August raid on Kenley recommended that the operations room should be moved from the station. It was soon agreed that this would be a good idea for all sector operations rooms. Laying miles of new telephone cables to destinations away from the bases placed further stress on the engineers. By late August, the daily survival of Denis Wissler and the rest of Dowding's pilots depended on the ability or willingness of Harbottle's engineers to lay and repair telephone lines whilst being bombed. They did not let him down despite seven-day weeks and twenty-hour days.

And luckily the weather helped: 21 August was the third successive day of poor flying conditions. The only plots on the board for Paul Richey, controller at Middle Wallop, were small raids and reconnaissance flights. At first Fighter Command had given strict instructions to shoot down all reconnaissance planes. Now they were a little more anxious about pilot losses and had forbidden chases out to sea. Nevertheless, Richey knew how important it was that the German decision-makers should be starved of accurate intelligence, and the plane that had been reported near Winchester looked like a suitable target. 'Who's at readiness in 234?' he asked. 'Bob Doe. The new Squadron Leader's asked to go up with him.' 'Good, Doe'll do. Phone through and tell them to scramble.'

Bob Doe was flying with a new squadron leader called O'Brien to show him the ropes. Already, after only a week in action, Doe was one of the squadron's leading pilots. Paul Richey vectored them towards the interloper and eventually they spotted him, a lone Junkers 88, dodging in and out of clouds. Doe dived in and fired a quick burst at the bomber and the squadron leader followed suit. Neither appeared to have any effect and so Doe curved back in and settled behind the bomber, creeping up on it slowly. The Germans fired back, but not for long. With the rear gunner silenced, Doe pulled even closer and launched a savage attack, filling the bomber with his bullets, practically emptying his magazines into it. It sank slowly away and came down in a field not far from Middle Wallop.

'Did you get him, sir?' the ground crew chorused as they helped Doe from the plane. One of them also pointed out that a bullet had gone through the main spar of Doe's Spitfire, which would need repair. 'Yes, I got him,' answered Doe. 'That's five, sir! Two Me 110s, two Me 109s and . . . what was this one?' 'A Ju 88.'

As usual after the stress of combat Doe was tired, but Squadron Leader O'Brien was impressed, excited and keen. 'Let's go and take a look at it, shall we? I've got a car.' Doe agreed.

As a child Doe had read a lot of W. E. Johns's stories about Biggles, the heroic pilot. He remembered that when you got five kills, you became an ace. He couldn't say anything to anyone, but he was thinking, Good God, I'm an ace. It would be particularly satisfying to see the wreckage of this plane.

When they found the Ju 88 near the village of King's Somborne, it was surrounded by Local Defence Volunteers, keeping away inquisitive children out souvenir-hunting. One old soldier was as excited as a child himself. With ghoulish delight he told the pilots, 'You didn't half sort this lot out. There must be five bullet holes in every helmet. Come and take a look.' Doe was sickened by the consequences of his moment of triumph in the sky. What had felt like a victory, the sum of all his skill and daring, now seemed more like a kind of execution. An execution with eight machineguns. Biggles hadn't turned people into a bloody mess like this. He turned away. He would not come sightseeing again.

Even so, later that evening Doe felt the need to mark his secret self-satisfaction. Only a week or so before he had been the worst pilot in the squadron. Now, before he turned in for the night, sitting on his own in the mess, he had a private celebration. Slowly, and with relish, he drank a pint of beer.

In the morning, he had to fly his damaged Spitfire to the Supermarine repair depot at Hamble, near Southampton. The ground crew were standing around waiting for him to appear. Something was different. And then he saw what. They had painted a neat little row of five swastikas along the side of the aeroplane. He smiled. Somebody had noticed. They were a wonderful lot, so efficient and so keen. A great warmth surged through him as he realised that his crew were taking pride in what he was doing – drawing strength from him. Him! But it seemed less extraordinary all the time.

There was thick cloud and a squally wind. Not much would be

happening today. Doe was not disturbed when told that the repair would take about five hours – would he like to wait? The foreman invited Doe to his home for some lunch. He and his wife were in their forties and very chatty, and it turned out that the foreman's wife had been watching the air fighting from her garden. He was the first pilot she had ever met. 'She was saying how grateful they were and that they could see this and that going on above them. And it was the first time it struck me that people could see what was happening in the air. It hadn't entered my head that we were doing something that ordinary people could see and admire.'

Courage and communication. Radar, rubble and repairs. Another layer of the Fighter Command support pyramid was made up by Lord Beaverbrook's aircraft repair operation. Thirty-five per cent of all the aircraft issued to pilots during the Battle of Britain were repaired rather than newly built. Excluding the many small repairs like Bob Doe's in Southampton, 61 per cent of all Fighter Command's damaged planes were patched up and returned to service. The remaining 39 per cent of total wrecks were carefully dismantled and used for parts. Nothing recoverable was wasted. No air force at war had ever been supported with this kind of mechanical tenacity or ingenuity.

The central idea was that repairs should not be carried out by the aircraft manufacturers, who would be left to concentrate on making new aircraft. Instead motor-car manufacturers transferred their skills to aeroplanes, with the chief repair centre at the Morris car works at Cowley near Oxford. It was called No. 1 CRU (Civilian Repair Unit).

The RAF sent accident officers to every crash site to see whether planes were repairable. Under their command were maintenance units of which the principal was No. 50 MU, also based at Cowley. It had ten gangs in converted, canvas-topped, three-ton trucks. Each truck was a mobile workshop with tools of every sort and a gantry for smaller lifting jobs like the removal of engines. If a bigger lifting job was needed, a Coles crane would accompany the truck. Back at Cowley planes would be repaired or dismantled and the parts sent to the appropriate factory. From a strength of 800 in May the workforce of No.1 CRU had expanded to 1,200 by August. They repaired 150 seriously damaged fighters between mid-July and mid-October.

Near one of the Morris Motors blocks, they built a set of flight sheds and a small grass airfield on what had been allotments and a scrapheap. Less seriously damaged planes would fly in and out for the 'out-patients' service.

As Oxford buzzed with the energy of repair and cannibalisation, the other side of Lord Beaverbrook's industrial empire was producing new planes in impressive numbers: 163 Spitfires were made in August, a new record, and 251 Hurricanes.

On the day that he flew to the repair depot, Bob Doe went out for the only time that summer. The weather was thoroughly bad and they were stood down at about six in the evening. They were not a wealthy squadron, and they only had one car between them. Six of them piled in and went to look for a local pub. After a while they found a quaint thatched place with about a dozen farmers and labourers. The pilots went in and bought a round of beer without attracting much apparent attention, and naturally enough started talking about what was happening in the air. As they talked they began to sense that the pub was getting quieter, and gradually the locals began to edge closer and gather round. Then they began to ask questions. They knew nothing about vapour trails, and the pilots had to explain such things to them. They told the locals a bit about the fighting and what they were doing there. At closing time the landlord said, 'Thanks for coming, lads. I know we'll win.'

Iain Nethercott was on a torpedo course at HMS *St Vincent* at Gosport on the South Coast. The trainee torpedo-men, Fleet Air Arm gunners and signalmen had all been issued with Canadian Ross rifles and two hundred rounds, webbing and a bayonet. They were supposed to keep their rifles with them at all times in case of sudden alarm: 'when you were at classes you used to pile all these bloody rifles in the corner while you was studying the guts of a torpedo and the electrics'. When the courses finished for the day about six o'clock, they were bussed to a nearby aerodrome to guard it overnight against enemy landings.

In those warm sunlit summer evenings they would roll through the beautiful Hampshire countryside and see the farm labourers and tradesmen of the village mustering on their village greens with their LDV armbands, ready to take up their positions with shotguns and pikes to defend their villages during the night. They would cheer the old boys as they drove past, none of them knowing what the night would bring. 'It was very moving actually seeing them like that, you know. You felt that it was something worth fighting for then, seeing all these sort of people.'

At the airfield they manned slit trenches. Obstacles had been placed on the runways to deter German glider troops, and about an hour before dawn working parties cleared these away so the airfield could be used again. This went on until one night the Germans bombed the airfield. They were also hitting nearby Portsmouth. A raid by fifty bombers on 24 August took the RAF by surprise. Iain Nethercott was on the roof: 'amongst the slates and that, they'd built me a sandbag enclosure for a twin Lewis gun'. Hit by anti-aircraft fire, the bombers jettisoned their load all over the town. A hundred were killed, the worst British civilian casualties of the war so far.

On Sunday, 25 August the cloud closed in and 17 Squadron's pilots played cards in the Tangmere dispersal hut on which was proudly displayed the tailplane of Birdy's Ju 88. They were at readiness or at fifteen minutes' all day long. Then another large raid was detected heading towards Portsmouth; 152 Squadron from Middle Wallop, 609 from Warmwell and 17 from Tangmere were scrambled. An estimated 230 enemy aircraft were to be countered by three separate attacks, with 12 aircraft in each.

A mechanic had the engine started and another was holding out his parachute as Denis Wissler jumped up on to 'V' and stuck his arms through the harness. He eased into the Hurricane's cockpit. Engine oil, dope and hot leather – always the same smell. Pull the straps tight. All OK. The mechanic can't hear so you give him a thumbs-up and he slams the side door shut. Pull the straps tighter still. Helmet on. Plug in RT lead. Engine running OK. 'Chocks away, boys, see you later.' They can't hear so you wave. Open the throttle and away towards the current take-off position, trying to avoid the rough bits and the rubble. All line up. There goes the leader. Today we all follow Alf Bayne. Throttle open wide. The rush of gathering energy and away with a glance down at the ruins of Tangmere. Three minutes – not bad. 'Foxfire leader to control. We're in the air, where to?' 'Intercept 200+ Weymouth, Foxfire leader. Angels 19. Vector 260.'

17 Squadron is still climbing when they see the Germans above them over Portland Bill. A swarm of black specks. Flight Lieutenant Bayne is chattering away over the RT as usual. Swallow hard, time to be brave. Bayne puts Blue Section in line astern and leads them in a No. 1 attack, picking out a Messerchmitt 110 and attacking from below. Denis Wissler, flying Blue 2, sees the Messerchmitt whip up into a half-arsed kind of a stall turn right in front of him. Jesus, does this man want to die? Wissler presses with his right thumb and catches the German fighter with a long

burst straight in its double cockpit. For a second he's transfixed by the sight. The big two-engined plane seems to hang in the air, almost still, just like the top of a proper stall turn. That was one of the most graceful of all the aerobatic manoeuvres. You just hold it there, standing on its tail, and then kick the rudder over into a nice elegant dive away to one side. But not this fellow.

The Me 110 suddenly changed from slow motion, pitching forward into a disordered spinning dive straight down into the sea. No parachutes – no point looking. Then, out of the corner of his eye, Wissler saw Alf Bayne's plane with smoke trailing from the engine, spiralling down in the same direction. 'Mayday, Mayday, Blue 2 to Dervish control, Blue 1 down.' He looked. Yes, a parachute. 'Alf's OK.'

Ahead, some other Me 110s had formed a wide defensive circle. Wissler had seen this before and had worked out how to deal with it. He forced a plane out of the circle with a sharp burst from inside, caught it again with another and watched it go down too. Again he was aware of the RT: 'Red 1's gone. His wing's shot off. Oh God.' That was the squadron leader. Sounded like one head-on attack too many. Against cannon-firing fighters like these. Madness. 'Got him, got him, got him.' That was Pittman's voice, excited. At Debden Pitters had been Wissler's room-mate and neither of them had had much luck so far. Today was going to be a good day for them both. 'Look out behind you Blue 2!' Christ, that was Birdy! Concentrate. Wissler swerved violently as the Me 109 that had been moving on to his tail overshot and was then hunted down in its turn by Bird-Wilson. This was a real dogfight. The turn took him away into open sky. He was out of ammunition and he turned home for Tangmere, elated.

Bayne was all right but the squadron leader was dead. The target of the raid had been RAF Warmwell in Dorset, and none of the three British attacks had penetrated the two-hundred-strong fighter escort. Two hangars were destroyed, the sick quarters were burned out, and nine unexploded bombs had to be marked with flags on the grass airfield. Several cables were cut, knocking out the telephones and teleprinters, but 609 Squadron, whose home it was, still managed to land having claimed six of the German fighters themselves. Mr Harbottle's engineers had the phones working again by noon the next day.

But RAF Manston was now beyond help. The horribly exposed forward base near Ramsgate was temporarily abandoned on 25 August. After weeks of daily bombardment hardly any buildings were left standing, the field was littered with unexploded bombs, and all communications with 11 Group had been cut. It was only a small station, but its fate was a warning about what could happen to the rest of Fighter Command.

Edith Heap and Winifred Butler had twenty-four hours' leave, and they decided to spend a day in Cambridge. When they came off watch at four in the morning they went home and, instead of going to bed, scrubbed and polished the house until their faces were reflected in the floorboards. When it was passed fit by the sergeant they climbed into the baby Jaguar and set off, stopping in a wood to change out of uniform. The lovely university town was quiet and peaceful and the white stone of King's College Chapel shone against a clear blue sky. Sandbags had been piled up around the walls and there were wooden boards where the precious stained-glass windows had been.

The two WAAFs enjoyed being ordinary for a day. They had lunch in the King's Parade restaurant opposite King's. They went on to Eden Lilly, buying clothes, shoes, the latest Bing Crosby for Edith's wind-up gramophone player. Then to Fitzbilly's for cakes by the river. They overheard someone saying that the college dons were making a serious attempt to drink the wine cellars dry before the Germans got there. They laughed.

It was inconceivable that storm troopers might march down King's Parade.

They did not bother to change back into uniform since they had the guardroom well trained by now. But as they approached Debden in the darkness it was clear that something was wrong. An acrid smell was drifting on the breeze and smoke was rising. The road to the married quarters was blocked by craters and rubble. They drove by the MT sheds and found them wrecked, their beautiful lorries and tractors covered in brick dust and crumpled under fallen girders. As Heap manoeuvred the baby Jaguar through the rubble, people were running around everywhere, digging out equipment and marking unexploded bombs. The sergeants' mess was in ruins and the equipment section had gone the same way as the MT sheds. There was no mains water or electricity and the NAAFI canteen had also been hit. Heap tried to make a joke about the hated baked bean stores being blown up but neither of them laughed very much.

Bill, their sergeant, was certainly not amused. She had been waiting in the guardroom for them to return, since they no longer had a house. Their attire gave her a good excuse to release some pent-up tension. But the sergeant had a heart of gold and did not have it in her to put them on a charge. Instead she took them round to her house, where they all slept on the floor.

Next day they went to salvage what they could from the wreckage. Heap found the picture that had hung over her bed with a piece of shrapnel stuck in it. She realised how lucky it had been that she had not stayed at home to sleep off the working night. Five of the base personnel had not been so fortunate.

Behind it all was a simmering row. A squadron from 12 Group should have been guarding Debden while its own squadrons were elsewhere. But it had never turned up. Keith Park, in charge of 11 Group, was furious and blamed Trafford Leigh-Mallory, his opposite number in the more northern 12 Group. The two men had been squabbling about tactics for a while now, with Park generally winning Dowding's support.

The problem was that the Germans were now sending over a variety of different kinds of raid: hit-and-runs, thirty or forty bombers with mass fighter escort, like the one in which Denis Wissler had been tangled on 25 August, and sometimes large formations consisting only of fighters. Fighter Command's radar and observer plots were becoming confused. A new order went out asking squadrons to report the size and direction of enemy forces before they engaged, so as to help with the assessment of priorities.

Around 4 p.m. on 26 August, 17 Squadron was brought to readiness again and scrambled from Tangmere. As Denis Wissler took off, a Heinkel 111 crossed the airfield towards the coast at about 1,500 feet. Alf Bayne, rescued from the sea only the previous day, put Blue Section in line astern and they all roared after it. To their disappointment they saw that it was already being attacked by Spitfires and its undercarriage was down. They each gave it a burst anyway and watched it turn back towards land and dive slowly towards Ford aerodrome, where it crashed. Having landed, they found themselves spectators at the outcome of another fight. A Spitfire and a Hurricane landed on their bellies. The Spitfire pilot was badly wounded. Way above them there was a terrific battle going on very high up. Three of 43 Squadron had taken to their parachutes. They had been trying to stop another raid on Portsmouth.

Below the action at nearby Gosport, Iain Nethercott was on anti-aircraft duty when he saw a damaged German bomber coming low across the harbour quite close to the Gosport ferry. 'All I could do was cock me gun up and let fly both Lewis guns because he was about 200 foot above me. He shot straight across our gates and into this recreation field with his bombs. Right on top of these slit trenches, and cartwheeled right across this field, but the bombs had hit the trenches and practically everyone in them, all my mates, were all dead.'

Nethercott and the other survivors set about gathering up the bodies. Carnage seemed to follow him around. At sea, on shore, there always seemed to be some fresh horror with him in the middle of it:

> One of them, a friend of mine, he'd been at Dunkirk with me and his mum was coming down for the funeral, because they had a proper funeral up at Gosport, and they had these coffins and of course there wasn't enough of them to put in the coffins you know, there was all little bits of flesh here and there and gobbets of this, that and the other. And of course the blokes who'd done this job before, they was just chucking half bricks in. So you said to them at the funeral all solemn like, how sad it was about your son and all that, but all they were praying over was a few bloody half bricks . . . But it all looked the same once you'd screwed them down and put a Union Jack on it.

At eight o'clock on the morning of 31 August Edith Heap and Winifred Butler were just going on duty, sauntering across the parade ground a few yards behind the CO, Wing Commander Fuller-Good, when the sirens went again. In front of them the CO started to run and the two WAAFs sprinted after him to make the ops room just before the great steel door swung shut, as they knew it would at the start of a raid. They shot through the door just as Ops B was issuing the station attack alarm: 'This is operations. This is operations. Air raid warning. Enemy attack imminent. All station personnel proceed to shelters immediately.' They went down to the floor. 'Tin hats everyone,' said the controller. Heap said to Fay Swaine, 'OK, I'll take it,' but with no way of leaving the building Fay and Pam stayed on to label blocks.

Outside, the planes of 601 Squadron were taking off between falling bombs. Some were tipping into the fresh bomb craters. 601 had been withdrawn to Debden for a rest after a severe bombing at Tangmere. Some rest. This raid had taken them completely by surprise. The noise was terrible. The Bofors guns and antiquated three-inch anti-aircraft batteries that guarded Debden were pounding the sky. Most of the women continued to plot, trying to keep up with information that was suddenly fast-moving and confused. One was being held by the sergeant, weeping silently. Another was just sitting there, head bowed, hugging herself with clenched fists. Then, very soon, the sound faded away.

When Heap came off duty the aerodrome was still smoking. The airmen's mess was a pile of rubble. Next to one trench was a blanket that clearly covered bodies. She was warned not to look inside the slit trench where four fellow WAAFs had been sheltering. It had taken a direct hit. Some of the telephone cables had been severed, but down in the craters engineers were already working on them. Within minutes gangs of airmen were filling the bomb craters with rubble. 'Here we go again,' one of them said. A maintenance unit arrived to take away several planes that had been caught on the ground and damaged. Others were being repaired where they stood. Where did these people find the energy to keep doing this time and time again? Heap thought that it was just sheer bloody-mindedness:

> We were just not going to let them get away with it. We were just not going to let them win, it was as simple as that. It was chaotic but it got cleaned up. I've never known determination like it. I don't think there ever has been, before or since.

Now the place was seething with people hard at work, putting things right. People were going round flagging unexploded bombs. 'Hey! Be careful what you're doing! That's my car,' shouted Heap. There was a man putting a cordon around her car. 'You better not touch it, there's a UXB right behind it.'

Later, they tried to laugh off the shock on the grass outside the married quarters. A girl from Scotland, inevitably known as Scottie, was explaining that she had been in the bath when the siren went. There was no time to get out, let alone get dressed. 'So I pulled the plug so that I wouldn't drown if I was hit and injured and then I put my tin hat on and I just sat there. And thank God the door wasn't blown off its hinges or I would have been a sight.' They collapsed in giggles.

The men who ran the RAF had been very worried about how the WAAFs would behave once the bombing started. Now those who had been sceptical had to eat their words. The women were frightened. Who wasn't? But nearly all of them got on with the job, just like the men were doing. Some couldn't take it, but neither could a few of the men. They were no different really, all equally brave, all equally scared, all equally determined to keep their base and their pilots in the war.

Denis Wissler was one of them and he was in action again whilst Debden was being bombed. On the last of four patrols they intercepted a raid by thirty Dornier 17s and about the same number of Messerschmitt 109s. Wissler saw Alf Bayne get one. He got on the tail of an Me 109 and fired several bursts at three hundred yards with no effect at all. Then he found a German had got behind him and broke away. He succeeded in throwing him off in a steep turn but not before the German put a cannon shell right through his wing. Sergeant Steward was shot down but baled out safely. His was one of thirty-nine RAF fighters brought down that day. Fourteen pilots were killed.

Saturday, 31 August had been a good day for the Luftwaffe, who hit Debden and other sector airfields very hard. Biggin Hill's operations room had to be moved out to the basement of a nearby village shop but, as at Debden, the base was kept open, the cables were fixed, the craters filled. The RAF was still in the war, still meeting the raiders, still maintaining its front-line strength. But only just. The next day Debden's 85 Squadron was caught in the air by a large fighter sweep. Four planes were lost – Booth jumped with his parachute on fire, Ellis was never found, Patrick Woods-Scawen was killed and Gus Gowers wounded. More experienced men out of action, more new arrivals to be shepherded and trained on the job.

Both 85 and Denis Wissler's 17 Squadron flew back to Debden

on 2 September to find that the airfield had been bombed again earlier in the day. An emergency operations room was to be set up in a less conspicuous spot – a chalkpit just outside Saffron Walden. On 3 September 17 Squadron was airborne at 10.12 a.m. and flying down towards the Thames Estuary where they were guided on to a formation of some forty Dornier 215s with two groups of about thirty Messerschmitt 110s above them as escorts.

Wissler was following Alf Bayne as Blue 2, and together they got on the tail of a 110. Firing simultaneously, the pilots saw both of its engines burst into flames as the Messerschmitt dived straight into the ground somewhere near Colchester. Another two Germans killed, another 'half' added to Wissler's account.

Within seconds, Blue Section found another victim, a Dornier 215 bomber. Wissler and Bayne emptied their magazines into it and watched the port engine explode and bits fall off the fuselage. David Leary, who had been covering their rear, swooped in to finish the bomber off, and they all saw it crash in a field just north of the River Crouch. Two descending parachutes signalled the survival of half the bomber's crew.

The Dornier's rear gunner had managed to plant a bullet in Wissler's radiator and glycol was beginning to spray all over the front of his cockpit. He wheeled off and headed for home. A few miles short of Debden and Hurricane 'V' began to experience serious engine trouble, and so Wissler decided to land in the grassy meadow at the satellite field at Castle Camps. Determined to get back in the action as soon as possible, he borrowed a Hurricane from 111 Squadron and flew it back to Debden. When he returned he discovered that, during the morning, the squadron had lost another three planes. One pilot was dead and another was in hospital, badly wounded. That afternoon Wissler flew another sortie over Gravesend, where he watched Alf Bayne shoot down an Me 109.

For Fighter Command, late August and early September was the hardest time in the Battle of Britain. But it had brought Denis Wissler more victories and more confidence. He'd kept his nerve, consistently going into action against far superior numbers, he'd survived his first forced landing, and he'd added significantly to his score.

Wissler was able to do this because, across southern England, the many had continued to support the few. Despite the Luftwaffe's growing success, it never closed a single important Fighter Command airfield. One of them, Biggin Hill, had its capacity seriously reduced for over a week, but 11 Group's six other sector stations, Debden included, were kept in the battle at all times. The telephone engineers and the plotters, the crater-fillers and the bomb disposal squads, the repair gangs and the factory workers – like Denis Wissler, they'd all just kept on going.

Churchill was now a frequent visitor to 11 Group's Uxbridge control centre, where he found the cut and thrust of air warfare thrilling and inspiring. At weekends at Chequers he would stride about in a magnificent red-and-gold dressing gown – without false teeth but usually with a lit cigar. If the noise of aircraft came close he would rush out into the garden, so as to catch a glimpse of his enemy. Secretaries would invariably follow, carrying the prime ministerial tin hat and urging the reluctant Churchill to slip it on to his head.

The RAF was fighting a battle of survival, but Churchill was already thinking of the offensives he wanted to carry out in 1941. He asked his generals to plan large raids across the Channel, perhaps even to seize the Cherbourg peninsula. Other schemes included a landing in Italy and the seizure of one of the Low Countries prior to a descent upon German arms factories in the Ruhr valley.

A week before, on the night of 24/25 August, a few of the 170 German bombers flying over England had missed Thameshaven and Rochester and accidentally bombed central London instead. Churchill had immediately ordered a reprisal attack on the German capital. Eighty-one Wellington, Whitley and Hampden bombers were sent to hit Berlin's power and railway stations the following night. Only twenty-nine found the city and dropped their bombs. These did little damage, according to the American journalist on the spot, William Shirer, except to a school and a dairy farm in the suburb of Dahlem. Nevertheless, the psychological impact, coming as it did from a supposedly near-beaten enemy, was immense. Berliners had done little but celebrate for the past two months. The parades and parties that followed the fall of France had gone on for weeks.

Germany's economy was not yet geared to total war; many factories didn't work a night shift and there was little in the way of rationing or blackouts. After all, this was the capital city of the victorious Reich, not London. The RAF's attack – which was followed by more raids every night for a week – was particularly humiliating for Göring, who had promised the people of Berlin that they would never be subject to enemy bombing.

In an angry speech Hitler accused Churchill of escalating the war. He announced that if British bombers damaged German cities then the Luftwaffe would reply by exterminating British ones. The shared fiction in London and Berlin that the precision bombing of military and economic targets was the main aim of their air forces was wearing very thin. German propaganda stations were already threatening Britain with a repeat of Rotterdam.

Göring told his Führer and his aircrews that the RAF was down to its last reserves. The time had now come for the final turn of the screw. In revenge for the bombing of Berlin a series of huge raids would be launched against London. They would amaze the world, shatter the morale of the enemy's civilians and bring the remnants of Fighter Command out of their hiding places and up towards their final destruction in the skies over their capital.

Chapter 14

4–11 September

Wednesday 4 September was Bob Doe's best day so far. His 234 Squadron Spitfires had been vectored on to a formation of Messerschmitt 110s and they were having a real party. They knew how to fight this plane now. You just crept up underneath it and it was totally defenceless. It was like a pigeon shoot. As his third victim fell to earth trailing thick smoke, Doe realised that he had begun to enjoy this. That was his ammunition gone. He gave Budge Harker a thumbs-up sign and the two of them peeled off and headed for home. Although you couldn't help being nervous before action, he was totally confident in his own ability now. He was actually looking forward to the next fight.

The next day he and Harker joined the fight too late. The enemy were already on their way back and so the two of them flew to Dover to look for trouble. They found German fighters there, waiting to escort their bombers home. As Doe dived towards one there was an urgent shout over the RT: 'Bob, tighten up.' He turned sharply, just in time, and Harker swooped down on the Messerschmitt 109 that had just been on Doe's tail. Perhaps he was getting careless – arrogant and careless. Time to start thinking again. Still, the system he had devised with Harker had worked.

Alan Francis was ten years old. He lived with his mother and father and his brother Robin, aged six, in a newly built semi-detached house in the prim and proper north-west London suburb of Wembley. He went to Preston Park School, swam in the local swimming baths, fished in the pond at the top of Barn Hill and watched the Hurricanes circling as they rose from the nearby RAF base at Northolt.

The family took air-raid precautions very seriously. Alan's father William, a City of London policeman, had brought some steel helmets home for them all to wear and, like nearly every other family in London, they carried their gas masks at all times. They knew all about the detector pads that stood on poles in the street and went green if there was gas about. Alan checked every time he walked past.

The family had collected the set of Air Raid Precaution cigarette cards. Following the cards' advice, they drew lines on big sheets of brown paper, cut them up and pasted the strips across the windows to make diamond shapes. That was in case of bomb blast. The brown paper would hold the glass together. They had several goes at it before they got it right.

Alan Francis had cigarette cards of all the capital ships in the Navy and he knew the armament and characteristics of each one. He saved football cards too, but that summer his real passion was aircraft. Francis collected the set of cards that showed all the various aircraft in the RAF, and he knew what it said about them in the album by heart. The *Aeroplane* magazine taught him how to identify every plane from its silhouette, or even from parts. He felt that he ought to know the shape and size of wings and fins and engines and even the sound the various planes made. Such knowledge could come in really useful if ever he needed to help the authorities during a real air raid.

He imagined the RAF pilots: young men with fantastic co-ordination and fast scientific minds; all Oxford and Cambridge rowing blues; the nation's élite putting themselves at risk every day. He was desperate to see a dogfight but so far dogfights had been rare over north-west London.

He was fascinated by the barrage balloons. There were loads of them to the right over the RAF base at Stanmore. One night there was a thunderstorm. Alan crept to the window, wondering if the bombing had started. Suddenly there was a flash of fork lightning that went straight through one of the balloons. A ball of flame fell from the sky. He rushed downstairs to the living room, breathless, to tell his parents.

The journalists had a hunch that something was coming. Ben Robertson had heard about the bombs that had fallen on London on 24 August and about the British bombing of Berlin. A few days later he and several of his friends decided that it was time to leave Dover. Robertson was impressed with the London he returned to. It seemed somehow at peace with itself, prepared and waiting. The Mersey docks had suffered four heavy night-time raids but so far nothing much had happened to London. It could not be long, though. They had all read the reports of Hitler's speech on 4 September. To wild applause the Führer had pledged: 'If the British Airforce drops two or three or four thousand kilograms of bombs, then we will in one night drop 150, 250, 300 or 400 thousand kilograms. When they declare that they will increase their attacks on our cities, then we will *raze* their cities to the ground. We will stop the handiwork of these night air pirates, so help us God!'

Robertson had a new confidence in Britain. On 7 September he cabled *PM*: 'England has courage and spirit and I for one do not doubt any longer the ability of the Royal Air Force to hold out, and my opinion is held by practically every American in London.' That afternoon he, Jimmy Sheean and Ed Murrow drove out to the east of London. It was the sort of day that held the promise of air warfare, but they lacked a viewpoint like the cliffs at Dover. London was a big place and it was impossible to know for sure where an attack might come. They gambled and drove towards the mouth of the Thames, reckoning they would get a better view of any attack from outside the city.

The young Americans passed through Stepney and Limehouse across the river from the wharves and warehouses of the Surrey Docks. East London steamed and smoked in the late summer heat. It smelt of coal tar and wood resin. It was low tide and children paddled in the thick brown water. Old men picked amongst the driftwood, empty crates and abandoned bicycles that littered the river shore. Freight trains left trails of black smoke as they steamed away from the quaysides. They drove on, skirting the great East India dock on the Isle of Dogs. Everywhere the dark merchantmen were loading and unloading. Some had naval camouflage paint on their sides. They drove through Canning Town and Silvertown and past the huge Royal Victoria and Royal Albert Docks with their towering cranes and grain elevators, dozens and dozens more ships, the commercial heart of the greatest trading empire the world had ever seen.

At Woolwich they crossed the river and drove almost as far as the fighter base at Gravesend. Hornchurch, an RAF sector station, was just across the river too, so there were plenty of likely targets near by. In the distance they could see the oil storage plant at Thameshaven still burning from a previous raid. If there was to be any action they should certainly see some of it from here.

It was exceptionally hot. They bought three tin-hatfuls of apples from a farmer, and found a haystack. Then, following the example of so many they had seen on their journey to the mouth of the Thames, they lay back to enjoy the sun, periodically scanning the clear blue sky.

The first warnings came at four o'clock as small formations over

Calais were picked up by the radar stations, but Fighter Command completely misread their enemy's intentions. The group controller at Uxbridge assumed that these raids would follow the normal pattern and arranged his fighter squadrons accordingly; thinly spread over a wide area to protect the sector stations and aircraft factories. Then the controller and his WAAF plotters watched with horrified fascination as the plots took an unfamiliar shape. Instead of splitting they coalesced into two waves, the first sweeping up the Thames Estuary, the second heading straight for central London. By now each formation was being reported by the Observer Corps at '400 plus'. At RAF Debden, as the truth dawned, Edith Heap was thinking, Oh my God, 400 plus means anything between four hundred and a thousand, it means too many to count. And we've got three and a half squadrons up there facing them.

At 5.30 Denis Wissler was on patrol over Thameshaven with five other Hurricanes, one of the very few units anywhere near the path of the attack. Coming towards them they suddenly saw the most frightening sight: a huge flight of bombers, double or treble the size of the largest raid they had ever seen before and with layer upon layer of fighter escorts weaving high above them. With only six planes they saw no prospect of getting anywhere near, but they were not even given the chance. While they were still staring, they were attacked from above by what seemed like dozens of Messerschmitt 109s. Escape became the only sane priority. Twisting and turning, Wissler managed to get in one short burst at a fighter and then fled with the others.

Half an hour later Bob Doe, flying Red 2 behind Squadron Leader O'Brien, and climbing to 16,000 feet over London, was just below the bombers as they opened the bomb doors. 'I saw this load of bombs going down, I saw them hit the docks, I saw the docks erupt.' He couldn't believe what he was seeing. For a moment he watched the little black clouds puffing up from all over the East End. But only for a moment. Suddenly masses of Messerschmitt 109s were swooping down on him too, and Doe was turning as tightly as his Spitfire would go. Having thrown off the fighters he became angry. 'It was horrifying. I mean, I was appalled. I hadn't thought that this would happen. Having avoided being shot down, I started looking round for something to shoot down myself.' Eventually he pounced on a Heinkel 111 and added it to his score, before making his escape back to Middle Wallop. O'Brien was not so fortunate and nor was the Australian leading 'B' Flight. Both were killed that afternoon.

Most German bomber crews never saw an RAF fighter the whole afternoon. For them it was a thrilling moment. Here they were, flying almost unchallenged over the heart of the British Empire. Perhaps it was true after all, as the Reichsmarschall had said; perhaps the English really were down to their last fifty Spitfires. Certainly the escorts easily brushed aside the handful of planes that appeared between them and their target. Few fighters, near-perfect visibility, everything ideal for bombing. The shape of the Thames was unmistakable. It was a simple job for the aimers to pick out the warehouses and port installations that were their major targets. Sticks of black high-explosive bombs and baskets of silver fish-like incendiaries were soon falling towards them.

But alongside the Thames lay mile after mile of crowded tenements and mean little back-to-back terraces, the homes of the men and women who worked in the docks and factories that the Luftwaffe had come to bomb. The men who sent the bombers knew this. Whatever was said then or later about 'military and economic targets' the fact that civilians would inevitably perish was part of the philosophy of strategic bombing. A single devastating attack could break the morale of a country. It had happened in Rotterdam and now, Göring believed, it was going to happen in London. As the first raid began he told the German people: 'This is the historic hour when our air force, for the first time, delivers its stroke right into the enemy's heart.'

In Silvertown, close by the Royal Victoria Dock, Ada Taylor, her father Arthur and her uncle Bob had noticed that the balloon barrage around the London docks had suddenly been raised. Bob Taylor said, 'Arthur, what's up there?' Ada ran outside into the yard to have a look. 'It's just birds,' a neighbour said. Ada's dad disagreed. 'Get inside! Now!' he yelled at his daughter. Within seconds the balloons were squirming across the sky in their death agonies and bombs were exploding in the nearby streets. At the same moment the warning siren wailed. Within a minute Harland & Wolff's was on fire. It was only half a mile away. The Taylor family cowered on the ground in terror near whatever cover they could find. The raw and refined sugar barges at Tate & Lyle's were burning, the smell of caramel mixed in with the smoke.

The Silvertown rubber company's warehouse went up next and soon Beckton gas-works was on fire too. The foul, sulphurous odour that resulted was a further cause for terror. Many, catching the first whiff of it, sprinted for their gas masks. The rumour spread through Silvertown that the Germans had dropped mustard gas. Incendiaries were causing fires in the Taylors' own street now. People were running around, not sure whether to try to make it to the public shelters or take their chances under the kitchen table.

Rosie Lee stood with her sister Lily in Bermondsey, to the west of Silvertown and on the opposite side of the Thames. They could see flames and a huge column of dark smoke rising from the docks and filling the sky. As they walked to the railway arch that served as the local shelter, the sisters could see that the bombers were now concentrating on the Surrey Docks, less than a mile away. These wharves served Canada and the Baltic ports and contained 250 acres of pitch pine and fir wood stored in stacks twenty-five feet high. Now it was burning, all of it. Flames rose for hundreds of feet. The smoke, black and choking, drifted westward past Rosie and Lily and on over Tower Bridge until the whole city could smell it. Barges on the river were ablaze too. Rosie Lee's father, a veteran of the first war said, 'They'll be over tonight. You watch it. We'll all get it tonight.'

So this was it, the final escalation, something that had been expected and dreaded since the war began. Watching the bombs fall from the relative safety of London's rural fringe, Ben Robertson wondered how many people were dying at that exact moment, and he wondered how the survivors would react. Would they march on Westminster? Would they all go mad? The American journalists watched more bombers come over and saw that they all seemed to get through without much opposition. Could it be that the Luftwaffe had finally ground the British down? It hadn't seemed like that down in Dover, but then again none of them had ever seen such a large number of German planes on one mission. One of them came very low and they all dived for the ditches. They sat there, stunned, imagining bombs falling on the streets they had driven through an hour or so beforehand. Sheean was remembering Spain, remembering Guernica. Robertson just kept repeating over and over again: 'London's burning, London's burning . . .'

The Surrey Dock was linked by two roads to what locals called 'the mainland'. Soon it was an island of flame. Across London fire engines and the converted taxis of the Auxiliary Fire Service tore down streets suddenly emptied of all civilians, all with clanging bells.

Rotherhithe Street, one of the two roads into the docks, was soon hopelessly blocked by what seemed to be a wall of pure fire. Redriff Road, lined with fire engines and men striving to hold back the flames on either side of them, resembled an escape tunnel. Twenty- or thirty-foot-high loops and tongues of fire flicked out and over the heads of the men and women on the roadside. Splinters of burning wood landed on their clothes and faces. One block of dockside flats received a direct hit from a high-explosive bomb, but over a thousand people were brought down Redriff Road that afternoon, their clothing steaming from the proximity of the inferno on either side.

Smouldering barges, their mooring ropes burnt away, drifted down the Thames. River police and firemen tried to save some vessels from the fire, approaching the burning wharves with wet towels wrapped round their faces as protection against the heat and the sparks. Other boats creeping by on the far side of the river, three hundred yards away from the docks, had their paint blistered.

The steady two-minute blast on the siren that meant 'all clear' sounded at 6.40 p.m. The Taylors rushed to where the first bombs had dropped, a doctor's surgery in Haig Road. It was total confusion, with dozens of people milling around looking for their relatives. Ada Taylor's family returned to her grandfather's house, two doors from her own home. The whole family was there now. Then the air-raid wardens arrived. They told them there were a lot of unexploded bombs about and that the area had been declared unsafe. If they could they should all get under the Canning Town viaduct. They took some clothes and their gas masks and set off. There was already a crowd under the arches and, as they waited their turn to squeeze in, the warning sirens wailed again and a pub on the other side of the road disintegrated before their eyes. Soon much of Silvertown was on fire. A rumour was going around that West Ham council had ordered three thousand canvas coffins. Ada Taylor was terrified.

It was obvious that, guided by the huge blaze, the Germans would come back at night. Where Rosie Lee lived the light from the fires farther east was as bright as daylight, only red as she'd imagined hell to be. The urgent, undulating wail of the siren had the Lees running the hundred yards from their newly built flats in the Neckinger estate to the nearest railway arch on Abbey Street. Rosie walked around the sandbags at the entrance and into a press of bodies, packed and sweaty like a Tube train in the summer. People were twitchy, fearful. Some tried to make jokes or sing, others were praying. The Lee sisters sat on the cobbles, trying to work out if the bombs were coming nearer. There was condensation dripping down the wall. Mrs Parr, an old neighbour, was mumbling 'Hail Mary, Mother of God ...' over and over again. In the end it got on people's nerves. Rosie and her sister shouted, 'Oh Mrs Parr, for goodness sake ...'

By midnight there were nine huge fires rated by the fire service as '100 pumps plus'. One, in the Surrey Docks, was '300 plus'. There were nothing like enough fire engines to deal with them all, even if they could have reached the heart of them. Many were left to burn. On the fringes of the fires, epic efforts were made to control their spread. It took two to hold the fire hose and direct the jet of water. If let go under full pressure, the hose would twist like an angry snake and could injure anyone close by. So there was nowhere to hide when the bombers returned: the firemen had to keep holding the nozzle, wrapping their arms round the hose as it rested on knee and thigh. Bombs dropped into the fires they were trying to put out. Walls fell, and sometimes firemen and policemen got caught under them. New incendiaries span and spluttered all around them. Stacks of timber that had been soaked and drenched to stop them catching fire would quickly steam and smoke and then burst into flame. The stenches mingled: scent factories, candle-makers', rum stores, paintworks and tanneries – all the old riverside trades of London, their smells all mixed together with the oil and the smoke.

Nobody had ever seen anything like it and, on this first day of bombing, all sorts of things went wrong. Roads were blocked that should have been kept clear. People went to the wrong shelters. Willing workers attended the wrong incidents and the wrong fires: 448 civilians and rescue workers died; 1,337 were seriously injured. Everyone would get better with practice. And they were going to be given many opportunities to practise.

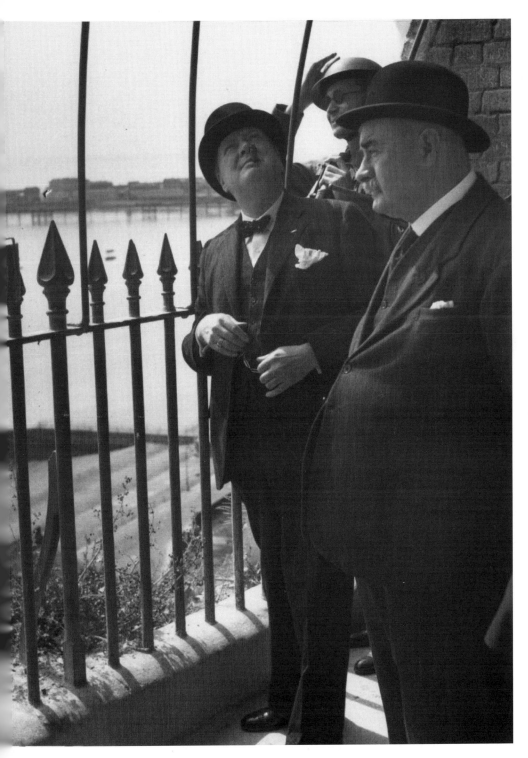

Winston Churchill watching a dog fight over Dover with the town's Mayor,
29 August 1940

New York Herald Tribune

TELEPHONE:
TEMPLE BAR 1972.

BUSH HOUSE, ALDWYCH,
LONDON, W.C.2.

August 21, 1940

Dear Mr Churchill —

I must send you a brief though belated note of thanks for your delightful luncheon at 10 Downing Street last week. The tribute you paid the work of the Herald Tribune was most heartening and should inspire it to ever greater heights. I only hope it can succeed in inspiring those destroyers!.

It is extraordinary that you should have time to ferret me out in the midst of your busy day — and I want you to know how deeply I appreciated both your kindness and the generous things you said about mother. ~~It was a great privilege to~~ meet you in your distinguished home ~~and~~ This takes with it much gratefulness and cheers for your superb speech yesterday. May your Mississippi roll on until it floods the nation!

Yours Sincerely,

Whitelaw Reid

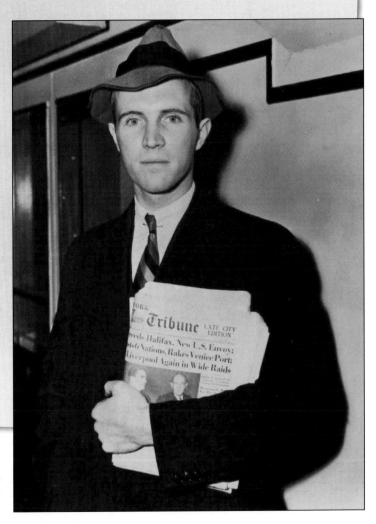

Whitelaw Reid and a
draft of his letter to
Winston Churchill

Planes arriving at Cowley were often as badly damaged as the Hurricane above.
Below, William Morris (Lord Nuffield), who masterminded the civilian repair programme,
admires a rebuilt Hurricane

Pilots of 17 Squadron awarding the 'Line Shooter's Medal' to Count Manfred Czernin on 20 August 1940. Denis Wissler stands to attention, third from the right

Edith Heap

Right above Anti-aircraft batteries in Hyde Park

Right below The front cover of an Air Raid Precautions cigarette card album

Alan Francis's home at 66 Beverley Gardens, Wembley

Alan (right) with Elsie Francis and his brother Robin

AIR RAID PRECAUTIONS

An Album
to contain a Series
of Cigarette Cards of
National Importance

W. D. & H. O. WILLS

BRANCH OF THE IMPERIAL TOBACCO COMPANY
(OF GREAT BRITAIN AND IRELAND), LIMITED.

PRICE ONE PENNY.

Ben Robertson, war correspondent for the newspaper *PM*

The *New York Herald Tribune's* team in London with Whitelaw Reid second from the left

The journalists came back to their haystack from a pub. Murrow remarked that 'The fires up river had turned the moon blood red.' Robertson thought that it was 'the most appalling and depressing sight any of us had ever seen. We were horrified. It almost made us physically ill to see the enormity of the flames which lit the entire western sky.'

As the Americans returned to London the next morning they passed small groups of people trekking in the opposite direction, the wealthy driving cars, the poor on foot, pushing prams and barrows, loaded with what little they had saved from the wreckage of their homes. They headed out to where they had relatives, to the hop-picking grounds where they got seasonal work, to the caves at Chislehurst. There were many homeless. Most had no idea what to do. Some were rounded up and sent to rest centres. From there, with varying degrees of efficiency or luck, the authorities attempted to evacuate them. Geoff Taylor, a policeman, spent 8 September convoying bus-loads of children to Epping Forest. He left them there, underneath the trees, as he had been told. Many were crying, tears running down blackened, sooty, faces. Taylor had no idea what was supposed to happen to them next.

Another convoy of buses was supposed to come and pick up the homeless of Canning Town and take them away from the dock area. Ada Taylor and all the others sheltering under the Canning Town arch had been sent by the relief officer to a temporary rest centre in Ada's old school on Agate Street, a few hundred yards to the east of the Taylors' abandoned home. The school had a reinforced concrete roof, making it relatively safe. On the other hand, it was close to the river and surrounded by factories. Lewis Webster, a volunteer ambulance driver, ferried more people to the school during the day. Some pointed out the closeness of the docks. They were told that they would not have to wait there long and that transport had been ordered to take them out of the dangerous areas. But the evacuation buses did not arrive.

On 7 September a Joint Intelligence Committee meeting noted alarming developments on the French coast. There had been a large movement of barges to forward bases in the Calais region. A secret intelligence decrypt revealed that dive-bombers had been transferred from Norway to France. They were also concentrated around Calais. There was a report that German Army leave had been stopped from 8 September. It was noted that moon and tide conditions were particularly favourable between 8 and 10 September. At 5 p.m., just before the bombing of London started, the Chiefs of Staff ordered defence forces to 'standby at immediate notice'. General Headquarters, Home Forces issued the invasion code word 'Cromwell' at 8.07 p.m.

Whitelaw Reid had been invited to spend the weekend with Anthony and Beatrice Eden at their country house at Elham. Eden, the Minister of War, had been particularly generous to Reid throughout his stay, letting him accompany him on all manner of inspections and fixing up special trips to see defence preparations and training camps. Reid had spent Saturday morning in the front garden with the Eden children, shooting bows and arrows and watching the occasional scuffle in the sky. Once a German fighter came streaking across the valley and crashed in the nearby Kent hills. Just the usual English weekend, thought Reid. But then Eden suddenly received word that 'Cromwell' was to be issued. He dashed back to London with a motorcycle escort, leaving Reid sitting on the biggest scoop of his career. He hurried off to Dover to try to get himself accredited.

Reid drove down to the coast and checked once more into Dover's Grand Hotel. In the streets outside he saw lorries packed with troops ready to go wherever a landing took place. Every so often he went out to check they were still there. Then all the church bells started ringing and everyone else knew too. All night he waited and watched. The weather was wild. There was a thunderstorm and lightning was hitting the barrage balloons and lighting up the whole countryside. Surely they couldn't come in weather like this?

In the morning the tension on the faces of those defending Dover was clear to see. Reid was about to take up his familiar station on Shakespeare Cliff to watch the invasion, or at the very least some more dogfighting, when he had a most unpleasant surprise. There was a hideous screech overhead and as he dived for a wall there was a loud explosion. Old Paddy, who grew potatoes up on the cliff, had been killed down on the beach. Shells! For a moment Reid thought the Germans really were coming, but the others told him that Dover had been sporadically shelled for weeks now.

Reid got permission to join the crew of a trawler on anti-invasion patrol. Art Menken loaned him his bullet-proof vest and with that and his tin hat Reid went aboard. They left port at sunset and stayed out on the water all night. On the far side of the Channel, British aircraft were bombing the barges. 'I remember the far coast being quite a sight . . . it was like the 4th July, all kinds of fireworks on the far side. And the reflection of it all came across a very still channel in the water right to the edge of the boat I was on.' The sailors had been doing this night after night all summer long, and they were really nervous. 'At one point a plane came overhead and they yelled at each other to be quiet and they got very mad because someone down in the bottom of the ship continued singing.'

'Cromwell' remained in force for twelve days, but the only German offensive was the one that continued to come from the air. On the day after the first raid, Churchill visited the East End and saw a ruined shelter in which forty people had died. Passers-by stopped and cheered him. Their Prime Minister cried. 'We can take it,' someone shouted, 'give it 'em back!'

But could the East End take it? The question preoccupied officialdom, whose observers and Home Intelligence agents were out in force to gauge the mood of the people in the worst-affected areas.

The rumours in Canning Town were correct. There were tens of thousands of coffins stacked in various council depots across East London. In 1937 the Air Ministry had estimated that 20,000 casualties would result from 600 tons of bombs. In reality the 600 tons dropped on 7 September caused only about 2,000 casualties.

The authorities had made their preparations in the expectation of huge numbers of fatalities. What they had not expected was large numbers of displaced, homeless people. Nor had they anticipated night after night of bombing and the need for large, permanent public shelters. Partly this was due to official concern that such air-raid shelters might produce a 'shelter mentality' with the occupants refusing to come back up to work.

Small private shelters were encouraged in gardens and allotments, but in the low-lying boggy land next to the Thames anything placed underground tended to flood. And anyway, the people packed into blocks of flats and East End terraces tended not to own any land in the first place. And so, in September 1940, the best the authorities had to offer were the arches of the huge Victorian railway viaducts. Sandbags were piled across the open entrances to protect those cowering inside from blast and shrapnel.

Some took control of their own safety. Their city was full of deep underground tunnels, tunnels with trains running through them. The Tube system looked a lot more secure than another night spent underneath the arches. On 8 September hundreds of frightened Londoners besieged Underground stations like Liverpool Street and Elephant and Castle. At first the gates were barred against them, but these soon gave way and bowed to the inevitable, as did the authorities. By the end of the month 177,000 people were taking nightly refuge in the Underground system. It was hot, crowded and insanitary, but the rumble of the bombs seemed a comfortable distance away. At daybreak the platforms were handed back to rail staff and commuters; by night the blankets and folding chairs and tables would return. Queuing for the evening intake would begin long before lunch-time.

In the London boroughs, where fires still blazed, confusion reigned. Coaches that were supposed to take away the homeless turned back. Some of the drivers, it was rumoured, were too frightened to go into that part of London at all. 'Canning Town? Sorry, mate, I thought you said Camden Town . . .'

Ada Taylor was still at the Agate Street school on the evening of 8 September when the bombers returned. The six hundred people there sang and shouted and prayed through repeated raids right until dawn. When the promised transport did not arrive on 9 September, about half of them were transferred to another school in nearby Frederick Street. Nobody seemed to know who was in charge and tempers were getting frayed. Ada's father Arthur had been drinking with a bunch of his mates. He collared the relief officer. 'Listen my brother, I want a word with you about these buses . . .'

But there were still at least three hundred people in the school when night fell on Monday, 9 September, and with darkness came yet more bombs.

They were crowded in the corridors, mostly silent, craning their ears for danger. Tilly Lloyd, sitting near Ada, was weeping, trying to stifle the noise because everybody else was silent and tense with fear. There were distant bangs. The building rocked gently. Tilly Lloyd's baby started to cry too. 'How do you want your eggs tomorrow, hard or soft?' Mrs Mac's loud voice, that was, with a joke for all to share. 'Have you got my Jimmy over with you?' another woman asked. Then a louder boom, very close – too close, much too close. As the noise receded Ada could hear mumbled prayers. The building shook violently. Everybody went quiet, waiting for the next bomb in the stick to fall.

There was a brilliant, multicoloured flash and the schoolroom doors flew past Ada Taylor's head. They landed farther up the corridor, followed by a shower of desks and chairs. Everyone seemed to scream at once, screaming in the blackness, screaming in complete hysterical terror. Then, with a strangely muted, shuffling sound, half the reinforced concrete first floor and the whole of the roof above fell in. There were fewer screams then, a lot fewer.

There was no way out, even for those who were not pinned down by the debris or the dead. When Ada regained her senses her first thought was for her father. Then she heard his voice. 'Ada, you all right?' Great relief but her mouth was choked with dust. 'Yeah.' 'Maud, are you all right?' 'Yeah.' 'Where's the old man?' 'I don't know.' 'Well where's Bob?' 'He was standing there with Frank.' Tilly Lloyd and her baby were dead. Many voices questioning, imploring, desperate to find those who didn't answer back. Tears, mounting screams again. Somebody climbed through with a light. 'Who's here? Who's here?'

As dawn broke the digging began in earnest. Maud, Arthur Taylor's stepmother, came out smothered in blood and dust. 'Arthur, what are we going to do? They've put the old man in hospital.' 'Which one?' 'I don't know. They said they didn't know.' Boy Day, the air raid warden, came by and a woman rushed up to him hysterical. 'There's Jimmy, that's him, with the brown jersey, that's him – he's got his scout medals on it!' Heavy rescue men ran up and started to lift the concrete. One gently pulled at the arm. It came away in his hand. The rest of Jimmy was somewhere else. At that moment Arthur Taylor spotted his brother Bob. He was being carried out dead.

Lewis Webster was woken with the news that a bomb had

dropped on the Agate Street school. He was mortified. Hadn't he driven half that lot down there himself two days ago? They were *en route* to the country or somewhere. Why were they still there? The same question was being shouted at the dazed policemen and council officials who were trying to keep grief-stricken relatives away from the scene when Webster's ambulance arrived outside the school a few hours later. It was like a taxi rank, Webster thought, as he waited for his turn to pick up the wounded and the dead. The Flying Squad, the best coppers in the Metropolitan Police, turned up. 'Move along now, nothing to see here, everything that can be done is being done . . .' There was anger in the air. A large policeman instructed the ambulance drivers not to talk about what had happened. It didn't do to have people panicking.

The rescuers were digging deeper now. The bomb had sliced the school in two and half of it had collapsed into the bomb's crater. The rescue workers were putting parts of bodies into rubble baskets. Then the baskets were put into the backs of the ambulances along with any complete bodies and taken by Webster and his colleagues to Romford Road swimming baths. The baths had been drained of water and put to use as a temporary mortuary. Easy to wash down and keep clean, someone pointed out. The seventeen-year-old ambulance man grimaced at the sight.

After the rubble baskets had been unloaded on to the tiled floor of the empty swimming pool, the mortuary attendants had to try to reconstruct complete bodies from them. The same thing was happening at the municipal pool in Drew Road. It was like a ghastly jigsaw puzzle. And, since nobody seemed to know who had been at the school in the first place, there was no way of knowing when the puzzle was done. There were all kinds of bits and pieces left over.

The community was in chaos. Missing friends and relatives might have been evacuated or might have been killed. Some turned up, most didn't. The formal casualty list that emerged was bad enough. Extended families were completely wiped out

– six Glovers, seven Gunns, four Jewells, six Lees. Seventy dead were recorded and buried in a mass grave. The search for bodies went on for twelve days. Then the whole scene was concreted over. Most local people believed and believe that more like two hundred died inside Agate Street school.

'Now Miss Sherlock, are you sure you are not frightened?' Marian Holmes blushed. She always did when Churchill teased her like this. Holmes, Sherlock Holmes . . . it was an obvious joke. And actually, yes, she was very frightened. But she would never admit as much in his presence. Who could? He who seemed oblivious to the danger. He who was forever rushing out to try to spot a bomber in the searchlights. During one of the first big raids Thompson the detective had pushed him to the ground and lain on top of him when a huge explosion from somewhere over the river rocked the whole of Whitehall. Churchill had given the policeman a real dressing-down for that.

This part of London was getting off lightly compared to the East End. But even so it was now painfully clear that Number 10 was a death trap. An incendiary had come right through the flimsy roof and landed in Marian Holmes's empty bedroom. They would have to move. The Central War Rooms, inside deep underground tunnels, offered the most secure accommodation. Secure, but also cramped and stifling. Churchill would go there during the worst raids but he hated the place. Sometimes his wife Clementine would order him to take more care of himself. Then he would go down the War Room stairs and quickly return to tell his staff that, if his wife was to ask again, they were to inform her that Mr Churchill had indeed gone into the shelter.

The 'Number 10 Annexe', about three hundred yards away in Storey's Gate, was chosen as Churchill's new London home. It was a solid building, and steel shutters had been installed over the windows of the ground-floor flat where the Churchills would sleep. From the roof there was a panoramic view of the whole city. Churchill was frequently to be found up there, with or without his tin hat. Number 10 was still used as an extra office, for Cabinet meetings and for entertaining, but from now on the business of government was principally directed from behind the more sturdy walls of the annexe.

Terrified, confused, sullen and depressed, more and more people trudged out of London. Oxford took in twenty thousand refugees bringing with them rumours that the capital was largely in ruins. But the Ministry of Information morale reports brought comforting news to the government. There was anger, plenty of it – at the Germans and also at the local authorities – but there was no serious desire for peace and little bad feeling directed at the government. What most people seemed to want was revenge.

The first few days of bombing confirmed Bess Walder's parents' worst fears. The Luftwaffe had not been stopped before they reached London. All through the first night the explosions had gone on, and the next, and the next. The family and their dog went across to the school and down a spiral staircase into the boiler house, where Mrs Walder laid out blankets and camp-beds. It was dark and smelt of coal, but everybody felt fairly safe. Bernard Walder, an air raid warden, spent half the nights rounding other people up and herding them into the nearby brick surface shelters that had been built the previous year.

When morning came and the 'all clear' sounded, the family returned home, seeing the exhausted fire crews returning to the school, their faces blackened, their eyes streaming with soot and the pollution of chemical fires.

The family had heard all about the docks – everyone knew

that hundreds were dying down there every day. All the main railway lines to the south were blocked. There didn't seem to be many fighters about, and they heard almost nothing in the way of anti-aircraft fire. London was going to be slowly bombed flat. Then, like a miracle, a letter arrived summoning the children to Canada. At last.

The Walder family went to Euston Station to put Bess and Louis on a 9 a.m. train for 'an unknown port'. The platform was full of parents hugging their children, and children crying. 'It was like an Italian opera.' Mr and Mrs Walder were very calm and collected. They said goodbye. Mrs Walder looked at Bess and said, 'Grow up to be a good girl.' And Bess thought, That's a funny thing to say. Bernard Walder looked at his daughter intently and said: 'Look after that young man,' gesturing to her brother Louis. Bess promised that she would. She puzzled over what her parents had said. Much later she realised that they thought they might never see their children again. The bombing had begun and they believed they were bound to get killed eventually. This was their sacrifice for their children's future. To be parted from them was a dreadful thing.

Bess had noticed the Grimmond family on the platform. Five of their ten children were on the train. Their house in Brixton had been reduced to rubble by a bomb the night before.

Once the train had departed, with parents waving from the platform, the crying stopped as if by magic and a wave of jollity and high spirits filled the carriages. Children were singing and laughing, getting to know new friends and the adult escorts who would take them all the way to Canada, new loving homes and a new life. 'Off we went, high hopes, here we go. We're going off and across the ocean.'

Bernard and Rosina Walder were not the only people in London worried about the city's ineffective anti-aircraft defence. Partly it was a lack of guns, partly it was the fact that up there blundering around in the darkness were the Blenheim and Beaufighter aircraft that made up the RAF's not very successful night-fighter force. After the first four nights a change in policy was ordered and dozens of new guns were rushed into the capital from the ports, factories and RAF bases that they had previously been protecting. On the night of 11 September they all opened up in an ear-splitting chorus of defiance: 13,500 shells were fired from within central London alone. All this noise and fury didn't do much to deter the night raiders, except perhaps to force them a few thousand feet higher, but it hugely encouraged the citizens of London.

This was a lot better than collecting cigarette cards. London was in the thick of the war at last and Alan Francis had a grandstand view. By day there were dogfights aplenty. And now, with all the big guns firing at night, there were loads of pieces of shrapnel just lying around to collect. You could hear shrapnel at night coming down all around the house. It made a kind of whirring, whistling sound. If it hit the roof it would bring some tiles down. In the mornings Alan would rush outside to be the first to get the biggest bit. The best thing was a complete shell cap, but he'd only seen one of those in somebody else's collection. It wasn't fair. This boy was thirteen and had been allowed to wander for miles looking for bits. Alan's parents were always making him stay inside. Being ten was awful sometimes.

He had not seen much of his father recently. He'd been doing twelve-hour shifts down at his police station. It was very close to the docks where all the fires were burning. His dad had been saving people's lives, he was sure of it, carrying them out of burning buildings on his shoulders. He used to come home looking very tired and his face was all black with little spots like a measles rash. It was burns from all the ash in the air, his mother had said.

If he was home in the evening, his father would stand with him outside the front door, looking out over the city.

> We could see six miles across and either side from the top of Barn Hill. We could see the German planes dropping flares and our machine gunning that used to try and shoot the flares out. You could see the tracer going up. I was told afterwards that the tracers are about one in every six bullets. To imagine that there was six times more ironware going up than we could see was really quite exciting . . . They dropped flares to light up the factories that lined the valley. The General Electric Company, the British Oxygen Company all doing vital war work.
>
> And there were no traffic lights, no shop lights, no background light of any sort and the whole thing was just pitch black so that you could see the firing so clearly. You could hear the German aeroplanes droning as though they were very heavily laden. And the searchlights would try to pick them up and we were willing these searchlights to do just that. And if they did pick up a plane it would shine up like a silver light in the sky and they would all switch on to it. Then all hell would let loose because the guns could see the target and they would fire more of these tracers. And they would get quite near the planes and that really was very exciting but very dangerous for people underneath because a plane caught in searchlights would dive and open its bomb doors to lessen its load and whoever was underneath at the time, that was their bad luck.

After the success of the 7 September raid, the Luftwaffe came back in force during daylight on 9 and 11 September. On both occasions the tactics were the same. They flew at a great height and they flew with at least two fighters for every bomber. Although it had some success on 9 September, Fighter Command had not yet come to terms with the new menace. On other days weather kept the bombers away, but they did come every night, carefully timing the raids so that the population of London received the maximum disruption and the minimum sleep. The Luftwaffe High Command were convinced that 20,000 feet below their Heinkels and Dorniers, inside a city whose fires were visible for a hundred miles, the population of London must surely now be getting close to breaking point.

Hitler and Göring felt that the moment of victory was near. On 14 September the *Völkischer Beobachter*, the Nazi Party's own newspaper, described the British capital as being in a state of social collapse:

> In spite of considerable resentment from the sorely tried population, after dark there is a nightclub atmosphere in the basement shelters of the luxury hotels. Bands play dance music, champagne and whisky flow freely. Those parts of London not already deserted have become pick-up places for good-time girls and prostitutes offering themselves to the playboy plutocrats who have dodged conscription. Meanwhile the abandoned women and children are left to find what shelter they can in a city largely gutted by fire.

Luftwaffe intelligence now calculated that the RAF had a hundred or so working fighters. But it still had over 1,000 in its squadrons, about the same number as in July. About 800 of them were serviceable and ready for action on 14 September. Over 200 more sat in storage units. For many weeks Dowding and Park had eked out their resources by spreading them thinly and playing a game of hit-and-run with the attacking force. Now, perhaps, they too would have to bring many hundreds of planes together at one time. Trafford Leigh-Mallory was the controller of 12 Group, to the north of Park's 11 Group. The two men disagreed about tactics. Leigh-Mallory favoured 'Big Wings' of four or five squadrons. During the August battles, Park had preferred manoeuvring with smaller units. But the German offensive over London might just be the moment to try something new.

Chapter 15

11–17 September

'My darling and most adorable mummy, thank you so terribly much for the heavenly case you gave me, it really is just heavenly . . .'

'Didit da didit da didit.'

There it was again. Rosemary Lyster started to scribble frantically.

'Didit da didit da didit.'

'E bar!' she shouted. And her heart was beating like crazy, because for all she knew they might be about to sink a ship and if she got it right she might save it. She ran upstairs, grasping her notepad, swerved past Control, who was on the phone to the other stations to see if they could get a bearing on the transmitter, and then burst straight through the door and into the back office where the 'Gestapo' lurked. She had no idea what they did with her transcriptions of the German naval Morse. Sent them somewhere even more secret than this listening station probably. She just hoped it was all doing some good.

She sat down again in front of her set in the lower receiving room. It was four in the morning. The 'E bar' had been exciting, they always were, but within a few minutes she was feeling very sleepy again. She had been on duty since eleven and would not be relieved till eight. Tomorrow she would get a good morning's sleep and then go riding on the Moors. Or cycling. There was absolutely nothing else to occupy her in Scarborough during the day, and she had to keep her weight down somehow. Last year, when she had been touring with the theatre company, her body had been lithe and taut and now what with all this sitting around it was slowly turning to fat. It would not do at all. She did a few hip rolls, partly to stay awake.

She went back to the letter to her mother. There was nothing much to do through the long nights of listening except write, and so she wrote reams. And they wrote back about all that was happening in Marazion. Daddy was in charge of the Local Defence Volunteers, the Home Guard, as everyone called them now. He had collected all the shotguns in that farthest extremity of Cornwall and locked them in the big cupboard in the hall. The tin hats were kept there too.

It seemed that they were pretty jumpy back home. Three times last week Daddy had been telephoned in the middle of the night by people who had seen strange lights or unfamiliar movements in some cove, and off he'd had to go with his patrol across the rocks to look for German spies or strange ships. Her mother would make the sandwiches. She had joined the local Red Cross, and even Rosemary's old nurse was in the St John's Ambulance Brigade.

Rosemary Lyster had asked for a rifle for her birthday to shoot the Germans when they came. Instead they had given her a birthday cake with a rifle on it made out of icing sugar. The other Wrens in Scarborough joked that she wouldn't be used for breeding the master race like the blonde girls would: being a brunette she would be allowed to keep her honour and just be shot instead. Gulp! But there didn't seem to be much chance of the Germans invading Scarborough. Nothing happened in Scarborough; she didn't imagine anything ever had.

Her little sister had been going to America. They had family out there. Her aunt had already sent her children away. But the news of the convoys was getting steadily worse. It wasn't safe to go and it wasn't safe to stay. She went back to her letter.

'It was very naughty of you to give me that and the britches. I'm going to stop eating now quite definitely. Well the night is wearing on, it's 0255 by our clock which means 0355 by ordinary time . . .'

The convoy system had worked well until the summer. Ships were gathered together into groups of forty, fifty or sixty and were escorted part of the way across the Atlantic by destroyers. From July the escorts went to 17° West or 47° North and then turned back. Across the vast mid-ocean the merchant ships were unguarded. As they neared Newfoundland the North American convoys were met by Canadian destroyers and brought into Sydney or Halifax in Nova Scotia. Some carried on south to Bermuda.

Other convoys went to Gibraltar, Sierra Leone and then on around the Cape towards the Indian Ocean. The system had worked because for the most part the German U-boats did not have the range to strike at the unguarded convoys in mid-ocean. But now things were much worse. The U-boats were operating from new bases in western France, which allowed them to attack convoys well out into the Atlantic or lurk for days off the Irish coast.

The other reason why things had changed is that there were practically no escorts any more. The destroyers were withdrawn to guard the coast against invasion and the vessels that replaced them were soft targets and ineffective hunters. The U-boats could easily pick off at will the so-called 'Armed Merchant Cruisers', old liners for the most part with the odd ancient gun welded to their decks and little in the way of anti-submarine capability. The U-boats had also begun to hunt in packs. The Navy tried to trap them as they left the Bay of Biscay by stretching a long, thin patrol line across it, but this proved highly dangerous for the Armed Merchant Cruisers asked to man the station.

Iain Nethercott's time in Portsmouth had been productive. He qualified in torpedoes, High and Low Power Electrics, Depth Charges and Demolitions and was told to put the gold Torpedo badge on his right arm. His pay of 18s 6d per week was raised by 3d per day. At nineteen he was also promoted to leading seaman. For a short time back at Chatham he had a quiet time as a sentry, standing guard among the cucumber frames outside the admiral's dugout, but that didn't last long. One day he was given a draft ticket, told to get his kit together and put on a train with about a thousand other sailors, most of whom had clearly only just joined the Navy.

The journey lasted all day. Several times they were held up by bombing and eventually it grew dark. 'Every time we stopped I kept looking out the window to see what station it was. But they were all blacked out.' Around dawn Nethercott woke to a juddering sound and leaned out of the window. The train was rolling along a jetty. He thought the place was familiar. Then Nethercott recognised the Liver Building opposite. Liverpool! At the end of the jetty was a liner, the *Duchess of Atholl*, and between the ship and the shore there were lines of military police. The sailors marched aboard and spent the day there because the Germans had mined the harbour entrance the previous evening. They waved at a party of children climbing the gangplank of another liner in the next berth. That night they sailed, but no one knew where they were headed. There was no escort. They were relying on the liner's speed.

Liverpool had been raided every night during the two weeks before the Luftwaffe turned its attention to London. Beth Cummings's widowed mother was becoming very anxious. For months she had agonised about whether to send Beth to live with her aunt and uncle in Canada for the duration of the war. Then, when the government announced the child evacuation scheme, she had made up her mind. If the government was setting it up then it must be advisable to send her away. One of Beth's brothers was in the Army and the other was training as an air gunner. Mrs Cummings wanted her daughter safe. The sooner she got her out of Liverpool the better.

It took the children much longer than usual to get from Euston to Liverpool because of the air raids. They arrived late at night at an orphanage in a great big hall with long white things lying on the floor. Bess Walder looked for guidance to the escorts who were looking after them on the trip to Canada, a combination of teachers, doctors and clergymen. One of them said, 'They're your beds, dear.' Bess had never slept on a straw palliasse. Before they went to bed the children had a medical inspection and one boy turned out to have measles and burst into floods of tears when he was told that he would have to go back home. Then the grown-ups said, 'Now you must go to sleep and tomorrow morning you will have a look at your ship.' Tired out with the excitement and the journey, but still tingling with anticipation, the children lay down on their straw mattresses and slept wonderfully well.

In the morning the children were divided into groups. In Bess's group there was a girl of a similar age. She had a similar name too: Beth. Beth Cummings.

The children had no idea what sort of ship they would be travelling on and when they saw her the next morning, moored up close to the famous Liver Building, they all gasped with delight. The *City of Benares* was magnificent. The 11,081-ton flagship of Ellerman's City Line, she was the pride of the peacetime run to

India. Now she was painted dark brown as camouflage for her first ever Atlantic crossing. Most of the ninety evacuee children had been on holiday steamers before, but never on an ocean-going liner. These streamlined beauties, decorated and fitted out to suit their normal destinations, were the ultimate in speed and luxury. The children had seen them on cigarette cards but they had only ever dreamed of sailing on one. Now they were going to do just that.

As they all lined up and marched up the gangplank, hundreds of sailors were lining the decks of the ship in the next-door berth, all waving and cheering them. That was another beautiful liner, the *Duchess of Atholl*.

At the top of the gangplank of the *Benares* the most amazing sight met their eyes: smiling men dressed in turbans, wearing full Indian dress with huge blue sashes around their middles and shoes that turned up at the ends. The men bowed to the children and welcomed them aboard. Bess Walder was impressed. 'They called us little madam and little sir. And they looked after us just wonderfully well. We were in seventh heaven. We felt that we'd stepped into the *Arabian Nights*. It was a floating palace.' And not only was it like a movie: it was a movie. A famous documentary director called Alice Grierson was filming the children for the National Film Board of Canada.

They sailed from Liverpool on Friday, 13 September 1940. The tide was right, the convoy was ready, there could be no delay. And so, despite some misgivings among the superstitious, they glided off down the Mersey and into Liverpool Bay. As they sailed out, the children all stood on the deck and sang 'Wish me luck as you wave me goodbye'. It was a lovely sound. And all the ships in the harbour saluted with their foghorns. It was thrilling. They sailed towards the coast of Ireland with high hopes and great excitement.

They were given an immediate guided tour of the ship. Bess would share a cabin with two other girls. The cabins were just above a row of bathrooms that were set aside for the children. The bunks were comfortable, the wardrobes were spacious, and the escorts were as attentive as any parent. The boys were put on one side of the ship, and the girls on the other. Bess was immediately worried that she would not be able to carry out her father's instructions to look after her brother, but he seemed to be in good hands. And actually, since he was quite a lively little boy, it was a secret relief that someone else was taking responsibility for him.

The stewards of the *Duchess of Atholl* were still on board and the food wasn't bad. All the way across the Atlantic they played Crown and Anchor, an old naval gambling game. The majority of the seamen were conscripts who had only been in the Navy for a couple of weeks. Some of them had never even seen a ship before. Iain Nethercott took shilling after shilling off them.

The weather was poor, but the liner kept up a good speed. Going fast in rough seas wasn't very comfortable, but it was one of the best defences against U-boats. They reached Halifax, Nova Scotia, without incident, and were all billeted underneath the grandstand of the city's racecourse. Two days later, led by a Canadian naval band, they paraded through the streets to where three American destroyers awaited them. There was a handover ceremony and, with the lowering and raising of flags, the USS *Yarnall*, built in 1918, became HMS *Lincoln*. For the next three days Nethercott was shown its secrets by his American counterpart. The man kept making apologies. Nethercott was partly responsible for electrics and worried that American ships were AC rather than DC. The American reassured him. 'I shouldn't worry about it. The whole lot'll go out when you get to sea.' 'Why?' 'Have you seen the cabling down below in the boiler rooms?' Sure enough, when Nethercott touched the rubber insulation it crumbled away in his hand.

After that there was the small matter of trying to train an entire crew before setting sail back across the stormy Atlantic.

Göring's pilots and aircrew were in good spirits. Their problems over the previous week had been with bad weather rather than British fighters. Then 15 September dawned cloudless and clear – good bombing weather, a chance to finish the job.

But this was the day when Fighter Command got its tactics absolutely right. The organisation that Hugh Dowding had nurtured worked as he had dreamed it would. The fighters, the men who flew, repaired and maintained them, the radar chain, the Observer Corps, the communications and plotting systems, Pip Squeak, IFF – all the interlocking cogs, wheels, flashing lights and ringing bells of this strange new three-dimensional war. And Churchill was there to see it happen, sitting with Dowding's right-hand man Keith Park inside 11 Group's Uxbridge control room.

Fighter Command knew how these raids worked now. Park left his sector airfields undefended and threw everything he had at the single bomber stream heading towards London. The first raid was met by eighteen squadrons of Spitfires and Hurricanes, over two hundred fighters in all. All but one of the squadrons made contact with and attacked the enemy. As the Germans fought their way north-eastwards over Kent, individual bombers were gradually forced out of formation by sudden glancing attacks and then, once separated, were set upon by larger numbers of prowling British fighters. There were few individual dogfights. This was a kind of warfare best summed up by the advice given to new pilots by South African ace Adolf 'Sailor' Malan: 'get in fast, punch hard, get out'. The RAF ignored the German fighters when they could. It was the bombers everyone wanted, those same bombers that for a week now had been trying to burn down London town.

When the raid did finally reach the capital, it was met by a remarkable, chilling sight: 12 Group's 'Big Wing', sailing serenely into view. On this day there had been time to assemble the rather unwieldy five-squadron formation and bring it into action at exactly the right moment.

Göring had begun to coax the Luftwaffe some time ago with the idea that there were only fifty Spitfires left. Having been harried all the way from the coast, to see more than fifty new fighters lined up against them confirmed the doubts that had begun to take root among the crews. It was with a new and sour irony that they joked, 'Look out, here come the last fifty Spitfires again!' It was a decisive moment. By the time the survivors returned home, the force that had torn into them over London had grown in their minds to 100, 150, 200.

The fighting over London seemed particularly savage. Hurricanes and Spitfires almost crashed into each other in their eagerness to get at their prey. Some flew through their own side's anti-aircraft fire. Those Londoners who had not taken to the shelters stood and cheered as bomber after bomber began to plunge towards the ground. Ray Holmes, a Hurricane pilot with ammunition spent, intentionally crashed his aircraft into a Dornier, sending both planes spinning to the ground. Holmes parachuted to safety. So too did his enemy, but the Dornier pilot had the misfortune to come down in Kennington, an area that had received more than its fair share of German bombs over the past week. A crowd of civilians attacked him and inflicted fatal injuries; people ran out of their houses with pokers and kitchen knives to join the screaming mêlée around the dying pilot, all caught up in the same avenging frenzy that was being played out thousands of feet above their heads.

That afternoon, the Germans came again, with a larger force this time. But the response was the same. Almost three hundred fighters were sent against this second raid, twenty-eight squadrons in all, and every one made contact, Fighter Command's best performance of the war so far. And once again the Big Wing was brought together and found its target. This time the wing was not quite in the right position and was itself engaged by a large number of Me 109s. But it more than occupied the bulk of this raid's fighter cover, allowing other squadrons to fall upon the bombers.

Fighter Command claimed 185 confirmed kills. The real total was nearer 60, but it was enough. As Londoners rejoiced and as Churchill shook hands and patted backs in Uxbridge, the surviving German aircraft limped slowly home full of bullet holes and dead and dying crewmen. The German pilots, gunners and bomb-aimers who had shared those terrifying minutes over London now knew that the RAF was still in business. Within a few hours, so did their masters: 15 September decisively ended Hitler's belief that Britain could be deprived of her air force and forced to come to terms. There would be no air superiority, no peace deal and no invasion. Although they didn't realise it at the time, and although they still had much hard fighting before them, RAF Fighter Command had just won the Battle of Britain.

The facilities on board the *City of Benares* were superb. They even had a school, not that anyone could concentrate on lessons with the Atlantic flowing past the window. Some of the little ones were too young for school. They had a wonderful playroom all to themselves. The older children were forbidden to play in there. From outside, Bess Walder could see a beautiful rocking horse. It had two baskets, one on each side, like huge panniers, and it took three children, one riding the horse and one in each basket.

There were other adults aboard as private passengers. Some of these were accompanied by their children, but the government-sponsored evacuees mostly stayed together: a tight band of brothers and sisters all enjoying one another's company and making very good friends.

Anything they wanted, they got. Bess was partial to ham, and she hadn't had a good ham sandwich for ages. At home sandwiches were usually bits of Spam wedged between huge doorsteps of gritty bread. Now they had proper York ham in beautiful fresh rolls, and the ham hung right over the edges! The stewards would come to them and they would bow and they would say, 'What would little madam like?' Little madam might request a ham roll. Up would come a silver tray covered with a lace cloth upon which two ham rolls would sit. Louis was very fond of chocolates. 'What would little sir like?' 'Chocolate.' Up it would come. On a silver tray, underneath the lace cloth, would be a box of Cadbury's Dairy Milk. Back home, sweets were rationed and they hardly ever saw chocolate. Louis had a wonderful time. Oranges, apples, pears, grapes, bananas. It was heaven. And this wasn't even dinner. This was 'extras'.

The *City of Benares* was the commodore ship, in charge of convoy OB213. The other nineteen ships were smaller and slower. They had left Liverpool with the destroyer HMS *Winchelsea* and two sloops to escort them to 17° West. But the hard-pressed escorts were summoned away on 17 September to escort an inbound convoy. That morning the adults on board the *Benares* were discussing the previous day's news, elated by the great victory being claimed in the air over Britain: 185 shot down! Imagine. The weather message from the captain depressed them only slightly. After all, heavy seas were to be expected in autumn in the Atlantic Ocean.

'That was a Dornier, Daddy.'
'Alan, why aren't you asleep?'

Alan Francis was wedged underneath something his granddad had built. It looked a bit like a cross between an ironing board and an old trestle table, and it went right over the settee. His brother Robin was near by. Their mother and father lay beside them, on a mattress under the dining-room table. The family slept fitfully inside their improvised air-raid shelter, behind the windows with the little brown paper diamonds on them, listening to the planes and the sound of the bombs. The boys prided themselves on knowing the different airplanes by their engine noise. Dorniers had a special note, a kind of rhythmic, droning sound.

After 15 September, large-scale daylight raids on London rapidly dwindled away, but the bombers came back just about every night. They came, more and more frequently, to Liverpool too, and to Swansea, Hull, Southampton, Bristol, Birmingham and many other provincial towns and cities. Night fighters and anti-aircraft fire made little impact. As summer turned into a cold and cloudy autumn, families all over Britain were soon learning to live like Londoners.

In Wembley the air-raid siren went every evening at about eight o'clock. People joked that you could set your watch by it. At first Alan Francis's family all gathered downstairs in their makeshift dining-room shelter. But half the time the siren went for a raid somewhere else, and so they would spend the whole night trooping up and down the stairs and never even hear a bomb within five miles. After a while they decided to stay in their proper beds until the bombing came close. There were mobile anti-aircraft guns near by and they would always open up if any bombers were near.

In the mornings, there would be discussion about what bombs had dropped where, whether Mill Hill or Hendon had been hit and whether Mrs Jacobs down the road had been hit by splinters when her windows blew out. The children continued the great shrapnel hunt. The school term had started now, about the same time as the bombing had. Some mornings a teacher would organise a sweep of the school playing field searching for unexploded incendiaries. The boys and girls would line up and walk along in a line, looking for little holes in the damp grass.

> In the football pitch they would make an inch and a half diameter
> hole and you could tell by whether the hole was burnt or not,

if the incendiary bomb in there was live or had caught fire two or three feet below ground. If anyone saw an incendiary bomb hole we had to raise our hand and the teacher blew a whistle and the whole line had to stop and then that was logged.

And of course shrapnel played hell with the school lawnmowers. Because when they came on with the tractor to mow the field had to be searched again before, otherwise it would wreck the blades.

One of the 15 September bombs hit Buckingham Palace. Queen Elizabeth wrote: 'I'm glad we've been bombed. It makes me feel I can look the East End in the face.' Only a few days before she and her husband had visited the site of the Agate Street school disaster. The royal family had found the East End in a grim state, and in a grim state it would remain. For weeks to come an average of 160 bombers dropped an average of 200 tons of bombs and 182 canisters of incendiaries every night. Most fell upon the poor.

A hundred East Enders demonstrated outside the Savoy Hotel, comparing the lavish air-raid facilities of the rich to their own squalid and inadequate provision. But this was a peculiarly polite form of social protest. An air raid developed, the protesters were all invited in, and after the 'all clear' siren had sounded, they all quietly left. The West and the East Ends returned to their usual divided existence.

Harold Nicolson at the Ministry of Information saw all the official reports on popular morale. 'Everybody is worried about the feeling in the East End, where there is much bitterness.' Ed Murrow was making nightly broadcasts on CBS about the defiance and solidarity of London's population. But he also came across stories of petty crime and looting:

> Considerable surprise has been expressed over the amount of looting in bombing areas. It hasn't reached large-scale proportions, but the British are always surprised at any increase in lawlessness. The matter is further complicated by the fact

that many of the articles picked up from the bombed houses are of little intrinsic value, a book or a piece of ribbon or a bucketful of coal – that sort of thing.

The activities and attitudes of the rich and the poor preoccupied observers. But between the extremes of Savoy and Silvertown, Britain possessed many social layers. Alan Francis's family and the other middle-class inhabitants of Wembley were closer to the average than any top-hatted plutocrat or East End docker. Teachers, technicians, tradesmen and women, skilled workers of all kinds – this was the Britain of 1940. And it was a Britain that, according to all official polling and eavesdropping, seemed in September to stand firmly behind its government and the war.

Even in the worst and most demoralised areas, chaos never became anarchy. Many people, most people, stayed at their posts, looked after their neighbours, went out of their way to be brave. There were inspirational stories aplenty for the papers and the pub. Bomb disposal men, rescue squads, nurses, volunteers of all types, all working together to look after their community.

And some Londoners watched the slow destruction of their city with a feeling that something strangely positive was taking place. They hoped that the instincts and institutions of an older, unfairer Britain were being burnt and blown away along with the warehouses and the tenements, the offices and the shops. This was the people's war now, the citizen's war, and it was being fought for more than King and Country.

At the height of this September night blitz the writer J. B. Priestley made a remarkable broadcast on the BBC. Harold Nicolson listened to it with some aristocratic friends:

> Priestley gives a broadcast about the abolition of privilege, while I look at their albums of 1903 and the Delhi Durbar and the Viceroy's train. Priestley speaks of the old order which is dead and of the new order which is to arise from its ashes . . . I glance at the pictures of the howdahs and panoply of the past and hear the voice of Priestley and the sound of the guns.

In Washington, American Cabinet minister Harold Ickes admired a more old-fashioned British quality: the stiff upper lip. After a dinner at the British embassy he wrote:

> I was tremendously impressed with the self-control of these Britishers. One would not have realised from their talk and actions that London was being subjected to the most terrible bombardment in its history and that England was fighting for its very life ... When Lord Melchett came in, Lord Lothian remarked that two of his homes had been destroyed by bombs ... and Melchett took it as if reference had been made to the loss of a game of cricket.

One of the Luftwaffe's favourite new weapons was the parachute mine. The large, thin-skinned blast weapons could flatten an entire street. Churchill ordered the RAF to use similar mines in their smaller-scale but now almost daily attacks on Germany. Impossible to aim, the mines would drift with the wind and could hardly be called a precision weapon. Both sides were slowly becoming hardened to making war against civilian life and property.

Jock Colville watched the bombing on one mid-September evening:

> The night was cloudless and starry, with the moon rising over Westminster. Nothing could have been more beautiful and the searchlights interlaced at certain points on the horizon, the star-like flashes in the sky where shells were bursting, the light of distant fires, all added to the scene. It was magnificent and terrible: the spasmodic drone of enemy aircraft overhead, the thunder of gunfire, sometimes close, sometimes in the distance, the illumination, like that of electric trains in

peace-time, as the guns fired, and the myriad stars, real and artificial in the firmament. Never was there such a contrast of natural splendour and human vileness.

Left home at 10.15 for Liverpool St, we left in an air-raid which reached its height at the moment we arrived. We had to go down to a hotel shelter, and missed the train. Eventually caught the 2.20. I went out to the pictures in the evening with Birdy, now D.F.C. and Steve. Bed at 10.30 thinking very hard of Mummy & Pop as I could see a hell of a barrage over town. God Damn and blast Hitler.

Denis Wissler set down his pen and went to brush his teeth. Yes, he thought, God damn that bastard Hitler. London was in a terrible state, getting it night after night, and there was nothing much the RAF could do. Wissler knew a couple of the Debden night-fighter boys, and he knew how hard they had been trying to get some of those bombers. But they said it was like looking for a needle in a haystack with all the lights turned off. He wished his parents would move.

The bombing wasn't the only reason he was feeling low. Birdy was his friend, his best friend on the squadron, but it was hard to see him get a medal and have nothing himself. He just needed a couple more clean kills, and no more of these stupid halves and shares.

We did a couple of patrols today but neither came to anything. I feel very depressed tonight. I don't know why. Just a passing mood.

Birdy tried to cheer his friend up. He asked Wissler if he fancied coming out to dinner at Bishop's Stortford. He was rather fond of a girl named Winifred Butler. Winifred had a friend called Edith and Birdy wanted Wissler to look after her.

The girls turned out to have rather a fine sports car. They let

Birdy drive it. Although Birdy had got Winifred out with a story that he wanted to introduce her to his friend Denis, nobody was surprised when he insisted that she sat with him in the front. Which left Edith Heap in the back with Denis. She was the one who used to drive the tractor, the one who'd given him a right telling off for stalling her engine with a handful of sand. How funny.

They had wine, there were candles, it was a fantastic evening. Edith and Denis never stopped talking to each other. On the way back they stopped the car at the sight of a fire and walked over a ploughed field to investigate. A racing stables had been hit. Some bomber had jettisoned its load over the nearby fields. Edith was very worried about the horses, but they were all safe. Walking back across the field, Denis took her hand.

Edith Heap was very taken with the young pilot from London; she even liked his smile. Silly boy, there was nothing wrong with his teeth. But Winifred told her that she thought Denis already had a girlfriend. Shame.

The children had been sent to bed early because of the bad weather and by now all the girls in Bess's cabin had gone a peculiar shade of grey. The *City of Benares* was pitching and tossing all over the place. The weather got worse and worse until the rain was battering horizontally against the portholes. The captain made another announcement. There were sailing, he said, through what he called a 'force eight gale', but the passengers were not to worry, the liner could easily handle seas a lot rougher than this one. The girls groaned at the thought.

Most of the adults had decided to turn in too. Just as the ship was settling down for an uncomfortable and bilious night, there came the most terrible explosion. Everyone in Bess's cabin woke with the force of it. The ship rocked violently, more violently even than it had done before. The alarm bells started to sound, the whole ship shuddered again, and all the lights went out. Bess realised what had happened. The ship tipped right over to one side, wardrobes fell across doors, cabin furniture splintered. The torpedo had gone right through the ship, directly underneath the cabins where the children were sleeping, shattering the row of bathrooms.

It all depended on what you meant by the word 'convoy'. The parents of the evacuees had been promised that their children would be looked after in a convoy. Every one of them assumed that meant a group of ships with a proper Royal Navy escort. When she was torpedoed, the *Benares* was in a group, but one whose escort had left twenty hours ago. And if she wasn't to be protected by an escort, why then wasn't she allowed to use her natural advantage, her speed? If the *Benares* had been allowed to go fast, like the *Duchess of Atholl* was doing at that exact same moment, then she would have been just about invulnerable. U-boats found it very difficult to hit zigzagging fast ships in rough seas, as the Admiralty well understood. When this terrible night was over and the letter-writing and parliamentary questions began, it soon became clear that more care and thought had gone into transporting a thousand sailors than those ninety young evacuees.

The children knew the drill: 'Lifejackets on, get out of the cabin, go along the corridor and up the steps, and onto the boat deck to the assembly points where the sailors would be ready to lower the appropriate lifeboat.' Rule number one: 'don't panic'. As the girls from Bess's cabin started climbing the stairs, the emergency lights came on. The ship was still heeling over steeply and people were being thrown about. Some lucky ones made the boat deck without calamity. The escorts were looking after the younger children and some of the older ones like Bess were caring for as many children as they could find and leading them by the hand.

'Don't worry, don't worry, come on.' There was no shrieking and no crying.

Out on the decks adults and children alike looked around at the other ships in the convoy. Surely one would come to their aid. But no, on a rocket signal from their own bridge the other ships scattered. That was standard procedure – you didn't hang around when there were U-boats about or you risked losing another precious ship. The crew of a stricken merchant vessel had to take their chances and hope a rescue boat would find them later. Standard procedure again. No one had thought it necessary to modify it to take account of the somewhat unusual and special cargo on board the *Benares*.

They were doing what they had been drilled to do. The only trouble was that they had been drilled to do it on a stable ship in daylight or in the full glare of the ship's lights. It was rather different on a sinking ship in a pitch-black night in a raging gale. And some of the children were so exhausted by the struggle to reach the decks they had to be half carried, half dragged along. Beth Cummings and Bess Walder both tried to support a very seasick girl called Joan. One little girl was bleeding heavily. Others had now begun to sob.

The ship was falling to pieces and the gangways they would normally have used were no longer there. As Bess reached a flight of stairs, it collapsed before her eyes. An adult took her by the hand and said, 'Come on,' and led her somewhere she had never been before, up steps she'd never seen before. He must have been one of the crew. They emerged on the boat deck to a scene of total confusion.

The deck was slanting violently. Lifeboats were swinging wildly about from their davits. Some of them were being smashed against the sides of the ship. Those that were now full of people were being lowered into the sea. But in the swirling wind and with the lurching of the ship, the lowering gear and the ropes that held the boats kept getting snagged and jammed. Boats were tipping up at one end, people were falling out, screaming, into the water below. Bess saw children in their lifejackets, bobbing around in the sea, waves breaking over their heads. She thought about Euston

Station. She had been told to look after her brother. But where was he?

Louis Walder was in the water, one of a large group of children who had been shepherded by their escorts into one of the first lifeboats to be launched, one of those boats that had just spilled its human contents down the side of the ship. But Louis was lucky. His lifeboat landed in the sea somewhere near him, and an older boy who was still aboard reached down and plucked him out of the water. He was called George Crawford and he came from Sunderland. A few minutes later he was lost over the side trying to rescue somebody else. Louis Walder came under the protection of a young theology student escort called Michael Rennie. Rennie dived into the sea time and time again to drag children back into the unsteady, waterlogged lifeboat.

Back on the deck Bess and Beth were picked up and almost thrown into one of the last remaining boats. As it was being lowered, Bess saw crewmen trying to climb down rope ladders.

> Many of them tried jumping, it was hit and miss, it was a gamble whether they managed to get in to something like a boat, or land on a raft. Most of the time it didn't happen and they were thrashing about in the water and not many of them could swim.
>
> An ocean going lifeboat is about the size of a London bus. And this one was grossly overcrowded. It was unstable, it was rocking violently from side to side and it was only a matter of moments before the whole thing became waterlogged. The ship by now had gone down and we were rowing away from it when the lifeboat, as we knew it would, turned upside-down. And everybody inside was flung out into the sea.

In Scarborough Rosemary Lyster was, as usual, listening for E bars when a Morse SOS call with an enemy sighting report came over the huge receiving set that was permanently tuned to the distress frequency. The chief petty officer went upstairs to phone the Admiralty. He came down rather startled. 'I don't know what that was, but when I phoned it through the duty officer just said "Good God!" and slammed the phone down.'

Chapter 16

17–30 September

Wind W.N.W. Force 10. Barometer: 29.76. Whole Gale.
High precipitous seas. Shipping heavy seas fore and aft.
Labouring heavily. Fierce squalls.

From the log of the Richard de Larrinaga, *sailing in convoy
with the* City of Benares, *17 September 1940*

Bess Walder, thrown clear of the capsizing lifeboat, was carried up
a towering wave and hurled off its precipitous peak. Her father had
taught her to swim in the sea and as a child she had jumped off
harbour walls without fear. She told herself that she was a good
swimmer. She told herself to remember her father's advice: 'You
will go down, down, down and when you do you will then come
up, up, up, because people are like corks. And it is when you come
up like a cork that you must begin your work and swim.' Bess sank
down inside a vast green, shiny tunnel of seawater. She didn't try
to swim or thrash about. She just waited to turn into a cork.

Suddenly there she was, surging up again, bursting to breathe
by now, and as she hit the surface the first thing she saw was the
upturned lifeboat almost within her reach. She dived towards it and
clutched for the keel. It was sharp and metallic but she clung to it
with both her hands as the next wave threw her diagonally across

the clinker-built hull. Most of her upper body was out of the water now, but the crashing waves threatened to drag her back in at any moment.

She looked around. It was almost pitch black apart from the occasional flare in the distance. Near by she could make out other hands grasping the keel. As her eyes adjusted to the darkness, she could see the face of another girl on the opposite side of the hull. Her hands were like a mirror image of her own. She knew this girl. It was Beth Cummings. Looking farther down, she could see a row of arms on her side and a row of gripping knuckles on the other. From her side of the boat Beth could see the hands of an older lady who wore the most incredibly beautiful rings on her fingers. Bit by bit those fingers lost their grip and the elegant old lady slipped away.

Bess and Beth were both young and strong and determined. They had come this far and now they had made up their minds that they were going to survive. Over the sound of the wind, they told each other that help would surely come in the morning, that the rest of the convoy couldn't be far away. Some of the adults with them knew better. They might get a single search vessel if they were lucky, but God knew how it would find them in seas like these. Logic told them that their situation was utterly hopeless. They were on top of an upturned lifeboat in the middle of the Atlantic in a force-eight gale and surging, ice-cold seas. No food, no water, not even a slim hope of rescue. Perhaps it was this demoralising knowledge, or perhaps it was because the adults simply lacked the fierce resolve of youth, but, for whatever reason, one by one the grown-ups slipped quietly away.

Louis Walder's lifeboat was still afloat, but as the night went on waves kept breaking over the heads of its soaking, sick and exhausted occupants. One by one they succumbed. When the heroic theology student Michael Rennie died, worn out by the effort of saving so many from the water, the children whose lives he had already saved, and whom he had attempted to console and cheer, now seemed to give up hope themselves. The other adults attempted to lift their spirits, but only two out of the fifteen evacuees in that lifeboat would survive the night.

After a while the girls stopped speaking very much. 'First, you had to shout against the noise of the storm. Second, if you opened your mouth it was likely to fill up with sea-water. Third, unless it was something vital it was best to keep your mouth shut and to concentrate on holding on.' Bess told herself that she had to get back to her parents. She must get back. They had already lost their son and she had to explain what had happened and how it was that her brother was no longer alive. It wasn't her fault. There was nothing she could have done. But he must be dead. She knew that he was dead. She had seen so many of the younger children die. Beth Cummings was thinking of her mother who was a widow and of her two brothers, who were serving in the forces thousands of miles away. If she died then her mother would be left alone. It was not going to happen. They clung on.

They saw the dawn break. It revealed a vast and empty sea. By mid-morning there were only four of them left: Bess, Beth and two Indian sailors. One was talking to himself in a language that meant nothing to the two girls. He called out to the skies and his eyes rolled in distress. The other seaman was tied to the boat but he didn't move or speak. After an hour or so they realised that he was dead. They clung on. Two girls, a corpse and a man who was going mad with fear.

They were flung up and down, their bodies raised by the waves and then dropped back so that they hit the sides of the hull over and over again. They found a rope which ran the length of the keel. That was something else to hold on to when they were lifted up into the air. Soon they were bruised all over. Every impact made them wince and catch their breath. If this coincided with another wave then they would breathe in some seawater and have to cough to clear their lungs. They clung on. They were thrown against the hull of the boat until their chests and thighs were beaten insensible. The fronts of their bodies felt like jelly. Their feet were swollen and frozen. The man raved and howled. Bess was no longer sure what she was seeing. 'I thought I could see, out in the distance, that wonderful rocking horse going up and down on the waves. There were basket chairs floating by, but it was the rocking horse that I remember from the children's nursery.'

Their faces were swollen, their tongues enormous. There was nothing to drink. There was nothing to eat. Their eyelids were beginning to close. 'We were very near death. I said through my swollen lips to Beth, "We'll hang on." And she said, "Yes."' From time to time they both nearly fell asleep, only to be wakened by a suffocating panic as water broke over their heads.

The weather improved slightly; the big waves came less often. They clung on. The Indian man was listless and silent now, his tongue too fat for noise. The girls looked at each other. The waves hurled them against the white hull once more. They were linked, joined in mutual peril – they needed each other's strength. If one went, the other would too, and neither wanted to be first to let go. Knuckles clenched, they clung on. But both had the same unspoken thought – they would not last through another night like the last one.

It began to get dark again. The weather was getting worse. Dark clouds were scudding across the sky. And then suddenly and quite unaccountably Bess saw something moving on the horizon. 'Now so far nothing had moved on the horizon except clouds or waves, not even birds. And this was a small speck and it was getting larger. It looked black.'

Although she was almost unable to speak by now, Bess leant as close to Beth as she could and mouthed, 'Ship.' The other girl shook her head. They had both seen things that didn't exist. Sailing ships, flying fish, mermaids – mirages all, which quickly disappeared. But this little black speck of hope didn't disappear; it just kept getting closer and growing bigger.

Over Beth's shoulders, Bess watched the speck approach and watched it grow larger and larger until it became one of His Majesty's destroyers. 'Ship,' she mouthed again. Finally Beth craned her head around and almost lost her grip. There it was, a sleek grey-and-brown destroyer, steaming towards them, battered by the waves, going as fast as any ship could possibly go without tearing itself to pieces. They were too close to death to make a sign. And waving would mean taking one hand off the keel. The ship stopped. Had it missed them?

For a moment they watched with horror in case it turned round or disappeared. The Indian crewman had managed to lift his head and he was looking too. All three watched a large rowing boat, a navy whaler, being lowered from the side of the destroyer and then saw it row towards them, powered by the arms of six hulking young men.

> Closer and closer it came and then men inside it were cheering and shouting and saying, 'Hang on, hang on, we're coming'. We could hear noises coming from the destroyer too and it sounded like a rugby crowd. Men were cheering and shouting. These sailors had been picking dead children up all day and to find us alive was like a miracle. The coxswain of the lifeboat, to whom I shall ever be grateful, a chap called Albert Gorman, stretched his hands out and said to me, 'Come on darling, let go.' Do you know I couldn't. I couldn't let go. My hands were stuck tight.

Gorman carefully edged round until he could prise Bess Walder's glued fingers back and away from the keel, lifted her gently up and sat her inside the whaler. She was huddled up in a blanket. Other sailors did the same for Beth Cummings, the crewman and the corpse.

On board the destroyer, HMS *Hurricane*, they were treated like princesses. Nothing was too good for them. A young surgeon lieutenant on his first posting spent hours with them every day.

They were housed in the officers' cabins while the officers went to sleep in the ordinary sailors' mess. They headed back to Gourock in Scotland, HMS *Hurricane*'s home port. The surgeon lieutenant became concerned about Bess. He said, 'Come on Bess, get better quickly.' She said that she was trying to work out what to say to her parents about her brother. He said, 'You shouldn't worry about that. They'll be so pleased to have you. Some mummies and daddies won't have anyone.' Bess thought about it, but she still felt sick at heart. And then the next day the captain banged on the cabin door and shouted to her, 'Sit up, miss!' As he bustled in he said, 'I've got a present for you.' Bess gasped. 'From behind his back he produced my brother!'

Louis Walder had been rescued some time before his sister, but no one had realised they were related. And then days later, as Louis was being led through the ship by an officer and was shown the boiler room, full of the survivors' drying clothes, he said, 'Hey! That's my sister's dressing gown!' 'And now there was my brother sitting on my bunk, and he was saying to me, "What are you doing lying there?" And just like a very cross mother I said, "Where have you been?" And then of course we had a big hug, and I kissed him which, just like my brother, embarrassed and disgusted him.'

The Walder family were incredibly fortunate. Out of 406 people on board the *City of Benares*, 256 died, including 77 of the 90 child evacuees. 'An official called on my parents wearing a bowler hat, from the Civil Service department that sent the children out and said to my father: "I've come to tell you that your children are safe". "Thank God", said my father, "it's about time". Because he expected us to have landed in Canada already. When he found out what had really happened he was absolutely shattered. My brother and I were the only brother and sister of all the evacuees to have been saved. Some of the evacuees came back, but their sisters or their brothers weren't with them.' The official overseas evacuation scheme was immediately cancelled and no more ships sailed with evacuees on board.

Night after night, night after night, the bombardment of London continues . . . I am nerveless, and yet I am conscious that when I hear a motor in the empty streets I tauten myself lest it be a bomb screaming towards me. Underneath, the fibres of one's nerve-resistance must be sapped. There is a lull now. The guns die down towards the horizon like a thunderstorm passing to the south. But they will come back again in fifteen minutes. We are conscious all the time that this is a moment in history . . . I have a sense of strain and unhappiness; but none of fear.

One feels so proud.

Diary of Harold Nicolson, 19 September

For the American journalists living there, London during its 'Blitz' acquired a kind of glamour in its blacked-out defiance. All the correspondents soon had plenty of colourful stories of their personal brushes with death: being bombed out of their flats or finding themselves suddenly face down in a gutter. There were funny stories too, stories that played upon Londoners' good humour and steadiness under fire. CBS's Ed Murrow and his friend and fellow broadcaster Larry LeSueur played golf on Hampstead Heath some mornings. The rules committee there decided that a bomb crater counted as a natural hazard and that any players unfortunate enough to land a ball in it would be entitled to a 'free drop'.

PM's Ben Robertson soon became tired of running for the fetid, air-less shelters and decided that the small chance of his West End apartment receiving a direct hit merited the risk of staying there in comfort. Even so, the night was not without its terrors:

> You must determine not to mistake the backfire from buses
> for falling bombs and not allow the sound of an icebox motor
> to send you hurtling to the floor with fingers in ears and

mouth wide open to keep your teeth from breaking when the bomb explodes.

As he lay in his bed, Robertson's mind would wander back to America and he would imagine how the citizens of New York might cope under such a bombardment. He also thought of the German pilots overhead with their hands on the bombing switches. 'Think of the fantasy chance of this war, of some German up there with a hand on a lever which he either pulls or doesn't pull and you accordingly either kick the bucket or don't.'

Robertson wrote stories for *PM* about the rich mingling with the poor. He'd seen débutantes and shopgirls huddling together for safety. 'The silk stocking district got it last night,' one article began, and concluded by pointing out how Londoners saw their shared suffering as a template for a new and more equal world: 'From the ruins of this bombed city there are signs pointing to a bigger and better future.'

> We made a tour of a southeast suburb where a church and houses had been demolished during the night. The desolation was exactly like that I had seen in Georgia and Carolina after a tornado had passed. A crowd of people had assembled, and a woman pushing a baby-carriage said to us: 'It will take a million bombs to get London down'.
>
> Everywhere there were craters and ruin, but the city in this crisis had rediscovered itself; it was living as it never had lived. Everywhere there was courage, and six million people who had lived humdrum lives now learned what it was like to live for civilization.

Whitelaw Reid had managed to talk his way into the smartest air-raid shelter in town, the basement of the Savoy Hotel, right across from the *Herald Tribune*'s London offices.

I remember there was still music at the Savoy. I slept in the basement for a while. One or two nights I slept next to David Bowes-Lyon, the Queen's brother and he couldn't have been nicer or more friendly. There were a lot of mattresses laid out, like fifty or a hundred in rows and you found your way between the mattresses to the one that had been assigned to you. It was a good barracks we had in the bottom of the Savoy Hotel.

I got in trouble with the chef because I wrote up how ingenious he was in preparing all kinds of different foods and that what used to be good for the pigs now got made into interesting things like hors d'oeuvres. And a member of the Board of the Hotel Savoy sent a great complaint to the Tribune asking how I could say such a thing about their chef and the food he was supplying?

The American reporters tended not to experience, nor to write about, the uglier side of London's Blitz. But what they did write certainly made an impact. According to one American opinion poll, less than a quarter of respondents wanted to send more aid to Britain at the beginning of September. By the end of the month more than a half did.

At 8.30 in the morning of Tuesday, 24 September, 17 Squadron was scrambled to intercept bombers over the Thames Estuary. It was clear and sunny. They flew down the regular route from Debden to the mouth of the Thames, climbing all the time. Denis Wissler was happy, humming to himself as he flew, feeling fresh. On Friday night at a party in the sergeants' mess he had met 'a sweet little WAAF named Margaret Cameron'. They had danced, and when the party ended he had walked her home and they had had 'quite a kissing session' on the way. He smiled at the memory. That had been followed by London and a day's leave.

His mother and father had just moved to a flat in Dolphin Square. The family, Swiss-German in origin, owned the factory that made Marmite. Pop wanted to be near the factory in case anything happened. He made jokes about the Germans having better things to do than bomb the British out of Marmite, but anybody could see that whatever the Germans thought they were doing with their night raids they weren't hitting anything with very much precision. Bombs had been landing all over the place.

Yesterday had been an easy day – just one 'flap' and nothing seen. They didn't seem to come over very much in daylight any more. So they had given up and come home in time for him to take Margaret out. They had just gone for a walk in the lanes in the autumn sunshine and found a nice quiet spot for some more kissing. She was nice, but he wasn't sure that she was quite his sort, or he hers. He thought for a moment about the girl he had met with Birdy. Edith. She had been so funny. Very sharp too – she had teased him mercilessly in the car. All about the sand he'd thrown into her engine. God, that seemed a long time ago. And then she had been so anxious about those horses in the burning stables, so tender about them. But she seemed to belong to Jeffers. Denis didn't believe in stealing other people's girlfriends, and anyway, there didn't seem to be much prospect of taking a girl from someone like Jefferies, who had been one of 17 Squadron's star pilots.

'Bandits on the run, Blue leader; new vector 100, angels 16.'
'Understood control.'

Almost at Southend. Better start scanning the skies. To his right he could see Birdy leading Green Section. He had been presented with his DFC this morning for his ninth kill. That was far more than Wissler could claim, even at the most optimistic count. He kept missing out. Whenever the squadron had an easy day's killing, he seemed to be on leave. And when he was there you could be sure that Ops would ask them to do something impossible. Ahead, he kept his eye on Alf Bayne. Over the Thames now. They should be able to see the bombers soon.

'Tally ho.'

Birdy was curving away to the right and Bayne was swinging Blue Section round too. Wissler concentrated on holding formation in the turn. Jesus, what was that? Spitfires. Spitfires were diving through them from above. Hang on – bullets. 'Mayday, Green 1 on fire.' The Spitfires have got Messerschmitts on their tails, lots of them. They've led them straight down on to us. Birdy's on fire. Leary's voice: 'He's out. There's a parachute. I'm going to circle him to guard him down.' 'Roger Green 3.' A 109 straight ahead. I can't catch him up. Have a go anyway. Blast – missed. I'm going to have one of these bastards. There must be one somewhere. Four, up above. Right. Climb, you sweet little engine, climb. I'm going to stall. Level out. That's better. Oh, shit! A blinding flash on the port wing and Wissler felt a blow on his left arm, and then blood running down into his flying suit. Dive, for Christ's sake, dive! He's gone. Better get back.

'Blue 2 to control. Do you receive me?' 'We hear you, Blue 2.' 'Been hit and coming home. The wing's damaged. I think I can get there but I may have trouble landing.' 'We'll have the fire engine waiting for you.' 'Is Birdy all right?' 'The Navy have sent an MTB. We hope he's OK. Vector 340 Blue 2. Happy landing.'

Down in the chalkpit operations room it was more tense than the controller's calm voice suggested. The CO was furious with the Spitfires. They'd wrecked the mission and caused serious losses. It sounded like one pilot dead and two wounded for no enemy losses. A bloody awful morning's work. The rest of the squadron had pulled out now, and they were limping back to Debden in ones and twos. Edith Heap and Winifred Butler exchanged glances. 'Green 1 on fire' had been a heart-stopping moment. They knew that was Birdy's normal spot, and sure enough it had been him. They both recognised Blue 2 as well. He was Birdy's friend Denis, the boy in the back of the car. Would he make it back?

Past Great Dunmow and circling Debden. Wissler had lost a lot of blood and was feeling rather faint. Just the landing now. Never done one without flaps. Could he stop? Perhaps he should bale out. No, he would get them both down, himself and 'V for D'. Landing without flaps – another first. Give it a long run. Come in as shallow as possible. Shallow and fast. Come on, 'V', come on, don't let me down now. On the deck. Christ, I'll never stop. I can hear the fire engine. Seems to be a gap in the hedge there. Come on, brakes. Thump!

As Denis Wissler lay in Saffron Walden General Hospital, Sam Patience was on board his battleship, HMS *Resolution,* off the West African port of Dakar. General de Gaulle had persuaded Churchill that the French garrison there could be brought into the war on the Allied side and an expeditionary force had been sent to encourage them to do so. The whole thing was a farce. Intelligence about the attitude of the French was hopelessly over-optimistic. Memories of *Resolution*'s previous anti-French action at Oran had poisoned all relations between Britain and such outposts as Dakar. Instead of coming over to de Gaulle, the local commander demanded that the British and Free French forces leave his waters immediately. On 23 September Swordfish torpedo bombers dropped leaflets in a vain attempt to persuade the garrison to change their mind. A poorly planned amphibious attack followed. The French shore batteries opened fire, damaging a British cruiser and two destroyers. The next day *Resolution* and other warships bombarded the base and *Ark Royal* launched a torpedo and dive-bombing strike on the French battleship *Richelieu*. Five out of the eight attacking aircraft were lost to anti-aircraft guns and French fighter planes.

On 25 September the Royal Navy shelled the harbour again. *Resolution* hit some shore batteries on an island where a great pile of groundnut husks sent a huge cloud of brown dust into the air. Sam Patience was watching this bizarre scene as the French submarine *Bévéziers* slipped out of harbour. One of the Fleet Air Arm pilots up above saw torpedoes running towards the battleship, but by the time he got his message out in Morse one of them had struck. 'There was a hell of a bang and a shudder. There was panic on board. Everyone ran up ladders to get on the upper deck. She heeled over. The torpedo had hit the boiler room and the ship couldn't get underway.' The crew rolled vast numbers of shells over the side in an effort to right the ship. Admiral Cunningham's fears about losing an old battleship and hundreds of lives had very nearly come true. *Resolution* limped back to Freetown for repairs, the only British battleship to be seriously damaged during the whole of 1940, hit not by Germans or Italians but by Britain's former allies.

At Freetown most of the crew dispersed. Sam Patience was sent back to Chatham, convinced that nothing could be worse than sitting on that old thunderbox in the sweltering heat off Africa. Within sixteen hours he was on the train for Liverpool where the *Duchess of Richmond* was waiting to take him to Canada.

Patience was being rushed out to supplement the crew of HMS *Lincoln*, one of the first of the old American destroyers to be handed over to the Royal Navy in Halifax, Nova Scotia. The few professional sailors then on board her certainly needed his help.

Iain Nethercott first mustered his trainee mariners in the *Lincoln*'s No. 2 mess. There were thirty of them, and at nineteen years of age he was in charge. He said: 'I don't know if you lot understand what a Leading Seaman is, but you've got to do what I tell you. And I don't want any old nonsense. I've never run a bloke before an officer in my life and if any of you make trouble we'll just hop up on the fo'c'sle and I'll give you a bloody good hiding and that'll save mucking about with Naval discipline.' Before delivering this speech he had checked that there was nobody in the mess of a build more imposing than his own. 'Now, I want your full names, and your previous occupations.' He had factory hands from the Midlands, office workers from London and Glasgow, 'keelies' from the Glasgow Gorbals, a well-spoken solicitor and one ugly, pug-faced Yorkshireman who claimed to be 'the best burglar in Barnsley'. He put the burglar and the solicitor on the same watch. They would have plenty to talk about. Only two in Nethercott's mess were regulars, both just out of detention for drunkenness and fighting the Shore Patrol.

Over the coming days, whilst the ship ran simple sea trials and waited for extra help to arrive, Nethercott taught his men rope-splicing, wire-splicing, semaphore, Morse, how to tie knots, how to raise and lower anchors, and how to cook on board ship. They were keen to learn, and there was no need for any strong arm stuff up on the fo'c'sle. Above all he taught them how to row and how to handle small boats in rough seas. They were all destined for convoy escort duty, and in a few weeks they might have to pull alongside a burning oil tanker. After a few early disasters, Nethercott was confident he had a good crew for the *Lincoln*'s wooden six-oar 'whaler'. He was less confident about the *Lincoln* herself.

> The ship was bloody awful, when she got out in a decent swell she was so low in the water that she was kind of half-submarine, half-destroyer. How they expected her to live in a full Atlantic gale, I have no idea. She looked like a packet of Woodbines with four long thin funnels, a glass-fronted bridge, which would be a death trap in a strafing attack from low-flying aircraft. She had no fire control, so each gunner would attempt to do his own thing. It would be completely impossible to man the foc'sle 4-inch gun in bad weather or at speed because the crew would be swept over the side.

Down aft, on what the Americans called the 'fantail', Nethercott came across a three-inch gun with a brass label proudly describing it as an 'anti-zeppelin' gun.

Edith Heap and Winifred Butler went to visit Denis Wissler in Saffron Walden. He was sitting up in bed with big bandages on his left arm and plasters all over his forehead. The arm wounds had come courtesy of the Luftwaffe cannon shell that had blown most of 'V for D''s port flaps away; the cuts to his head were from the collision with the pile of rubble at the side of Debden's main runway. The WAAFs told Wissler that 'Birdy' Bird-Wilson was all right – he had been fished out of the sea with slight burns and taken to a hospital in Haywards Heath.

Wissler was discharged on Friday, 27 September in time for

another party in the sergeants' mess. He tried to be nice to Margaret Cameron, but then he spotted his two hospital visitors. Making the most of the rawness of his wound, he disengaged and slipped over to buy the two WAAFs drinks from the bar. Soon they were chattering away. Edith Heap was witty and quick and he liked her – yes, he liked her a lot. When he said goodnight to Margaret she left him in no doubt about her displeasure. There was no kiss.

Heap liked her injured pilot too. Liked his funny half-smile, his confidence, liked the way he had a quick rejoinder to everything she said. Most men weren't like that, not with her anyway.

On Saturday Wissler had the stitches in his arm taken out because the wound was slightly infected. The doctor told him that he was staying on the ground at Debden until his arm healed properly and he was going to get seven days' sick leave. On Sunday he lay around all day waiting for the evening. The band would be playing in the mess as usual but Edith was on duty in Ops until eight and Ops was now in some chalkpit in Saffron. When the band packed up he went over to the sergeants' mess. He had a few drinks, just waiting for Edith to arrive. Finally she came through the door with Winifred, looking absolutely radiant. This must be love. He walked over to make sure he was the first to ask her to dance. In the morning Denis went home on leave. The world was a wonderful place. For the first time he couldn't wait to get back to Debden.

The war came home to everyone at a different time. It came to 66 Beverley Gardens, Wembley on the night of 29 September 1940. Whilst Denis Wissler and Edith Heap were dancing the polka, Alan Francis was sleeping under an ironing board, dreaming of sugar lumps. Elsie Francis was going to make rhubarb jam in the morning. Alan had made a mental note that she had left the family's precious hoard of rationed sugar out close to him, and he might be able to raid the jar for a handful during the night. His parents had kissed him goodnight before making up their own bed in the

345

dining room. Tonight sounded pretty serious, so they had not even bothered going upstairs.

Alan woke about two in the morning, very confused. People were shouting. This was the perfect opportunity. He reached down to pick up a piece and popped a lump of plaster into his mouth. Yuk!

His grandfather was doing the whistle, the one with his fingers in his mouth that Alan couldn't master. He was doing it out in the garden. You couldn't normally see into the garden. But you could now. You could see right into the house next door too. 'My father was OK, my mother who was lying next to him under the table was hit by the middle wall which came through and just crushed her.'

The war came home to everyone at a different time, but not in the same way. British civilian losses in World War II were minor compared to what would happen in Russia, in the Ukraine, in Germany, in Japan. Most British schoolboys and schoolgirls could and would continue spotting planes and comparing battleship cards without ever seeing what war was really like, without ever fighting for their lives in the middle of an Atlantic gale or waking up next to their dead mothers. Most could and would. These would be the best days of their lives.

Life or death? Plaster or rhubarb jam? It was just luck really.

> I was carried out of the building by a police inspector and my brother was carried out by a fireman. I remember saying to him that I knew what all this stuff in the road was called, it was called debris. I felt very proud of the fact that I could use that word and know what it was. Oh yes, he said, that's debris all right.
>
> And we were taken to this house opposite. My father went to the hospital and was told that my mother had been killed. He came back to the house and his hair was standing straight up on end, just like it used to in the children's comics, anyone who'd had a shock, straight up as though electrified. I didn't really comprehend the immensity of it. I was determined at the time that I wouldn't react, strange as it may seem, I kept a stiff upper lip. I get more upset about it now than I did then.

Chapter 17

October

Everyone had heard about the poor bastard stuck in a burning cockpit, wailing and screaming over the RT, or the guy who'd somehow got back down with his arm off and an eyeball hanging out, only to expire on the tarmac, or the one who'd baled out with his thigh cut most of the way through and who kept kicking himself in the face with his flying boot as the bottom half of his leg spun about at the end of a tendon.

Some started to crack, some didn't – you could never really predict it.

'Twitch', a bad case of the 'twitch', or the 'shakes', 'nervous exhaustion and the shakes' – that would be it. 'Been putting a few extra mirrors in the cockpit, always a bad sign. Haven't seen him in the mess much either. Needs to go out and get absolutely blotto with the rest of the boys. Can you have a word with him? Maybe he needs to go away for a bit, pressure's off a little now, let's give the poor chap a rest. Come back right as rain, you'll see.'

Denis Wissler had kept going. He'd been in this ghastly war for five months now and he wasn't an ace and he still hadn't got a medal but he'd kept going. Halves, shares, wild-goose chases but no twitch, no shakes, no kindly suggestions from above that he should take a bit of a break, not even after he was shot down.

Although the bombers rarely came in daylight any more, the Luftwaffe kept sending over fighter sweeps, or fighters armed with single nuisance bombs, and so Fighter Command scrambled people to go up and drive them away. A job for Spitfires really, but 17 Squadron's Hurricanes had their share of the action. As soon as the medical officer passed him fit, he'd be back up there in 'V for D' with the rest of the boys. He still wanted that DFC.

The phone rang and the guard summoned Edith Heap. It was Denis, back from sick leave. 'Are you coming to the squadron dance?' She knew that 17 Squadron was going to be moved to Martlesham again and they were having a special dance down in 'B' Flight's dispersal hut. 'Yes, we've been asked already. Actually we're on duty till eight down at the emergency Ops Room so we'll all come afterwards.' How exciting – so much for that other woman.

Edith expected that Jefferies would be there. They had been going out together but she hadn't heard from him recently, he hadn't written once, and anyway, she didn't care much for him now. When they came off duty quite a flood of WAAFs turned up at the hut. Denis was waiting for her at the door and so Edith never got as far as the bar at the other end of the room. He caught her in his arms and whirled her off and they danced and danced and then just talked again for ages. He was so funny and considerate. He spoiled her in a way that she could definitely get used to.

Out of the corner of her eye Edith saw that Jefferies was dancing with Winifred, and she couldn't care less. She felt completely bowled over by someone for the first time in her life, and it was wonderful. Denis said he wanted a photograph. They went back to her billet to fetch one and they kissed for the first time as they crossed the grass. They laughed when they noticed that another couple was already using the back of Edith's Jaguar for some privacy. And then it was midnight and they all left. At the door Jefferies appeared, cross because Edith had not spoken to him all night. Edith asked Denis to step back while they had a private word. She told him that it was his job to make the moves, not hers, and that she hadn't seen him making any for weeks. She walked home with Denis and they agreed that they would write to each other every day and meet as soon as their duties would allow.

Marian Holmes was sitting in the ground-floor air-raid shelter inside Number 10 Downing Street. As usual most of the explosions were distant and muffled. But then one wasn't. There was a roar, a rush of warm air, and the whole building shook around them. Holmes was temporarily stunned by the noise and by a strange feeling inside her ears, as if she had put her head under water. Air pressure, she thought in a dull, stumbling way, the bomb's pressure wave. Then, as her head cleared, she realised that the force of the blast had also smashed her temple against the brick wall.

The bomb that gave Marian Holmes concussion had landed on the Treasury, right next door. It exploded on top of a shelter very much like her own and killed three civil servants inside it. It shattered most of the windows in Downing Street too. Shards of broken glass were sent flying all over the Prime Minister's kitchen. Minutes earlier Churchill had ordered his cook and her maid to stop hiding under the tables there and to join him and the others. He had saved their lives, or at least that's what everyone in the house believed. The force of the blast had even buckled the heavy steel door to the underground passage that linked Downing Street to the Treasury – 'the Chancellor's Back Passage' as it was known inside Number 10. Falling bombs and sleepless nights seemed to make people want to share that kind of dirty joke.

But it just went to show that moving to the annexe had been

a good idea. Stupid, really, to keep using Number 10 at all, but Churchill did so love to entertain there.

Bob Doe and the rest of 234 Squadron had been pulled out of the front line and sent back to Cornwall for a well-deserved rest. Only three of the pilots who had flown up with Doe in mid-August flew back. Four had been killed in action, two were POWs, and the rest were injured or had been found wanting in some way and 'posted'.

In Cornwall Doe spent a lot of time sleeping. He was terribly tired and felt that he should preserve his strength for the next challenge. His respite, although welcome, was short. He was sent back to Chilbolton, a satellite base of Middle Wallop, as a new flight commander with 238 Squadron. The major catch was that 238 flew Hurricanes. He took one up for half an hour's familiarisation and there didn't seem to be anything particularly difficult about it. 'How did you find D, sir?' Naturally, Doe had demanded 'D' for Doe again. 'Not like a Spit but she'll do. Flaps a bit stiff. Sort it out, would you!' 'Yes, sir.' And then, as the new officer retreated: 'He's a bit grumpy, isn't he?' Bob Doe, so unsure of himself a few weeks before, was now very confident about his own abilities, and rather less confident about the abilities of others.

His new squadron had taken heavy casualties. Two died on the morning he arrived. But Doe soon added to his own account with a Messerschmitt 109 and a Junkers 88. The Junkers had been startling. It was part of a small raid towards Yeovil or Bristol. 'I must have hit an oxygen bottle, which blew the tail off, and out of this hole people started coming out and pulling their parachutes. The last one out pulled his parachute too soon and it caught fire and I saw this parachute burning away as it went down.'

He now had fourteen swastikas on the side of his plane and scramble calls kept coming.

One came on 10 October. Doe led them off the ground. The early morning fog had gone but there was thick cloud. 'Hello control, Koda squadron calling. Koda squadron airborne making Angels 20, over.' A little later: 'Hello Koda leader, Bandy here. Vector 220, Angels 20.' The raid seemed to be aimed at either Warmwell, the forward airfield, or else at nearby Portland harbour. The enemy were flying high, too high for Hurricanes, which were not good at top altitudes. It sounded like another lightning attack by bomb-carrying Messerchmitt 109s. If so, God help the kids he had with him.

'For Christ's sake be careful in the cloud, do you hear. And see you up above. Good luck!' Then into the cotton wool, climbing steadily with nothing in sight for six nerve-racking minutes. Wondering whether the others would still be following when they came out of the cloud. Knowing that from above you can see planes two or three hundred feet deep in cloud, though if you're in the cloud you can't see a blind thing. A hint of light ahead. Almost at the top now. Would they be waiting?

'Shit!' Something shot over Doe's shoulder and into the petrol tank in front. 'Christ, will it blow?' Another bang. 'Ah, my foot! Shit, I can't move it. Where the hell was that bang?' Thud. A sledgehammer to the left side of the chest. 'My heart! Oh my God, I'm dead. No, my shoulder, not dead, not yet. How are they shooting me from in front and behind at the same time? Where are they? Ow, my hand! The bastard's smashed my watch. What do I do? Think, Doe! Down. Hit stick. Straight down.'

Bunting, they called it in flying school. Leaning on the stick and doing a kind of half-loop forwards and downwards. You pulled an awful lot of negative G, your engine would probably cut and you might well pass out for a second or two, but it was the best and quickest way to get out of the kind of serious trouble that Bob Doe was in.

By now he was back deep inside into the cool, wet, enveloping cloud. Time to take stock. Hurricane 'D' was mortally wounded even if Doe wasn't. It was extremely lucky that the fuel tank hadn't

blown up already. It still might. He had to get out. Pull the release
pin. It hasn't worked. The Sutton harness is still holding me. Christ.
Tear at it. Thank God, it's free. I've fallen out. Where is the hood?
I never opened it. Shot clean away. Get clear of the plane, count
and pull. No, not yet, you chump, this is wonderful! What a lovely
sensation! Free fall. Woosh. But how can I tell where the ground is
when I can't see anything? How long have I been falling? Where's
the parachute handle? Thank God I can still use my right arm. Here
it comes. Good, but not that good. That bang underneath me. The
shell must have exploded near the parachute pack. There's hardly a
single panel without a rip in it. Still, I'm coming down a bit more
slowly. Quite a lot more slowly really. The bottom of the cloud
coming. Then we'll see what we're in for. Christ, I'm in paradise.
It's gorgeous. They don't have blue lagoons like this in England.
Will it be better to go into the sea? It must be better to hit water
than land at this speed. Hang on, I'm drifting towards that island.
Will I clear it? Ugh, this is foul.

Brownsea Island in the middle of Poole harbour was a nature
reserve. Mrs Mary Bonham-Christie, who owned the island, was
a great believer in nature. She didn't approve of sewage treatment,
for a start. All of the sewers on the island ran into a central drainage
pit, and it was this quagmire that had broken Bob Doe's fall. The
impact knocked him out for a moment. When he came round
he was aware first of the stench and then of an enormous,
fierce-looking man standing over him brandishing an iron bar.

The man spoke in a broad Irish accent. 'What are yer?' Doe
wondered what would happen to him had he been German, and
thought just in time to answer 'British' rather than 'English'. The
Irish giant pulled him out, threw him over his shoulder and carried
him eight hundred yards to the jetty. He then gently put the pilot
down. Doe lay with his head resting on a wild rose bush and
thought how beautiful Poole harbour was, how beautiful England
was, how beautiful life was. He'd come up smelling of roses after
all – well, sort of.

He would have a job living this story down when the squadron found out, as they inevitably would. The immortal Doe, the 'gen man', the cool killer, saved by what had seemed uncommonly like a cesspit. The Navy sent a boat to pick him up and, holding their noses theatrically, the sailors took him over to a hospital in Poole. Perhaps he had been a bit arrogant and short-tempered recently. Well, he'd got his comeuppance all right. You had to see the funny side, though. He laughed and it hurt.

On 8 October Denis had driven over to Martlesham with the adjutant and another pilot, having been given ground duties for three more days. They stopped at a number of excellent pubs. In the evening he dropped in on Edith, but she had just come off duty and was on again in four hours' time. She gave him a watch list, so that he would know where she was. He and Pittman went to the cinema. On 10 October he was passed fit for full flying and straight away he was back on patrol.

Experienced pilots were like gold dust now. On his first flight a straggling newcomer was picked off by a lone Me 109. They were patrolling London. Wissler found it difficult to adjust yet again to the routine of risking his life two or three times a day. On Sunday, 13 October he wrote in his diary: 'The weather again was clear and bright, oh for some clouds and rain.' Finding time to write to Edith was not easy. He had to get the letter right. It was an important one. His thoughts were always with her. He was also bothered about his parents. He had not told them about Edith. Would they understand? They must have been in love when they were young. But it would not have been quite like this.

Denis wrote and said that he wanted to see her on Friday and for them to go out and do something special. He had some leave. He wondered if they could spend some of it together, away somewhere, in a hotel. He wanted her to ring to discuss it. On Thursday, 17 October, after two patrols over London and a fruitless chase after an intruder with Alf Bayne, he sat in the mess waiting nervously for a call from Edith. It came. Tomorrow, she said. She would meet him at Debden. Yes, she'd come away with him.

Edith waited eagerly for Friday evening. Nothing like his had ever happened to her before, and not quite knowing where it was going to lead only added to the excitement. He arrived on time and she drove him to Cambridge in her car. He directed her straight to the Garden House Hotel and marched in, but came back looking anxious. 'They've only got a double room and I said that wouldn't do. That's right, isn't it?' She said decisively, 'Oh yes,' wondering if this was the invitation to spend the night together, wondering if she should, wondering what he would have thought of her if she had said, 'Oh come on, it's late, let's take it anyway.'

They drove out of town and at the Red Lion at Trumpington they got lucky. There were two single rooms free. They had dinner and talked and laughed and smiled at each other. Then he said, 'I've got something I want to say to you, privately.' They went up to her bedroom. She looked carefully to see if anyone had noticed. 'You never had a man in your bedroom, you just never did it.'

'Denis sat on the bed and I leant against the dressing table, and he said, "Will you marry me?" So I said, "Of course".' Denis went downstairs and ordered a bottle of champagne and the landlord brought it up and never said a thing. Edith was quite surprised. Eventually the champagne was gone and they both felt happy and light-headed. It was a night of possibilities, the beginning of a lifetime of possibilities.

They both grew suddenly quiet and nervous. Neither wanted to spoil the moment, neither wanted the other to think less of them. It was Edith's move really, and she signalled her decision with silence. Denis put his glass down, kissed his fiancée goodnight and went to his room.

Next morning he said, 'We'll go and buy the ring first, but I want to take you to see my parents, because they don't know anything about you.' Suddenly Edith was stymied. As a result of some misdemeanour, her watch had been penalised twelve hours of their twenty-four hours off camp as a punishment. After they had chosen a ring she rang Bill, her sergeant, and said, 'Look, I've just got engaged to Denis and he wants me to go down to see his parents, is that all right?' 'Where are you?' 'Cambridge.' So Bill said, 'Yes, that's all right.' 'Do you want me to come and book out?' 'No, no,' she said, 'off you go.' Denis stopped in Quendon to ring ahead and announce their impending arrival. He just said he was bringing a girlfriend for the night. Edith waited in the car, beginning to think, 'Oh my God, what are they going to say? They don't know anything about me.' The nearer they got to London the more apprehensive she became.

Edith parked in Dolphin Square, they climbed the stairs to the first-floor flat and she was trembling as they walked down the long corridor. Denis took hold of her hand to give them both courage, and rang the bell. There was a shout of welcome and they came out and he said, 'Get in there,' and pushed Edith into the bathroom just inside the door to wait. And she heard him tell them, and there were whoops and yells and they came and fetched her from the bathroom and that was it. She was accepted and it was absolutely fantastic. Edith had the nicest evening she had ever had in her life, because Denis's family were so funny and so friendly and soon they would be her family too.

While Denis stayed on in London, Edith had to drive back to camp. She told Winifred the news and it was not well received. Winifred thought that Edith had treated Jeffers badly. Within a week she was engaged to him herself. Then Edith realised that she had better ring her own mother. Long-distance calls were limited to three minutes before you were cut off by the operator, so you had to think what you were going to say, and say it fast. 'So I rang her up and said, "I'm engaged!" "Oh!" she said, and, "what's all this?" I said, "Well, actually all you need do is to go down the road and see Aunt Florrie who happens to be related to his aunt. He's writing to you".' Edith's sister told her later that their mother got her coat on and went storming down to see her old friend Florrie and eventually she came back and said, 'Well that's all right then!'

Rosie Lee's father was a middle-aged docker. As more men volunteered or got conscripted, the busier he became. Now he had a regular job at Butler's Wharf. When it became clear that the Germans were going to bomb London every night, the company offered to house their workers' families in one of the deep cellars under the warehouses. And so for several weeks Mr and Mrs Lee, Rosie, Lily and Charlie would all walk down to the docks when the siren went and climb down a long spiral staircase to the vault that was to be their overnight quarters. There wasn't much in the way of home comforts – the toilets were two metal buckets behind a piece of rough sacking.

It was a damp, joyless, smelly old place, it was a long way from home, and the girls soon grew to hate it. And besides, as Rosie and Lily kept pointing out, there was a great shelter under the arch by Druid Street. All the young people went there now. Somebody had dragged in a piano and every night there would be some kind of a party. Tonight was Friday night, 25 October, the end of the week, and it would be an especially good party. 'Oh. Come on Mum.'

Mr and Mrs Lee caved in to their daughters' nagging and they all walked down to Druid Street. Sadly, it was already full. Inside they could hear singing and laughter. The girls were very cross and quietly sulked as the family trudged miserably on towards Butler's Wharf again. The siren wailed once more and the searchlights began to perform their nightly dance across the sky.

In the morning, they all came home to wash and change. As they walked back down Druid Street, there were ambulances stretched right across the archways, completely blocking the entrance. The policeman would not let them come close. He said they wouldn't want to see inside. Rescue workers were in tears and ambulancemen sat around with dull eyes and pale, haggard faces. A bomb had gone straight through the railway line and penetrated the shelter from above before exploding right inside it. A big bomb. Seventy-seven people were officially dead but, as usual, nobody knew how many had been there in the first place.

'I'm sorry, can't you see that I'm busy.' The shopkeeper turned her back and continued talking to the lady with the large handbag.

'You're all a bunch of bloody snobs!'

Ada Taylor could feel the tears welling up, but she wasn't going to give another stuck-up woman the pleasure of seeing her weep. She turned and flounced out of the door. It made a satisfying slam behind her. Then she started to cry.

She hated Finchley. It was the worst place in the whole world. Her father had been cautioned by the police for singing and carrying on in the pub, the family next door just looked the other way whenever they went in or out, and just about every shopkeeper made a point of serving someone else first or saying that they were saving this or that 'for our regulars'.

'Snobs, snobs, snobs!'

She missed Canning Town so much. Missed the noise in the street, the funny old woman up the road with the donkey in her yard, the muffin man coming round, her dad and his brother sitting out on the step talking to the neighbours. Neighbours! They didn't know the meaning of the word around here. Poor Uncle Bob, killed in that stupid ruddy school. That hateful school. She cried some more. A kindly old lady stopped and asked whether she could help. Ada thanked her, pulled herself together and walked home.

They weren't all bad. The policeman who'd taken her father away had turned on some of the locals and told them that he'd been down the East End and that it could have been people like them under those bombs, and they should all give these newcomers a chance. And the woman whose house she and her sister were staying in was really generous. She'd even let

Ada bring her pet dog. But by and large Finchley had signalled its disapproval of the East End refugees from the start. The local relief officer seemed more concerned with delousing them than getting people somewhere decent to stay. Families had been broken up; people that were used to living in a large, loud community were separated and spread out right across this big unfriendly suburb, a handful here and there. Ada's father, Arthur, was put half a mile away with her granddad. When the evacuees tried to get together in the pubs it would soon be 'Throw all these East Enders out!'

After weeks of complaining, the Taylors were reunited in a large family house of their own. Others were not so fortunate. October had brought no relief from London's nightly ordeal by fire and high explosive. On 15 October Balham Underground station was hit and of the six hundred people sheltering there sixty, seventy – again no one was ever sure how many – died under the rubble. There were more homeless people every day.

Jock Colville and Clementine Churchill visited the Prime Minister's parliamentary constituency in the London suburb of Chingford: 'The saddest sight was the homeless refugees in a school. One woman, wheeling a baby in a pram, told me she had twice been bombed out of her house and kept on saying disconsolately, "A load of trouble, a load of trouble." One woman said: "It is all very well for them," (looking at us!) "who have all they want; but we have lost everything."'

Sam Patience joined HMS *Lincoln* as quartermaster for her Canadian sea trials because they were short of people who could steer the ship. The first few days were enough to put him off. The four funnels made it look top-heavy, and the slightest Atlantic swell confirmed the impression. They had hardly left Halifax harbour before the ship started rolling unsteadily back and forth. The thing was falling to pieces, was barely watertight, and Patience very much doubted if it would even make it back to England. Besides, there was hardly

17 Squadron 'B' Flight, Blue Section:
left to right 'Birdy' Bird-Wilson, Alf Bayne, Denis Wissler

Members of 17 Squadron at Debden on 12 August 1940.
Left to right: flight sergeant (unknown); Denis Wissler, Jack Ross, 'Birdy' Bird-Wilson;
Cedric Williams; David Leary

Main picture Tower Bridge with the docks on fire, 7 September 1940
Above East End homes being evacuated, 8 September 1940
Left The ruins of Agate Street School after it was bombed on 10 September 1940

Sam Patience

Right Patience's certificate signed by the senior surviving officer of HMS *Jervis Bay*, verifying his injuries and his sobriety

Rosie Lee

CANADA

Certificate for Wounds and Hurts

These are to Certify ~~the Honourable the Minister of National Defence of the Dominion of Canada~~ that

(Name in full)	(Rank or Rating)	(Official No.)

SUTHERLAND PATIENCE   A.B. R.N.R.   X 19818A
SAMUEL   "

belonging to His Majesty's ~~Canadian~~ Ship " *JERVIS BAY* "

being then actually upon His Majesty's ~~Canadian~~ Naval Service in

Here describe the particular duty.   HAMMER P1

"Injured" or "Wounded." †Date.   was* Wounded   on† Nov. 5th 1940   by

Here describe minutely the nature of the injury sustained and the manner in which it occurred—as required by articles 1207, 1318, 1354 of the King's Regulations.

the explosion of an 11" shell from the enemy which landed on the Forecastle as she was putting a smoke float over the bow. He was blown on to the well deck. He sustained 2nd degree burns on the left hand involving the dorsal and palmer surfaces. Also a puncture wound to the Right 3rd and minor wounds by a piece of shrapnel. 2. Loss of Partial Lower denture

1"Sober" or "not sober."   He was† Sober   at the time

Age about 21 years. Born at or near Aboch, Sc. Htland Height 6 ft ½ ins.

Personal Description.   Hair Brown   Eyes Blue   Complexion fresh

Particular marks or scars.   { Rear right ~~~~ about 2" long ~

Date 7/No. 27.   19 40

~~Senior Surviving~~
Signature of ~~Commanding~~ Officer of Ship.   NEwood

Rank Lieutenant RNR (T.124)

Signature of person who witnessed the accident. }

Rank

Signature of Medical Officer. }   R Webster

Rank Surg. Lt RCNVR

NOTE:—The grant of a Hurt Certificate to a Petty Officer or Man is to be noted on his Service Certificate.

C.N.S. 2435
5a—3-40 (4135)
N.S. 815-9-2435

The photograph of herself that Edith Heap gave to Denis Wissler on the night of 7 October 1940

Denis Wissler with Hurricane 'V for D'

enough room, quite literally, to sling a hammock. In a bar in Halifax, Patience met another quartermaster from a liner called the *Jervis Bay* which had been converted into an Armed Merchant Cruiser. The man wanted to get home in a hurry and *Jervis Bay* had to wait for a convoy. *Lincoln* was now ready to leave. How would Sam fancy a swap? As a boy, Patience had dreamed about steering an ocean liner. He said yes immediately, the two captains agreed the deal, and Sam Patience bade HMS *Lincoln* a not particularly fond farewell.

As soon as they were at sea, water began to leak through the rivet holes underneath. The pumps were working all the time. And the *Lincoln* seemed to have a mysterious kink in her so that whatever you did with her she carried about ten degrees of port wheel. To steer a straight course you had to add ten degrees of rudder all the time.

And then the weather turned rough. South of Greenland they ran into a terrible storm.

It soon became a struggle for survival. A big wave would catch the bow and sweep it around. In daylight you could see them coming, but not necessarily at night. The man on watch at the wheel would turn the ship towards the wave, put her nose in and hope she would climb it. Iain Nethercott and the other experienced sailors on board had never seen anything like it. 'It scared me at night on the bridge watching giant rollers sixty and seventy feet high rearing ahead in the darkness and nursing the old girl's bow up into them so that they wouldn't sweep us broadside where we might broach to and roll over.'

Down below, Nethercott's mess was a disgusting shambles. With one exception his novice sailors were hideously seasick. The experienced hands got them in their bunks and lashed them round and round with ropes and just left them with their heads hanging over. Soon they were just bringing up green bile and wishing they were dead. Then oil started leaking up through the manhole covers. All the portholes and scuttles were leaking too because the rubber seals had perished. The mess deck was awash with two feet of seawater, oil and vomit, with coats and boots and cups all floating around in it. 'As the ship rolled, this lot just rolled with it and you could hear this great roar and crash as it washed from side to side in the messes.' Nethercott slept elsewhere. The sailors who could still stomach their rum ration toasted President Roosevelt and Winston Churchill for providing them with such a ship as this.

When finally they reached Devonport, one of the four funnels was hanging over the side and they'd lost one of the guns completely, washed right off its rusty bearings. One of the whalers had vanished too:

> A tug brought us in and once we got alongside the great clear up started, you know, because I wasn't having any bloody nonsense then. They'd had their sea trip and they were out of those bunks in no time and down on their bloody hands and knees scrubbing and cleaning and washing stuff over the side and getting the place ship shape. Otherwise they'd have lost all bloody heart. But once we'd got the ship clean and nice and smart again, they did take heart. And I said to them, 'Well you've had the worst, you'll never get worse than that. You've been through it now. You'll be all right next time' and most of them were.

ACTION THIS DAY.
Pray let six new offices be fitted for my use, in Selfridge's, Lambeth Palace, Stanmore, Tooting Bec, the Palladium and Mile End Road. I will inform you at 6 each evening at which office I shall dine, work and sleep. Accommodation will be required for Mrs Churchill, two shorthand typists, three secretaries and Nelson [Churchill's cat]. There should be shelter for all and a place for me to watch air-raids from the roof. This should be completed by Monday. There is to be no hammering between office hours, that is between 7 a.m. and 3 a.m.

W.S.C.

31.10.40

The secretaries' spoof memo entirely convinced many of the people who worked in the annexe.

When he got the chance, Jock Colville loved to ride in Richmond Park early in the morning. By late October there was frost on the grass and mist gathering in the hollows and around the fringes of the plantations. Over Putney and Roehampton, columns of smoke rose from the latest night raid.

Colville had served Chamberlain loyally; he'd approved of Munich. On the evening Churchill came to power he'd sat and drunk and grumbled in the Foreign Office with Rab Butler. What was it he'd called Churchill? 'Adventurer', 'talkative but inefficient', something like that. Colville smiled.

Actually the great man could be much worse than that. In many ways he was a terrible boss: inconsiderate, demanding, petulant. Plans would be changed at the last moment. Complaints would rain down, usually about delays, usually about delays he had caused himself. He'd continually press for all kinds of personal comforts too, giving much trouble to people who were already overworked.

But he'd saved them all, of that Colville had no doubt. Saved them by being adventurous and talkative and unpredictable. He had 'some strange intuitive power which . . . might induce him to take a line contrary, as it appeared, to logic and contrary to the normal mental workings of everybody else'. Someone else could, maybe would, have done the deal, the logical, obvious deal. Back in May or June, that had been the moment.

Nazi terror weapons and Nazi terror politics had seemed so frightening and so crushing then. But then Churchill lit the beacon, wrote and spoke a different ending to the story. Colville had sat in the House for the last speech. The man next to him said it made him shiver.

We must be united, we must be undaunted, we must be

inflexible. Our qualities and deeds must burn and glow through the gloom of Europe until they become the veritable beacon of its salvation.

His script, their performance. Yes, by now most of Churchill's people were drunk on pride, thrilled to act out the noble parts he'd written for them. Even those poor people in Chingford. To be the only ones left standing – imagine! Us! Undaunted, yes, undaunted.

Sunlight was sparkling on the frost. Colville pulled on the rein and cantered back towards the stables in Wimbledon. He'd already applied for permission to leave the civil service and join the RAF, but in the meantime there would be plenty for him to do in the annexe.

Denis Wissler did not have much time to plan his wedding. He was now well and truly back in action, frequently flying long patrols at extreme heights of over 25,000 feet. It got very cold up there. On Sunday, 27 October he wrote:

> We went over to North Weald this morning and did three patrols, two of which were at 28,000 ft. I did 5½ hours, and am I tired tonight? or am I? I am going to bed early tonight but I shall be just as tired tomorrow morning. We saw some Me 109s and chased them, but failed to get close enough. There was a flap as soon as we landed back at Martlesham (which was bombed by 109s today, no bad damage) and we all took off again to make a dusk landing.

The next day was equally draining:

> I led Blue section at about 7.30 this morning, we went hun chasing, lost Blue 2 in a cloud and finished up at Debden in dreadful weather for breakfast. Took off again and saw a Do 215. Leary got there first and got it. Landed at Martlesham and went to North Weald with squadron, did patrol, came

back to Martlesham, took off again in terrible weather. Saw a Hun through a convoy balloon barrage. Landed again at Martlesham in the dusk. In all 6 hours flying. Pictures in the evening with Pitters.

Whitelaw Reid was getting near to the end of his time in Britain, but there was still one thing he really wanted to do. As usual he decided to go right to the top. He fixed to see Sir Archibald Sinclair, the Secretary of State for Air. Could he fly with an RAF bomber crew over Berlin? No, he couldn't. He went to see Lord Beaverbrook instead. Could he fly with an RAF bomber crew over Berlin? No, he couldn't, but maybe something else could be arranged.

Eventually the call came. If he still wanted to go flying he was to drive up to an airfield near King's Lynn in Norfolk and report to Flight Lieutenant Cunningham of Coastal Command. Within a couple of days Reid was crouching behind the pilot's seat of a long-nosed Blenheim fighter-bomber, one of a section of three on a regular long-range patrol over the North Sea. Their job was to watch out for enemy shipping and submarine movements. Along the way they passed a Wellington bomber coming back from a solo mission somewhere over Germany.

They flew at about 2,000 feet, just below the base of flat, misty cloud. After about an hour they could see Denmark. Then they turned south-west, skirting the little islands of the German coast: Norderney, Langeoog, Spiekeroog. Reid had sailed in these waters. It wasn't far from Wilhelmshaven, Cuxhaven and the western end of the Kiel Canal. That's where he had climbed the mast whilst the others had fed a German policeman peaches out of a tin.

Now they were off northern Holland. Reid had never heard of most of the places on the navigator's map: Harlingen, Holwerd, Den Helder. There were German troops down there, German troops and policemen too. He imagined what the sound of the Blenheims' engines meant to the inhabitants of these coastal towns.

'They came again yesterday, father, definitely British planes.' Somewhere down there people were sitting in attics, listening for the British engines, trying to find the BBC on their radios.

He looked back towards the long-vanished coast of Britain. Not just here; it meant something in Paris too, and Prague, and Warsaw, Copenhagen and Oslo. Those few bombers overhead, the sound of resistance, the sound of hope. The single undeniable fact that for the very first time Hitler had said he was going to do something and, guess what, he hadn't.

It was something Reid had been thinking about for some weeks now, in London, down under the Savoy, but flying in this Blenheim decided it for him. As soon as he got back to New York, he was going to learn to fly.

They turned for home, over the open sea wrinkled with white surf, then back over the mudflats of the Wash and the familiar hedge-lined countryside of East Anglia. It was getting dark now and the pilot broke into a loud and rollicking version of 'Show Me the Way To Go Home' with completely disgusting lyrics. Then the mess and the bar and two excellent Scotches courtesy of the squadron leader. Then America.

Chapter 18

November onwards

If the Skipper fell into the oggin,
If the Skipper fell into the sea,
If the Skipper fell into the oggin,
He'd get no fucking lifebelt from me.

Swim back, swim back, swim back you bastard to me, to me.

'Oi, Nethercott, what have you done with the Yorkshire? We need another 15 pints of Guinness over here.'

Swim back, swim back, swim back you bastard to me.

The senior man ashore was, by the immutable law of the sea, responsible for collecting and spending the 'Yorkshire'. All the sailors had put their half-crowns and ten-shilling notes into Iain Nethercott's hand as they gathered at the base of the gangplank. Ma Stanley's was first – great big black frying pans thick with bacon grease. 'Oh it's Iain back, how many eggs do you want?' 'Oh, about six to begin with.'

Eggs and bacon and sausage and black pudding and the whole of Londonderry at your disposal. Across the border and into the Republic too. You weren't supposed to but no one really cared.

No blackout there, and look at all the shops, full of biscuits and chocolates and tins of things unseen in His Majesty's Navy. And the village dances. All the country girls down one side of the hall and all the wicked sailors down the other and a 'diddly diddly' band up on the stage. 'They were nice girls, very pretty, ever such pretty girls. But Catholic, there was no funny business.' Not like shore leave in Portsmouth, with the Commercial Road thick with whores.

The Yorkshire. Nethercott struggled to remember. There had definitely been plenty of it left in his pocket several pints ago when they'd all rolled and pitched their way into Riley's, the favourite pub, the singing pub, the best bleeding pub this side of the River Foyle. 'Any port in a storm, eh lads. Line 'em up Bridget.' But now, where was it . . . ? He had a feeling he'd been buying for more than his own twenty-odd shipmates. No, wait . . . A single soggy ten-shilling note emerged from under a stray pint glass. On your feet, Leading Seaman: 'My dears, it would be my enormous pleasure to purchase the beverage of your choice.'

Swim back, swim back, swim back you bastard to me, to me.
Swim back, swim back, swim back you bastard to me.

It got a bit like the Wild West sometimes. Scottish sailors, Canadian sailors, Free French sailors, Norwegians and Poles too, all shouting and singing, and half the time there'd be some kind of a punch-up. Tattooed arms passed over another round, others supported someone's unsteady shoulders. Outside for a quick spew. Best thing for it. 'Get it up, lad, you'll soon feel better. Anyone for an omelette later? Let's have another bloody song!'

Can a Dockyard Matey run, yes by Christ we've seen it done,
At five o'clock you'll hear the bell, you see them run like fucking hell.

What do you say when you're dying? 'You say, "Why is this

366

happening?" "What on earth have I done?" "Do you reckon I'm worth saving?" This sort of thing. Unless you've been there you don't realise.' That time drifting away in the water off Dunkirk with a bullet through his knee, Nethercott had remembered something they'd all been taught on the training ship:

> Strength now my fainting soul and play the man
> and through such waning span of life is still to be trod
> prepare to meet thy God.

Someone would cry. You could never predict who. Just sit and weep and shake. There was a rhythm to the sad thoughts, a drinking rhythm. Happy, loud, sad, happy again later when you'd got rid of it, when you'd spewed it all out and made yourself feel better. A mournful song about some ship lost at sea, that would set them off. The U-boat crews that chased them back and forth across the Atlantic probably sang the same kind of songs when they got a bit pissed up. Sailors had for years. Nethercott preferred the funny ones, the dirty ones. Swim back you bastard to me.

Number 1 Escort Group was hardly the pride of the British fleet. There was the *Lincoln*, Nethercott's old American destroyer, refitted and stabilised now but still retaining many of her unique semi-submersible qualities. Then there was an old Great War destroyer, the *Keppel*: 'she was leader, a load of old rubbish she was'. There was one decent destroyer too and a couple of corvettes of the old sort which could only do fourteen knots flat out. A handful of armed tugs completed the security screen for the fifty or so merchant ships and tankers that had to be shepherded halfway to Halifax six or seven times a month.

The trouble would start as soon as the escorts left Londonderry. On the Irish Republic's side of the River Foyle, men from the German embassy in Dublin would watch them pass. Snipers from the

IRA would take pot shots too. They never hit anyone. Nethercott would give them Churchill's old V for Victory sign as he passed, only with his fingers the other way around.

The convoy would come out of the Mersey or the Clyde. Soon after they picked it up, the German aircraft would usually arrive: Condor spotter planes that could stay up there for hours and hours. What with the planes and the audience at the riverside, Nethercott and his shipmates used to wonder why they just didn't save everyone the trouble and send a cable straight to Berlin whenever they sailed.

The spotters would sometimes swoop down and try to bomb a tanker, but the real threat came from beneath the waves and came after dark. Waiting for them was the worst part. Actually, no, being hit and trying to abandon a burning ship in a high Atlantic sea would definitely be the worst part. Thankfully that hadn't happened to the *Lincoln* so far. But sometimes the waiting felt like a deferred death sentence:

> When I lay in my bunk during a middle watch or something I used to think that it was only about three foot above the water and think, well, if a torpedo slams into me now I'm already trapped down below, there's no way I can get out from here, I'll just stay there and go down in me bunk.

After an attack the red flares would go up, the nearest escort would turn towards where it thought the U-boat was and try to get an Asdic fix on it. The escorts had their orders and their priorities. Sinking U-boats was more important than rescuing survivors:

> If you did get an Asdic ping and they were right over the top of it you still went in and dropped your depth charges right amongst them and blew them all to pieces in the water. And there was one or two occasions where these poor buggers thought that they were going to be picked up and they were all waving and the ship just ploughed on straight through them and fired their charges.

Nethercott just kept going: joking with the hairy-arsed stokers, complaining about the terrible food, cursing the idiot at the wheel when the ship lurched between a wave or 'took it green' over the iron decks. There was an old washing machine on board, a luxury unheard-of in the British Navy. Everyone used it until the motor burnt out. Then one night, during another depth-charge attack, Nethercott told someone to heave it over the side. The sailors joked about the U-boat, which had escaped as usual, returning to Germany with a brand-new British secret weapon stuck to its conning tower. *Achtung* – the washing-machine bomb. Now we have to surrender.

What mostly kept him going was training up his lads. With the seasickness of the first crossing behind them, they were turning into decent sailors. He was particularly proud of their prowess in the ship's whalers: 'You've got five men in a crew on a whaler and they've got to be ready to be dropped from the davits into the Atlantic and pull over to a ship where men are jumping into the sea . . . off a tanker that's on fire or anything like that, you've got to be ready to pull alongside practically and pull them out. And you've got to know the drill properly.'

The only time Nethercott got a bit worried about their seaman-ship was when they were trying to pick up some men from a sinking ship at the back of the convoy and the *Lincoln*'s skipper got an Asdic reading and had to chase off after it, leaving Nethercott and five others pitching around by themselves. 'And he shouted out from the bridge as she tore off, he said, "I'll come back for you later if I can find you". And I thought, "Bloody heck!".'

The Yorkshire's long gone now. Nethercott is back in his bunk when he hears a familiar Barnsley accent: 'Do you want another drink?' Under the influence of far too much Riley's Guinness, the burglar-turned-sailor has temporarily reverted to his former profession. Somehow he's rolled a barrel of the stuff down to the dock and up into the ship and he's filled up a big mess kettle with it. 'Come on, have a cup.'

Any rate we managed to get rid of it before the morning but I said you've got to get that barrel over the side before anyone bloody notices it and we did and it floated away down the river Foyle. But we had the old constabulary aboard first thing, there must have been a trail of booze I think leading from where they'd nicked it. So they came down with our First Lieutenant and he says, 'Has anyone been stealing beer?' and, of course, the place reeked of it. And we all looked wide-eyed and said, 'No, no!'

For their sake – Iain Nethercott is telling the story for their sake. 'Because no-one really has, not really . . .'

Often, you couldn't pick people up, the seas were so rough, and if they weren't in boats or anything, if they were just in the water you just had to leave them.

You only went for survivors when you could actually see them or they'd got a boat down. You didn't run around the ocean looking for them. If a ship had disappeared and you saw a lot of heads bobbing about with red lights on the life jackets you could go for them if the skipper thought it was alright. A lot of them you had to leave behind anyway. A lot of them were very badly burnt, especially with steam burns, and if you got hold of a bloke's hand and the whole of his arm came off leaving you holding a bit of white bone, you'd know that he'd been broiled alive in the engine room. So you'd just let him go, because they were in so much agony it was best to leave them.

And sometimes if it was very, very rough, you had to leave them anyway, you couldn't get a boat down. We had survivor's nets but they'd never be able to hang on to them. And they knew it as you swept past them. I remember one bloke, he must have been a very brave man. In the night, there was two or three of these blokes and we were speeding up to get in with the convoy. They'd got lifebelts on but they were going to die. And this bloke realised it, and he was shouting out 'Taxi! Taxi!, Taxi!', just taking the mickey, like, because he knew he was going to die, he knew we couldn't stop.

And all we could hear in the distance was him shouting 'Taxi! Taxi!'. And it just faded away.

And it made hard men weep.

At the beginning of November the new ops room was ready and Edith Heap moved to a school in Saffron Walden. The plotters were housed in the main building with a watch to each dormitory. Ops itself was in the glass-roofed school gymnasium. Looking up, the plotters could hardly believe their eyes. Typical, they thought. What idiot sanctioned that? Still, in contrast to the emergency operations room in the chalkpit, it was a spacious place with a nice balcony for the controller. Edith and Winifred had just been elevated to the balcony themselves. They sat either side of the controller, Winifred charting the course of the enemy and Edith keeping track of their own squadrons.

Life was pretty good in the school, except for the consistently awful RAF food. Edith had a slow-simmering argument with one of the cooks. Once they ended up shouting at each other.

She met Denis whenever she could. On 30 October she picked him up from Martlesham. Pittman covered for him so that the engaged couple could spend the afternoon together. They larked about around the planes, and she noticed that he was having difficulty with the release pin on his harness. It was bent and it wouldn't come undone easily in the way that it should. 'You must get them to straighten that,' she said.

They went to Ipswich and in the evening they bought Pitters dinner at the Pig, as they called the Great White Horse. Next day they went to London and had another raucous time with the Wisslers. They made their wedding plans. Edith's discharge would come through soon. They decided the day would be 4 January, the anniversary of Pop and Ma Wissler's own wedding. When they got back to Martlesham, Edith was invited to the squadron dinner in the mess, but she couldn't go in uniform and hadn't got a dress. She drove the Jaguar back to Debden instead through the late autumn gloom.

Early November was thick fog or at best low cloud and rain. Not much flying was done, though what they did was dangerous. On 6 November Wissler tried to fly low over Edith's billet, but the cloud was down to 200 feet and he couldn't find the place. The next morning they drove to Yorkshire together to meet Edith's family and celebrated all over again. They got back to the news that the squadron had scored an enormous success in a battle with some unescorted Stukas. Every one of the blokes had got at least one. Fifteen destroyed in all plus some probables. Denis was crestfallen. 'That'll put me even further behind,' he said. 'You know, I'm the lowest scoring pilot of my intake in the squadron.'

> You see it mattered. Some people could be a bit nasty, if somebody wasn't scoring very highly and one person in particular, who was a nasty little squirt as a matter of fact, he was horrid to Denis and I think that affected him.

Sam Patience wore the smile of a man who'd achieved his lifetime's ambition. He turned the wheel to keep the big liner correctly trimmed. Of course, this particular liner was wearing camouflage paint and called an Armed Merchant Cruiser now, but even so . . .

Armed Merchant Cruiser. She was armed with seven six-inch guns of which the newest was dated 1896. There were three either side and one up on the high poop in the stern which could be trained in either direction.

Patience was the quartermaster. At sea he steered the ship, in harbour he was responsible for keeping a check on who was ashore and who came on board. They seemed a good crowd on this ship, very friendly. The usual mix of regulars, reservists, merchant navy men like himself and hostilities-only ratings. He filled in the logbook and recorded the wind strength and visibility. He piped people aboard and relayed messages with his boatswain's call. He made the hand signals that brought small boats alongside. It was a responsible job, a proper sailor's job. Thank God for the Froggie who'd blown a hole in that awful battleship, and the bloke who wanted to get to Britain in a hurry.

As soon as Patience had taken the wheel, Captain Edward Fegen had come to speak to him. He asked him where he'd been and what he'd done. Fegen was very interested in the Norwegian campaign and all the business with the French. The captain always seemed to be on the lookout for something or somebody. But then his was the only escort for Convoy HX84: thirty-eight ships with gasoline, kerosene, fuel oil, crude oil, steel, pit props, scrap iron, lumber, trucks, newsprint, wool and maize outward from Halifax, 28 October. Sooner or later there would probably be submarines below or Condors above such a tempting target.

One day they saw a battleship. It was 5 November, Fireworks Day, Sam Patience's eighth day behind the wheel. When she appeared on the horizon at 4.55 p.m. Patience was midway through the first 'dog watch'. The chief yeoman signalled with the Aldis lamp to the unknown warship. There was no reply. The crew looked through the eyesights of the guns. They could see the silhouette plainly. Someone suggested it was an 'R'-class battleship, but Patience explained that it couldn't be because they had a distinctive 'tiddly top' on the funnel. They were still speculating when the first salvo whistled over their heads and exploded in the sea about a hundred yards away.

Nobody had even considered that this might be a German warship. All of the large German ships were supposed to be bottled up in the Baltic, and had been for months. But not the *Admiral Scheer*, which had sneaked unobserved out of Brunsbüttel on 27 October. Up on the bridge they typed out a sighting report and ordered the convoy to scatter to starboard. Action stations! Patience handed the wheel to another sailor and went to man the port forward gun. The crew was told to throw smoke floats over the side – big containers like dustbins. They pulled the stoppers out and hurled them over, soon generating a satisfyingly thick, black screen that was meant to protect the convoy as it dispersed. Then the *Jervis Bay* steamed to port, away from the smoke and straight towards the *Admiral Scheer*.

The second salvo fell short but shrapnel from an exploding shell decapitated the man standing next to Patience. The Germans were about 25,000 yards away and firing fourteen-inch guns. The range of their own six-inch guns was about 10,000 yards, but they never got a chance to fire them. The third salvo caught the *Jervis Bay* amidships, smashing the wireless office and much of the deck superstructure. The captain ordered full steam ahead, and steered towards the enemy. More explosions rocked the liner. Patience looked up to see the bridge alight and Captain Fegen with one arm partly severed. There were fires everywhere now. Men were on fire, too. Screaming, they jumped over the side. The next salvo blew the S1 gun opposite Patience right off the fo'c'sle, along with its mounting and its crew.

The shells arrived at a horrific velocity. The huge ship bucked and rolled under the impact. The next one had to kill him. Instead its blast blew him off the gun platform and down on to the well deck, dazed but only slightly injured. The sick bay was on fire and a leading seaman said, 'Get that bloody hose and try and get in there.' Another sailor called Bill Storey picked the hose up by the nozzle and Patience held it up behind him as together they aimed the jet. Another shell came over, the doors slammed shut, and Patience was left holding a severed hosepipe. 'It just happened like that. Woodwork, steelwork and him as well, all got blown to pieces.' There was a terrible smell of cordite and burnt flesh.

The shelling went on and on. In the past Armed Merchant Cruisers, not designed to withstand shelling, had sunk so fast that their crews hadn't had a chance to escape. So their holds had been filled with empty barrels to increase buoyancy in an emergency. Those empty barrels saved the convoy, every bit as much as the courage and quick thinking of Captain Fegen and his crew. The ship stayed afloat for a long time and, whilst it did, the *Admiral Scheer* was strangely immobile, sending shells into her useless hulk long after it served any military purpose. Meanwhile the rest of the convoy was steaming away in every possible direction.

Almost all the officers were dead. The chief officer, George Roe, hobbled forward with a bad injury to his leg and shouted to the crews of the four forward guns, 'Abandon ship. Every man for himself!' Patience did not see him again. He suddenly regretted not having written to his parents to let them know where he was. Some of the life-rafts were on fire but they stopped burning when they hit the water and men threw themselves in after them.

Like a lot of sailors, Patience couldn't swim: 'I thought, well I've got to make a decision here, I either go down with the ship or get over the side.' First he went to the carpenter's shop under the fo'c'sle. He had seen some bags of shavings there. He took one, thinking it would make a float, but when he threw it over the side, the bottom fell out and all the shavings drifted away. He had another look round and found a lifebelt in a shattered glass casing. He took it to the side. There seemed to be only two of them left now. The ship was going down by the stern and they were on the steeply rearing bow. Patience urged the other sailor over the side. 'He said, "No, I can't swim." I said, "Well neither can I but I'm going in anyway."' He put the lifebelt around his neck and slipped down what he took to be a rope. It turned out to be a wire hawser and when he reached the sea forty feet below he had cut his hands to the bone.

Until he hit the water he had thought that with the lifebelt he would be strong enough to survive until the morning. But he soon realised that he could not last the night: 'it was so cold, it was bitter bloody cold'.

Flames from the *Jervis Bay* lit the scene for a while and then, with a great sucking glug, she sank. For an hour and a half, Patience was thrown about by the huge seas, feeling colder and weaker all the time. The German battleship was now chasing after some of the convoy members and firing at them. As he rose up the side of another wave, Patience could see distant flashes. He was convinced that he was going to die.

Fifty years later, sixty years later, long after he'd met and married Rosie Lee and they'd had their family and they'd all grown up and left home, Sam would kick his wife out of bed. Just thrashing about in his sleep: fighting the Germans, staying afloat, keeping his head above the waves.

Suddenly a lifeboat appeared. One of the ship's own boats had not been smashed and had got safely away. The other survivors dragged him aboard, lifebelt and all. They drifted for another hour or two and then in the distance they saw a ship. They took it for a German prison ship, following up after the battleship, and when they heard foreign voices from the boat it seemed their fears were confirmed. Then suddenly a Scottish voice rang out, 'You're all right now lads!'

Captain Sven Olander of the *Stureholm* had reckoned that his ship, laden as she was with steel and scrap, would be too slow to escape. So when all the other ships scattered he stayed put. He had hidden in the *Jervis Bay*'s smokescreen for four hours until the German raider was far away. Then he'd crept out and not long afterwards seen a small torch signalling SOS. He'd put his Scottish stoker on the ship's boat to communicate with survivors. 'Magnificent, oh they were brilliant. They came down, carried me up to the officer's quarters and they laid us down on the deck. Filled us with a tot of vodka or rum or whatever it was and they put raw iodine on me hands and me burns and bits of shrapnel wounds I had.'

All but five ships in the convoy escaped. The tale passed immediately into legend, the epic of the *Jervis Bay*. One of the merchant ships caught by the battleship, the tanker *San Demetrio*, was abandoned when it caught fire, but then subsequently reboarded by its own crew. They put the fires out and limped home with the ship, cargo and all. A propaganda film was made about them all. Fegen was awarded a posthumous Victoria Cross and became an icon of duty and self-sacrifice. And Patience? When Sam Patience came out of a Canadian hospital he was put on board another Armed Merchant Cruiser and just carried on.

'London has changed you, Whitey. You've become a serious young man.' Whitelaw Reid would smile and nod. They were right. Sure, it was nice to ride in taxicabs down Madison Avenue, go dancing in a brightly lit nightclub or share the cocktail hour with his smart, amusing friends. But there was always something else on his mind now, something that hadn't been there before. It was Britain, it was the war, it was the future. Everyone agreed: Whitey had found a cause.

Looking back, he felt vaguely guilty at the blindness of them all. His generation had been canoeing and horse-riding and flying out to Hollywood for a vacation whilst the rest of the world was going to hell. All that had to change. And it could – it just took a bit of imagination and a bit of courage. Yes, there were terrible things happening in Europe, but there was hope and heroism out there too. Dover and London had taught him that. So too had those remarkable young men who had flown him over occupied Europe. They were determined to bring light and freedom back to that darkened continent and so was he. He signed up for a private flying course. When the time came he wanted to be ready. And in the meantime he decided to push his own vision of the war and the future.

He sat in the drawing room on East 82nd Street. This was where he'd listened to Churchill on the radio and heard Herbert Hoover announce that Britain was finished. That was before the customs officer and the fishing-pole people and actually meeting Churchill himself. Now he was typing out notes for his latest lecture: 'Is not our only hope to win the war so we can have a community of nations; then to organise that community so as to prevent war and permit democratic institutions to develop?'

Whitelaw Reid's talks became very popular very quickly. He was good-looking, confident and eloquent, and he was straight back from the war. He was also 'one of us', from the same world as the men and women of the societies, committees and luncheon clubs that were the engine-room of East Coast political life.

He talked to the British War Relief Society, the Women's National Republican Club, the New York State Editors and the American Association of University Women. He talked to the English Speaking Union at a lunch to promote its destroyer-adoption scheme. This was aimed at linking American communities to the former US destroyers that now carried their names – like *Bradford*, *Newport* and *Lincoln*. Reid felt a special pride in this. He'd discussed those ships with Churchill and the paper had pressed for their delivery. Then there was the Bundles for Britain committee, WYNC Radio, the Foreign Policy Association, the Woman's Press Club, the 'Committee to Defend America by Aiding the Allies', the Deke Fraternity Dinner. He had barely a day free.

On one of them Reid wrote a long article for the *Herald Tribune* entitled 'War Is Not the Worst Evil': 'The world, as some of us realize and all of us must realize in the near future, has become a community in which we have a stake. It is now a sick world.' Reid's main point was that going to war in defence of a great cause did not mean the end of everything: indeed, it could be a positive national experience. He described how such a process was happening in Britain: 'Living has been intensified – it has been given a rudder – but it has not stopped . . . life in England has been uplifted rather than degraded by the battle.'

He described the America he had returned to: 'today the country is torn and racked by divergent views as to whether we should help or how much we should help the only people in the world who are fighting for our way of life against a bunch of bloody bandits'. He concluded by urging more than aid: he wanted the use of American troops to cleanse the world of gangsterism. Such an opinion was still very rarely voiced in America.

More invitations to lecture and debate came thick and fast. So did the thank-you cards. Mostly from young women, his friends pointed out with a smile. On one elegant page of bespoke notepaper an impressed female listener wrote: 'I am writing this, my first, but assuredly not your last, fan letter . . . You've made up your mind that our place should be in the war and in what will be left of the world that follows and you have ideas as to how we should obtain that place and hold it, and you're not afraid.'

He had been afraid before. He'd thought that war would be the end of everything, he'd wondered whether he would be able to hold his own in a trench or up in a plane, but not now.

On 5 November President Roosevelt won the American presidential election. From Ottawa, Mackenzie King, who had spent months observing the to and fro of opinion in Washington, predicted more help for Britain: 'This clears the air and the skies, and makes possible a certainty of assistance to Britain and ourselves which could not possibly have come otherwise. Meanwhile the British will be given fresh heart. It means that we have the U.S. with us for the next 4 years.'

To remain in this war, Britain needed American help. But London was running out of money fast. By November there was just about enough left to cover outstanding orders for the rest of the year. After that Churchill would have to place himself entirely in Roosevelt's hands. Diplomats had already started talking about the cash squeeze. Washington pressed the British to liquidate all her remaining dollar assets. Beaverbrook complained bitterly about asset-stripping.

Roosevelt was preparing to launch a credit scheme that would attach the anaemic British to the drip-feed of American economic support. It didn't have a name as yet, but the world would soon know it as Lend-Lease. Arms and materials would soon flow in ever increasing quantities, billions of dollars' worth. America would become, in Roosevelt's own ringing phrase, 'the arsenal of democracy', and take another step towards entering the war.

More streets flattened, the water system in ruins. Commuters on Waterloo Bridge pass groups of exhausted, dull-eyed firemen. The river is full of sewage, chemicals, the occasional corpse. Somewhere rescue workers are struggling to drag people out of collapsed buildings before they drown in the rising water from a burst main. Swimming pools are mortuaries again. Londoners have woken to many mornings like this since early September. As autumn turns to winter, many other ghastly dawns will have to be faced in Coventry, Sheffield, Hull, Swansea, Southampton . . .

Denis Wissler clambered out of his Hurricane as a WAAF with a tractor and bowser approached to refuel it. 'Nothing there, sir?' 'No, nothing.' One and a half hours over the convoy, just circling round. Why did the Jerries never send over unguarded Stukas when he was flying? They had got a small fire going in the dispersal hut and they huddled round as Squadron Leader Miller outlined the plan for the next patrol. Denis would lead Blue Section.

'Scramble 17.' In Saffron Walden Edith Heap looked up through the glass roof. Up there, her man, up there soon. She took a new sheet of tracing paper, fixed it to the grid map and marked the start point: Martlesham Heath, 11.45 a.m., 11 November 1940. 'Show me the bandit plot, Win,' said the controller. 'Right. They must be heading for the convoy. We should get them off Burnham. Vector 190 Angels 20, Red leader.'

Every five minutes Edith plotted the fighters. Winifred plotted the enemy. The two lines were converging towards the mouth of the Thames. 'You should be over the convoy now, Red leader, how's the visibility?' 'Not bad.' 'Bandits coming from the usual direction. Estimate sixty. Look out for fighters.' For now Edith's job was done. She listened.

Two formations of twenty Stukas. 'Tally ho. I'll take the one on the right. Blue, you take the one on the left. Yellow, guard our backs. All clear. Let's go.' 'Yellow 4 look out behind you.'

'I can't hold them, Red leader.' 'Messerschmitts, bloody hundreds of them coming out of the clouds.' 'Take them, Yellow 1.' 'Yellow section, form on me.' 'Abort attack, abort attack, break right.' 'Who's that? Come back you can't attack on your own!' 'Blue section, abort, do you hear? Abort!' 'Yellow 3 on fire.' 'Got the bastard.' 'Blue 1 going down into the drink.' 'There's a plane down and there's no parachute.' Edith froze. 'Reform over the convoy.'

Everyone else went off for lunch, keeping their distance. She walked from the school up at the top of Saffron Walden to the camp just out of town. She watched the first plane come down. Then she couldn't face it and walked on. Even now, in the middle of the day, the grass was crisp underfoot from the first hard frost of winter. The leaves, turned dull brown, were still clinging to the oak trees. The pale blue sky was streaked with clouds. If only it had been raining, they would not have flown. Perhaps it wasn't him. She knew it was. Charging in after them, wanting a Stuka of his own. He should have got that release pin sorted out.

She stopped at the MT yard and tried to talk to some old friends, but she felt sick. In the end she walked back to the school dormitories where they were living. Bill was waiting for her outside. She said, 'Edith, Denis is missing.' Edith said, 'Yes, I know. No parachute?' 'No. I'm sorry. You better take the night off. I'll get someone else to do the midnight shift.'

Always there would be the 'should haves' and the 'might have beens': the release pin, the nasty little squirt in the mess. Sailing off by himself, chasing glory, he so wanted that medal. And always imagining the last seconds. Her name on his lips.

There was nobody around. Winifred had disappeared with Jeff. In the end she went to bed but couldn't get to sleep. In the small hours her enemy cook came up with a cup of tea and sat by her bed and talked to her. In the morning she went in for duty. The controller wanted to see her but she asked Winifred to see him for her and to ask him not to send a telegram to the Wisslers. She would tell them herself.

> I knew Ma Wissler was dreading it, and so I went and saw Bill and my wedding release had come through, so I cancelled that and they gave me a fortnight's compassionate leave and I went off to London to tell them.
>
> And everybody is so kind but . . . do you know what I mean if I say 'kind at a distance'? They don't cramp you with it. And yet they would say just a little something, which encouraged you. We were used to it, so everybody knew how to treat it and they gave you strength.

For his sake – she's telling the story for his sake. She took the pilot's wings from his dress uniform and sewed them into the inside of her own, so that they would always press against her heart.

Britain could not win the war alone, but in 1940 she refused to lose it.

Denis Wissler died on 11 November 1940, Remembrance Day. Jock Colville placed a wreath at the Cenotaph on behalf of his Prime Minister. In Paris there was a small demonstration by the eternal flame under the Arc de Triomphe. It was only a gesture but it would grow. Hitler had said he was going to crush the Tommies too, but he hadn't. He'd been confounded for the first, decisive time. Confounded, frustrated, beaten. By Denis Wissler and George Gristock, by Bob Burroughs and Dickey Lee, by Elsie Francis and Bob Taylor.

Hurricane 'V for D' was never recovered, nor was its pilot's body. That's lost at sea, out there somewhere with Captain Fegen and the 'Taxi! Taxi!' man who made hard men weep. Denis Wissler is a name on the Runnymede RAF memorial now. Panel number ten, down on the left. He's a picture by the side of a bed in Yorkshire too. His wings against her heart, her name on his lips. Lost at sea but still within reach. All of them, all the hard brave men and women, still just within reach.

Epilogue

Harold 'Birdy' Bird-Wilson

After many distinguished years in the RAF, and a DSO to add to his 1940 DFC, he rose to the rank of air vice-marshal. He retired from the service in 1974 and now lives in Surrey.

Jock Colville

Left Whitehall in 1941 to serve as an RAF pilot. Returned to the civil service and worked again for Churchill, for Clement Attlee, for Princess Elizabeth and then for Churchill once more. He died in 1987.

Bob Doe

One of the RAF's highest-scoring fighter pilots of the Second World War, he served in many theatres and finished the war in Burma. He stayed on in the service and, altogether, has flown over 150 types of aircraft. Now retired, he lives in Surrey. His youngest daughter is a commercial pilot.

Alan Francis

After National Service in occupied Germany, became an officer in the Metropolitan Police. Now retired, he lives in Kent.

Edith Heap

Became an intelligence officer working with bomber squadrons. After the war she worked as a social worker. She was married and is the mother of two daughters. In 1991 she decided to place Denis Wissler's Battle of Britain diary in the Imperial War Museum. She now lives in West Yorkshire not far from where she was born.

Marian Holmes

Rose through the Downing Street ranks. Worked closely with Churchill throughout the war and attended Yalta and other 'Big Three' conferences. After a distinguished Civil Service career, she is now retired, and lives in West London.

Dickey Lee

Dickey Lee died on 18 August 1940. On 18 August 1999 a wreath was placed in his memory at the Runnymede RAF memorial. The anonymous message read: 'To Dickey Lee, who inspired such love and admiration that even after 59 years just the mention of his name brings forth a smile to all who knew him'.

Kenneth 'Hawk-eye' Lee

After the Battle of Britain he trained other pilots and then served in the Western Desert. In 1943 he was shot down over Crete and became a prisoner of war. He lives in South Yorkshire, where he is still a close friend of his 501 Squadron comrade, Johnny Gibson.

Ernie Leggett

Did walk again although the surgeon's prediction that in later
life his wounds would trouble him proved accurate. He lives in
Norfolk, still regularly attending St Peter's church, Clippesby, is
active in the Dunkirk Veterans Association, and plays the bugle
at Remembrance Day services.

Martin McLane

Served with distinction in Burma with the Durham Light Infantry
and ended his career in the Army as a much decorated regimental
sergeant-major. In 1999, some time after the death of his wife,
Annie, he decided to move from Newcastle to become a Chelsea
Pensioner.

Iain Nethercott

Transferred to submarines in 1941 and was engaged in the
Mediterranean, the Malacca Straits and the South Pacific. He
lives in Essex, painting ships and writing poetry during nights
when his memories prevent him from sleeping.

Sam Patience

Transferred to destroyers in 1941 and served on the Malta and
Arctic convoys. He met Rosie Lee in 1942. They are still married
and live in East London.

Whitelaw Reid

Served as a pilot in the United States Air Force in the Pacific.
Afterwards returned to journalism and was president and editor
of the *New York Herald Tribune* during the 1950s. He lives in
upstate New York and is a regular competitor, and winner, on
the American veterans tennis circuit.

Paul Richey

Returned to action in 1941 as a Spitfire pilot. Later he became a wing commander, serving in the Far East, and then a senior officer with the Allied air force High Command in Europe. After the war he was an oil executive, a deep-sea diver, and an air correspondent. He died in 1989.

Ben Robertson

In 1941, he interrupted his career as a war reporter to write a classic account of life in South Carolina, *Red Hills and Cotton*. In February 1943 he was killed on board a transatlantic 'clipper' flight which crashed into Lisbon harbour.

Ada Taylor

Returned from Finchley to the East End where she still lives, the matriarch of a large family of her own.

Peter Vaux

Before the end of 1940 his battalion joined a convoy bound for the Middle East. He fought in the desert and in Italy. After the war he reported on the help that he had received from M. Gilis and the Belgian received an award for courage. The two men became lifelong friends. He retired from the Army as a brigadier and currently lives in Hampshire.

Bess Walder

After the war, she worked as a teacher and, later, as a headmistress. Became the sister-in-law of her friend and fellow *Benares* survivor Beth Cummings when she married Beth's brother, Geoff, in 1947. The couple now live in Gloucestershire.

Acknowledgments

─────────────

Our first debt of gratitude is to all those who have consented to be interviewed or have volunteered information that has helped us with the television series and with this book:

Ada Allen; Paul Ashwell; Joan Bright Astley; Tom Barter; Jean Bekaert; Alice Bentley; Harold Bird-Wilson; Tony Bishop; 'Danny' Boulger; 'Charlie' Brown; Terry Bulloch; Betty Cook; 'Oscar' Cornish; Bess Cummings; George Dakin; A. D. Daniels; Dennis David; Peter Dawbarn; Bill Deedes; Bob Doe; Michael Foot; Peter Gannon; Mr and Mrs J. Gartside; Johnny Gibson; Irene Gray; Dorothy Green; 'Griff' Griffiths; Richard Grumberger; Cecil Halliday; 'Pat' Hancock; Ronnie Hay; Norman Hayes; Sir Arthur Hezlet; 'Taffy' Higginson; Eustace Holden; Harry Jacobi; Tom Johnson; 'Jogs' Joughin; Alan Kerr; Bill King; Edith Kup; Alan and Leslie Le Claire; Kenneth Lee; Ernie Leggett; Roger Legroux; Larry LeSueur; Daphne Lumsden; Rosemary Lyster; Iain McIntosh; Martin McLane; Richard McMillan; André Merck; Don Milburn; Geoffrey Mills; Brian Mobley; Eric Monk; Vera Morley; Robert Moy; Iain Nethercott; Sam and Rose Patience; Colin Perry; James Radcliffe; Constance and Huw Reece; Whitelaw Reid; Michael Richey; Dickie Rolph; Jack Rose; Frank Scrivener; Jessie Smith; Derek Smyth; Mary Soames;

Sidney Sole; Marian Spicer; Alan Sutton; Harry Swanson; Geoff Taylor; Vice-Admiral Tony Troup; Mr and Mrs Turner; Peter Vaux; Tim Vigors; Hilaire Wadoux; Robert Walsh; John Welsh; Beth Williams; Page Wilson; Ted Wilson; F. T. Yates.

We are grateful to all those who have helped. We hope that anybody who has inadvertently been omitted from this list will forgive us.

We owe another big debt to the television production team whose work has been a considerable resource and whose critical comments have been most helpful: Steve Bergson; Jason Berman; Paul Burgess; Pat Butler; Andy Cottom; Michael Davies; Clare Healy; Brian Lapping; Gregor Murbach; Tim O'Connor; Iain Overton; Nick Read; Sarah Sapper; Kari Wallerstein; Nick Ward.

Finest Hour has taken several years to produce and, along the way, has relied on the goodwill and support of a number of BBC executives: Peter Grimsdale; Michael Jackson; Adam Kemp; Jane Root; Peter Salmon. Our thanks to them all.

Special thanks go to Sir Martin Gilbert, who agreed to act as series consultant and gave the project a great deal of help and sound advice. We are also very grateful to Warren Kimball, who advised on questions of American politics, and Alfred Price, who did the same on the war in the air.

We appreciate the many friends and colleagues who have read drafts of this book and have offered their advice, in particular: Pat Butler; Frances Craig; Simon Firth; Richard Klein; David May; John Stevenson; Nick Ward; David Wilson.

Various individuals and institutions have gone out of their way to help us. In particular we would like to thank Charlie Brown of the Dunkirk Veterans Association; David Brown, head of the Naval Historical Branch; Noreen Chambers of the Medway Queen Preservation Society; Mike Craig; Commander David Hobbs of the Fleet Air Arm Museum; Commander Jeff Tall of the Submarine Museum; Captain Pat Tyrrell; George Cross Island Association; Robert Miller and the committee of HMT

Lancastria Association; Rover (Oxford) Sports & Social Club Retirees Section; the Tank Museum, Bovington; Richard and Ros Basey of the friends of MTB 102; Jean Lindsey; Lucien Dayan of the Musée du Souvenir, Dunkirk; Didier de Liedekerke; Emile Rans; Hélène Sabard; Dot Jackson.

In the course of research we have received generous support from the staff of various libraries, in particular Leslie Morris, Curator of Manuscripts, Houghton Library, Harvard; Sarah Montgomery, National Archives of Canada, Ottawa; the staff of the Bodleian Library, Oxford; the staff of the Imperial War Museum library.

Inevitably we have had dealings with every department of the Imperial War Museum and we would like to extend our thanks to all who helped us; initial introductions were effected by Dr Chris Dowling, who has been supportive throughout. We have had most contact with the Sound Department to whom we are especially grateful: Margaret Brooks, Peter Hart, Joanna Lancaster, Richard McDonough, Rosemary Tudge, Conrad Wood. Terry Charman made helpful suggestions.

We are particularly grateful for the generous help of Diana Richey, and for her hospitality during a memorable evening in Dorset.

For permission to quote from published works and manuscripts we would like to thank the following. For Harold Nicolson's diary, HarperCollins Publishers Ltd; Hodder & Stoughton for the diaries of John Colville and Sir Bernard Freyberg; for *PM*, the General Research Division, the New York Public Library, Astor, Lenox and Tilden Foundations; for Violet Bonham-Carter's letter to Churchill, Jane Bonham-Carter; Whitelaw Reid. Winston Churchill's speeches are reproduced with permission of Curtis Brown Ltd, London, on behalf of the Estate of Sir Winston S. Churchill. Copyright Winston S. Churchill. Other Churchill material reproduced with permission of Curtis Brown Ltd, London, on behalf of C & T Publications Ltd. Footnote from the Churchill War Papers Volume 2 by Martin Gilbert copyright C & T Publications Ltd.

For the loan of and permission to reproduce photographs we are indebted to Peter Wright; Neil and Mary Clayton; Imperial Tobacco Limited; Centre for the Study of Cartoons and Caricature, University of Kent, Canterbury; Edith Kup; Whitelaw Reid; Peter Vaux; Ernie Leggett; Harold Bird-Wilson; Alan Francis; Martin McLane; Sam and Rose Patience; Beth Williams; Solo agency; Marian Walker Spicer; Iain Nethercott; Diana Richey; Bess Cummings; Dr Alfred Price; the Lancastria Association and the late Frank Clements; the Imperial War Museum; Grosvenor Prints; Page Wilson; Dot Jackson; Newham Archives and Local Studies Library.

Every reasonable effort has been made to acknowledge the ownership of the copyrighted material included in this volume. Any errors that may have occurred are inadvertent, and will be corrected in subsequent editions provided notification is sent to the authors.

We have received substantial encouragement and support from Hodder and Stoughton, in particular from our editor Rupert Lancaster and his assistant, Helen Garnons-Williams. Kerry Hood, Briar Silich, Roland Philipps and Martin Neild have also been a source of enthusiastic help and advice.

Our American publishers, Simon and Schuster, have been similarly supportive. We're particularly grateful to Bill Rosen and his assistant Sharon Gibbons.

Our agent Elaine Steel made much of the above happen and our copy editor, Ian Patten, made sure that the final product contained at least a modicum of proper English grammar.

Finally, and most importantly of all, we'd like to thank our respective families: Juliette and William; Frances, Alex, Helen and Jenny. In recent months we have seen a lot less of them than we would have liked to. Despite this fact Juliette kindly provided the author photograph, Frances the index.

Bibliography

Manuscript

Imperial War Museum (IWM)
Sound Archive: see notes
Denis Wissler, pocket diary for 1940 (91/41/1)
Edith Kup, 'Memoirs of a wartime WAAF' (88/2/1)
Graham Lumsden, 'One Man's War at Sea' (66/24/1)

Public Record Office (PRO)
No. 17 Squadron, operations record book
No. 501 Squadron, operations book
Air 214593/3A report on evacuation of No. 98 Squadron by Pilot Officer J.F. Castle
Air 214593/11A report on events of 17 June by Squadron Leader J.C. More commanding 73 Squadron
Air 214593/13A report on return journey from Nantes to the United Kingdom by Wing Commander D. Macfadyen
WO167/352 war diary, 2nd battalion Royal Norfolk Regiment.

Library of Congress (LC)
Papers of Harold Ickes
Papers of Cordell Hull

National Archives of Canada (NAC)
William Lyon Mackenzie King Diaries, MG 26 J 13
Records of the Department of External Affairs

Houghton Library, Harvard University, Cambridge, MASS (HL)
Papers of James Pierrepoint Moffat

Privately supplied memoirs
George Dakin, diary for 1940
Geoff Taylor, account of experiences as a policeman in 1940
Don Milburn, account of experiences as a policeman in 1940
Brian Mobley, journal made by his father while working for 50MU
Beth Williams, 'City of Benares – Beth's story'
Harold Bird-Wilson, '17 May–19 June No. 17 Hurricane Squadron'; logbooks
    and intelligence patrol reports for 17 Squadron

Printed

Newspapers and current periodicals, notably the *Aeroplane*; *New York Herald Tribune*; *PM*; *Picture Post*; *The War Illustrated*.

Anon, *Fleet Air Arm*, London, HMSO, 1943
Anon, *East of Malta West of Suez: The Admiralty Account of the Naval War in the Eastern Mediterranean September 1939 to March 1941*, London: HMSO, 1943
Anon, *Ourselves in Wartime*, London: n.d.
Arthur, Max, *There Shall Be Wings: The RAF 1918 to the Present*, London: Hodder & Stoughton, 1993
Astley, Joan, *The Inner Circle*, London: Hutchinson, 1971
Atkin, Ronald, *Pillar of Fire: Dunkirk 1940*, London: Sidgwick & Jackson, 1990
Barker, Ralph, *Children of the Benares*, London: Methuen, 1987
Barnett, Corelli, *Engage the Enemy More Closely: The Royal Navy in the Second World War*, London: Hodder & Stoughton, 1991
Bickers, Richard Townsend, *Ginger Lacey, Fighter Pilot*, London: Robert Hale, 1962
Blaxland, Gregory, *Destination Dunkirk: The Story of Gort's Army*, London: William Kimber, 1973

Bloch, Howard (ed.), *Black Saturday: The First Day of the Blitz*, London: T.H.A.P., 1984

Briggs, Asa, *History of Broadcasting in the United Kingdom*, Vol. 3: 'The War of Words', Oxford: OUP, 1970

Brooks, A.J., *Fighter Squadron at War*, 1980

Brown, David, 'The Road to Oran: Anglo-French Naval Relations, September 1939 to July 1940', unpublished MS.

Bussy, Geoffrey, 'Blackburn "Skua" et "Roc": les gros vilains canards', *Le Fana de l'Aviation*, 344 (July 1998), pp. 12–21, and 345 (August 1998), pp. 34–47.

Calder, Angus, *The People's War*, London: Jonathan Cape, 1969

——, *The Myth of the Blitz*, London: Jonathan Cape, 1991

Carne, Daphne, *The Eyes of the Few*, London: Macmillan, 1970

'Cato', *Guilty Men*, London: Gollancz, 1940; ed. J. Stevenson with preface by M. Foot, 1998

Charmley, John, *Churchill's Grand Alliance: the Anglo-American Special Relationship 1940–57*, London: Hodder & Stoughton, 1995

Cloud, Stanley and Olson, Lynne, *The Murrow Boys: Pioneers on the Front Lines of Broadcast Journalism*, New York: Houghton Mifflin, 1996

Collier, Richard, *1940: The World in Flames*, London: Hamish Hamilton, 1979

Colville, John, *The Fringes of Power: Downing Street Diaries 1939–1955*, London: Hodder & Stoughton, 1985

Costello, John, *Ten Days that Saved the West*, London: Bantam Press, 1991

Deighton, Len, *Fighter*, London: Granada, 1979

Delmer, Sefton, *Black Boomerang*, London: Secker & Warburg, 1962

Dilks, David (ed.), *The Diaries of Sir Alexander Cadogan O.M, 1938–1945*, London: Cassell, 1971

Divine, David, *The Nine Days of Dunkirk*, London: 1959

Doe, Bob, *Fighter Pilot*, Selsdon, Surrey: CCB Associates, 1991

Dundas, Hugh, *Flying Start: A Fighter Pilot's War Years*, London: Penguin, 1990

Fairfax, Ernest, *Calling All Arms*, London: Hutchinson, 1946

Feiling, Keith, *The Life of Neville Chamberlain*, London: Macmillan, 1946

Fleming, Peter, *Invasion 1940*, London: Hamish Hamilton, 1957

Forrester, Larry, *Fly for Your Life*, London: Frederick Muller, 1956

Foster, Reginald, *Dover Front*, London: Secker & Warburg, 1941

Franks, Norman, *Double Mission*, London: William Kimber, 1976

——, *The Air Battle of Dunkirk*, London: William Kimber, 1983

——, and Richey, Paul, *Fighter Pilot's Summer*, London: Grub Street, 1993

Gardner, Charles, *A.A.S.F.*, London and Melbourne: Hutchinson & Co., 1940

Gilbert, Martin, *Finest Hour: Winston S. Churchill 1939–1941*, 1983 (1989 edn)

——, *Second World War*, 1989

——, *The Churchill War Papers*, Vol. II: 'Never Surrender May 1940–December 1940', London: Heinemann, 1994.

Glover, Michael, *Invasion Scare 1940*, London: Leo Cooper, 1990

Harman, Nicholas, *Dunkirk: the Necessary Myth*, London: Hodder & Stoughton, 1980

Hart, Peter, *At the Sharp End: From Le Paradis to Kohima,* 2nd Battalion The Royal Norfolk Regiment, Barnsley: Leo Cooper, 1998

Higham, Charles, *Trading with the Enemy*, New York: Barnes & Noble, 1995

Hinsley, F.H. and Stripp, A., *Codebreakers: The Inside Story of Bletchley Park*, Oxford: OUP, 1993

Hinsley, H.H., Thomas, E.E., *et al.*, *British Intelligence in the Second World War: Its Influence on Strategy and Operations*, London: HMSO, 1979–88

Howard, Anthony, *RAB: The Life of R.A. Butler*, London: Jonathan Cape, 1987

Hull, Cordell, *The Memoirs of Cordell Hull*, 2 vols, New York: Macmillan, 1948

Ismay, Hastings, *The Memoirs of General the Lord Ismay*, London: Heinemann, 1961

Jackson, Dot, 'Gentle Ben', *Clemson World Magazine*, fall 1992, pp. 16–21

Johnson, David Alan, *The Battle of Britain*, Conshohocken, PA: Combined Publishing, 1998

Kaplan, Philip and Collier, Richard, *The Few: Summer 1940, the Battle of Britain*, London: Blandford, 1990

Keegan, John, *The Second World War*, London: Century Hutchinson, 1989

Kessler, Ronald, *The Sins of the Father: Joseph P. Kennedy and the Dynasty He Founded,* London: Hodder & Stoughton, 1996

Kimball, Warren F. (ed.), *Churchill and Roosevelt: the Complete Correspondence: The Alliance Emerging, October 1939–November 1942*, Princeton: Princeton UP, 1984.

——, *Forged in War: Roosevelt, Churchill and the Second World War*, New York: William Morrow, 1997

Longmate, Norman, *The Way We Lived Then*, London: Hutchinson, 1975

McMillan, Richard, *Mediterranean Assignment*, New York: Doubleday, Doran & Co., 1943

Mackenzie, S.P., *The Home Guard*, Oxford: OUP, 1996

Marchant, Hilde, *Women and Children Last*, London: Gollancz, 1941

Martin, Sir John, *Downing Street: The War Years*, London: Bloomsbury, 1991

Middlebrook, M. and Everitt, C., *The Bomber Command War Diaries*, London: Viking, 1985

Murrow, Edward R., *This Is London*, London: Cassell 1941

Nicolson, Harold, *Diaries and Letters 1939–1945*, ed. N. Nicolson, London: Collins, 1967

Padfield, Peter, *War beneath the Sea: Submarine Conflict 1939–1945*, London:

John Murray, 1995

Perry, Colin, *Boy in the Blitz: The 1940 Diary of Colin Perry*, London: Leo Cooper, 1972 (1980 edn)

Pimlott, Ben (ed.), *The Second World War Diary of Hugh Dalton 1940–45*, London: Jonathan Cape, 1986

Pollock, Fred E., 'Roosevelt, the Ogdensburg Agreement, and the British Fleet: All Done with Mirrors', *Diplomatic History*, 5, no. 3 (summer 1981), pp. 203-19

Pollock, George, *The Jervis Bay*, London: William Kimber, 1958

Ponting, Clive, *1940: Myth and Reality*, London: Hamish Hamilton, 1990

Poolman, Kenneth, *Armed Merchant Cruisers*, London: William Kimber, 1985

Price, Alfred, *The Hardest Day: The Battle of Britain 18 August 1940*, 1979 (Cassell edn 1998)

——, *Battle of Britain Day: 15 September 1940*, London: Sidgwick & Jackson, 1990

Priestley, J. B., *Postscripts*, London: 1940

Robertson, Ben, *I Saw England*, New York: Alfred A Knopf, 1941

Roskill, Stephen, *The War at Sea, 1939–1945*, Vol. I, 'The Defensive', 1954.

——, (ed.), *The Naval Air Service*, The Naval Records Society, 1969

Sheean, Vincent, *Between the Thunder and the Sun*, New York: Random House, 1943

Shirer, William, *Berlin Diary, 1934–41*, London: Hamish Hamilton, 1941.

——, *The Rise and Fall of the Third Reich*, New York: Simon & Schuster, 1960

Stevenson, John, *British Society 1914–45*, Harmondsworth: Penguin, 1984

Stewart, Graham, *Churchill and Chamberlain*, London: Weidenfeld and Nicolson, 1999

Stewart, James D., *Bermondsey in War 1939–1945*, n.d.

Taylor, A.J.P, *Beaverbrook*, London: Hamish Hamilton, 1972

Terraine, J., *The Right of the Line: The Royal Air Force in the European War 1939–1945*, London: Hodder & Stoughton, 1985

Texier, Prosper, *Avec le Branlebas vers Dunkerque et l'Angleterre*, Boissise-le-Roi, 1994

Thompson, Julian, *The Imperial War Museum Book of the War at Sea*, London: Sidgwick & Jackson, 1988

Thompson, Laurence, *1940: Year of Legend, Year of History*, London: William Collins, 1966

Thompson, W. H., *Sixty Minutes with Churchill*, London: 1953

Townsend, Peter, *Duel of Eagles*, London: Weidenfeld and Nicolson, 1970

Wood, Derek and Dempster, Derek, *The Narrow Margin: The Battle of Britain and the Rise of Air Power 1930–40*, London: Hutchinson, 1961

Wynn, Kenneth, *Men of the Battle of Britain*, Norwich: Gliddon, 1989, 1992

Ziegler, Philip, *London at War 1939–1945*, London: Mandarin, 1996

Notes on Sources

The action described in this book was based principally on interviews conducted for the television series *Finest Hour*. The principal interviews used were with Ada Allen (Ada Taylor), Harold Bird-Wilson, Oscar Cornish, Bess Cummings (Bess Walder), George Dakin, Bob Doe, Alan Francis, Edith Kup (Edith Heap), Ken Lee, Ernie Leggett, Rosemary Lyster, Martin McLane, Iain Nethercott, Rose Patience (Rosie Lee), Sam Patience, Whitelaw Reid, Dickie Rolph, Frank Scrivener, Marian Walker Spicer (Marian Holmes), Peter Vaux, Lewis Webster, Beth Williams (Beth Cummings) and Page Wilson (Page Huidekoper).

Several of our interviewees had already been interviewed by the Sound Department of the Imperial War Museum and occasionally quotations or details taken from these very full and graphic interviews were also used. The reference numbers for the most important are: Harold Bird-Wilson 10093, Edith Kup 13927, Ernie Leggett 17761, Martin McLane 10165, Iain Nethercott 7186 and 11068, Sam Patience 11729, Peter Vaux 6614. A great number of other IWM interviews were consulted in the course of research.

Graham Lumsden's account is taken from 'One Man's War at Sea' (IWM 66/24/1) and Daphne Lumsden's from correspondence with the authors. The character of Paul Richey was reconstructed from his books *Fighter Pilot* and *Fighter Pilot's Summer* and from documents supplied by Diana Richey. Ben Robertson was based principally on his autobiographical *I Saw England*. Denis Wissler was based on his diary (IWM 91/41/1) and on information from Edith Kup and Harold Bird-Wilson.

All reconstructed dialogue, thoughts and feelings were based closely on the above sources. On rare occasions, comments made at different times have been grouped together for dramatic effect. For example, the 501 pilots' jokes about 'penguins' and plotters may not have been told inside the Chez Moi nightclub on the same evening that Ken Lee was teased about a past encounter with one of the waitresses.

Quotations taken from other sources are listed below:

Chapter One

p. 16   'I hope that it is not too late', Thompson, *Sixty Minutes*, p. 44.

p. 21   'A half-breed American' and other remarks, Colville, p. 122.

p. 22   'Crazy Gang', Martin, p. 9.

p. 22   'My wish is realised ... .', Gilbert, *War Papers*, II, pp. 2–3.

p. 22   'I have nothing to offer', speech in House of Commons of 13 May (*Hansard*).

Chapter Two

p. 29   'I spent the day in a bright', Colville, p. 129 (13 May).

p. 30   Supersubmarines and other phantoms, LC, Hull papers.

p. 31   Sumner Welles from his report, 12 May 1940, cited in Costello, p. 70.

p. 31   'the President said', LC, Ickes papers, Ickes' diary, 12 May 1940.

p. 31   Moffat and Butler, HL, Moffat papers, diary for 13 March 1940.

p. 32   'the voice and force', Churchill papers, cable from Churchill to Roosevelt of 15 May in Gilbert, *War Papers*, p. 45.

p. 32   'the road to Paris was open', Premier papers 3/188/1 in Gilbert, *War Papers*, p. 35.

p. 33   'Situation very serious', NAC, Mackenzie King diary, 17 May.

p. 39   'the foulest and most soul-destroying', broadcast of 19 May, Churchill papers, in Gilbert, *War Papers*, p. 83.

p. 39   'It is refreshing to work', Colville, pp. 135–6.

Chapter Three

p. 44   'England passed her peak', Kennedy to Roosevelt, 30 September 1939, in Kessler, p. 201.

p. 44   'It is a gigantic impersonal war machine . . .', Shirer, *Berlin Diary*, 1941, pp. 289–90 and 297–8.

p. 46   'Wait. Barclay told us to wait for his signal', Hart, pp. 51–2.

p. 49   'I feel more confident than I did', Churchill to Reynaud, 21 May, Foreign Office papers 800/312 in Gilbert, *War Papers*, p. 102.

p. 49   'I don't know whether . . .', Nicolson, p. 88.

p. 50   It is usual for the Mark II tank to be designated the 'Matilda' but it inherited this name in the desert after the Mark I tank had been withdrawn from service. According to Peter Vaux, tank crews knew the Mark I tank as 'Matilda' during the campaign in France.

p. 52   'I have not seen Winston so depressed . . .', Colville, p. 138.

Chapter Four

p. 68   'If members of the present administration . . .', cable from Churchill to Roosevelt, 20 May, Churchill Papers 20/14 in Gilbert, *War Papers*, p. 93.

p. 68   'the main type of problem', HL, Moffat diary, 21 May.

p. 69   'Germany has got into the hands', NAC, Mackenzie King diary, 10 May.

p. 69   22 May headline from LC, Hull papers.

p. 69   'the object of the proposed meeting', NAC, records of the Department of External Affairs.

p. 70   '[He] asked me if I could send', NAC, Mackenzie King diary, 24 May.

p. 75   'There are, therefore, so far', LC, Hull papers, George Messersmith from Havana to James Moffat.

p. 76   'There is no doubt in my mind', LC, Ickes diary, 26 May.

p. 76   'Things are so desperately serious . . .', Barnett, pp. 143–4.

p. 81   'A dramatic afternoon . . .', Colville, p. 139.

p. 83   'let no one be mistaken', Atkin, p. 120.

p. 83   'if one side fights . . .', memo, Churchill to Ismay, 24 May, Churchill papers 4/150 in Gilbert, *War Papers*, p. 138.

p. 84   'just as gloomy as usual . . .' Dilks, p. 289 (Saturday 25 May).

p. 84   'the situation, according . . .', Costello, p. 166

p. 84   State of morale from Home Intelligence Report of 25 May in Calder, *Myth of the Blitz*, p. 123.

p. 85   Prayers from *A form of prayer to Almighty God at this time of war to be used on Sunday, May 26th, 1940*, London, 1940.

Chapter Five

p. 87   'with a view to exploring', Gilbert, *War Papers*, p. 144n.

p. 88   'opposed to any negotiations', Cabinet papers 65/13 in Gilbert, *War Papers*, p. 153.

p. 88   'We must take care not to be forced' and following account, Cabinet papers 65/13 in Gilbert, *War Papers*, pp. 157–8. The Cabinet minutes normally employ the conventions of reported speech (The Prime Minister said that '. . . our prestige in Europe was very low' . . .). To aid clarity we have occasionally switched tense to recapture the flavour of what was actually said (Churchill said '. . . our prestige in Europe is very low . . .').

p. 89   'WSC too rambling and romantic', Dilks, p. 290 (Sunday 26 May).

p. 90   'Bullet in neck' telegram with kind permission of Diana Richey.

p. 97   'Facing an air superiority', 'Report of a discussion of possible eventualities' prepared by Keenleyside, 26 May 1940, NAC, records of the Department of External Affairs.

p. 98   'I question if ever', NAC, Mackenzie King diary, 27 May.

p. 99   'Opinion in the republic', NAC, Keenleyside's 'Report of . . .'.

p. 99   'For a moment it seemed', NAC, King diary, 27 May.

p. 106   'The United States had given', Cabinet papers 65/7 in Gilbert, *War Papers*, p. 163

p. 107   'increasingly oppressed' and following quotations, Cabinet papers 65/13 in Gilbert, *War Papers*, pp. 167–9.

p. 108   'I can't work with Winston any longer', Dilks, p. 291 (Monday 27 May).

p. 108   'We had a long and rather confused discussion' in Gilbert, *War Papers*, p. 170.

Chapter Six

p. 114   'a frank statement', Cabinet papers 65/7 in Gilbert, *War Papers*, p. 177.

p. 114   'the House should prepare', speech in House of Commons, 28 May (*Hansard*).

p. 116 'slippery slope' and subsequent quotations, Cabinet papers 65/13 in Gilbert, *War Papers*, pp. 180–81.

p. 117 'clawing-down rate' and subsequent quotations from Dalton's account, Pimlott, pp. 27–8.

p. 131 'In these dark days', Premier papers, 4/68/9 in Gilbert, *War Papers*, p. 187.

p. 131 'the President has decided', Gilbert, *Finest Hour*, p. 426.

p. 132 'an empire which was practically', LC, Ickes diary, 26 May.

p. 133 'it may well be the most significant', NAC, Mackenzie King diary, 30 May.

Chapter Seven

p. 142 'theatrically bulldoggish', Cadogan, p. 292 (29 May).

p. 143 nobody leaves . . ., Martin, p. 11.

p. 143 'the Prime Minister thought', War Cabinet, 30 May, Cabinet papers 65/7, Gilbert, *War Papers*, p. 250.

p. 144 'This struggle was protracted', speech of 4 June in House of Commons (*Hansard*).

p. 148 'Worth 1,000 guns', Gilbert, *War Papers*, p. 248.

p. 148 'Even repeated', Gilbert, *War Papers*, p. 250.

p. 151 'When Skelton came over', NAC, Mackenzie King diary, 4 June.

p. 151 'It was a great speech', LC, Ickes diary, 5 June.

p. 151 'British situation vastly improved', Premier papers, 4/43B/1 in Gilbert, *War Papers*, p. 254–5.

p. 152 'If we go down', Churchill to Lothian, 9 June, Churchill papers 20/14 in Gilbert, *War Papers*, p. 270.

p. 152 'Nothing is so important', Churchill to Roosevelt, 11 June, Churchill papers 20/14 in Gilbert, *War Papers*, p. 287.

p. 155 Dunkirk naval losses from Barnett, p. 161.

p. 156 'Interesting censorship report', Colville, p. 149.

p. 156 'The completely defensive', Churchill to Ismay, 4 and 5 June, Churchill papers 20/13 in Gilbert, *War Papers*, pp. 249 and 251.

p. 156 'To-morrow it is proposed', Premier papers 3/188/1 in Gilbert, *War Papers*, p. 265.

Chapter Eight

p. 166 '. . . and yet the politicians', LC, Ickes diary, 23 June.

p. 167   '1500 desperate characters', Gilbert, *Finest Hour*, p. 498.

p. 167   'Machines will one day', Gilbert, *Finest Hour,* p. 509.

p. 167   'If there is anything you can say', Churchill to Roosevelt, 11 June, Premier papers 3/468 in Gilbert, *War Papers*, p. 307.

p. 168   'He said, in his best French', Ismay, p. 143.

p. 168   'I personally believe that the spectacle', 15 June, Churchill papers 20/14 in Gilbert, *War Papers*, p. 341.

p. 169   'Dinner began lugubriously', Colville, pp. 157–8.

p. 170   Robertson details from Jackson, 'Gentle Ben'.

p. 170   'We are against people . . .', *PM* mission statement, 22 April.

p. 173   Westrick details from Whitelaw Reid interview and personal archive, and Higham, p. 97.

p. 177   'A prayer for protection', Robertson, p. 16.

Chapter Nine

p. 181   'lying in his bed', Colville, p. 158.

p. 184   'I wish to repeat my profound conviction', Churchill to Pétain and Weygand, Churchill papers 20/14, in Gilbert, *War Papers*, p. 359.

p. 185   Account of the sinking of the *Lancastria* indebted to the two collections of eye-witness accounts compiled by the HMT Lancastria Association, 'HMT *Lancastria* Narratives' and 'HMT Lancastria: Narratives 2 and other things'; also to interviews with Oscar Cornish and George Dakin and to reports in the PRO.

p. 187   'Mr Butler's official attitude . . .', *Daily Express* (11 September 1965) in Howard, p. 97.

p. 188   'I do not at all underrate', speech of 18 June 1940 in House of Commons in Gilbert, *War Papers*, pp. 360–8.

p. 189   'Butler held odd language to the Swedish Minister', Foreign Office papers 800/322, 25 June in Gilbert, *War Papers*, p. 419.

p. 189   'My heart aches', NAC, Mackenzie King diary, 16 June.

p. 190   'there is a great deal of thinking', HL, Moffat papers, letter to William Emerson, 12 July 1940.

p. 191   'I don't think words count', Churchill to Lothian, 28 June, Churchill papers 20/14 in Gilbert, *War Papers*, p. 436.

p. 192   'I have taken more . . .', recalled by Marian Holmes.

p. 193   'Peace Moves Heard', *PM*, 28 June.

p. 195   'People seem suddenly to realise', *PM* , 28 June.

p. 195   'Stop Hitler Now', *PM*, 18 June.

p. 195   'Keeping enemy nerves twitching' *PM*, 25 June

Chapter Ten

p. 201   'Tis better using France than trusting France', Colville, p. 181.

p. 202   'As long as I can issue orders . . .', Brown

p. 202   'There is a good deal of Anglophobia', Colville, p. 173 (27 June).

p. 202   'the withdrawal of the Eastern', CAB 79/5, COS 40, 183rd meeting, Min. 3 in Barnett, pp. 209–10.

p. 206   'He [Churchill] emphasised that the great invasion', Colville, p. 192 (12 July).

p. 207   'The big aerial onslaught is expected', Colville, p. 197 (17 July).

p. 207   'Winston . . .is contemplating', Colville, p. 175.

p. 209   'Waves broke against Dover', Robertson from Dover in *PM*, 10 July.

p. 209   'Twilight hangs heavy', *PM* editorial, 28 June 1940.

p. 213   'said that he had never seen', Colville, pp. 183–4.

p. 213   'It is with sincere sorrow', speech of 4 July in House of Commons in Gilbert, *War Papers*, pp. 469–75.

p. 214   'England gave the world today . . .', *PM*, 7 July.

p. 216   Details on internees chiefly from Calder, *People's War*, pp. 130–3, and *Myth of the Blitz*, pp. 110–18.

p. 217   'In reply to a request', Colville, p. 177.

p. 220   Freyberg's evening with Churchill, 8 July, Gilbert, *War Papers*, pp. 494–5.

Chapter Eleven

p. 223   'A great Empire will be destroyed', Shirer, *Rise and Fall*, p. 754.

p. 223   'Let me tell you what', Delmer, p. 17.

p. 225   Czernin story, Wissler's diary, 2 August, and interview with Harold Bird-Wilson.

p. 228   Account of Dover Cliffs indebted to Foster, Marchant, Robertson, Sheean.

p. 229   'could be in the midst of life', Robertson, p. 89.

p. 232   Sheean's feelings, *Between the Thunder and the Sun*, p. 157.

p. 233   'The flash of the Spitfire's wing', Sheean, pp. 200–1.

p. 233   'I was for freedom', Robertson, p. 93.

p. 234   'Destroyers are frightfully vulnerable', Churchill to Roosevelt, 30 July, Premier papers 3/462/2/3 in Gilbert, *War Papers*, p. 594.

p. 235   'a terrible misfortune', NAC, Mackenzie King diary, 18 July.

p. 235   'Churchill has . . .been begging', LC, Ickes diary, 4 August.

p. 235   'nervous and irritable', Colville, pp. 209–10 (6 August).

p. 235   'The President has sent a message', Colville, p. 223 (15 August).

p. 236   'long step towards coming . . .', War Cabinet, 14 August, Cabinet papers 65/8 in Gilbert, *War Papers*, p. 667.

p. 237   'The defence of Southern England . . .', Kimball, *Forged in War*, p. 63.

p. 242   Churchill's phrase-making in his car, Ismay, p. 179.

p. 243   Discussion of Ogdensburg is based on Kimball and Pollock.

p. 243   'Congress is going to raise hell', Kimball, *Forged in War*, p. 58.

p. 244   'I am deeply interested', Churchill to Mackenzie King, Pollock, p. 218.

p. 244   'Morgenthau said at dinner', NAC, Mackenzie King diary, 30 August.

Chapter Twelve

p. 247   Description of 18 August indebted to Price's full and exciting account in *The Hardest Day*.

p. 253   ' "There they are", exclaimed Moyra', Colville, p. 225.

p. 257   'Never in the field', speech of 20 August in House of Commons (*Hansard*).

p. 258   'It was less oratory than usual', Colville, p. 227.

p. 259   'Dear Mr. Churchill . . .', Whitelaw Reid's private papers.

p. 261   'there is considerable risk', Cunningham to Pound in Barnett, p. 219.

Chapter Thirteen

p. 263   Denis Wissler's assessment was made and shown to him on 15 February 1940. He recorded it in his pocket diary.

p. 267   Harbottle from Wood and Dempster, p. 173.

Chapter Fourteen

p. 287   Journalists from Murrow, p. 171 and Robertson, pp. 119–23.

p. 290   'This is the historic hour . . .', Wood and Dempster, p. 338.

p. 295   'The fires up river', Murrow, p. 171.

p. 295   'the most appalling and depressing', Robertson, p. 121.

p. 307   'In spite of considerable resentment', *Völkischer Beobachter*, 14 September, quoted in Price, *Battle of Britain Day*, p. 11.

Chapter Fifteen

p. 321   Savoy hotel demonstration, Calder, *People's War*, p. 167.

p. 321   'Everybody is worried', Nicolson, p. 114 (17 September).

p. 321   'Considerable surprise has been expressed . . .', Murrow, p. 232.

p. 322   'Priestley gives a broadcast', Nicolson, p. 117 (22 September).

p. 323   'I was tremendously impressed', LC, Ickes diary, 15 September.

p. 323   'The night was cloudless', Colville, pp. 248–9.

p. 325   Account of the *Benares* indebted to Barker.

Chapter Sixteen

p. 331   Log of the *Richard de Larrinaga* from a letter to the *Liverpool Echo and Evening Express*, 28 September 1965.

p. 337   Americans playing golf, Cloud and Olson, p. 94.

p. 337   'You must determine not to mistake . . .', Robertson article in *PM*, 24 September.

p. 338   'The silk stocking district', Robertson article in *PM*, 17 September.

p. 338   'We made a tour . . .', Robertson, *I Saw England*, pp. 136 and 131.

p. 339   Details of opinion polls, Cloud and Olson, p. 92.

Chapter Seventeen

p. 349   Treasury bomb, interview with Marian Spicer (Marian Holmes).

p. 358   'The saddest sight . . .', Colville, p. 257 (4 October).

p. 360   Spoof memo, Colville, p. 280 (31 October).

p. 361   'some strange intuitive power . . .', Colville, p. 125.

p. 361   'We must be united', speech of 8 October in House of Commons in Gilbert, *War Papers*, p. 922.

Chapter Eighteen

p. 378   'War Is Not the Worst Evil', from Whitelaw Reid's personal archive.

p. 379   'I am writing this', letter from Barbara Crim, from Whitelaw Reid's personal archive.

p. 379   'This clears the air and the skies', NAC, Mackenzie King diary, 6 November.

p. 379   'arsenal of democracy', Kimball, *Forged in War*, p. 72.

p. 382   Paris demonstration, Gilbert, *Second World War*, p. 140.

Index

San Demetrio, ss, 376
St.Abbs, Admiralty tug, 134
St Venant, 94, 103, 119, 141
St. Vincent, HMS, 272
Scharnhorst, (German
  battlecruiser), 207
Schöpfel, Gerhard, 249
Seclin airfield, 7, 37
Severeid, Eric, 232
Sheean, Vincent 'Jimmy', 232,
  233, 287–288, 292
Shirer, William, 44–45, 161,
  223, 283
Simson, David James Robert, 80
Sinclair, Sir Archibald, 363
Skipjack, HMS, 134
Somerville, Admiral Sir
  James, 212
Somme, river, 26, 63, 96–97, 99,
  125, 156
Soper, Sgt. F. J., 91
Stevens, Leonard 'Pip', 219
Storey, Bill, 374
Stratton, W.H. 'Stratters', 91
Stureholm, ss, 376
Swaine, Fay, 248, 278
Sylvester, Edmund John Hilary,
  231–232

Taft, Robert, 166
Taylor, Ada, 291, 293, 295,
  299–300, 357–358, 386,
Taylor, Arthur, 291, 299,
  300, 358
Taylor, Bob, 291, 300, 357, 382
Taylor, Geoff, 295
Tournai, 35, 40, 54–55
Thames, river, 1, 111,
  112, 281, 288, 289,

290, 291, 293, 298, 339,
  340, 380
Thompson, Dorothy, 165
Thompson, Detective Inspector
  W.H., 302
Townsend, Peter, 157, 158, 255
Tully, Grace, 243

U-boats, 71, 121, 194, 206,
  211, 311, 315, 326, 327, 367,
  368–369

Valiant, HMS, 211, 212, 261
Vaux, Peter, 3, 26–28, 40–41,
  49–52, 55–59, 60–63, 85,
  96–97, 99–102, 125–129, 147,
  171–173, 195–196, 206, 386
Venetia, HMS, 82
Venomous, HMS, 80, 82
Vimiera, HMS, 82
Vimy, 41, 49, 59, 60, 61, 196
Vimy, HMS, 73, 77, 80
Völkischer Beobachter, 307

Waalhaven airport, 10
Wakeful, HMS, 121, 122
Wake-Walker, Rear-Admiral
  W.F., 122, 123
Walder, Bernard, 246–247,
  303–304, 336
Walder, Bess, 245–47, 303–304,
  313–315, 318–319, 325–328,
  331–336, 386
Walder, Louis, 245, 246–247, 304,
  319, 328, 332, 336
Walder, Rosina, 246–247,
  303–304
Walker, P.R. 'Johnny', 91
Webster, Lewis, 295, 300–301

417

This was our hard day
being at 15 mins and
readiness the day long. At
about half past seven
we had a hell of a scrap
over Portland, in which
about 100 a/c were engaged.
F/L Bayne made an attack
below and astern quarter, the
He 110 whipped up in a stall
Turn and I gave him a long
burst while he was in a stalled
condition, it fell over and
went down. I then went on
my own and made a Me 110
brake formation, I gave it
another burst and it went
down towards the sea. F/L
Bayne shot down but OK. S/L
Williams lost. Wing shot off